BEHAVIORAL INVESTMENT MANAGEMENT

An Efficient Alternative to Modern Portfolio Theory

GREG B. DAVIES
ARNAUD DE SERVIGNY

New York   Chicago   San Francisco   Lisbon   London   Madrid   Mexico City
Milan   New Delhi   San Juan   Seoul   Singapore   Sydney   Toronto

ISBN: 9780071746601
MHID: 0071746609

e-book ISBN: 9780071748353
e-book MHID: 0071748350

This publication is designed to provide accurate and authoritative information in regard to the subject matter covered. It is sold with the understanding that neither the author nor the publisher is engaged in rendering legal, accounting, or other professional service. If legal advice or other expert assistance is required, the services of a competent professional person should be sought.

> —*From a Declaration of Principles jointly adopted by a Committee of the American Bar Association and a Committee of Publishers*

McGraw-Hill books are available at special quantity discounts to use as premiums and sales promotions, or for use in corporate training programs. To contact a representative please e-mail us at bulksales@mcgraw-hill.com.

This book is printed on acid-free paper.

CONTENTS

INTRODUCTION

This book is a result of the recent 2007–2009 and 2011 financial crises, one consequence of which was greatly increased skepticism among investment professionals about the "received wisdom" drawn from modern portfolio theory and its later developments. The combined collapse of Goldman Sachs Asset Management (GSAM) quantitative funds during the summer 2008 and then the formal academic recognition in 2009 that a $1/N$ (i.e., equally divided) asset-allocation strategy performed better than any statically optimized portfolio strategy[1] cast serious doubts on the capability of modern finance, relying as it did on quantitative analytics, to provide value to investors. Modern portfolio theory (MPT) suddenly appeared terribly old-fashioned and out of date for a very simple and straightforward reason: It did not work!

Finance and economics are not like physics. In finance, there are very few systematic "laws of nature" to be observed. We instead observe the effects of compounded human behavior on asset prices in an open environment where exogenous shocks take place on an almost continuous basis. MPT tackled this complexity through some rather extreme (and, as it proved, untenable) shortcuts. These included, for example, the assumption that the dynamics of asset prices are random and that the distribution of possible outcomes follows a Gaussian law.

These shortcuts made it much easier to build an elegant theory. Convenience and parsimony in presentation became more valued than an accurate representation of reality. Many academics therefore were encouraged to spend a massive amount of time constructing and refining concepts and findings related to this theoretical framework, most of the time without even testing their results on a fresh, untouched data set. Until recently, only a few courageous people, such as Mandelbrot, exerted themselves to argue consistently that the axiomatic hypotheses on which MPT was established were flawed—and they were not listened to.

Why did this happen? The main reason probably was that the construction of a theoretical framework dominated by efficient markets was not inherited primarily from observation of the world around us but instead was a construction of the mind. When in 1954 Arrow and Debreu came up with the concept of complete markets, such markets did not exist. They were aspirational. In a way, we might better characterize their idea as an intellectual abstraction that took off when it began to be taught on a large scale in universities. By establishing a common framework within which to think of and understand markets, we narrowed the gap with what was expected to happen. Complete, fully efficient markets were on their way, and every day that passed was expected to move reality closer and closer to the conceptual ideal. The fascinating, and ironic, aspect of this was that the combination of individual attempts to outperform the market by using more sophisticated insights or more complex modeling and forecasting techniques in fact would lead to a reinforcement of the efficiency of financial markets. Modern finance had borrowed from classical economics the thinking that the pursuit of individual selfish interests inevitably would lead to the realization of common welfare. In other words, modern finance was expected to provide a very stable environment because every attempt by individual agents to actively engage in challenging it would only strengthen it.

It is remarkable that within about 50 years in the Western world, an almost ubiquitous common understanding of finance has been established, and this has led to the development and expansion of financial markets to an extraordinarily large and complex scale (facilitated enormously by the development of communications technologies and global integration). Thus we now find ourselves in a very interesting situation where the plans of the financial market architects largely have been followed, the infrastructure exists, but the foundations on which these plans were grounded have been shown to be less sound than they appeared initially.

The reason for this, we would argue, is primarily because deep understanding of human individuals and of their behavior has been neglected. Initially, it might have been thought that there was no place for human irrationality in a world dominated by the sciences. Let us remember in this respect that many people's concept of modernity is very much linked to the Enlightenment (in the eighteenth century), "*le siècle des Lumières*," during which philosophers focused on hard sciences and the laws of nature as a way to gain freedom and empowerment vis-à-vis religion and the mainstream Greek philosophies. Whether intended or not, *behavioral finance* also has been influenced by this background, with its emphasis on the numerous biases (i.e., deviations from rationality) attached to the otherwise exemplary rational individual. The acknowledgment of emotional forces in individuals was almost a limitation that needed to be hidden. To put it in blunt terms, the frequent expectation is that the modern investor should be able to master his or her own feelings, and as a result, his or her satisfaction, as expressed in the economic jargon of the utility function, should result only from rational financial decisions. If this is not the case, the diversity of emotions in financial markets at least should have limited import for the transmission of information on prices, thanks to the enormous number of individuals exhibiting different emotions in markets averaging each other out, in the absence of systemic biases. Modern finance thought-leaders by and large were happy to live with these overly simplistic assumptions on human nature and thought it better to concentrate on their more serious studies aggregating the decisions of rational agents, that is, constructing the axiomatic principles of modern finance.

Following the multiple market bubbles we have experienced over recent centuries—inflated whenever human beliefs and behaviors aggregated to a point of disequilibrium—we now have almost completely lost respect for the current theoretically driven architecture for analysis of the financial universe. The time has come for two things:

- First of all, we need to be more empirical and to resist the temptation to invent laws of nature where they do not exist. At best, there may be some stable patterns that are conditional on specific current states of the world and the economy. Thinking that we can find unconditional patterns in finance is probably way too ambitious—a legacy of a more antique or medieval way of thinking where truth was to be synonymous with stability. Our cultural mental universe instead has evolved toward constant innovation and rethinking of the world and of its perceived common understanding. It is noticeable that with the acceleration of communications and thus the development of new ideas, the shelf life of any global intellectual consensus is becoming shorter and shorter.

This has developed to the point where getting consensual buy-in to a common conceptual closed framework (e.g., any next incarnation of modern finance) may be not just uncertain, but impossible. This, in itself, could become an interesting new problem.

- The second aspect is that we can no longer consider finance to be separate from human behavior. Humanity, with all its limitations, may well be the source of the stability we lack in our more abstract conceptions in the universe of finance. In this respect, such financial laws of nature that do exist much more likely may be related to investors rather than to investments. We do not wish to imply by this statement that we negate statistical or quantitative methods. On the contrary, we believe that the emergence of virtual communications channels such as the Internet create a massive opportunity to better understand human behavior, applying the full statistical tool kit we have at hand. To a large extent, the age of scientific enlightenment therefore may be coming to completion, paving the way for a new age focusing on the complexities of human interactions and decisions.

The ambition of this book is considerable and in practice threefold:

- To "de-silo" finance from the other areas of knowledge, such as human behavioral science, economics, and mathematics. In this respect, we use various techniques that correspond to best practices in these different fields.
- To plead that we should understand financial systems from a more empirical perspective rather than as idealistic theoretical constructs. Something may not be true purely because it works, but something certainly cannot be true only because there is a tidy theory to which to relate it.
- The last aspect we emphasize is business applicability and strategic consequences. New ideas not only must work but also must be implementable and influence the financial industry and, ultimately, the satisfaction of individuals in a positive manner.

However, we would like to make it clear that this book does not try to set a new holistic standard, a so-called successor to modern portfolio theory. We focus only on incorporating time and human adaptability into a practical investment framework.

Before you start the book proper, we would like to summarize its structure. The first four chapters constitute a detailed review of modern portfolio theory

(MPT). In Chapter 1 we review the functioning of finance as a science largely independent from economics and human psychology. In Chapter 2 we assess the implicit choices that have been made by MPT in terms of human psychology and identify very serious shortcomings. In Chapter 3 we go through a thorough scientific and abstract description of MPT to ensure that we really grasp what it is about at the heart. Chapter 4 presents a fairly systematic analysis of why MPT does not work empirically.

This leaves us with a largely ruined portfolio-construction landscape and sets the stage for reconstruction. In the next four chapters we rebuild a conceptual framework that appears reasonable given actual common knowledge and the fact that it improves the capability of a financial investor to generate performance. In Chapter 5 we revisit concepts of risk using the perspective offered by behavioral science to place the objectives of the investor at the heart of the framework. In Chapter 6 we look at the dynamics of asset prices, hoping to develop an understanding that goes beyond a pure assumption of randomness. Then, in Chapter 7, we combine the findings of Chapters 5 and 6 to establish a new paradigm for best practice in portfolio construction. In Chapter 8 we examine how this paradigm could be used and extended to incorporate and compensate for the inevitable emotional reactions of investors. We finish the book with some strategic thinking on how all these new findings may affect, challenge, and also create opportunities for the wealth management and pension fund industries.

We would like to thank the people who have directly helped us in this book: Shweta Agarwal, Peter Brooks, Pierre Dangauthier, Prosper Dovonon, Daniel Egan, and Ricardo Feced. As testimony to their contribution we have included their biographies right after this Introduction and have also indicated the chapters where they contributed most. We would also like to thank our editor, Graham Richardson, who has spent a great deal of time bringing our words to the right level of fluidity. We would like to pay a specific tribute to the people in our professional environment who have led us to the intellectual framework which underpins this book. In this respect Tom Kalaris, Kevin Lecocq, and Mitch Cox have been inspirational. Lastly, but most importantly, we offer very grateful thanks to our wives, Elena and Marie, who very kindly supported our effort despite the considerable 'non-work' time commitment it entailed.

Please note that the content of this book may not reflect the position of the firms we work for.

Note

1. DeMiguel, Garlappi, and Uppal (2009).

ABOUT THE AUTHORS

Greg B. Davies

Growing up in South Africa, Greg completed his undergraduate degree at the University of Cape Town. He holds an MPhil in Economics and a PhD in Behavioural Decision Theory, both from Cambridge University. His PhD dissertation combined research into the psychology of decision making with finance theory to examine financial behavior and the psychology of risk.

Between his Master's and Doctorate degrees he worked at the financial services strategy consultants Oliver, Wyman & Co. Throughout his PhD he was a director of Decision Technology, a consultancy originating in the cognitive psychology work of Warwick University, which specializes in developing commercial applications from academic decision sciences and behavioral economics. Today he heads both the global behavioral and quantitative finance teams at Barclays Wealth, and is responsible for the design and global implementation of Barclays Wealth's Investment Philosophy.

He has authored academic papers in multiple disciplines of economics, psychology, decision theory, and management science, holds an honorary Research Fellowship at University College London (UCL), and lectures intermittently at Oxford's Said Business School, and the London School of

Economics (LSE). He also presents regularly at academic and industry conferences and is a frequent media commentator on behavioral finance.

In earlier days he sang with the World Youth Choir, the London Philharmonic Choir, and the BBC Symphony Chorus, and is now a member of one of London's top chamber choirs. He also trained as a foot guide for dangerous game areas in South Africa – which has not yet been terribly useful in finance.

For queries related to this book he can be reached at g-force@cantab.net and followed on Twitter at @GregBDavies.

Arnaud de Servigny

Arnaud de Servigny is a Managing Director and the Global Head of Discretionary Portfolio Management and Investment Strategy at Deutsche Bank Private Wealth Management (DB PWM). He and his portfolio management teams around the world have $55 billion under direct management. His Investment Strategy team supports the DB PWM's Global Investment Committee and its dynamic asset allocation process.

Until mid-2010, Arnaud was a Managing Director at Barclays Wealth, where he was in charge of Economic and Behavioural Research, Investment Strategy and Asset Allocation. He also ended up chairing the bank's investment committee. He was focused on three main areas – positioning research and strategy as the cornerstone to the investment proposition at Barclays Wealth, bringing to life cutting-edge developments related to asset allocation and, finally, developing a common Investment Philosophy within Barclays Wealth, based on innovative techniques in the area of behavioral finance.

From 2001 to 2006 Arnaud was the Global Head of Quantitative Analytics at Standard and Poor's. He was responsible for developing and implementing advanced technology within the firm's Credit Market Services department. This was centered around the creation of portfolio solutions, early warning indicators, and stress testing tools.

Prior to joining Standard and Poor's, Arnaud worked in the Group Risk Management Department of BNP-Paribas, focusing on credit risk-related portfolio management and control.

Arnaud is also an Adjunct Professor of Finance at Imperial College Business School in London, where he co-launched their Master of Financial Engineering and Risk Management programme in 2005.

Arnaud holds a PhD in Financial Economics from the Sorbonne University, an MSc in quantitative finance (DEA) from Dauphine University, and a Civil Engineering MSc from the Ecole Nationale des Ponts & Chaussées in Paris.

Publications include many papers and articles as well as five books: the first on monetary policy and fixed income, the second and third on credit risk management, the fourth on structuring and the last on asset management.

Arnaud has received two awards for his work.

For any query on this book, you can reach Arnaud at the following address: a.deservigny@imperial.ac.uk

Contributors

Shweta Agarwal

Shweta Agarwal is currently a PhD student (AXA Research Fellowship) at the London School of Economics (LSE). She is pursuing research on decisions under risk and uncertainty and its implications for risk management.

Shweta works periodically for Barclays Wealth as an analyst in their Investment Philosophy and Behavioural Finance team, helping to develop and implement commercial models that integrate mathematical techniques with real world behavior. She has designed risk rating tools for Barclays Wealth's structured products and business management & strategy teams, in order to evaluate the inherent risk of various financial products and their suitability for clients with different risk attitudes. Shweta also works on projects for a consultancy, Decision Technology, focusing on the commercial applications of the psychology of human decision making.

Shweta holds an MA in Mathematics from the University of Cambridge and an MSc in Decision Sciences from the London School of Economics. Her Master's thesis at Cambridge explored alternative mathematical approaches in the field of mechanism design, highlighting the limitations of quantitative methods when studying human behavior. Her Master's thesis at the LSE was a collaborative project with the Behavioural Finance Team at Barclays Wealth, exploring and modelling alternative measures of financial risk.

Peter Brooks

Peter Brooks is Head of Investment Philosophy and Behavioural Finance, Asia for Barclays Wealth. In this role, Peter works with a team of experts to develop and implement commercial applications, drawing on behavioral portfolio theory, the psychology of judgement and decision making, and decision sciences.

Since his relocation to Singapore in February 2011, Peter has been providing specialist support to the Barclays Wealth's private banking business across Asia. He also provides research commentary on how investor attitudes are affected by prevailing market conditions and how this links to investor behavior.

Peter holds an MSc in Economics and Econometrics, and a PhD in Behavioural and Experimental Economics, from the University of Manchester. His PhD thesis focused on experimental research into individual attitudes to monetary gains and losses.

Following his PhD, Peter worked as a Senior Research Associate in Behavioural and Experimental Economics at the University of East Anglia, where his research involved designing and running experiments on the ability of repeated market outcomes and experiences to "teach" individuals to overcome psychological biases. He has also contributed research articles to the Journal of Risk and Uncertainty and the Wiley Encyclopedia of Operations Research and Management Science.

Pierre Dangauthier

Pierre Dangauthier is a quantitative analyst specialized in machine learning. Pierre was previously a member of the Quantitative Analytics team of Barclays Wealth and now works for Credit Suisse. Pierre designs statistical models and machine-learning algorithms with application to financial markets. His area of expertise combines modern applied statistics, computer sciences and financial engineering.

He has a PhD degree in Bayesian statistics from Inria, the French national institute for research in computer science and control. He also holds an MSc in mathematics from Ensimag, a high profile French engineering school, and an MSc in robotics and computer vision. During his PhD, Pierre collaborated with Microsoft Research to improve features of the Xbox Live gaming system. In addition to publishing papers, he registered a patent dealing with chess player ranking. He also designed an expert system to improve the "ambient intelligence" of homes for Philips Research.

Prosper Dovonon

Prosper Dovonon holds a PhD in Economics from the University of Montreal and is currently Assistant Professor at Concordia University in Montreal. Before joining Concordia University, he was in charge of statistical modelling of asset allocation strategies at Barclays Wealth.

Prosper's research interests include fields such as econometric theory and financial economics. His research contribution includes several papers in leading academic journals.

Daniel P. Egan

Daniel Egan is Head of Investment Philosophy and Behavioral Finance, Americas at Barclays Wealth. His previous commercial experience includes analysis at a stem-cell research firm, research at the University of Pennsylvania into optimal health insurance reimbursement plans, and work as an economist for Chiliogon, a corporate finance advisory.

While completing his undergraduate degree at Boston University, Daniel used his senior year to pursue an independent research project on wind power and electricity markets. Daniel later continued his academic career at the London School of Economics, where he completed his MSc in Decision Science and investigated its applications to financial theory and investing.

Daniel has authored papers on investor decision making and behavior, regularly gives lectures at universities, and presents at both academic and industry conferences.

Ricardo Feced

Ricardo Feced is responsible for the general quantitative framework underlying Barclays Wealth's asset allocation proposition and, in particular, strategic and tactical asset allocations and early warning signals for portfolio risk control.

He graduated in Telecommunication Engineering at the Universidad Politecnica Madrid (ETSIT), and then completed a PhD in Electronic and Electrical Engineering at King's College, London. Before joining Barclays Wealth in 2005, Ricardo worked as a senior researcher at the Optoelectronics Research Centre (Southampton University) and at Nortel Networks, modelling and designing optoelectronic systems. He has been granted five US patents for technological innovations.

Ricardo also holds an MBA (Finance) from Cass Business School (City University, London). He has published 20 articles in peer-reviewed journals and contributed 34 conference papers.

Chapter 1

QUESTIONING THE CURRENT INVESTMENT PARADIGM

The past 10 years have proved challenging for the asset management industry. To put it very simply, traditional portfolio-construction procedures have not produced results capable of consistently outperforming a naive portfolio in which all risky assets are equally weighted.

In addition, the claim that in the long term, risky assets and in particular equities should revert to a stable, positive risk premium has been questioned over the last 10 years, a period during which three major troughs have occurred: the technology/Internet crisis between March 2000 and September 2002, which led to a 45 percent fall in global equity prices, the credit crisis between October 2007 and February 2009, which led to a 54 percent drop and the sovereign debt crisis in 2011. Overall, the period has not been characterized by the benefit of any long-term positive equity return but rather by extreme spikes of volatility. Investment professionals have lost a lot of respect from their clients, and, more fundamentally, the capability of these professionals to articulate credible investment solutions in response to the crises has been close to nonexistent.

In the opening chapters of this book we will sharpen our diagnosis by identifying the many weaknesses of the well-established modern portfolio theory (MPT) paradigm, and it is surprising how many flaws and simplistic approximations it is possible to spot. A positive take on this would be to claim that a lot of knowledge has been acquired over the past 50 years since MPT, the capital asset pricing model (CAPM), and the efficient market hypothesis (EMH) were first expounded—now we have to work out how best to apply what we have learned.

This book is not intended to be a blow-by-blow discussion of technical issues. Instead, we want to take a more fundamental look at the principles of portfolio management, particularly in the light of what has been learned over the past 10 years, and to suggest, as a result of our analysis, some possible ways forward.

We believe that any reformulation of portfolio-construction techniques should meet the following four requirements:

1. A clear understanding of the behavior of investors
2. A realistic representation of the dynamics of investment returns
3. A sound and sophisticated blending of these two positions
4. A robust empirical testing framework

In this chapter, and in the three that follow it, we are not going to provide a ready-made solution but rather will focus our attention on reasons why the traditional approaches have not delivered. In Chapters 5 through 9 we set out the details of our proposed new approach.

We start here by articulating the link between investors and investments. We then focus more specifically on investors and subsequently on investments.

It is important to accompany any theoretical approach to portfolio construction with an understanding of what goes on in the real world and of what purpose financial assets actually serve. In practice, the savings of individuals and institutions are invested in a great variety of assets, including both real assets (such as real estate) and financial assets (such as equities and bonds) for the purpose of storing and increasing their stock of wealth. Financial intermediaries reallocate idle resources from savers to those in need of investment to fund profitable projects by transforming, repacking, and redistributing the cash flows generated by the producers, issuing liabilities in exchange. The interaction of many optimizing agents theoretically allows financial markets to reach equilibrium, setting the prices of financial assets.

In terms of understanding the behavior of investors, things are not as simple as they look. Consider first a specific problem—how we establish a link between the decision-making process of any individual investor and the process by which the community of investors behaves as a whole. The essential insight from the discussion of this problem below is that the concept of a *representative investor* (much used in the current financial literature) is largely flawed. This has major implications because it means that slavish use of the MPT/CAPM (see Chapter 2) will produce suboptimal results for individual investors. This is an unresolved (and usually unremarked) problem that lies right at the heart of current approaches to investment.

Our third area of focus, which is more of a *tour d'horizon* related to the dynamics of investments, highlights the necessity of incorporating different time horizons and combining different academic disciplines. We review long-, medium-, and short-term time horizons and outline what economics, MPT, and quantitative analytics, respectively, can tell us about each. All disciplines have notable weaknesses specific to each of them. We claim that it is essential to combine the disciplines to form a more realistic picture of the situation.

Investors and Investments

In this section we introduce the main agents in the economy, together with their typical portfolios and the assets and liabilities commonly held in their balance sheets. The main agents in an economy can be broadly classified in six groups:

1. Households
2. Corporations
3. Government
4. Retail and commercial banks
5. Other financial intermediaries
6. Central banks

Households

The objective of households is to maximize their consumption and wealth along their life span (and possibly beyond in the case of bequests). Their current consumption typically is financed by an annual income together with mortgage and consumer credit agreements that sit on the liability side of their balance sheets (Table 1.1).

Households store wealth to allow for future consumption by means of a variety of real and financial assets. The main real asset is usually property (real estate), but this category may include other valuables, such as cars, jewelry, and art.

Of the financial assets, cash is the safest and most liquid and includes currency (paper money and coins) and non- (or low-) interest-bearing

Table 1.1

Households' Assets and Liabilities

Assets	Liabilities
Real estate	Mortgage
Cash deposits and currency	Consumer credit
Government bonds	
Corporate bonds	
Public equity	
Private equity	
Other funds (hedge funds, commodities, etc.)	
Insurance/pension	Net worth

instant-access deposits at banks (checkable accounts). A broader notion of cash includes time deposits that reward investors with interest for not being able to access their deposits for a stipulated period of time.

Additionally, households typically own government and corporate bonds, public and private equity, and other funds such as hedge, real estate, and commodity funds. These financial assets are claims on future cash flows generated by other economic agents such as corporations or governments—they correspond to liabilities of other economic agents. Finally, households also hold claims on insurance and pension benefits.

Corporations

The fundamental objective of corporations is to maximize shareholders' value, measured as the present value of the cash flows generated as a result of their business activity. The annual performance of a corporation is summarized in its profit and loss account, where the earnings from its operations are stated together with how these earnings are allocated as payments of interest to the finance providers, tax to the government, and dividends to shareholders or else retained by the company for reinvestment.

Corporations have liabilities with respect to their sources of finance (Table 1.2). Bondholders provide firms with capital in exchange for interest (coupon) payments and repayment of principal at the end of the agreed periods of time. Shareholders provide capital in exchange for shared ownership of the corporation, which translates into a stream of periodic dividend payments.

Prices of corporate bonds reflect the ability of the company to honor its obligations (credit risk). The two main credit-risk categories are *investment*

Table 1.2

Corporations' Assets and Liabilities

Assets	Liabilities
Cash deposits Corporate assets	Bank loans Corporate bonds Public/private equity

grade and *subinvestment grade* (also known as *junk/high yield bonds*), with the second type exhibiting higher credit risk in exchange for higher yields.

Smaller corporations have more difficulty in financing themselves through bond issues and therefore usually rely on bank loans as the source of funds. In this case, companies depend on the appetite of banks to lend and on the price at which they're prepared to lend. This is related to their required return on capital, which is itself constrained by the regulatory environment (e.g., the Basel II and Basel III agreements).

Bondholders' and banks' claims on the cash flows of corporations precede those of shareholders, making equity a riskier asset class than corporate bonds. Public equity is a more liquid asset class than private equity because it can be traded in secondary markets.

Governments

Governments finance their activities by means of taxes and the issuance of bonds (Table 1.3). Public-sector borrowing requirements depend on the government's ability to match annual tax income with expenditures. Expansive fiscal policies usually give rise to government budget deficits, but these may be essential to reactivate the economy in periods of recession. However, continuous budget deficits increase a country's national debt, reducing eventually the government's ability to borrow owing to perceived higher credit risk.

Table 1.3

Governments' Assets and Liabilities

Assets	Liabilities
National assets	Government bonds Net worth

Government bonds can be classified with respect to their maturity (or duration[1]). Long-dated bonds are riskier than short-term bonds in the sense that their prices will fluctuate over time owing to changes in the general level of interest rates (interest-rate risk). If we bought an AAA-rated 10-year-maturity government bond today and sold it in one year, we might incur a loss owing to either increasing interest rates or a change in credit risk. However, if we bought an under-one-year-maturity bond issued by the same government, the main possibility of a loss would be related to credit risk.

Government bonds from developed countries (*high-grade sovereign bonds*) are considered to be the safest assets with regard to credit risk, whereas those from emerging markets (*emerging market bonds*) are somewhat riskier, although this assessment has to be made on a case-by-case basis, and the gap with developed markets has been narrowing gradually in recent years.

Retail and Commercial Banks

Retail and commercial banks are financial intermediaries that, in a simplified picture, capture savings in the form of cash deposits or other relatively liquid accounts (their liabilities) and benefit from lending those funds over longer time horizons (*maturity transformation*) taking onboard possible credit risk (Table 1.4). The important role of banks is to intermediate between individuals with spare savings and those in need of funds for consumption or potentially profitable investments.

Besides cash deposits, banks also fund themselves in the capital markets by issuing long-term bonds or even seeking short-term financing in money markets. The equity owners of the bank earn the yield differential between its assets and its liabilities, which appears in the annual profit and loss account as the net interest income.

Table 1.4

Retail and Commercial Banks' Assets and Liabilities

Assets	Liabilities
Bank reserves and currency	Cash deposits
Mortgages	Bonds and money-markets funding
Consumer credit	Equity
Corporate loans	
Government bonds	

Table 1.5

Central Banks' Assets and Liabilities

Assets	Liabilities
Government bonds	Currency in circulation Banks' reserves Net worth

Banks have to keep a given percentage of their clients' deposits (*reserve ratio*) as cash deposits with the central bank (*reserves*).

The financial health of a bank always has received a high degree of scrutiny. There are two main aspects to monitor. The first is related to the degree of credit and market risk on the bank's balance sheet. The second is related to the liquidity mismatch between assets and liabilities resulting from the maturity transformation operated by the bank. Regulation has primarily focused on providing safety rules related to the minimum amount of capital to be held by banks in order to withstand losses resulting from these aforementioned risks.

Central Banks

Central banks are public institutions, usually independent from governments, with responsibility for monetary policy. The central bank directly controls the monetary base of the economy, which includes both the currency in circulation and the banks' reserve accounts with the central bank (Table 1.5).

Other Financial Intermediaries

There are many other financial institutions that act as intermediaries, offering customized financial assets to their clients in exchange for a premium. Intermediaries usually take exposure to a set of risky assets and transform their payoff characteristics to adjust the degree of risk of the cash flows associated with the financial products sold to their clients (Table 1.6).

Insurance companies and pension funds are typical examples of this type of financial intermediary, where client cash flows are triggered either by an insured event or by clients reaching retirement age. These institutions invest in a variety of assets to be able to hedge their potential liabilities.

Other intermediaries such as mutual funds give small investors access to diversified portfolios that they would not otherwise be able to buy. Structured

Table 1.6

Other Financial Intermediaries' Assets and Liabilities

Assets	Liabilities
Real estate	Insurance liabilities
Mortgages	Pension liabilities
Consumer credit	Fund units/shares
Government bonds	Structured products/securitized credit
Corporate bonds	
Public equity	
Private equity	
Commodities	Net worth

products repackage the risk of a pool of financial assets, engineering a set of transformed cash flows that may be able to better match the risk features desired by investors.

The Market Portfolio: Consolidated Private and Institutional Investors

In preceding sections we described the balance sheets held by the various agents in the economy. Let us focus now on the consolidated portfolios of private and institutional investors—mainly households and some financial intermediaries such as pension funds and insurers. Their consolidated assets and liabilities are summarized in Table 1.7.

Table 1.7

Private and Institutional Investors' Assets and Liabilities

Assets	Liabilities
Currency and cash deposits	Mortgage, consumer, and other credit
Government bonds (short/long duration)	
Corporate bonds (investment grade and high yield)	
Securitized credit	
Public/private equity	
Hedge funds	
Commodities	
Real estate	Net worth

In the balance sheet, we observe two main components:

1. *A long or short position in the riskless asset.* Banks allow private and institutional investors to establish the desired level of cash or debt (leverage) in their investment portfolios.
2. *A variety of risky real and financial assets.* Private and institutional investors absorb the issues of financial assets by governments and corporations in the primary capital markets and will further trade them in secondary markets. They also invest in other financial assets, such as securitized credit or hedge funds, which can be thought of as assets repackaged by financial intermediaries.

It is important to have in mind this systematic approach of economic intermediaries operating in a partial-equilibrium setup. Analogous to what takes place in physics with the principle of connected vessels, the demand for and the price of assets depend directly on the relative appetite for them by private and institutional investors. This balance is referred to in macroeconomics as the *budget constraint*. This constraint is not soft but is binding. Disequilibria may lead to a breaking of a constraint and, as a result, to serious crises.[2]

Zooming In on the Microeconomic Investor

In the preceding we showed that even at a macroeconomic level, we cannot easily talk about a single investor. Investors can be households, corporations, governments, commercial banks, and central banks. Each of these investor types, and individual entities of each type, may have very different preferences and very different amounts of capital to deploy. In this section we focus on disentangling the unclear links assumed between the microeconomic preferences of individual investors and the overall macroeconomic behavior of the market.[3]

In MPT, as well as in the CAPM, there are a few key elements that guide the construction of an optimal portfolio for any investor. First, there exists a set of particular combinations of all assets that offers optimal returns for any given level of risk.[4] Second, depending on their risk tolerance, all investors should hold a combination of a single one of these optimal portfolios and cash (or leverage for highly risk-tolerant individuals).

However, this neat solution where all investors simply hold an appropriate portion of their total wealth in a single, well-defined portfolio depends heavily on a very strong assumption—that there exists a *representative investor* who is a single market agent that represents the aggregated beliefs and preferences of all investors in the market combined. Without this, there will be no clear way of aggregating either the beliefs about future risks and returns of multiple market participants or their preferences (degrees of risk aversion). Risk aversion helps us to define the attitude of an investor faced with investments, the financial outcomes of which are uncertain. It defines how much uncertainty is tolerable in any risk/return tradeoff and thus determines the marginal price of risk. It would be very useful if a representative investor did exist because then there would be a direct relationship between establishing the optimal portfolio allocation for any individual and for that of the market as a whole in equilibrium. Without this representative investor, there is no simple notion of equilibrium to which the market can converge to represent the risk/return preferences of market participants.

The Elusive Representative Investor

While this concept of a representative investor sounds useful enough, it is important to think carefully about what exactly happens when we try to aggregate different beliefs and different risk-tolerance levels to create this beast.

Problems with Preferences

In equilibrium, the expected return of each asset will adjust according to the laws of demand and supply—the supply fixed by the amount of the asset available and the demand by the price the representative investor will pay given its risk. Assets with overly high expected returns relative to their risk will increase in price, reducing the expected returns, and the opposite will happen for those with low expected returns relative to their expected risk. All assets will adjust so that marginal demand equals marginal supply.

The notion of a representative investor simplifies this progress toward equilibrium because we can represent the combined preferences of all market participants in the preferences of a single individual, who becomes the marginal investor for all assets. Without this, we have no way of representing the marginal investor and thus no way of determining the expected returns of each asset.

This is all attractively neat and tidy, but we need to be sure that we can make this subtle shift from a market optimum to an individual optimum. It certainly should not be taken for granted. Can we aggregate the risk/return preferences—in effect, the degree of risk aversion—for all market participants into a single measure of risk aversion for the market as a whole? There are two problems. The first is not that the efficient frontier cannot be determined but that it is inherently unstable. Just why should this be? Many investment professionals frequently put the blame on the lack of predictability of the assets themselves, but this might not be the major issue, at least under the hypothesis of efficient markets. Instead, the key point is that the preferences of the market tend to evolve over time in a way that is not predictable. This boils down to a simple calculation: Assuming that all investors have a stable, well-defined degree of risk aversion (as is assumed by classical economics[5]), the risk aversion for the representative investor can be derived from the aggregation of the coefficient of risk aversion of each of the underlying individuals weighted by their level of consumption and wealth at any given time. Note, however, that since the distribution of consumption and wealth among individuals is time-dependent, the risk aversion for the representative investor itself must be time-dependent and stochastic (i.e., not wholly determined by predictable events). It is therefore not realistic to assume that the representative investor is in any sense an "average investor" with stable risk/return dispositions.

The second problem comes from behavioral science. The classical model assumes that all market participants are perfectly rational all the time, that their preferences are stable and well defined, and that each has a clear degree of risk tolerance. We don't have to look around the real world too hard to notice that not only are we not all rational all the time, but that many of us are quite irrational quite a lot of the time. Preferences are complicated: They alter moment by moment and from context to context. Indeed, there is considerable evidence that for many decisions, we don't have clear preferences that we can draw on when making decisions, but rather we *construct* our preferences on the fly when we decide,[6] and we are all prone to a range of behavioral biases that can distort our risk tolerance away from whatever fundamental attitudes actually do exist. We will discuss these behavioral issues in some detail in Chapter 2. In the meantime, though, we simply note that they cast considerable doubt on the notion that we can represent the aggregate risk attitude of the market through a representative investor or, if we can, that the resulting risk attitude is either stable or reflective of anything fundamental rather than merely of behavioral biases.

This point should make us look afresh at the current best practices in optimal portfolio construction. It tells us that it is unlikely that we can define a profile of the preferences for market outcomes (*a utility function*) that can describe appropriately, over time, the community of investors forming the market. This is so because while it should be possible to create such a utility function at any point in time (albeit at a cost), this may not be very helpful in identifying the parameters of the utility function of the representative investor over the next period.

Nonhomogenous Expectations of Investors

The portfolio perceived to be optimal by an individual investor depends on his or her expectations of the distribution of forward-looking returns of the financial assets evaluated. If we assume efficient markets and complete information, then everybody should have similar expectations, but as we know from the literature (and we show in the analysis presented in Chapter 2, which provides a behavioral analysis of how individuals approach investment decisions), this assumption does not hold in practice. Individuals will have different representations of the future distribution of asset returns. Typically, *bearish people* (pessimists) will position their distribution of returns around a low expected mean, whereas *bullish people* (optimists) will do so at a higher level. Furthermore, different investors may have quite different perceptions of the expected riskiness of assets in the market. For example, most investors tend to ascribe lower risk to assets that are familiar to them (e.g., local stocks, familiar names, etc.). This means that different investors may have quite different risk expectations for the same assets. In addition, we are all influenced by the opinions of those around us—peers, experts, and the media. It is not difficult to find economic "experts" who disagree fundamentally on the future potential returns of even the most well-understood asset classes.

Even if we discount the role of psychology, there is little reason to expect different market participants to perceive expected risks and returns identically. First, information is rarely complete or symmetric across individuals, and different participants will have different amounts of time, resources, and expertise in using the information available to them. Even sophisticated financial institutions, which have the sorts of resources to use the information as effectively as possible, frequently come to quite different conclusions about the future expectations for asset classes: Economic and quantitative financial modeling involves complex mixes of art and science that involve dozens of subjective assumptions and choices. The outcomes reflect the quite disparate opinions of many individuals and should not be expected to lead to identical (or even particularly similar) conclusions despite drawing on the same information.

The representative investor's distribution of returns therefore will be the wealth-weighted average of subjective future return distributions considered by individuals at any particular point in time. However, this will be prone to two systematic discrepancies to that considered by any individual investor. First, this distribution is likely to exhibit a *larger* variance than that of individual investors because aggregating quite different prior beliefs (be they bearish or bullish) leads to an exaggerated perception of the range of possible asset returns, which magnifies uncertainty. The second discrepancy relates to the unavoidable incorporation of market sentiment in forming the aggregated expected asset returns. As market sentiment evolves—that is, more bearish investors become bullish or vice versa—the aggregated mean itself may exhibit substantial volatility over time around the unobservable "objective" distribution of returns.

The general point here is not that the representative investor may be more biased than any individual investor (in fact, the opposite is probably true most of the time) but that the incorporation of market sentiment and shifting beliefs means that the risk and return expectations of the representative investor are bound to be unstable and to differ from those used by any individual investor.

Last, even if the beliefs of individual market participants can be adequately aggregated, it is important to question what this means for the program of optimal portfolio construction. A single set of beliefs that aggregates those of all market participants is very useful when trying to determine the *equilibrium* state of the market. However, we have no reason to believe that the market will reach a stable equilibrium—individual beliefs will shift dynamically over time, and the share of wealth will shift, causing changes in aggregate beliefs—both of which will trigger constant fluctuations in the equilibrium state itself.[7] Thus the aggregated beliefs of the representative investor may never reflect the actual situation.

Even if the beliefs of the representative investor did reflect reality at any given point, how would actual investors use them in portfolio optimization? By definition, these beliefs are the combined beliefs of the market, so unless all investors individually share the same beliefs as the representative investor (which we've already dismissed), each investor will have his own beliefs that differ from the (unobservable) beliefs of the representative investor. Thus the beliefs of the representative investor are an attractive abstract construct but are not accessible to or usable by any given investor as practical input into a portfolio-optimization procedure.

The conclusion from this, unfortunately, is that the only case where a representative investor can be seen as a useful concept corresponds to the case described by Rubinstein and Brennan and Kraus,[8] where in addition to having all the same characteristics in terms of risk aversion, investors all have homogeneous beliefs about market dynamics. These conditions are clearly not realistic.

Implications

Because of these problems surrounding the use of a representative investor, we must be suspicious of any holistic portfolio theory that claims to define, for all investors, best investment practices based on a single objective methodological outcome. The practical consequence of this quick analysis of the validity of the representative investor is that the simplicity and elegance of MPT/CAPM—the very factors that have been very important to its mass adoption—are bound to lead to suboptimal results for individual investors. This analysis also fundamentally questions what has become "received wisdom" and serves as a basis for seminal models such as Black-Litterman—the belief that, in the absence of any view, the optimal choice for an individual investor is to "buy the market," adjusted for risk.

Fortunately, although these issues are highly problematic for any attempt to define a single equilibrium portfolio to be used by all investors, they are not in fact a major hurdle for our primary goal in this book—*individual optimal portfolio construction*. To determine the optimal portfolio for any particular investor at a point in time does not require that the markets are in equilibrium, does not require that all investors or the market agrees on the distribution of future returns, and does not require that the risk aversion of all investors either is stable or can be aggregated to a single representative investor. It requires just two things:

1. That the investor has a clear notion of her own preferences for risk and return and, by implication, of her degree of risk aversion.
2. That the investor's assessment of the expected risks and returns of available assets to be used in constructing the portfolio is relatively accurate—only if the assumed future returns distribution is reasonable will the optimal portfolio constructed from it perform well in reality.

No single investor, no matter how sophisticated his models, can hope to exactly foresee the returns distribution at any one point. Indeed, if any investor had perfect foresight, there would be no distribution—the right solution simply would be to put 100 percent in the asset with the best future return—but none of us has a crystal ball. The best we can do is base our own assumptions on the best use of the evidence before us. In the next section we shall review some of the traditional attempts to form expectations based on assumed investing laws of nature.

What Are the Dynamics of Investments?

Events in the last few years have led to increased questioning of many assumed laws of nature regarding asset pricing that have had a major part in forming opinion about investor best practices. Here are three of the most important laws of nature that have come under scrutiny:

1. The assumption that there is a stable level of *long-term risk premium* associated with certain asset classes (e.g., investors should obtain a premium of x percent from being invested in equities over bonds) and that, because of this, it makes sense to hold stable portfolios over time and to rely on risky assets to be able to capture the benefit of these risk premia, typically at a 5- to 10-year horizon.
2. The assumption that because markets are efficient, the returns that result from macroeconomic-based relative allocation to the various asset classes observed in the market (also called *equilibrium returns*; see Chapter 3) are the best rational expected returns. This assumption implies that one should make investment decisions and portfolio allocations on the basis of these returns.
3. The assumption that because time series of asset returns are well behaved in terms of risk and return (i.e., jointly normally distributed), the recourse to historical data provides a sound basis for the stable estimation of their comovements.

Over the past 10 years, investment strategies that have relied on these three paradigms have not been particularly successful. This leaves us with two choices: Either we continue to believe in these laws of nature and assume, as an act of faith, that the required time horizons over which they apply just need to be very much longer for them to be proved true, or we focus on achieving a more in-depth understanding of the dynamics of markets before making any assumptions.

We think that we must go down the second path because we believe that the three investor laws summarized above no longer hold. This is one of the central themes of this book.

As we will show, we believe instead that the main point to bear in mind is the existence of different individual investment factors at play corresponding to different time horizons, some being very short term and others being much longer term in nature. We believe that investment decisions should take into account the effects of these different time horizons. In this section we distinguish among three:

1. The long-term, structural picture, typically 10 years and above
2. The traditional asset-allocation horizon, 1 to 10 years
3. The short-term horizon, 1 second to 1 year

We now review each of these horizons from a return and risk perspective so as to show that each of them has something to teach us about the formation of asset prices.

The Long-Term, Structural Picture—The Contribution of Economics

When we look at this time frame—typically 10 years and above—we need to focus on likely macroeconomic developments and their long-term implications for asset prices. In a long-term view, low frequency of observations means that one has to be governed by the principle of *nonreplicability*—it is very difficult to be able to identify with any certainty the existence of laws of nature. Structural changes to the global economy over time will also make it very difficult for such laws of nature to exist. However, it is possible to identify three megatrends that will contribute to the evolution of asset prices.

Growth, Innovation, and Regulation

Over the past 100 years, we have observed the emergence of a multipolar world, now represented by three major regions (the Americas, Europe, and Asia), that is increasingly well balanced in terms of relative gross domestic product (GDP; Table 1.8). This multipolar world has been essential to individual wealth creation because it has provided access to cheap goods thanks to classical free-trade economic principles. As a result, markets for real goods have become more effective, more accurately reflecting productivity gains. The breadth and depth of markets, and, in particular, of financial markets, have increased considerably. Back in the 1950s, when Arrow and Debreu[9] were talking about the notion of *market completeness*, these concepts looked very abstract and remote from reality. Today, thanks in particular to the explosion of derivatives markets, we can observe market prices for many existing financial assets at many different time

Table 1.8

A Multipolar World

2009	United States	European Union	Developing Asia	Japan
GDP, $US, trillions	14.3	16.4	8.9	5
GDP as a % of global GDP	24.8%	28.4%	15.4%	8.7%

Source: Asian Development Outlook Database.

Table 1.9

An Increasingly Urban World

	1970	2000	2006
Urban population/total population	36%	46%	50%
Global life expectancy	59 years	67.2 years	68.5 years

Sources: United Nations, World Bank.

horizons. Because of this, prices have become more transparent, and the incorporation of new information has become more immediate and efficient. As a result, the allocation of limited capital resources has become increasingly efficient, and better selection of projects with the greatest profit potential has been instrumental in generating macroeconomic growth. The global economy is currently benefiting from a year-on-year GDP growth in the region of 3 to 5 percent. We tend to take such high and sustained growth as a given, but we would do well to remember that in humankind's history there have been prolonged periods of stagnation or recession.

The consequences have transformed the status of the populations of many regions: Urban concentrations have developed (Table 1.9), life expectancy has increased for almost all of us, and systems are in place in developed economies to help us maximize our lifetime consumption, whether we are talking about credit, savings, pensions, or social security.

Growth has benefited from two core factors—population growth (Figure 1.1) and innovation—both of which have boosted demand. Innovation has become the primary engine of growth in the developed world (Figure 1.2). In an economic environment where *rents* from artificial restrictions and oligopolistic organizations are not favored, the only way to maintain high profitability is to use innovation to stay one step ahead of price pressures from competitors. The prioritization of research and development (R&D) funding and the overall availability of cheap funding for investment are critical requirements if a firm is to maintain a high level of innovation.

However, as a result of years of growth and innovation, economies are organized in increasingly complex and diverse ways and require appropriate regulation. In the financial industry, we have recently been able to measure the massive impact on asset prices of the 30-year regulation/deregulation cycle in the wake of the Reagan/Thatcher period: An increased pace of innovation has come at the price of devastating asset-pricing bubble and burst periods.

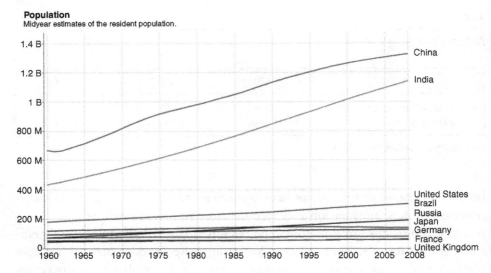

Figure 1.1 Population growth trends.
(*World Bank.*)

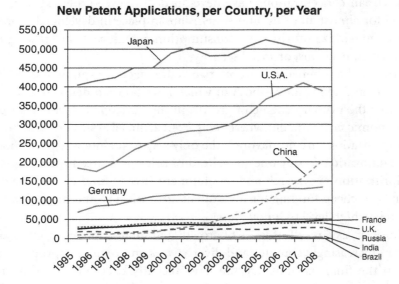

Figure 1.2 Innovation and patent applications.
(*World Intellectual Property Organization.*)

Excessive availability of credit has led to asset bubbles in Northern Europe, Japan, and the United States and will probably soon result in another in China. This phenomenon has been so significant that well-regarded economists[10] have coined the terminology of a *credit supercycle*.

The creation of a regulatory environment that is sufficiently open to innovation—and sufficiently nimble to adapt to evolving market dynamics—is necessary to stabilize what has become a complex, "unstable economy," to use part of Hyman Minsky's book title.[11] The belief that free markets can and should be left to organize themselves has been increasingly challenged recently, and the quality of the regulatory/governance environment gradually is being perceived as a key public good that will drive the value of assets. One example of the positive contribution to the economy of such regulatory/governance measures has been the global effort over the last 20 years to grant more independence to central banks, thereby reinforcing their credibility in the fight against inflation and inflation expectations (Figure 1.3). These measures have led to a structural decrease in the level of interest rates, allowing (among other things) safe assets to be made available in the economy at almost all maturities.

In summary, in a complex society such as ours, the price of assets will be constantly affected by the tension between growth and innovation (which is the

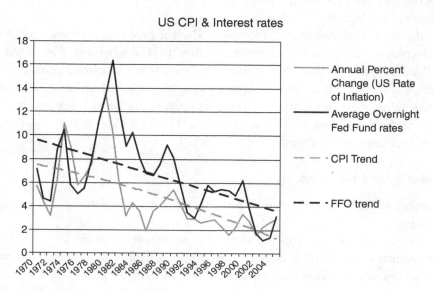

US CPI & Interest rates

——— Annual Percent Change (US Rate of Inflation)

——— Average Overnight Fed Fund rates

— — · CPI Trend

— — · FFO trend

Figure 1.3 The effect of central bank action on inflation containment.
(*Federal Reserve Bank of Minneapolis, Federal Reserve Bank of New York.*)

source of future profits), on the one hand, and the need for regulation that, *inter alia*, has an impact on discount rates and valuation, on the other hand.

The Political Aspect of Globalization and Its Implications for Portfolio Diversification

The second point to consider is the *political* aspect of globalization. Political inter-action across countries has a massive influence on asset prices. This has been long evident, for example, in the European and Middle Eastern wars of the twentieth century. Thanks to technology, perceptions of distances and borders have been fundamentally altered. Voice communication is almost instantaneous around the world, and physical transportation has become much quicker. This transforma-tion has been the source of massive productivity gains in an environment where the probability of major conflicts between large nations seems to have decreased, where the long-term trend is for gradually receding trade protectionism, and where financial exchanges and interdependencies have increased dramatically.

The practical consequence of this is that the investment opportunity set available to individual investors has widened, offering greatly increased oppor-tunities for diversification. As a result, diversification has become a significant component of investment management best practice, and the benefits of asset decorrelation are increasingly being priced into new asset classes, which could otherwise have lagged.

But here, as elsewhere, the solution is also the problem. As trade and finan-cial interconnections develop, as diversification increasingly is considered to be a positive, the independence of regional dynamics tends to diminish as a direct result. Claims of "decoupling" have begun to look increasingly untenable (Figure 1.4 provides an example). Thus we must continue to think about what diversification really means for asset prices. This is a subject that by its very nature is continually evolving.

Imbalance and Disfunctionality

A number of structural imbalances remain in the global economy. Let us high-light a few.

First, consider one problem related to the stability of prices over time. We have benefited considerably over the last 20 years from a clear policy commit-ment to keeping inflation under reasonably tight control. However, a separate, more recent trend has been for central banks to assume a dual role as both driv-ers of monetary policy and chief regulators. The risk here is that central bank independence gets gradually eroded. While governments should remain at arm's

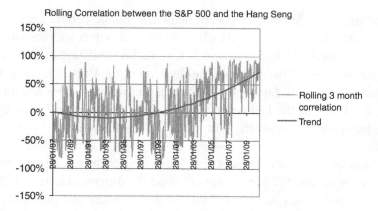

Figure 1.4 The increasing correlation between two country-specific equity indices.

length from monetary policy, they will naturally become involved in regulatory activities.

Another primary source of risk in the global economy relates to future uncertainty and, as a result, increased volatility owing to excessive leverage (Figure 1.5). Nowadays, debt overload affects all major macroeconomic actors,[12] whether

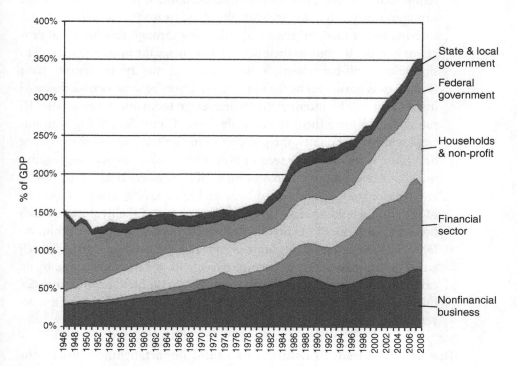

Figure 1.5 Composition of U.S. debt between 1945 and 2009.

we are talking about leverage of governments and public entities (as in the 2011 crisis), corporate leverage (as in the early 2000 Internet bubble), or consumer leverage (as in 2007 in the United States, with households exhibiting negative savings). In the figure we present the details of the situation in the United States. It is worth noting that elsewhere, in Japan and in Europe, the situation does not look vastly different from that of the United States. The situation looks tricky; its dynamics not fully under control, to say the least, for at least two reasons:

- *Deficient indicators to track risk.* Measuring credit risk has become an issue. Since the 1970s, we have relied on third-party players to help us assess credit and counterparty risks in the economy and ultimately to help us to price them—the rating agencies. As a result of the 2007–2009 crisis, rating agencies have lost a lot of credibility, but it is fair to say that there is no credible alternative in place, apart from the financial markets themselves, however illiquid or thinly traded they may be. The consequence is higher volatility of credit spreads, often driven by market sentiment.
- *A virtuous temptation to shrink the economy.* The second issue we are currently facing is the appetite of all macroeconomic players to deleverage simultaneously, each for individually good reasons. Governments are entering into a mode of sustained tightening through tougher fiscal programs in order to contain their deficits, to manage the impact of their pension-related off-balance-sheet liabilities, and to try to restore their credibility as borrowers by the same token. Over the same period, financial institutions will be incentivized to deleverage too, with the new Basel III rules likely to force them to gradually do so. Consumers facing high unemployment uncertainty, the prospect of higher taxes and ever-increasing healthcare costs (as can be seen in Figure 1.6), and a long-lasting negative wealth effect owing to the loss in value of their assets (real estate, stocks, and pensions) are bound to head toward higher saving, to a readjustment of their household leverage given a reassessment of their future net cash flows, and therefore to tighter control of their consumption. The joint effect of all these actors acting rationally on an individual basis carries in itself a real deflationary risk that is counterbalanced, for the time being, by an extremely accommodative monetary policy. With luck, the nonfinancial business activity in the developed economies and the buoyancy of the developing countries will give us some room to maneuver.

This last point leads us naturally to a third important uncertainty—the questionable stability of the international currency system. To present the

Consumption-to-GDP Ratio (%)

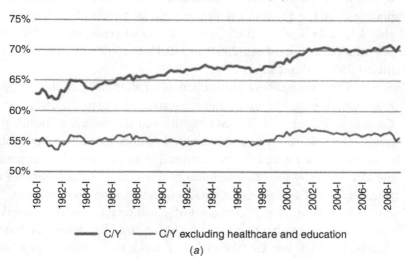

——— C/Y ——— C/Y excluding healthcare and education

(a)

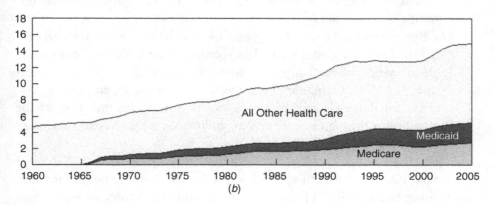

Figure 1.6 (a) The increasing weight of healthcare in U.S. consumption. (b) A more detailed look at the cost of healthcare in the United States as a percentage of GDP (1960–2005).

(*Congressional Budget Office, based on data on spending on health services and supplies, as defined in the national health expenditure accounts maintained by the Centers for Medicare and Medicaid Services.*)

situation in a simple way, we can say that the world currently relies on five major currencies, with a very special role attributed to the U.S. dollar, which is the dominant international reserve currency. Let us consider the situation:

The U.S. dollar. The status of the U.S. dollar as the dominant international reserve currency is tied to the continuous balance-of-payments deficits of the United States, which have allowed surplus countries to increase their U.S. dollar reserves. In addition, though, the U.S. dollar must be managed by the Federal Reserve to meet domestic objectives—to provide adequate liquidity and, in a situation of crisis, to avoid deflation. For this reason, between 2008 and 2010 the U.S. monetary base was multiplied by about 2.5.

The euro. The euro has been positioned as an alternative to the U.S. dollar. However, the recent and ongoing crisis of Portugal, Italy, Ireland, Greece, and Spain (PIIGS) has highlighted the peculiar "political currency" status of the euro and has raised doubts about its future stability.

The renminbi. The renminbi is nonconvertible and more or less harnessed to the U.S. dollar by the Chinese authorities in a way that supports the competitiveness of Chinese goods, thereby creating monetary surpluses (as of 2009, China controlled 27.3 percent of global foreign-exchange reserves).

The yen. The yen has been affected for some time by Japan's deflationary situation, which has translated into a weak international position, as well as by a very accommodative monetary policy meant to address domestic circumstances.

The British pound. The British pound used to be the dominant currency before 1914. Its global status has receded along with the diminishing global weight of the United Kingdom in the world economy. In addition, the United Kingdom recently has been using its currency extensively for domestic purposes as a means to mitigate the effect of the credit crisis through heavy purchase of long-term gilts as part of a *quantitative easing* (QE) program.

In this global situation, there is no doubt that there will be continuing tensions relating to the ability of money to be a stable repository of value. As a result, the pricing of assets could be influenced by the risk of inflation in the long term or at least the perception of such a risk. The increase in the value of gold serves as a good indicator of investor skepticism vis-à-vis these main currencies, particularly because it is clear that gold will never regain its past monetary reference status (Figure 1.7).

Among other structural imbalances, we can think of the cost of access to productive resources. There are obvious bottlenecks, for example, related to the availability of a skilled workforce; in particular, access to education is a real challenge in Asia. Consider also the competition for commodities between regions, especially developing ones (Figure 1.8), which has resulted in a short-lived (2003–2008) so-called commodity supercycle that could reappear in the future, as soon as global GDP growth regains strength.

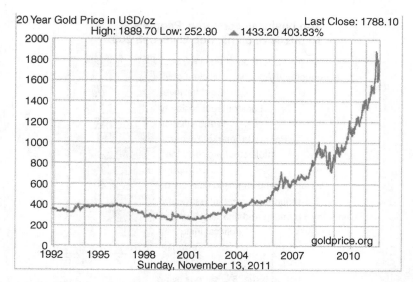

Figure 1.7 Twenty-year gold price history in U.S. dollars per ounce. (*Goldprice.org.*)

One last source of difficulty relates to possible shifts in the demand for financial assets owing to the aging of Western populations, leading to an increasing demand for safe assets over more risky ones. What is well understood is that the demand for fixed-income assets will expand, probably at the expense of equity assets. What is less analyzed is the impact on real estate. A recent Bank of International Settlements (BIS) working paper[13] shows a significant potential negative impact on the change in value of houses related to a change in the demand/offer equilibrium as the population gets older (Figure 1.9).

This snapshot of the structural evolution of the world economy is, of course, very incomplete, but it is probably sufficient to demonstrate that there is a clear indirect impact of these long-term macroeconomics trends on asset prices. Let us first summarize the analysis in Table 1.10.

From this it is clear that the dynamics of asset classes cannot be represented by a random walk. The long-term directions of macroeconomic indicators are bound to have an effect on the performance of these asset classes. But the link between these macroeconomic trends and the prices of assets is indirect and complex. So we start by presenting a stylized vision of what is going on.

One way to do this is to consider the reaching of an economic equilibrium as the result of a stylized multiple-period game[14] among three actors: governments, consumers, and corporations. In this "game," governments and corporations react to expected consumer demand. Corporations focus on the adjustment

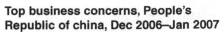

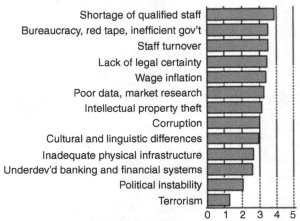

1 = not an issue, 5 = serious issue

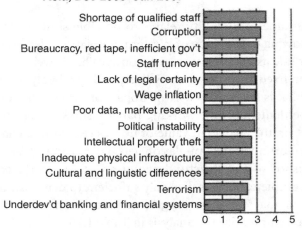

1= not an issue; 5 = serious issue

Figure 1.8 The evidence of a shortage of qualified staff in Asia.
(Based on an Economist Intelligence Unit 2007 survey.)

of production, inventories, and investment to expected consumption trends. Governments adjust monetary and fiscal policies to achieve the right balance between maximum economic growth and policy and structural credibility (e.g., through holding down budgetary or external imbalances). At each period of this

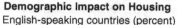

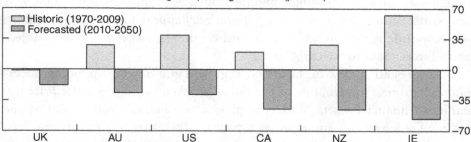

AU = Australia; CA = Canada; UK = the United Kingdom; IE = Ireland; NZ = New Zealand; US = the United States.

Figure 1.9 Forecasted price changes over the next 40 years.
(Takats, 2010.)

dynamic game, we can therefore infer a view on the state of the economy, expressed as an expectation of future GDP growth as well as an associated level of uncertainty. This multiple-period game is affected by a country's economic history because elements such as credibility can only be gained gradually over time as the track record of the players is established. The game obviously factors in the major trends identified earlier.

The interest in using a game theoretic conceptual framework to derive GDP growth expectations and corresponding uncertainty is that it helps us account for the fact that across time periods, the conditions of equilibrium can shift in a discontinuous way. In recent economic global history, it is possible to

Table 1.10

A Summary of the Impact of Some Long-Term Macroeconomic Trends on Asset Prices

	Equities	Fixed Income and Credit	Real Estate	Commodities
Developed financial markets	↑	↑	↑	↑
Increasing population wealth	↑	↑	↑	↑
Real economy innovation	↑	↑		↑
Tighter regulation	↑	↓		
Risk of joint deleverage	↓	↑	↓	
High level of leverage		↓	↓	
Poor risk measurement		↓		
Monetary instability	↓	↓	↓	↓
Aging of the population	↓	↑	↓	↓

identify such somewhat lasting periods of unstable equilibria: Asia in 1997–1998, the United States in 1997–2000, and developed economies in 2007–2009. It is also worth adding that although equilibria may appear to be decoupled from one economic region to another, in reality, they are deeply interconnected, which further adds to the complexity.

This resulting view on future GDP growth and on corresponding uncertainties becomes, in turn, one of the three core factors that drive the price dynamics of financial assets. This view plays a considerable role in setting the degree of risk aversion among market players. The other two factors are, first, the quality of financial news flow related to corporate profitability and the outlook for this and, second, the liquidity conditions of the financial markets. Liquidity conditions play an important indirect role in the financing of risky assets, supporting the valuation of low-yielding asset classes such as equities, real estate, and commodities by encouraging or discouraging leverage. They also set a reference point by affecting the pricing of risk-free assets.

The fundamental point here is that when we try to understand the impact of the macroeconomic environment on asset prices, we should move away from a linear perspective and from any assumption that the normal state of affairs is for an indefinite period of growth punctuated only by some unexpected periods of disturbance. It is interesting to note in this respect that empirical evidence has shown us that the dynamics of prices tend to follow a multiple-regime pattern, as was well documented by Ang and Bekaert (2002) and others for equities in the early 2000s.

It therefore does not look reasonable to develop an asset-allocation process that does not incorporate in a formal way the impact of long-term macroeconomic trends and the dynamics of the macroeconomic evolution.

The Traditional 1- to 10-Year Asset-Allocation Horizon: The Contribution of Finance

Over the past 40 years, finance has emerged as a well-established discipline, largely independent of economics. During this period, financial theory has evolved toward providing prices or portfolio-construction rules almost independent of economic forecasts.

Some of the founding principles of finance have been

1. *Market efficiency.* This makes forecasts useless because current prices are believed to be the best mechanism to aggregate all market participants' forecasts instantaneously.

2. *Static portfolio construction.* This is seen as the way to mitigate risks through diversification.
3. *A long-term focus.* This is needed because a regular rebalancing of the asset allocation would be susceptible to market timing and the associated risks. It is also assumed that a stable allocation should enable us to benefit from excess returns over cash generated by risky assets, thanks to the existence of a risk premium toward which returns revert to over the long term.
4. *Asset class indices as the basis for asset allocation.* Under the CAPM approach, active managers can add value only if they can rely on superior information.
5. *The existence of a single optimal asset allocation.* This occurs once the risk tolerance of an individual has been determined.

These principles have greatly influenced the investment thinking of the financial community. But their credibility has been dealt a big blow recently with the empirical observation that if one applies all the principles just described and uses standard modeling techniques, it is very difficult to outperform a naive equally weighted portfolio on a risk-adjusted basis.[15] Thus it is worth revisiting all these principles one by one.

Questioning the Assumption of Market Efficiency

If markets are efficient, then the best allocation is precisely that of markets as a whole. By assuming that we know the relative weights across asset classes as well as the risk-aversion parameter of the representative investor, we can establish the expected returns from efficient markets by computing the corresponding *equilibrium returns* of assets as in the CAPM or Black-Litterman approaches (see Chapter 3).[16]

Assuming that we can overcome the problems associated with such calculations—which, by the way, are considerable—we usually arrive at the surprising observation that equilibrium returns generally depart massively from the historical average returns. This is not an intuitive conclusion and must prompt further analysis. Is it worth questioning, for example, one's assessment of the relevance of the relative weight of some asset classes in the light of their dynamics? Should Asia have a much larger relative allocation in the future than now? Will the appetite for fixed income in the future diminish if there isn't much potential for further gains after 20 years of successful inflation fighting by the newly established independent central banks? How can we reliably assess the size of the less-liquid over-the-counter (OTC) markets?

But by asking such questions, we implicitly start to depart from the assumption of efficient markets. And an even more fundamental question comes quickly to the fore: Are the equilibrium returns corresponding to current information relevant at the horizon of a second, a month, a year, or 10 years? The longer forward we look, the more suspicious the results implied by the CAPM appear.

Dependency Patterns Are Fact Time-Varying

The implicit belief is that there exists, to be discovered, a stable diversification level across asset classes and that this corresponds with an optimal way to protect from downside risks and maximize the satisfaction (utility) of investors. A number of events over the past 20 years, however—for example, the 1997–1998 sovereign contagion and the 2007–2009 sharp rise in comovement across asset classes—have meant that these implicit beliefs increasingly have been questioned. In parallel, there have been many mathematical refinements around the definition of multivariate risks, focusing on extreme events and fat tails rather than on volatility and covariance, as well as around the definition of adequate estimation methods.

Now that all these refinements have been incorporated into portfolio construction without yielding any major breakthrough, though, it is an appropriate time to confess that there is no Holy Grail static methodology. Any such modeling framework looks, at best, very weak when used to make future decisions and prone to *overfitting* on past information (i.e., it describes random past events rather than establishing any robust underlying relationship).

As an example, let us focus on the recent 2007–2009 credit crisis. Credit portfolio modeling relied very heavily on portfolio diversification. Thus, squeezing the value generated from diversification through securitization [collateralized debt obligations (CDOs), residential mortgage-backed securities (RMBSs), etc.] became the name of the game. In the credit universe, the benefit of diversification was assumed to be massive because it was observed that default correlation typically was 10 times lower than the corresponding equity/asset correlation. The idea was that it was possible to reliably measure and benefit from a stable, low, "through-the-cycle" correlation level among individual credit assets. This has proved to be an empirical dead end. Conscious of this precarious situation even before the crisis, the credit industry had spent a fortune on R&D, trying to identify a stable dependency framework that was more refined than simple correlations. It failed because there is no such law of nature waiting to be discovered that can describe fundamentally stable dependency patterns across assets and asset classes. Multiasset dependency is clearly time-varying.[17]

Assumptions On Stable Asset Performance and The Short and Long Term

Although it claims fierce independence from macroeconomic thinking, modern finance in fact makes significant implicit macroeconomic assumptions, among which is the belief in a reasonably stable increase in the price of risky assets over the long run (mean reversion toward the long-term risk premium). However, if you consider the case of Japan, for example, it might appear that this assumption holds only in the very long run—or not at all. In *Wealth, War and Wisdom*,[18] Barton Biggs notes that one of the most promising emerging markets before World War II was Argentina. It has consistently failed to deliver performance since then. Even in countries such as the United States, the assumption of a stable trend has been questioned recently, as can be observed in Figure 1.10. Overall, the assumption of a fundamental independence between the long-term performance of risky assets and the dynamics of the related macroeconomic environment does not seem to hold.

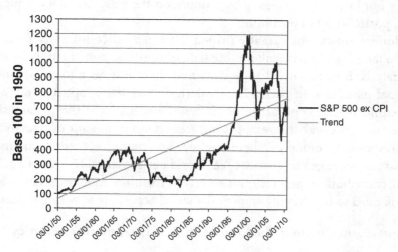

Figure 1.10 A changing pattern of mean reversion of the Standard & Poor's 500 Index (S&P500) over the past 60 years.

Active versus Passive Asset Management

With only around a quarter of mutual funds typically outperforming their benchmark on an annual basis after fees and only 5 percent managing to do this over three-year periods in developed markets, active asset managers have not been very successful in proving the benefit of active stock picking. This is an important point, and the recent dramatic growth of the exchange-traded funds (ETF) industry is a testimony to the increased acceptance of the value of passive management. (As an aside, this point about the virtues of passive versus active asset management generally is used to back the efficient market hypothesis, something that is more questionable—believing that the alpha of a stock over its index follows a random walk does not mean that the excess return over cash of that same stock is bound to follow a random walk too.)

More Evidence Against a One-Size-Fits-All Approach

We have seen earlier in this chapter, using behavioral finance, that because of the weakness of the concept of a representative investor, we should not consider a one-size-fits-all optimal portfolio. In addition, empirical evidence shows that such a portfolio, when computed according to best practices, is very sensitive to the definition of the time period over which it is estimated, as will be detailed in Chapter 4. A method recently employed to mitigate this issue is to perform time averaging of portfolios computed over different periods using a process called *resampling* (or *bootstrapping*). Such a procedure enables us to limit spurious accuracy but by its very necessity casts doubt on the existence of a unique, truly optimal portfolio/set of portfolios.

Modern finance has greatly helped the financial community to adopt a common language, in particular in the field of portfolio construction. From our brief analysis, it is, however, quite clear that there is a need to go beyond this traditional paradigm. In particular, modern finance has adopted a very principle-based normative approach, that is, describing things as they ideally should be rather than the way they empirically are, often for reasons of tractability of the corresponding models. Where applied, however, this theoretical environment has not managed to generate real-world performance. In order to produce a useful contribution, any technique derived from the modern finance framework will need to be carefully empirically tested according to best practices.

The Short-Term Horizon: The Contribution of Quantitative Analytics

Relatively high-frequency *quantitative analytics* (QA) emerged in the early years of this century as a new driving force on the buy side, beyond the closed world of hedge funds. After a short period of excitement, however, it was dealt an almost fatal blow with the Goldman Sachs Asset Management (GSAM) quant fund quasi-collapse during August 2008.

Does this mean that there is no future for QA? Let us have a look at both the facts and our intuitions before drawing a conclusion.

Modern finance maintains a focus on market efficiency. QA may be able to drill down further in this area if it can use its tool kit to analyze with care the process of aggregation of new information into prices, and thus we can benefit from it to enhance returns.

Some people, such as Andrew Lo,[19] have suggested a Darwinian approach to market dynamics, coining the term the *adaptive market hypothesis* to replace the efficient market hypothesis. We have, however, a less ambitious perspective and focus here instead simply on observation.

A way to describe this process of understanding market dynamics is to break it down into four features:

1. *Inertia.* The word used commonly in finance to characterize inertia is its opposite, *momentum.* The basic premise is that future market movements can be deduced from what has happened in the recent past.
2. *News incorporation.* If you observe financial markets from a trading desk, it is clear that unemployment numbers, activity surveys [purchasing manager index(PMI), the Institute for Supply Management (ISM) new order index, etc.], GDP updates, and so on have a significant impact on prices.
3. *Feedback loops.* New information often leads to prices under- or overshooting and then subsequently correcting. The corresponding concept is that of mean reversion toward a drift/moving-average level.
4. *Market receptivity.* There are periods when the financial news flow from corporations, for instance, significantly affects market prices and other periods during which similar information does not seem to have much influence. During the latter periods, markets can seem to be polarized by other systemic issues and worries. Practitioners have put together risk-aversion indices or sometimes use market volatility as a gauge for this concept of market receptivity and its influence on the price of risky assets.

Let us review these four features in more detail.

Implicit Reliance On Inertia

Modern finance relies on the principle of market inertia much more than it thinks. This principle underpins the estimate of a covariance matrix using

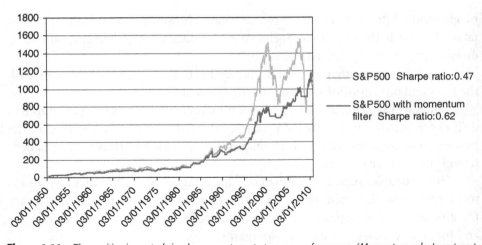

Figure 1.11 The positive impact of simple momentum strategy on performance. (*Momentum rule:* Invest next month if cumulative past five-month return has been positive; otherwise, do not.)

historical information. What is to some extent reassuring is that when using the most recent past information to make near-term decisions, we generally obtain better results than when we rely on a longer historical period. With respect to time-series forecasting, momentum always has been a weed in the garden of modern finance because it contradicts the hypothesis of market efficiency (Figure 1.11). It has already found its way into traditional Fama-French-type factor models. [20]

There is a striking finding related to the use of momentum that can be illustrated by the following experiment: Consider a traditional equity/bond portfolio corresponding to a standard geographic diversification. The first option consists of estimating an out-of-sample yearly covariance matrix and rebalancing an optimal portfolio on a yearly basis. The second option consists of estimating the covariance matrix on a monthly basis and rebalancing the portfolio dynamically every month. The finding, over the past 20 years, is that instead of generating a Sharpe ratio over that period in the area of at best 0.3 with option 1, we can reach a Sharpe ratio in the region of 1.0 with option 2. In other words, by more frequent observation and rebalancing, we should be able gain an increase in excess return for a given level of risk. Naturally, the impact of transactions costs is relevant in this context because they will eat into gains slightly, but there remains a broader point here.

One specific asset-management field, commodity trading advisor (CTA) hedge funds, has relied heavily on the principle of momentum with some success. Can we therefore say that momentum constitutes one of our elusive laws of nature? The higher frequency of observations possible here lends itself better to the identification of such laws of nature—if they exist—and there is certainly a role for momentum in such analysis. However, the intensity with which momentum comes into play appears to be time-varying. In periods of high volatility, for instance, during which the flow of time seems to accelerate, momentum may play a lesser role.

News Incorporation

It is obvious that new information affects market prices. The question is whether there exist relatively stable patterns corresponding to the incorporation of news in prices. Will, for instance, a GDP number announced this month affect the value of the equity index next month in a stable and predictable manner? The theoretical answer to this question is "No," because if there were there such a relationship, many investors would chase this abnormal return until it disappeared. However, identifying such patterns is usually costly, so as long as would-be investors do not overcrowd the space, it is possible that there do exist some undiscovered relationships of this type. The number and size of investors involved and aware of such patterns are important here. Take the case of the GSAM quant fund mentioned at the start of this section. At some stage, several similar large funds [e.g., Barclays Global Investors (BGI) and JPM Highbridge] were using equivalent techniques called *factor models* to track such resilient patterns, leading to overcrowding in this investment space, decreasing performance, and in turn resulting in higher risk-taking. This is one of the reasons why people working on tracking the mechanisms for news incorporation tend to do so in a secretive manner and invest large sums of money on innovation in order to keep an edge over the competition. This being said, static factor models that seek to find stable relationships over time related to news incorporation tend not to be successful for long—once such patterns are identified, their usefulness diminishes. There are in fact no laws of nature to expect here. It is interesting to note, in this respect, that time-adaptive factor models typically do a much better job of forecasting. This is certainly an avenue for niche players on proprietary trading desks for CTA and hedge funds but is not likely to become a mainstream profitable practice in asset management.

Feedback Loops and The Concept of Mean Reversion

At times, markets get carried away by a piece of news, by market sentiment, or just by prolonged momentum and tend to deviate substantially from "fair value" on commonly accepted valuation standards. In the high-frequency space, this fair value can take the shape of a drift or moving average. At some stage, there is usually a convergence back toward this fair value. This mechanism is called *mean reversion*. Like momentum, mean reversion seems to be a persistent feature, although, again, this is not a feature that comes into play with the same strength at all times.

Market Receptivity

Markets are driven by supply and demand. At certain times, demand for risky assets becomes more limited—with, for instance, retail investors fleeing to "safe" assets. This typically influences the expected risk premium that is demanded by investors and hence prices. The prices of assets are sensitive to the expected modification of future cash flows signaled by new information, as well as to the variation in the discount factor that translates the cash flows of tomorrow into a price today. These two random variables compete and get combined into price formation.

In addition to providing deeper insight into the dynamics of markets and prices than the EMH paradigm, a short time horizon also offers some interesting insights from a risk management perspective. The more the frequency of observation increases, the less time series of returns look normally distributed, which implies that a focus on tail risks, rather than just volatility, becomes even more important.

Being able to fully specify a measure of risk that incorporates all the information about the returns distribution is crucial to avoiding an excessively narrow focus just on certain aspects of tail risk—for example, a VaR (value at risk) 95 percent measure means that we are blind, from a risk perspective, on 99 percent confidence level risks. In this respect, we believe that using behavioral finance techniques to estimate risk measures specific to individuals' risk/return preferences constitutes a significant improvement over existing rule-of-thumb practices. We will discuss this later in this book.

QA as Potential But Limited Solution

As is obvious from this section, QA seems to have some real potential in investment management. Thus one should not be surprised by the recent interest in higher-frequency rebalancing of portfolios.

Beyond this, we need to ask ourselves whether news incorporation, which in reality is another name for the usually dreaded *market-timing problem*, offers some hope. Expressing this issue from a mathematical perspective, this all means that we, as finance professionals, are, in reality, in the business of explaining the residual error term in the dynamics of returns because returns generally are not well characterized by Brownian motion. However, it should not be possible to generate consistently excess returns over the market without relying on high-conviction views. These views can be derived from qualitative as well as quantitative observations, factors, and patterns.

Conclusion: What This Means for Future Trends in Asset Management

Paraphrasing a well-known sentence in the sphere of monetary policy, we did not abandon modern portfolio theory; it abandoned us.[21] Over the next chapters, we are going to investigate, with care and following an objective review process, what has gone wrong. In the second part of this book, we then will recommend a new framework to replace MPT. But before we move on to this, let us summarize the key points from this chapter.

First, we should realize that behavioral finance has a lot to add to the subject of traditional finance. Behavioral finance does not need to be confined to an endless identification of human biases and irrationality. It also need not be set up exclusively in opposition to classical finance—the traditional tools have considerable value and should not be discarded simply because their assumptions are too rigid, but they speak only to nonexistent ultrarational investors, not real humans. Rather, by allowing us to really understand how investors make decisions and why any claimed universal optimal investment solution should be treated with suspicion, behavioral finance can contribute to creating value and raising investment performance. This, after all, is what investment management should be all about. Instead of thinking in terms of behavioral finance versus classical finance, we prefer the phrase *behavioralizing finance.*

Second, we should accept that the attempt by finance to disentangle itself from economics and rely on a stylized configuration of the world and of financial assets has failed. We need to rethink the way we combine economics and finance.

Third, we have to move beyond the efficient market hypothesis. Some 40 years ago, it might have made sense to assume that at some stage of development of financial markets, full market efficiency would be within reach. In reality, while we have progressed toward efficiency, it is clear that there are major obstacles to moving further along this road. Instead, we need to fine-tune our understanding of the formation of prices in such a way that it becomes usable in an investment management process. Quantitative analytics should help in this respect.

Fourth, we clearly need to depart from a linear perspective of the global economy and asset prices, where we see them as characterized by steady growth and punctuated by rare periods of disruption. This has important consequences for how we consider asset diversification and dependency. The notion of a stable through-the-cycle dependency pattern across assets has proven wrong.

Fifth, we need to ground portfolio construction to a lesser extent than previously on regional and asset class diversification, the two aspects of diversification that have dominated debate for the last 20 years. To complement this shift in emphasis, we should investigate *time-horizon diversification*, achieved through blending investment strategies relying on different time horizons, because time series do not exhibit similar properties at different frequencies.

Chapters 2 through 4 explain the problems facing us in more detail; our new proposed approach to portfolio construction, which addresses the five points highlighted herein, is set out in Chapters 5 through 9.

Notes

1. Duration corresponds to the maturity of the equivalent zero-coupon bond. A simple way to compute duration is to compute the weighted-average maturity of all the payment flows corresponding to the bond (interest and principal).
2. For more details, see Leijonhufvud (2011).
3. We largely rely on the seminal work of Shefrin (2008).
4. See Chapter 3 for a thorough definition of the efficient frontier.
5. Classical economics assumes that all investors have stable, rational preferences that can be represented by expected utility theory. We will explore this idea extensively in Chapter 2.
6. See Slovic (1991).
7. In addition, disequilibrium may persist for substantial periods owing to considerable limits to arbitrage (Shleifer, 2000).
8. Rubinstein (1974) and Brennan and Kraus (1978).
9. Arrow and Debreu (1954).
10. See Bolton and Boeckh from BCA.
11. Minsky (2008).
12. This situation has been analyzed extensively in Reinhart and Rogoff (2009).
13. Takats (2010).

14. Following the spirit of the seminal Barro and Gordon (1983) article, which represented monetary policy as a game following rules established in the framework of game theory.
15. See in particular DeMiguel, Garlappi and Uppal (2009).
16. Using, for instance, various families of copulas, frailty models, higher moments, and so on.
17. Recently, several academic papers have looked at accounting for such time variations, thanks to dynamic multiperiod models. Apart from simple implementations, most of these multiperiod models (typically using stochastic dynamic programming techniques) stay largely theoretical because the difficulty of estimating parameters and the accumulation of error terms makes the process quickly intractable.
18. Biggs (2008).
19. Lo (2004).
20. See Carhart (1997).
21. The original sentence from G. Bouey, governor of the Bank of Canada, quoted by Mishkin (1999), was, "We did not abandon monetary aggregates; they abandoned us."

Chapter 2

INDIVIDUAL INVESTOR PREFERENCES AND BEHAVIOR

with Peter Brooks and Daniel Egan

An integral component of modern portfolio theory (MPT) is an evaluation of the individual's preferences and behavior in reaction to risky outcomes at an instant and through time. We start this chapter by describing *expected utility theory* (EUT), the foundation of classical economic and finance theory. Then we explain why the way EUT is used in MPT is unsatisfactory and can lead to investment underperformance. In the third section we look at the distinct problems of narrow framing and diversification. This is followed by attempts to develop an alternative descriptive theory of choice, but then we outline why such descriptive theories should not be used to guide behavior. For the remainder of the chapter we examine some of the additional complexities that we believe should be considered to achieve the best result for each investor, contrasting our *affective* and *deliberative* systems of decision making and also underlining why a number of investor psychometric traits need to be measured, not just risk tolerance.

Before we start, however, we need to draw a distinction between normative and descriptive models. *Normative models* attempt to explain how choices *should* be made by an individual, whereas *descriptive models* attempt to describe how choices actually *are* made. Any portfolio-optimization technique will be a normative model of how to achieve the best potential set of outcomes for the individual. However, to understand how individuals actually perceive and react to risky investment situations, we must turn to empirical evidence and descriptive models to guide our intuitions about what matters to real investors. We all have different preferences, and it is important to know how and why to measure differences between individuals when building up a model of how they should make investment decisions.

Expected Utility Theory and Observed Choices

Utility Functions as a Way of Representing Preferences Mathematically

Every day we each make numerous decisions that affect our well-being. Some may be small, such as which chocolate bar to purchase from an office vending machine; some may be large, such as the investment options in your pension plan. It is reasonable to assume that in your decisions you aim to maximize some measure of well-being, satisfaction, or pleasure.

Your preferences signal the relative attractiveness of the options you have available to you. You may prefer apples to oranges or tea over coffee. Economists use the abstract concept of *utility* to measure individuals' relative preferences. A *utility function* is a way to represent preferences in a mathematical form by mapping outcomes into real numbers so as to order the options in the same way as your preferences. Thus, if you prefer to have an apple rather than an orange, then at that moment the apple must have a higher utility value.

When making investment decisions, satisfying your preferences means trying to make choices that achieve the best possible financial outcome in your portfolio. Here we assume that more wealth (and hence greater ability to consume) is always the higher-utility outcome. However, financial decisions are not as simple as choices between fruits. They involve uncertain future outcomes and therefore involve trading off outcomes in various possible futures to achieve the best tradeoff between average or *expected* returns and the risk of the investment. To do this requires considering both the magnitude of future outcomes and their associated probabilities of occurring. In other words, we are required to trade off the chance of extremely good but lucky outcomes to ensure that we protect against extremely bad and unlucky outcomes.

Why an *Expected Value* Approach Is Unsatisfactory

A simple normative solution to evaluating such tradeoffs in economic theory is to maximize *expected value*—that is, to determine the potential gains and losses in wealth from all the potential outcomes—and then to find the portfolio that generates the highest expected wealth across all possible outcomes in the future, weighted by their probability of occurring. However, this expected value model delivers unrealistic and counterintuitive results because it requires that you weight negative outcomes exactly the same as positive outcomes.

To see this, imagine two separate investments:

1. A 50 percent chance of losing $10 and a 50 percent probability of gaining $10
2. A 50 percent chance of losing $10,000 and a 50 percent chance of gaining $10,000

Both these scenarios appear to be bad gambles to take. In probability-weighted monetary terms, you exactly break even in both, but you can get the same expected value without having to take the gamble in the first place. The first intuition we gain here is that it is a bad idea to take on potential losses for *no* expected (average) upside—a baseline criterion for an attractive investment is that it should have a positive expected value.

Even then, expected value fails as a description of how we evaluate investments. Imagine adding 1 cent to the $10,000 gain in the second scenario so that it becomes $10,000.01. Would this make it suddenly the obvious choice because it now has a positive expected value? Most people would still see the second scenario as very risky and less preferable. What we need to do, therefore, is to define a utility function that reflects the fact that potential losses hurt more than potential gains feel good. This would prevent us from accepting investments that have high potential losses, for zero or only marginally positive average gains (like either of those listed above). By understanding the level of utility investors apply to possible future outcomes, we can ensure that additional risks are taken on only if they, on average, result in higher *expected utility* (rather than just monetary gain) for the investor.

Properties Ascribable to Rational Long-Term Investors

Expected utility theory (EUT), the foundation of classical economic and finance theory, provides the theoretical underpinning for this. EUT in essence shows that if our preferences between choices (e.g., different investments) display some simple rational properties, then we can represent those preferences using a utility function that assigns each possible outcome a utility value. In this utility function, each specific possible future return, for example, 5 percent, is assigned a utility level regardless of which investment it comes from. When each outcome's utility (rather than merely value) is multiplied by the probability of its occurring to arrive at the expected utility of each option or investment, this numerical *expected utility* assigned to each investment will have exactly the same rank order as our preferences between the investments themselves.

Reversing this logic, if we can define the utility function and know the probability of each outcome, then we can calculate the expected utility of each prospective investment and thereby determine which one best satisfies our preferences. The optimal investment decision is the one that gives us the maximum probability-weighted (expected) utility, that is, the one that maximizes our preferences on average over all possible future outcomes.

Defining the utility function accurately is thus crucial to being able to determine the optimal investment portfolio. If the utility function is to assist the decision maker in making rational decisions, then it needs to be in some senses "well behaved"; that is, it needs to reflect rational assumptions about how an investor should value monetary outcomes and approach risk. The following are properties that may be sensibly ascribed to rational long-term investors considering how to invest their total wealth:

- *More is always preferred to less.* Each additional amount of money should always increase utility. Graphically, this means that the function is always increasing as wealth increases.
- *The investor should be averse to risk.* At each point on the utility function, the investor should place a stronger emphasis on losing one unit than on gaining an additional unit. In effect, this means that while more is preferred to less, each additional unit of money should yield less utility than the previous ones (diminishing marginal utility). A more risk-averse individual will feel this more strongly than an investor who is more risk tolerant. Graphically, this means that the function is concave—the curve at any point is steeper to the left than to the right. The more concave the curvature, the stronger is the risk aversion of the investor.[1]
- *There should be no sudden jumps in utility.* A well-behaved utility function for money should not have smoothly increasing utility up to some value of wealth and then a sudden surge in utility over this value. For such a surge to be rational, there would have to be other nonmonetary benefits to achieving this particular level of wealth, such as some social or psychological benefit from achieving some aspiration. Such nonmonetary benefits are certainly plausible, but for the purposes of investment strategy, we are concerned here with purely financial outcomes.

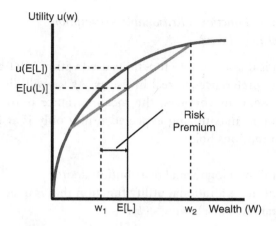

Figure 2.1 Utility gains associated with increasing levels of wealth.

Figure 2.1 shows a utility function (of wealth) that satisfies all these requirements: It is smoothly increasing with no jumps and gets gradually less steep as wealth increases. This concavity has the important implication that the expected utility of any uncertain investment is lower than the utility one would get by having that amount with certainty. So in the 50/50 investments described earlier, while the expected value of this is a breakeven (equal to your current wealth), the expected utility is negative because the potential loss of utility outweighs the potential gain. Or in the figure, the expected utility from a 50/50 lottery (L) between w_1 and w_2 is $E[u(L)]$, whereas getting the expected value $E[L]$ for certain gives higher utility of $u(E[L])$.

The more curved the utility function, the faster is the decline in utility at any point relative to an equivalent gain, and so the greater is the aversion to risk.

Problems with the Utility Foundation of MPT

Unfortunately, the utility function implicit in MPT fails to satisfy both the first and second properties outlined earlier at large wealth levels, as well as displaying other undesirable features. We discuss several of these failures below and argue that these problems cast doubts on the way in which EUT has been used in MPT. At this stage, we are concerned only with EUT's failures at a *normative* level—in other words, how it fails to adequately describe the choices that *should* be made. Later in this chapter we look at the behavioral difficulties associated with putting such normative recommendations in place in practice.

*Is a Quadratic Utility Function a Reasonable Assumption
for a Rational Decision Maker?*

The first problem is that the utility functions used within MPT are inaccurate in describing rational preferences of real investors. As we will discuss much more extensively in subsequent chapters, the mean variance optimization used in MPT is equivalent to maximizing expected utility only if at least one of the following two assumptions holds:

1. Returns follow a lognormal distribution and/or
2. Individuals have a rational utility function that is quadratic—that is, of the general form $u(w) = aw^2 + bw + c$.

Here we will focus on the second of these: whether quadratic utility is a reasonable assumption for a rational decision maker. A discussion on whether or not the assumption of the normality of returns is empirically justified can be found in Chapter 4.

Figure 2.2 shows the shape of the standard quadratic utility function. The most obvious failing is that it implies that above a certain point, investors start *losing* utility from better returns and will do so at an increasing rate.

The quadratic utility function also has implausible implications for how individuals' risk aversion changes as they become wealthier. Consider the following questions: Does risk aversion change as people get wealthier? Does their additional wealth lead them to take more or less risk?

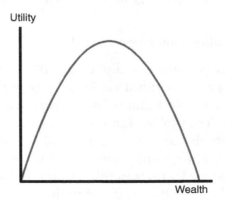

Figure 2.2   A quadratic utility function.

Problems Associated with the Assumption of Constant Absolute Risk Aversion

To explore this further, let us introduce the concepts of absolute risk aversion and relative risk aversion. An investor is said to have *constant absolute risk aversion* (CARA) if changes in wealth do not cause changes in the investor's willingness to take risks with a fixed amount of money—for example, decision makers with CARA will be just as happy to take a bet of plus or minus $10 on a fair coin toss regardless of whether they have only $100 to their name or are millionaires. This seems unlikely. Consider the implications of the following three scenarios.

First, imagine that an investor has a total wealth of $1 million and chooses to invest $100,000 in a single stock. Now what would happen if the same investor wants to invest in the same stock but his or her total wealth is now $2 million?

> *Scenario 1:* The investor still chooses to invest $100,000. This indicates constant absolute risk aversion.
> *Scenario 2:* The investor chooses to invest less than $100,000. This indicates increasing absolute risk aversion.
> *Scenario 3:* The investor chooses to invest more than $100,000. This indicates decreasing absolute risk aversion.

There is no right or wrong pattern of risk attitudes, and you may come across different individuals who exhibit each of these behaviors at certain times or in certain circumstances. However, the dominant behavior would appear to be *decreasing absolute risk aversion*. As individuals get wealthier, they tend to put a greater absolute amount at risk. Intuitively, this seems highly plausible. We may measure this curvature by the *Arrow-Pratt coefficient of absolute risk aversion*, defined as minus the second derivative of the utility normalized by its first derivative[2]:

$$-\frac{u''(w_0)}{u'(w_0)}$$

By contrast, an investor is said to have *constant relative risk aversion* (CRRA) if he or she invests the same *proportion* of his or her wealth in a risky asset irrespective of the level of his or her wealth. This may be measured by the *coefficient of relative risk aversion*, which is defined as

$$-w_0\frac{u''(w_0)}{u'(w_0)}$$

Reflect on the same situation as above, where the investor has total wealth of $1 million and chooses initially to invest $100,000 (10 percent) in a single stock. Now consider what would happen to the relative size of the investment (as a percentage) if total wealth is $2 million:

Scenario 1: The investor chooses to invest $200,000 (10 percent). This indicates constant relative risk aversion.

Scenario 2: The investor chooses to invest less than $200,000. This indicates increasing relative risk aversion.

Scenario 3: The investor chooses to invest more than $200,000. This indicates decreasing relative risk aversion.

Again, there is no correct pattern of behavior. Arrow (1965) hypothesized that individuals should exhibit increasing relative risk aversion, and the experimental evidence suggests that many people exhibit either slightly increasing or constant relative risk aversion. Examining the overall economy over the long run, it is clear that relative risk aversion cannot change much as wealth increases: Wealth and consumption levels per head have increased dramatically over the last few hundred years without any evidence of long-run trends in the costs investors are prepared to pay to avoid relative risks, that is, interest rates and risk premia. Thus, on average, over the long term, relative risk aversion must be approximately constant.[3] This also feels intuitively plausible. If an individual is willing to put 10 percent of his or her wealth at risk at one wealth level, then it seems reasonable that he or she would be willing to continue investing 10 percent of his or her wealth if he or she gets wealthier.

Let us return to considering the quadratic utility function that is consistent with MPT. Taking the quadratic utility function of the form

$$u(x) = x - ax^2$$

where x is the wealth level and $a > 0$ so that the function is concave, the function has an absolute risk-aversion coefficient of $-2a/(1 - 2ax)$ and relative risk aversion equal to $-2ax/(1 - 2ax)$. These are both increasing in x, so the quadratic utility function exhibits both increasing absolute risk aversion and increasing relative risk aversion. While the second of these implications *could* be reasonable, the requirement for increasing absolute risk aversion is generally unacceptable. As individuals get wealthier, it is unreasonable that they reduce their absolute exposure to risk. Thus, even if an individual is an expected utility maximizer (as individuals normatively should be), his or her utility function would never be quadratic. The assumptions are just too unreasonable to explain rational long-term investment behavior. By rejecting quadratic utility, we also reject the applicability of MPT, except in the highly specific case where returns are normally distributed.

Why Using a Quadratic Utility Function Prevents Consideration of the Full Returns Distribution

So why has a theory based on this function become so widely used in practice, even if it is easy to show that the assumptions on which it is based are unrealistic? Well, it has some very mathematically convenient properties that make it easy to use.

With many utility functions, expected utility can be rewritten as a tradeoff between expected return, which we can denote as $\bar{r}$, and a measure of risk, which we can represent as R. That is, we can rewrite the expected utility $E[u(x)]$ as a function of expected return $\bar{r}$ and risk R so that maximizing expected utility is equivalent to determining the optimal tradeoff between $\bar{r}$ and R, that is, $E[u(x)] = f(\bar{r}, R)$.

It turns out that for an investor with quadratic utility, the risk R of any investment can be completely expressed by the *variance* of the distribution σ^2, so the decomposition of expected utility into risk and return has a particularly simple form: $E[u(x)] = f(\bar{r}, \sigma^2)$. Quadratic utility implies that investors do not care about any aspects of the distribution of returns other than mean and variance. If log returns are normally distributed, then this is not a problem because the distribution can be fully described using only mean and variance. However, this is not true of investments in general—and for investments with significant deviations from normality (e.g., any derivatives or asset classes with fat tails in the distribution), investors would need more measures than just the variance of the distribution.

Variance is an odd risk measure to use for investors because it is a symmetric measure of the dispersion of a distribution around its expected value, so deviations both above and below the mean add equally to the "risk" of an investment. While the chance of negative outcomes should increase risk, it is far from clear why better than expected outcomes also *add* to the risk of an investment. Most investors would not consider returns that exceeded their expectations as being risky. To them, risk is psychologically a downside-oriented notion, and the use of variance in portfolio optimization therefore makes little sense. We need a better function than the quadratic to incorporate more sophisticated risk attitudes so that R can be represented by a measure that encompasses the risks of investment more comprehensively than variance.

Quadratic utility rules out any possibility that an investor has preferences regarding the kurtosis and skewness of a distribution (in other words, regarding the "peakedness" of a distribution, the size of the tails on each side, and whether or not the distribution is even around the center point). Quadratic utility ignores all these factors. It is entirely reasonable that an individual should dislike return distributions that have a significant chance of extreme outcomes (the so-called fat tails brought about by kurtosis). Disregarding this further diminishes the applicability of the quadratic utility function.

Biases and Paradoxes of Choice: Going Beyond EUT

Looking beyond the immediate problems of using quadratic utility as a normative model, it is also clear that it is wrong to assume that investors always decide rationally according to EUT. Behavioral science is full of examples of failure of EUT to describe real decision making, which tells us much about our practical preferences and biases.

Framing, Loss Aversion, and Risk-Seeking for Losses

A number of biases and paradoxes have been studied over decades by behavioral scientists, providing evidence of numerous violations of the axioms of EUT. Many of these use carefully constructed mathematical examples[4] to prove that EUT is regularly violated in the choice patterns of most people. But let's examine a much more general phenomenon that is ubiquitous in the psychology of perception as well as judgment and decision making and leads to such violations—*framing*.

The word, of course, stems from an art analogy whereby a painting may be appreciated quite differently if it is housed in a large, ornate gilt frame or in a thin, black minimalist frame. We all know that a room may appear dark if we've come into it from a bright exterior or bright if we've previously been somewhere dimly lit. And we've all come across many visual illusions that play on this effect of framing and relative judgment.

But framing can also lead us to make different judgments and choices in decision problems when the outcomes of the decision are exactly the same but are just presented to us differently. Here is a well-known but simple and effective example of this: Amos Tversky and Daniel Kahneman (who in 2002 became the first psychologist to win the Nobel Prize for economics[5]) presented two independent groups of university students with different descriptions of the same choice problem—their so-called Asian disease problem.[6]

Imagine that the United States is preparing for the outbreak of an unusual Asian disease that is expected to kill 600 people. Two alternative programs to combat the disease have been proposed. Assume that the exact scientific estimates of the consequences of the programs are as follows:

Program options presented to group 1:

If program A is adopted, 200 people will be saved.

If program B is adopted, there is a one-third probability that 600 people will be saved and a two-thirds probability that no people will be saved.

Program options presented to group 2:

If program C is adopted, 400 people will die.

If program D is adopted, there is a one-third probability that nobody will die and a two-thirds probability that 600 people will die.

It is easy to see that the outcomes of the options presented to each group are the same. The only difference is that one set is described, or *framed*, as saving lives, and the other framed as people dying. If individuals assess outcomes irrespective of the description of the problem, then we would expect the same choice patterns to emerge in each group. Explicitly, we would expect that the proportion of group 1 that prefers program *A* should be the same as the proportion of group 2 that prefers program *C*. This pattern does not emerge. Tversky and Kahneman found that 72 percent of group 1 preferred program *A* to program *B*, whereas only 22 percent of group 2 preferred program *C* to program *D*.

It is difficult to overstate how dramatic this result is. Group 1 and group 2 have essentially been given the *same* problem. The backstory is the same, and the option outcomes are identical. Also note that the expected value of the two options is identical—so a risk-averse individual normally should pick the option with lower variation (program *A* and program *C*). And yet the change in those opting for this option following a simple rewording of the problem—framing outcomes as losses (lives not saved) rather than gains—is fully 50 percentage points. Moreover, the majority choice has flipped from the more reasonable risk aversion to actively seeking risk.[7] It is impossible for EUT to capture these shifts in preference caused by framing the decision differently.

The tendency for decision makers to become risk-seekers when option outcomes are framed as losses, while not necessarily rational when structuring an investment portfolio with one's whole wealth, is a particularly robust finding of experimental decision theory and is a large part of the most persuasive descriptive choice theories.

Kahneman and Tversky recognized that individuals consistently make choices that cannot be explained by rational normative theories of choice such as EUT. Rather than considering the final state brought about by a risky situation, individuals tend to react to gains and losses differently—being generally risk averse in situations involving positive outcomes but risk-seeking for negative outcomes. For example, when presented with a sure gain of $100 or a risky 50/50 chance of gaining $0 or gaining $200, most individuals take the sure thing (they are risk averse). When presented with a sure loss of $100 or a 50/50 chance of losing $0 or losing $200, most individuals are more likely to take the risky choice (risk-seeking).

By observing the relative reluctance of individuals to accept 50/50 gambles (such as those on the toss of a fair coin) where they either win or lose a set amount, Kahneman and Tversky also recognized that "losses loom larger than gains." Risk-averse individuals will always avoid fair gambles, but when one of the outcomes is a loss and the other is a gain, this risk aversion can become significantly more extreme because the decision maker will require much more compensation to take on the risk of ending up with a loss. The way that losses are given greater weight psychologically in decisions is known as *loss aversion.*

Framing has particularly adverse effects for investors when the way in which the decision is framed is not aligned with the true objectives of the decision maker. *Narrow framing* occurs when the investor considers an investment decision in isolation from the broader context of that decision.

Narrow Framing in Time

Myopic loss aversion is an example of one sort of framing—narrow framing in time. We have a strong tendency to frame investment decisions by considering short time horizons, basing our decisions on how we think the investment will perform over a month or a week (or in extreme cases, a day or even less). This would be fine if these short time horizons were genuinely the same as our financial objectives—but most of us have financial objectives that are much longer than this. In practice, a specific investment horizon is very hard to determine because it is rare that we wish to completely terminate any investing on a specific date. In general, we want our saved wealth to continue growing indefinitely, even past our own lifetimes if we consider bequeathing our wealth to our children and later generations. Often, when we talk about time horizons, we are really talking about emotional time horizons, not practical ones.

Framing things in this way can have major implications. Consider a potential investment in the MSCI World Equity Index. From the beginning of 1970 to August 2011, this index produced a positive return 88.4 percent of the time, when considering rolling five-year periods. For an investor intending to hold the investment for five years, this may appear like a fairly limited risk. Unfortunately, investors are rarely so composed. And the difference, framing from misalignment of emotional and financial time horizons does influence decisions: The shorter the time horizon becomes, the riskier the investment looks. For example, if an investor looked at the performance over monthly time horizons, then that investor would observe a positive return in only 60.8 percent of months and a negative return in the other 39.2 percent. Thus, simply by observing investment performance more frequently, the same investment *appears* much riskier.

The myopic investor in the preceding example could quite reasonably decide that a 39 percent chance of loss was too great a risk to warrant investing. Note, though, that this decision could be made again next month . . . and the one after . . . and the month after that. One hundred and twenty months (10 years) down the line, the investor would be very likely to wish that he or she had invested at the very start.

Narrow Framing and Diversification

Narrow framing also occurs when an individual focuses too narrowly on a single decision or series of decisions in isolation rather than considering the effects of this decision or decisions in conjunction with the overall portfolio. This focus on each individual choice rather than the big picture tends to lead individuals to options that are suboptimal in combination.

Here again, behavioral psychologists have been able to construct sets of numerical choices that demonstrate how experimental subjects often fail to connect a number of concurrent options into a choice problem, resulting in suboptimal outcomes.

The obvious application to financial theory is to diversification— frequently a portfolio of investments behaves quite differently from any of its component parts, and yet, if we focus our decision making on one investment at a time, without considering the effects on our whole portfolio, we miss this and often make suboptimal decisions.[8] Narrow framing leads investors to assess the risk/return tradeoff of each and every investment independently rather than of their portfolio as a whole. By narrowly framing their investment options, investors could very well turn down investments that add valuable diversification to their portfolios.

In extreme cases, the investor may turn down *all* investments as being too risky even if a diversified portfolio of these investments would provide an acceptable risk/return tradeoff. Imagine a company with 10 separate business units. The head of each unit is presented with an investment opportunity that requires a substantial commitment of the total resources of the business unit and which has only a 10 percent chance of paying off $10 million but a 90 percent chance of losing $1 million. Despite having a positive expected value (of $100,000), the large probability and cost of failure may well incline each business unit head to decline this risk in favor of less chancy investments. Now consider the firm CEO, who may well jump at the chance of 10 such investments. Assuming that each opportunity is uncorrelated with the others, there is still a high risk of failure, but the CEO faces a compound bet where only one of the 10 investments needs to pay off for the collection to lead to a profit. Even if the other nine investments fail, the profit to the organization is $1 million, and the potential upside from more than one succeeding is substantial. Unlike the business unit heads, who individually face a 90 percent chance of failure, the CEO's combined gamble will fail only in the 35 percent chance that all 10 investments fail. Unless the CEO manages to induce the unit heads to take what to them appear to be unreasonable risks, though, this favorable portfolio will never come about.

This is precisely analogous to what happens with myopic loss aversion— dividing portfolio choices into too many slices in time raises the proportion of observed losses and causes loss aversion to kick in. Narrow framing in one's portfolio at a given point in time can lead to very similar failures—observe and evaluate each investment independently, and you could well end up turning away a portfolio that you would be very happy with holding if it were presented as a whole.

Toward a Descriptive Theory of Choice

These examples have encouraged academics to develop descriptive theories that fit better with observed choices and the psychological reactions to risk that individuals tend to display. In addition to loss aversion and risk-seeking for losses, it was clear that people have biased perceptions of probabilities. Individuals often tend to believe that rare events are more likely to occur than they actually are. For example, people perceive their chance of winning a national or state lottery as much higher than those chances actually are. In general, decision makers appear to systemically overweight the probabilities of extreme events—*hope* induces them to pay more attention to potentially very good outcomes and thereby overweight the likelihood of those extreme events occurring, and *fear* similarly causes individuals to overweight extremely negative events.

Dealing with These Issues in Cumulative Prospect Theory (CPT)

To improve on what they saw as the descriptive failings of EUT, Kahneman and Tversky proposed a descriptive theory of choice called *cumulative prospect theory* (CPT).[9] One of the key departures from EUT was to describe utility by reactions to *changes* in wealth (gains and losses) from their current *reference point* rather than upon total wealth—people appear to respond to changes rather than to absolute levels. The point at which there is a zero change in wealth is the reference point, which divides gains from losses. More generally, the reference point for decisions is typically the status quo position, whether that is current wealth or current consumption levels. Introducing a reference point within CPT means that individuals can have different attitudes towards gains and losses in different circumstances rather than having a single global risk attitude. This change massively increases the ability of the theory to describe actual choice.

This idea of a reference point is a crucial feature of CPT and indeed of most behavioral/descriptive models of decision making. It models the fact that individuals psychologically simply do not approach decisions by comparing their total wealth positions in each outcome, but rather they respond to what they perceive to be gains and losses from their current position. As an example, imagine that your total wealth amounts to $100,000. When trying to decide whether to take a 50/50 gamble where you can either win or lose $10, you don't naturally think of this as a 50 percent chance of ending up with $100,010 and 50 percent of ending up with $99,990. You just think of it as a gamble where you can gain $10 or lose $10. As we have seen, people have a deeply embedded tendency to treat losses quite differently from gains, and without a utility function that focuses on changes in wealth, rather than levels of wealth, we lose the ability to reflect these differences. With a utility function that has the zero point fixed at the investor's current reference point, we can provide a far better model of what is important to those investors.

Although the utility function in this approach (sometimes called a *value function* in CPT) is still required to be consistently increasing as wealth increases, it is concave in the gain domain (i.e., implying risk aversion in positive outcomes) but *convex* in the loss domain (i.e., implying risk-seeking over negative outcomes). Figure 2.3 provides a stylized example of this.

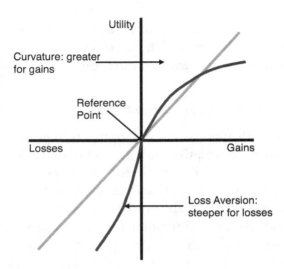

Figure 2.3 The utility function for CPT.

CPT models loss aversion by making the utility for losses suddenly steeper below the reference point—that is, the function has a kink at zero. Studies suggest the ratio of the slope of the utility function just below the reference point to the slope of the utility function just above the reference point falls in the range 2 to 2.5.[10] Thus it is often said, although it dramatically oversimplifies the evidence, that we make choices as if losses were twice as important as gains.

Recall that in EUT the *utility* of each outcome is multiplied by the probability of that outcome occurring. This prevents any distortion of probabilities from playing a role in the decision-making process. In CPT, Tversky and Kahneman introduced a *probability weighting function* that to a large degree captures the observed regularities in how decision makers tend to subjectively distort probabilities—overweighting of probabilities attached to extremely good or bad outcomes and underweighting of the likelihood of middle outcomes. This feature is familiar to those who observe market behavior—decisions truly seem to be driven much more by investors' hopes of great returns or their fears of dreadful returns than by setting up portfolios sensibly to capture the more likely middle ground effectively. The effect of a CPT probability-weighting function in transforming the standard normal distribution is shown by the heavier line in Figure 2.4: All probabilities in the center of the distribution are underweighted, whereas the tails of the distribution are overweighted—quite dramatically in the extreme tails.

—— Original Distribution --- Distorted Distribution

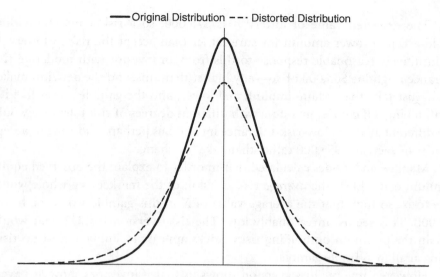

Figure 2.4 How CPT probability weighting changes the standard normal distribution.

Using CPT on the Equity Premium Puzzle

CPT is nowadays the dominant descriptive theory of choice. It can explain a rich set of quite distinct behavioral components of risk aversion[11] and a range of observed choice patterns that cannot be explained by EUT.[12] In particular, it can explain the *endowment effect*, where individuals place a greater monetary value on things merely because they own them, becoming less willing to divest assets at the price the market will pay for them; the *disposition effect*, which leads investors to hold onto losing stocks for too long and sell winning stocks too early[13]; and the *equity premium puzzle*,[14] where individuals would need to have implausibly high levels of risk aversion to justify the higher average return on equities over the return on government bonds.

Mankiw and Zeldes[15] approached the equity premium puzzle by posing a simple risky-choice problem. You are presented with two lotteries:

Lottery A: Receive $50,000 with 50 percent chance; receive $100,000 with 50 percent chance.

Lottery B: Receive $X dollars for sure.

What value of X would make you indifferent between choosing lottery A and lottery B?

The expected value of lottery *A* is $75,000, so a risk-averse individual would accept a lower amount for sure rather than accept the risk in lottery *A*. An intuitively reasonable response to this from an investor with moderate risk tolerance might be $65,000 or so—any higher than this, and the decision maker would just take the certain amount; any lower, and the gamble seems like it's worth taking. Of course, investors with different degrees of risk tolerance would give different answers, low-risk-tolerance individuals perhaps choosing to accept an offer of even just $55,000 rather than take the chance.

Mankiw and Zeldes calculated that in order to explain the observed equity premium using EUT, the *average* risk aversion of the market as a whole would have to be so high that the average value of *X* in this gamble would be below $52,000. This seems unreasonably low: The risk aversion in EUT that would explain the premium on holding risky stocks appears to imply almost no risk-taking at all in a simple gamble.

However, myopic loss aversion shows us that if investors show *loss* aversion as modeled in CPT, then if they evaluate their portfolios regularly—meaning that their performance is always observed over relatively short time horizons—we can explain the observed equity premium without having to assume that the average investor has such unreasonable levels of risk aversion. Because short time horizons exhibit a greater proportion of losses, this makes investors who display the behavioral deviations described through CPT highly averse to equities, driving down the price and driving up returns. Quite reasonable levels of risk aversion, coupled with an average decision time horizon for the market of one year, can quite adequately explain the equity risk premium.

Why Descriptive Theories Should Not Be Used to Guide Behavior

While CPT may provide a good descriptive fit for actual behaviors, it is in many ways an irrational way to invest—it describes behavior but should not be used to guide behavior. We are back again to the distinction between *normative* and *descriptive* theories described the start of this chapter.

CPT's failures as a normative theory relate largely to the fact that it is good at identifying short-term behavioral responses to risky outcomes, but these characteristics are not necessarily ones that investors would rationally wish to affect long-term portfolio choices. For example, while risk-seeking regarding losses may seem sensible in the short term (see above), this doesn't make sense as a rational solution for the long term—one simply should not take on additional risk without being compensated for it.

In other words, if an investor wants to have the best possible long-term portfolio solution, the utility function used to optimize the portfolio should eliminate short-term behavioral biases, not replicate them. Thus, although there have been attempts in the academic literature to optimize portfolios using CPT preferences,[16] one has to question why it would be a good idea to pander to an investor's short-term behavioral attitudes when what he or she is seeking is the best possible risk/return tradeoff to best satisfy his or her rational long-term preferences. Furthermore, it can never be the right solution to base a portfolio solution on distorted probability assessments. Individuals may well distort probabilities when making decisions—but the real probabilities are those they actually will face in the world, and using behavioral distortions will only result in lower expected utility in reality. The concept of a reference point also carries risks as well as advantages: Why should an investor want his or her long-term portfolio optimized to suit a set of short-term behavioral preferences relative to a momentary reference point that may be nowhere near where the investor's reference point is in 20 years?

Incorporating Short-Term Irrational Decision Making

Nonetheless, the CPT approach does have uses in describing quite accurately how an investor will feel about interim results along the investment journey. We all react emotionally to the month-by-month performance of our investments despite our rational financial objectives being much more long term. Even if the portfolio we're in is the best possible one to meet our long-term objectives, it will never get us there if along the way we get anxious and have extreme reactions to the month-by-month losses that are reflected in CPT. Chapter 8 examines how we should aim for long-term rational results while controlling short-term behavioral responses that could jeopardize those returns.

Investors in the real world display behavioral responses to short-term outcomes as they occur, and this can make the normative model of long-term preferences less relevant as as guide to ideal investment behavior. A rational investor—and indeed, classical portfolio optimization—may want to ignore such responses, but the way in which those responses affect his or her comfort and happiness along the way may be no less important to the investor in reality than long-term performance. We are, after all, complex human beings, not robots.

The conclusion must be that truly optimal portfolio-optimization strategies for individual investors should consider both the long-term *rational* self and its short-term *irrational* brother. To do so simply accepts the reality that investment decisions are complex—they involve not only probabilities, numerical returns figures, and time horizons but also the ability to assimilate those items with conflicting information, intuitions, and emotional reactions. Many of us have problems predicting what music we will like in five years, and predicting what portfolio has a return distribution that gives the best chance to satisfy our risk/return preferences is perhaps even harder. To understand why we are not hyperrational, we must understand the machinery we use to understand and predict our feelings about potential outcomes and to make decisions.

Affective and *Deliberative* Decision-Making Systems

In fact, there is considerable evidence from both behavioral science and neuroscience that our decisions result from the combined operation of two separate mental systems that work together when making these types of decisions.[17] The first is the *affective*[18] (or "hot") system, and the second is the *deliberative* (or "cold") system.

The affective system tells us what feels good or bad and what we are attracted to or fear. It is extremely fast, produces visceral feelings, and provides intuitive motivation to decide and act, frequently drawing on unconscious emotional responses to specific personal past experiences rather than rational assessments of the likelihood of outcomes. It is inherently "short-termist"—working alone, it cannot plan ahead, be patient, or forgo pleasure now for more at a later point. Neurologically, it appears to stem from more basic brain functions in the lower brain and midbrain and is what drives reactive responses in more primitive animals that lack the capacity for reasoning and deliberation. These brain functions are still present in our human brains, although they are supplemented by more contemplative cognitive structures (the neocortex, or "new cortex").

The second, deliberative, system enables us to reason about and contemplate future events, seeing how causes, effects, and actions can lead to different futures. It is more calculating than intuitive and permits structuring tradeoffs between conflicting preferences rather than allowing the single most accessible desire to dominate. This system is what we use for mathematics, strategy, planning, and general reasoning. Characteristics of the two systems are summarized in Table 2.1.

Most of the time in decision making there is little room for conflict between the two systems. When deciding on what to eat, we rely largely on the

Table 2.1

Our Two Decision-Making Systems[19]

Affective System	Deliberative System
• Based on similarity • Knowledge from personal experience • Automatic • Reproductive • Intuition, fantasy, creativity, imagination, visual recognition, associative memory	• Based on symbol manipulation • Knowledge from language, culture and formal systems • Strategic • Productive • Deliberation, explanation, formal analysis, verification, ascription of purpose, strategic memory

affective system—it has a much tighter link with how experiences feel, so it can make very good decisions very quickly. You don't need to trade off relative preferences for texture, sweetness, saltiness, and aroma to know that you'd prefer the chocolate to the orange—you just do. When you're dieting, however, you may draw on the deliberative system to compare the nutritional content of different options or to deliberately forgo pleasure now in the pursuit of longer-term goals. Conversely, some decisions are mostly deliberative—would you prefer $15 or 2^4? The difficulty of this problem is not affective ($2^4 = \$16$, which is plainly better than $15) but rather that we need to do the calculation to put it in a form that our affective system can use for the comparison. Thus the deliberative system shoulders the majority of the load, which makes the decision easier for the affective system.

Investment decisions require the affective and the deliberative systems to work together. When we make an investment decision, our deliberative system, aided by our economic and financial knowledge and tools, may help us to determine the best portfolio to satisfy our long-term preferences, but our decisions will always be influenced by our emotional responses and behavioral preferences to avoid short-term losses, even if these lead us to a poor tradeoff of risk and return and lower expected utility in the long term.

However, while the affective system receives help in understanding numbers from the deliberative system, it is an independent and powerful motivator that can genuinely lead us to decisions that would not be appropriate if we were making only "rational" assessments of our long-term preferences. And potential conflict between the affective and deliberative systems is strongly exacerbated in times of heightened emotion—times of stress, fear, regret, envy, hope, and enthusiasm. In fact, in market conditions where we most need a cool head, our decision making is most likely to be skewed toward shorter-term, emotionally driven responses.

Short-Sighted, Reactive, and Associative Traits in the Affective System

If we cannot simply ignore the affective system entirely, we must consider which aspects we should incorporate into normative models and which aspects we should avoid, control, or ignore. First, the affective system is *short-sighted*—it discounts (quite heavily) our future selves when making decisions (in other words, it doesn't pay much attention to results of current actions that occur some time in the future). Second, it is strongly *reactive*—it weights how we are currently feeling and how we have felt in the recent past very heavily when making decisions. Third, it is *associative*—it makes fast and strong connections between things to determine if they are perceived as good or bad, sometimes irrationally. Each of these has specific incarnations within investment decisions that can harm our chances of achieving our rational objectives.

In investing, short-sightedness evidences itself in several ways. As stated before, we discount the future heavily, which means that we care about the returns *this month* more than the returns over the next year. Furthermore, as we have already seen, we tend to frame investment decisions over a far shorter period of time than appropriate. Thus a shorter emotional time horizon and more frequent monitoring make investments appear far more "risky."[20] Since most individuals have true investment objectives of far more than five years, they should perceive the market as even less risky. However, their focus on the present and short-term future prevents them from making decisions for the long term.

Second, the affective system is *reactive*. The strength and simplicity of the feeling we get when reacting to a specific stimulus are very useful in more natural settings. A strong feeling of fear when we see a snake or lion is a very useful adaptation—it prevents us from being harmed. Similarly, when we have our fingers burned by a hot beverage, it is very hard to prevent our hands from snapping back quickly. However, reactivity is only useful when avoiding something unpleasant is actually beneficial. Injections are unpleasant, but in the long term, they are beneficial, and we overcome the initial pain because of our understanding that the benefit is worth it. This is an example of deliberative self-control overcoming our affective reaction.

The reactive nature of our decision making is disadvantageous to investment opportunities in a number of ways. Individuals tend to move money out of the markets *after* they have experienced a large fall.[21] This is counter to the very simplest of investing advice—buy low, sell high. Because individuals are feeling the unpleasant emotion of having a negative return, however, they seek to avoid the problem or end it by closing the position. The decision is rarely based on the individual's long-term expectations of subsequent market performance but rather on the immediate fear of losing more. This problem is especially pernicious because strong rallies frequently occur after sudden drops,[22] and we therefore can be worse off than if we had simply done nothing. The converse problem occurs during sustained bull markets. Individuals feel more comfortable with the recent pattern of returns, which appear to be high return, low risk. As a result, they invest more at the top of the market (after a sustained climb), when the assets are comparatively expensive. As a result of the combination of these two maladaptive reactions, it is not uncommon for self-directed investors to in fact buy high and sell low.

The final problem, of decision making being associative, is manifest in two obvious ways. First, individuals' investment habits are often formed by their experiences with asset classes in their formative investing years. Individuals who experience positive returns on an asset class continue to view those assets positively. Conversely, individuals who lose money on a particular asset class (e.g., American bonds during the inflationary 1970s) continue to view them negatively.[23] Once burned, twice shy.

A second facet of the associative nature of the affective system is that things that are perceived as familiar are viewed more positively. This has a number of interesting applications in investing. Our familiarity with domestic companies and stocks leads to a *home bias*, a tendency to overinvest in domestic stocks, even though we don't necessarily have superior information about those stocks.[24] Domestic stocks are seen as more familiar[25] or pleasant.[26] This occurs even *within* countries—Americans invest more in companies whose headquarters are close to them than those far away, even controlling for whether the person works there or not.[27] A stock's ticker symbol can also have a big impact. Ticker symbols that elicit affective responses (e.g., LUV for Southwest Airlines) or are fluently processed (e.g., GOOG for Google and IBM for IBM) tend to trade at a relative premium to those which don't (e.g., Uniqlo for Fast Retailing Company [9983 JT]). Amazingly, stocks with similar ticker symbols but with unrelated businesses (e.g., MCIC for MIC Corporation versus MCI for Mass Mutual Corporate Investors) tend to move together because individuals mistake one stock for the other.[28] Thus things that are familiar tend to benefit from a *halo effect* when we assess a fair price for a company's stock.

Overlaying Short-Term Needs on a Long-Term Strategy

The behaviors detailed earlier by the affective system are not, on their own, a good premise for investing. However, the affective system is what determines how we feel about our returns, which is an integral part of an optimal behavioral investment strategy. Thus we must carefully choose what expressions of our affective system we will use in our optimization procedures and which expressions we will attempt to mitigate. The starting point should be a long-term utility function that accurately reflects the downside risk aversion present in our deliberative preferences. But we should overlay strategies that ameliorate or satisfy our short-term preferences. How we formulate the short-term strategies depends critically on the individual and the relative strength of his or her short- and long-term systems.

Thus, rather than ignore our short-sightedness bias, we must find ways to satisfy our short-term selves just enough to prevent them from running the show entirely. To do this, we might express all figures in only annual or five-year terms, such that they accurately reflect the long-term decisions we are making. Second, we might reduce monitoring frequency to reduce the degree to which our perceptions of future risk are distorted by recent events. Finally, we might outwit our current selves by precommitting to changes in our investment strategy in the future, for example, by committing ourselves to future rises in savings rates, linked (say) to increases in personal income.[29]

We should clearly attempt to mitigate *reactivity*—investment decisions always should be forward-looking. However, the desire to avoid risk after a sudden loss may be too strong to control. Thus we should look to either minimize the possibility of these situations or form precommitment mechanisms to control our reactions to them. We can minimize the possibility of these situations by reducing the potential for severe or sustained drawdowns in the portfolio. These are the situations most likely to cause reactive behaviors, so minimizing their frequency helps us not to be tempted by our emotional selves. Second, low-liquidity products or products with a penalty for early withdrawal can help us to maintain a steady hand. If we simply cannot exit a position immediately without cost, it removes the temptation to be "short-termist," and it may actually increase satisfaction. When individuals have an open option to change their minds, they are frequently less happy with that option than when they have little ability to change it. The constant consideration of other options decreases both the ability to enjoy the benefits of the status quo and also increases stress on the individual.

Familiarity is the least problematic of the affective biases. When making decisions, especially at a portfolio level, we should be looking to minimize correlations across individual assets. Unfortunately, along with narrow framing, familiarity works directly against this, making large, domestic, and market-correlated stocks appear more attractive to us than diversified portfolios of smaller, international stocks. The problem is exacerbated by the fact that both our employment prospects and income are likely to be correlated with domestic markets. Thus, during a large bust, we may experience a double hit of portfolio losses and losses to our income stream. When tempted by a bias toward familiar markets, we should forcefully ask ourselves whether we actually have better information about domestic assets or whether we are simply being seduced by the familiar. Unless we genuinely have particular knowledge or expertise in familiar markets, a bias toward to international stocks over domestic ones is usually the better course of action on the basis that they will not correlate as highly with income streams or other domestic holdings.

In summary, we would not be completely better off without emotions or biases, but we need to make sure that they do not overwhelm us in the investment process as a whole. By either minimizing the opportunities for our short-term selves to make emotional decisions, or taking steps to make our short-term selves sufficiently comfortable with the journey to stick with a portfolio suited to our long-term objectives, or restricting the ability or set of options available to us, we can move closer to our long-term goals without putting ourselves on an investment path that feels tortuous in the intermediate phase.

Conclusion

We differ from each other in our preferences and behaviors in many ways, and there is no reason why investment preferences should be an exception to this. But MPT treats individuals as if they differ from one another along only one dimension—*risk tolerance*—and then makes some very restrictive and unreasonable assumptions about how this is reflected in the utility function that governs optimal risk/return tradeoffs for each individual. We have discussed in this chapter why the quadratic utility function assumed in MPT is inadequate as a representation of the preferences of our long-term rational selves. We will develop this theme in much more detail in Chapter 5 to show how we can put portfolio theory on a more sound footing.

In addition, simply assuming that all individuals with the same degree of long-term risk tolerance should have the same portfolio fails to reflect the true complexity of each investor. Some find it easy to overcome their short-term desires and pursue the rational long-term solution, and some find this very difficult. When it comes to the intensity of emotional response, some are highly composed and unaffected by short-term outcomes or monitor their portfolios less, whereas others are highly emotionally involved with the short term and easily get stressed or overexcited. Some are more loss averse, and some less.

Each of these individual attributes should have specific implications for determining the "right" portfolio for each individual—and in many cases it may make sense to deviate somewhat from the rationally optimal portfolio in order to help achieve this additional tailoring. It is better to be in a portfolio that is slightly suboptimal with regard to your long-term objectives but one that you can stick with sensibly throughout the journey than to be in a *technically* optimal portfolio that causes you to panic or respond emotionally at every step along the way. In Chapter 8 we will explore in some depth how we can use our understanding of short-term or behavioral preferences to ensure that investors' portfolios are not only an appropriate long-term solution but also consider their emotional comfort with the journey and strategies for controlling their own emotional and behavioral responses along the way.

Notes

1. Expected value is equivalent to a straight line with no curvature: Equivalent increases and decreases in returns or wealth are treated as having the same effect on utility, and thus there is no risk aversion. A convex line, which gets steeper as returns increase, reflects risk-seeking because utility increases faster for a gain than it decreases for a loss.
2. Risk aversion at any point on a utility function is determined by the degree of curvature, which we can measure using the second derivative. However, because the same utility function can have different units while still describing the same preferences, we need to divide by the first derivative to ensure that the risk-aversion measures are comparable.
3. Campbell and Viceira (2002), Chapter 2.
4. For example, in the Allais paradoxes (Allais, 1953).
5. Tversky, Kahneman's longtime collaborator, died before the prize was awarded.
6. Tversky and Kahneman (1981).
7. Incidentally, this example provides an immediate riposte to those who claim that objective psychometric assessments of investors' levels of risk tolerance are unnecessary on the dubious grounds that "investors know how risk tolerant they are." Even without the bias imparted by the financial

advisor (salesperson), individuals' self-assessments of risk tolerance are heavily influenced by framing—the current state of the market, recent investment outcomes, influences of media and peer groups—and focus on the short term rather than true investment objectives. If rewording a problem can push risk attitudes around so extremely, it is naive to believe that investors have a stable grasp of their true risk tolerance in the face of such a wide range of influences.

8. William Shakespeare captured this idea of diversification a long time before the advent of MPT or behavioral finance. As Antonio says in *The Merchant of Venice* (1596–1598), "My ventures are not in one bottom trusted / Nor to one place; nor is my whole estate / Upon the fortune of this present year / Therefore, my merchandise makes me not sad."
9. Kahneman and Tversky (1979); Tversky and Kahneman (1992).
10. Tversky and Kahneman (1992); Abdellaoui (2000).
11. Davies and Satchell (2006).
12. Although, in turn, academics have produced a number of experimental choice problems that require even greater sophistication than CPT from a descriptive theory (e.g., Birnbaum, 2004), there is not as yet, and quite possibly never will be, a single descriptive theory that captures all systematic deviations from EUT.
13. Barberis and Huang (2001).
14. Benartzi and Thaler (1995).
15. Mankiw and Zeldes (1991).
16. For example, He and Zhou (2011).
17. For example, Sloman (2002).
18. *Affect* is a word used in psychology to describe how good or bad we feel or whether a given stimulus is felt to be good or bad.
19. Adapted from Sloman (2002).
20. Benartzi and Thaler (1995).
21. Friesen and Sapp (2007).
22. Estrada (2008).
23. Malmendier and Nagel (2007).
24. French and Poterba (1991).
25. Huberman (2001).
26. Head, Smith, and Wilson (2009).
27. Coval and Moskowitz (1999).
28. Rasches (2001).
29. Thaler and Benartzi (2004).

Chapter 3

MODERN PORTFOLIO THEORY

with Ricardo Feced

As discussed in Chapter 2, this book breaks down into two halves. In the second half of the book (from Chapter 5 onward) we discuss ways in which we think portfolio theory and implementation can be improved to deliver better results for investors.

In the first half of the book, however, we set out in some detail the current state of play, looking first (in Chapter 1) at how modern portfolio theory (MPT) has been developed and then (in Chapter 2) at how the study of investor behavior and preferences has tried to keep pace. In Chapter 4 we ask the all-important question: Does MPT, in its current form, deliver good investment performance?

Traditional economic theory considers individuals as rational consumers whose main objective is to maximize consumption and wealth along their lifespan. To achieve these goals, they regularly face financial decisions with important consequences for their future welfare.

The variety of investment opportunities open to investors has naturally led to systematic study of how they select optimal investment strategies. The *normative* objective of private and institutional investors is to maximize their subjective benefits (or utility) from potential future consumption and accumulated wealth. In any period of time, they receive cash flows in the form of income from their work and dividends and interest payments from their financial investments. These cash flows contribute to their accumulated stock of wealth. The first decision that the investor faces is what portion of this wealth should be consumed in the next period and what percentage should be saved to fund future consumption. A second decision is how to invest the savings in an optimal way so as to maximize purchasing power when future consumption needs arise. This chapter, and the majority of this book, will focus on this second optimal portfolio investment decision.

Investment decisions are very sensitive to changes in the macroeconomic environment over time, as we have already commented on in Chapter 1. Financial assets promise a stream of future cash flows to their owners, but the final value of these is uncertain. Investors can choose from many financial assets exhibiting different risk/return characteristics, and it is critical for them to choose the right mix to meet future financial targets and liabilities. Portfolio theory studies optimal strategies to select both real and financial assets to meet these objectives.

In the second section of this chapter we present the nomenclature of key elements and ratios that we will use. Then we describe the classical mean variance optimization framework. In the fourth section we present the capital assets pricing model (CAPM), and we end the chapter with an explanation of the Black-Litterman approach. These are the foundations of modern portfolio theory (MPT).

Risk and Return, Defining the Notations

Chapter 1 set out the variety of financial assets available to investors and explained where they typically sit on the balance sheets of the different economic agents. Financial assets entitle their owners to a stream of future cash flows. However, there is some risk associated with the magnitude of these cash flows because the prices of securities evolve randomly over time (market risk) and debt issuers could default on their contractual obligations (counterparty or credit risk). Consequently, the risk/return characteristics of financial assets have to be described by means of statistical models. The objective of this section is to introduce simple statistical models for financial assets that will enable us to develop portfolio theory later in the chapter.

Probabilistic Models

The financial state of the world can be described by the value of a number of macroeconomic and financial variables (the information set at time t). Because these variables evolve over time in a nondeterministic way, the best possible description of the financial state of the world in the near future (at time $t+1$) is through statistical models. Let us consider here a one-period model for financial asset returns described by

1. The universe U_t of all the events at time $t + 1$ that we can realistically think of given the information set I_t that we have at time t
2. The ex ante probabilities of these events, the way we see them at time t (We represent these probabilities by a generic p, also called the *probability measure*.)

Events are the sets of possible future states of the world. We name each of these possible states ω. The granularity of the universe U_t depends on the amount of information incorporated at time t and on the detail available in the framework to characterize the potential future financial states of the world.

Expected Returns—Notation

Asset returns for a given period can be defined as simple returns or as logarithmic returns. The first definition is more appropriate when calculating the return of a multiasset portfolio over one time period, whereas the second is more suitable to the study of single-asset returns over long time periods.

If the world ends up being in state ω at time $t + 1$, we calculate the arithmetic return $\tilde{r}_i(\omega)$ for asset i over the $(t, t +1)$ period in terms of the current price of the asset $P_{i,t}(\omega)$ and its final price $P_{i,t+1}(\omega)$, which includes both capital gains and all income cash flows:

$$R_i(\omega) = 1 + \tilde{r}_i(\omega) = \frac{P_{i,t+1}(\omega)}{P_{i,t}}$$

Equivalently, the logarithmic returns $\hat{r}_i(\omega)$ can be calculated as

$$\hat{r}_i(\omega) = \ln\left[\frac{P_{i,t+1}(\omega)}{P_{i,t}}\right]$$

We shall use these extensively in later chapters, but here we will focus simply on describing the system of notation for arithmetic returns—log returns have an analogous system.

Owing to its important role in MPT, we also introduce special nomenclature for the risk-free rate of (arithmetic) return:

$$R_F = 1 + r_F$$

The risk-free rate has the important property of being independent of the state of the world ω and is known at time t. The risk-free rate is used to calculate the risk premium of an asset. We define the excess return (over the risk-free rate) $r_i(\omega)$ of an asset as

$$r_i(\omega) = \tilde{r}_i(\omega) - r_F$$

Generally, we will deal with a set of risky assets, so we stack the excess returns in a vector of size N (the number of assets excluding the risk-free rate):

$$\tilde{r}(\omega) = [\tilde{r}_1(\omega) \quad \tilde{r}_2(\omega) \quad \cdots \quad \tilde{r}_N(\omega)]^{tr}$$

where tr stands for transposed. Similarly, we can define the vector of excess returns as

$$r(\omega) = \tilde{r}(\omega) - r_F\bar{1}$$

where $\bar{1}$ is a column vector of ones of size $N \times 1$.

In the remainder of this chapter, while keeping in mind the probabilistic characteristic of these returns, we will simplify the notations and write[1]

- $\tilde{r}_i(\omega) = \tilde{r}_i$
- The vector of total returns, $\tilde{r} = [\tilde{r}_1 \quad \tilde{r}_2 \quad \cdots \quad \tilde{r}_N]^{tr}$
- $r_i = \tilde{r}_i - r_F$
- $\bar{r}_F = r_F\bar{1}$
- The vector of excess returns, $r = \tilde{r} - \bar{r}_F$

Finally, at time t we can calculate the *expected* excess returns for the next period of time as the weighted average of the returns in each state of the world multiplied by the probability of realization p, as seen from time t, of each of these states:

$$\mu = E_p^t(r) = \int r \, dp$$

We can also simplify this expression, writing

$$\mu = E(r) = \int r \, dp$$

Volatility—Notation

The value of financial assets fluctuates over time depending on the financial state of the world. *Risk* generally refers in some way to the spread of the distribution of the asset returns across the different final states of the world. A simple way of doing this is by calculating the *volatility*, which we define as the standard deviation of the distribution of excess returns for each asset during the period.

$$v_i = \sqrt{E(r_i^2) - [E(r_i)]^2}$$

If the distribution of excess returns is normally distributed, then we know that there is a 68 percent chance of getting a return in a range within 1 standard deviation (v_i) on either side from the expected value and a 95 percent chance of getting a return in a range within 2 standard deviations ($2v_i$). In the case of normally distributed (Gaussian) returns, the description of the distribution is complete once we specify expected returns and volatility. However, the assumption of normality is not essential to the definition of volatility.[2]

Correlation and Covariance—Notation

One of the main benefits of investing in a portfolio of assets is diversification, a consequence of the absence of perfect comovement among assets. Some assets will perform better in some states of the world, whereas others will perform better in other states of the world. Mathematically, the correlation among the excess returns of the assets is characterized by the correlation matrix ρ_{ij}:

$$\rho_{ij} = \frac{E(r_i r_j) - E(r_i)E(r_j)}{v_i v_j}$$

A correlation ρ_{ij} of 1 means that the excess returns on asset i can be reproduced with a combination of asset j and a certain amount of cash in all the final states of the world. Assets with correlations close to 1 are essentially the same asset and do not provide diversification benefits. The correlation ρ_{ij} can range from −1 to 1; two assets are said to be *uncorrelated* if their correlation is 0.

As a simple example of the diversification benefits, let us assume an equally weighted portfolio of N assets with equal volatility v. As previously explained, if the assets were perfectly correlated, we would be dealing essentially with a portfolio of one asset with volatility v. However, if the assets were uncorrelated, then the volatility of the portfolio would decrease to $v/\sqrt{N}$—the benefits of diversification!

We also introduce here the covariance matrix Ω, which combines correlation and volatilities in vector notation:

$$\Omega = E(rr^{tr}) - E(r)E(r^{tr})$$

The covariance matrix is used extensively in portfolio theory because informa-tion on both correlations and volatilities is important in assessing the final risk of a portfolio.

Mathematical Model for Returns—Notation

It is convenient to introduce a simple mathematical model for asset returns to be able to develop portfolio theory in a more concrete way. As we will indicate later, some parts of the theory are independent of the actual model for returns, but the reader will benefit generally from the derivation of many results in the context of a specific model. Here, we assume that excess returns in one period follow a multivariate Gaussian distribution driven by a vector of M independent unit-variance and zero-mean random factors $W(\omega)$ depending on the states of the world ω.

Notation-wise, we write

$$W(\omega) = W$$

$$E(W) = \overline{0}$$

$$E(WW^{tr}) = I$$

where $\overline{0}$ is a column vector of zeros and I is the identity matrix.

The model for arithmetic excess returns for the N risky assets (the risk-free asset is not included here) is now expressed as

$$r_i = \mu_i + \sum_j \sigma_{ij} W_j$$

or, alternatively, in vector form:

$$r = \mu + \sigma W$$

We can easily find the expected excess returns for the assets:

$$E(r) = \mu$$

and the covariance matrix:

$$\Omega = E(rr^{tr} - \mu\mu^{tr}) = \sigma\sigma^{tr}$$

This model is used extensively in the financial literature. Multiperiod and continuous models are usually built from the concatenation of this one-period model, generally assuming that the return distributions are independent and identically distributed across different time periods. Aggregated distributions of returns over long time horizons then become lognormal distributions (i.e., the log of the return follows a normal distribution).

The equivalent of the preceding model for logarithmic excess returns for one period could be expressed to some degree of approximation as[3]

$$r_i^{\log} = \mu_i - \frac{1}{2}\sum_j \sigma_{ij}^2 + \sum_j \sigma_{ij} W_j$$

This approximation will be used in later chapters, in particular in Chapter 5.

Risk and Return for the Asset Classes Considered

In this section we present a simple case study. The main asset classes and indices used are

- Cash (Treasury bills [TBs])
- Bonds (government [Gov], investment grade [IG], high yield [HY])
- Equities (U.S., developed countries excluding the United States [DEVexU.S.], emerging markets [EM])
- Commodities
- Real estate
- Hedge funds (HF)

We present the main characteristics of these assets and indices in Tables 3.1 and 3.2. Figure 3.1 shows the positioning of all the assets considered in the risk/return space.

Portfolio Optimization: The Classical Framework

In the preceding section we introduced a statistical characterization of the risk and return features of assets. We now address the natural question of what is the optimal mix of financial assets (i.e., the optimal portfolio) that each investor should hold to achieve a given financial objective.

For the moment, we assume that all the parameters that characterize the statistical model for asset returns are known. They should reflect our best guess of the probabilities of the possible future financial states of the world (possible scenarios) for the next period of time. In later sections we will discuss how to

Table 3.1

Mean Returns and Volatilities

	Gov Bond	IG Bond	HY Bond	U.S. Equity	DEVexU.S. Equity	EM Equity	Commodities	Real Estate	HF
Index	U.S. Treasury Master	U.S. Corp Master	U.S. High Yield Master II	MSCI USA	MSCI World ex USA	MSCI Emerging Markets	S&P GSCI Commodity	FTSE EPRA/ NAREIT USA	HFRI FUND OF FUNDS COMPOSITE
Annual Excess Return (%)	2.6%	3.0%	3.9%	4.7%	5.6%	12.5%	5.7%	8.9%	4.6%
Annual Volatility (%)	5.7%	7.1%	9.0%	15.7%	17.4%	23.6%	20.0%	20.7%	5.7%

Table 3.2

Correlations

Correlation	Gov Bond	IG Bond	HY Bond	U.S. Equity	DEVexU.S. Equity	EM Equity	Commodities	Real Estate	HF
Gov bond	1.00	0.86	0.27	0.14	0.08	-0.04	-0.08	0.19	0.04
IG bond	0.86	1.00	0.63	0.34	0.26	0.19	0.02	0.38	0.26
HY bond	0.27	0.63	1.00	0.56	0.46	0.50	0.08	0.58	0.42
U.S. equity	0.14	0.34	0.56	1.00	0.63	0.63	0.06	0.56	0.48
DEVexUS equity	0.08	0.26	0.46	0.63	1.00	0.66	0.16	0.44	0.46
EM equity	-0.04	0.19	0.50	0.63	0.66	1.00	0.18	0.39	0.65
Commodities	-0.08	0.02	0.08	0.06	0.16	0.18	1.00	0.05	0.30
Real estate	0.19	0.38	0.58	0.56	0.44	0.39	0.05	1.00	0.27
HF	0.04	0.26	0.42	0.48	0.46	0.65	0.30	0.27	1.00

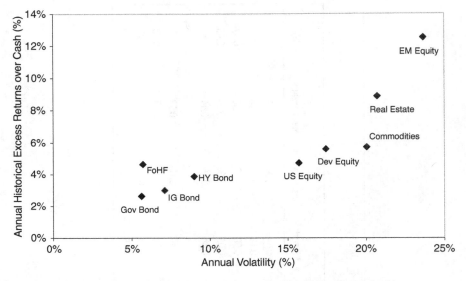

Figure 3.1 Risk/return diagram for the various asset classes. (FoHF = funds of hedge funds)

gauge these parameters from the assumption of equilibrium in the financial markets, as well as how to introduce views or tilts in the models if we differ from the market views and believe that our information set is superior.

Portfolio Basics

A portfolio of assets is characterized by a vector that describes the proportions allocated to the different assets in the portfolio. Let us introduce two types of portfolios:

- Long or fully funded portfolios
- Partially funded portfolios

In *long* or *fully funded portfolios*, a positive amount of initial wealth is invested by distributing it in certain proportions among the assets in the portfolio. The asset allocation x_L verifies two conditions. First, the sum of the weights adds to 1, that is, $\overline{1}^{tr}x_L = 1$, and second, only long (positive) positions are allowed, that is, $x_L \geq \overline{0}$. x_L is a vector of size $N + 1$ that contains both the weights of the N risky assets x and the weight of the risk-free asset x_F, and $x_L = [x_F, x]^{tr}$.

Partially funded portfolios are similar to long portfolios, but short (or negative) positions now are allowed for some of the assets. A partially funded or leveraged portfolio with allocation x_V can be described through its balance sheet, where

- The equity (net worth) still adds to 1, that is, $\overline{1}^{tr}x_V = 1$.
- The sum of short positions w_S corresponds to the liabilities.
- The assets side will be the sum of liabilities plus net worth, $1 + w_S$.

The *leverage ratio* usually is defined as the ratio of the liabilities to net worth w_S. With this definition, a 100 percent leveraged portfolio is constructed by borrowing an amount equivalent to the initial funds available for investment.

Expected Return and Risk

Given the statistical model of asset returns introduced in the preceding section, let us now examine what the expected return and volatility of these portfolios will be. The total simple return $\tilde{r}_x(\omega)$, noted $\tilde{r}_x$, of a *partially* or *fully funded portfolio* for the final state of the world ω is calculated as the product of the asset weights and their corresponding returns (with the previously introduced notation):

$$\tilde{r}_x = x_F r_F + x^{tr}\tilde{r} = r_F + x^{tr}r$$

And the corresponding excess return r_x is

$$r_x = x^{tr}r$$

The expected excess return μ_x for the portfolio now follows by averaging over all possible future states of the world:

$$\mu_x = E(r_x) = x^{tr}\mu$$

A plausible measure for the risk is provided by the volatility for the excess returns v_x, which is calculated through the covariance matrix for the risky assets (the allocation to the risk-free asset does not contribute to the volatility):

$$v_x = \sqrt{E(r_x^2) - [E(r_x)]^2} = \sqrt{x^{tr}\Omega x}$$

Portfolio Performance Measures: Sharpe Ratio

Portfolio performance measures combine expected returns and risk in a single number to characterize the attractiveness of the investment. These numbers can be calculated based on actual historical returns of the portfolio (ex post) or can be constructed based on expectations and assumptions about the future (ex ante).

The main performance measure traditionally used is the *Sharpe ratio,* which measures the ratio between the expected excess returns over the risk-free rate and the volatility of the portfolio:

$$\text{Sharpe ratio} = \frac{\mu_x}{v_x} = \frac{x^{tr}\mu}{\sqrt{x^{tr}\Omega x}}$$

As we will see later, the objective of classical portfolio optimization is actually to maximize the Sharpe ratio.

Mean Variance Optimization

In groundbreaking work in 1952, Markowitz proposed the idea of characterizing portfolios in terms of two features: their expected returns and their volatility. The implicit assumption, obviously, is that investors will be concerned only about expected returns and volatility as measures of profitability and risk. Markowitz then discovered the existence of a set of efficient portfolios that maximized the expected return for given levels of volatility. Investors always will select portfolios along this "efficient frontier," in particular, the one that matches their level of risk aversion.

Markowitz's analysis was carried out in the one-period setting we are considering in this chapter (also referred to as *myopic optimization*). However, we should emphasize that myopic optimal portfolios can be valid over longer time horizons for certain types of investors and models of asset returns.[4]

Mean Variance Utility

Let us characterize investors by parametric functions that capture their attraction for profits but their dislike for risk, that is, their subjective tradeoff between expected return and volatility. These utility functions have been discussed already in Chapter 2, and we shall return to them in depth in Chapter 5. In this chapter we shall use them fairly loosely. Markowitz did not discuss what type of utility function would best characterize investor preferences for risk and return; he simply assumed a quadratic utility function on the grounds that it assumes that investors care only about expected returns and volatility and not about any more complex characterizations of the returns distribution. This simple mean variance utility function (MVU) will depend linearly and positively on the expected excess returns and negatively on the square of volatility (the variance):

$$\text{MVU}(\mu_x, v_x) = \mu_x - \frac{1}{2}av_x^2$$

The constant a measures the risk aversion of the investor, with low values indicating that the investor is mainly concerned about the expected return (more risk-neutral) and high values being appropriate for investors more worried about the associated risk (more risk-averse).

Optimal Portfolio That Includes the Risk-Free Asset

Let us go back to the problem of finding the optimal partially funded portfolio for investors characterized by the mean variance utility function. The optimization program aims to determine the vector of allocation weights x to the risky assets that maximizes the mean variance utility:

$$\underset{x}{\text{Max}}(x^{tr}\mu - \frac{1}{2}ax^{tr}\Omega x)$$

where we have used the expressions previously derived for μ_x and v_x.

No further constraints are necessary because the allocation to the risk-free asset simply will be the remainder necessary to verify that the sum of the weights add to 1, that is, $x_F = 1 - \overline{1}^{tr}x$. The solution is calculated from the first-order condition that equates the derivative of the mean variance utility to zero:

$$x = \frac{1}{a}\Omega^{-1}\mu \tag{3.1}$$

The vector of allocation weights to risky assets is directly proportional to the vector of expected return and inversely proportional to the covariance matrix (risk). Also, the magnitude of the exposure depends on the risk-aversion parameter, with highly risk-averse investors reducing their allocation to risky assets.

By normalizing the weights of the previous portfolio, we can express the solution in terms of the portfolio M with weights adding to 1:

$$x^M = \frac{\Omega^{-1}\mu}{\overline{1}^{tr}\Omega^{-1}\mu} \tag{3.2}$$

Notice that portfolio M does not depend on the investor's risk aversion a.

We now can express the allocation to the risky assets in terms of this portfolio M as

$$x = w_M x^M$$

where w_M depends on the risk aversion:

$$w_M = \frac{\overline{1}^{tr}\Omega^{-1}\mu}{a}$$

Finally, including the allocation to the risk-free asset, the final partially funded portfolio weights x_V are

$$x_V = \begin{bmatrix} 1 - w_M \\ w_M x^M \end{bmatrix} \qquad (3.3)$$

The optimal portfolio is a combination of the risk-free asset, with a weight $1 - w_M$ and the previously introduced portfolio M (w_M). The proportions between these two portfolios depend on the risk aversion a of the investor. This is our first example of a two-fund separation theorem because the optimal portfolio can be decomposed in a mixture of two subportfolios or subfunds.

The set of optimal portfolios has been found as a function of the risk-aversion parameter a. This set constitutes the so-called efficient frontier and is a straight line when represented in a volatility (v_x)/expected return (μ_x) graph (see Figure 3.2). The equation of the line is given by

$$\mu_x = \sqrt{\mu^{tr}\Omega^{-1}\mu}\, v_x \qquad (3.4)$$

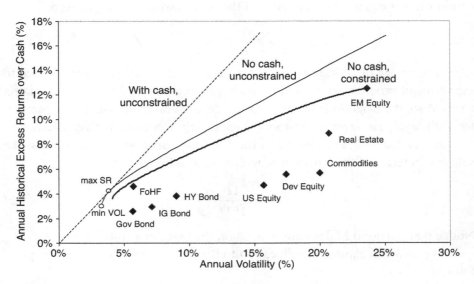

Figure 3.2 Optimal mean variance portfolios, assuming that historical return is a good proxy for forward returns.

The portfolio M is the portfolio with maximum Sharpe ratio that contains exclusively risky assets. We notice that $\sqrt{\mu^{tr}\Omega^{-1}\mu}$ is the Sharpe ratio corresponding to M and that if other portfolios of risky assets exhibited a higher Sharpe ratio, we could obtain an efficient frontier entirely above the one just found by mixing it with the risk-free asset.[5]

Optimal Portfolio Without the Risk-Free Asset

Let us now examine how the efficient frontier changes when there is no risk-free asset in the economy (or this is not allowed in the portfolio). If x is the vector of weights for the risky assets, the optimization problem is now to maximize the mean variance utility:

$$\underset{x}{\text{Max}} \left(x^{tr}\mu - \frac{1}{2}ax^{tr}\Omega x \right)$$

subject to the constraint that the sum of the weights should add to 1:

$$\overline{1}^{tr}x = 1$$

Note that we allow for potential short positions (negative weights) in some of the risky assets, so the optimal portfolio will generally be a partially funded portfolio.

The optimal portfolio is calculated by the Lagrange method of introducing a multiplier to take into account the constraint. The solution is the linear combination of two portfolios: m and M. Portfolio M is the maximum Sharpe ratio portfolio previously described, whereas portfolio m now takes the role of the risk-free asset:

$$x = w_m x^m + w_M x^M = (1 - w_M)x^m + w_M x^M \tag{3.5}$$

Portfolio m is actually the portfolio of minimum volatility (or variance) that meets the previous constraint of weights adding to 1 (i.e., the best substitute for the risk-free asset):

$$x^m = \frac{\Omega^{-1}1}{\overline{1}^{tr}\Omega^{-1}\overline{1}} \tag{3.6}$$

We could verify that this is effectively the minimum variance portfolio by solving the same optimization problem as before but removing the term associated with the expected return of the portfolio.

Portfolio M is still the maximum Sharpe ratio portfolio that we have already seen in the last section:

$$x^M = \frac{\Omega^{-1}\mu}{\overline{1}^{+}\Omega^{-1}\mu} \tag{3.7}$$

The proportion of wealth allocated to each of these two portfolios (w_M and w_m) is a function of the risk aversion of the investor a:

$$w_M = \frac{\overline{1}^{tr}\Omega^{-1}\mu}{a} \tag{3.8}$$

$$w_m = 1 - w_M$$

Since the risk-free weight is null, the final partially funded portfolio will be

$$x_V = \begin{bmatrix} 0 \\ (1 - w_M)x^m + w_M x^M \end{bmatrix} \tag{3.9}$$

The optimal portfolio verifies a two-fund separation theorem, where the two funds now correspond to the minimum variance and the maximum Sharpe ratio portfolios.

The efficient frontier will represent the set of optimal portfolios in an expected excess return versus volatility diagram and can be built by recording the expected excess return and volatility of the optimal portfolios for each risk aversion a.

Let us assume a portfolio on the efficient frontier with expected excess return μ_x. Since this portfolio is a combination of the two funds, we can work out the corresponding weights of the minimum variance portfolio and the maximum Sharpe ratio required to generate this portfolio. For this purpose, let us first calculate the expected excess returns of the two funds μ_m and μ_M:

$$\mu_m = \mu^{tr}x^m = \frac{\mu^{tr}\Omega^{-1}1}{\overline{1}^{tr}\Omega^{-1}\overline{1}}$$

$$\mu_M = \mu^{tr}x^M = \frac{\mu^{tr}\Omega^{-1}\mu}{\overline{1}^{tr}\Omega^{-1}\mu}$$

From the expression for the expected return of the portfolio μ_x,

$$\mu_x = \mu^{tr}x = (1 - w_M)\mu_m + w_M\mu_M \tag{3.10}$$

we can recalculate the weights w_m and w_M as a function of μ_x:

$$w_m = \frac{\mu_M - \mu_x}{\mu_M - \mu_m}$$

$$w_M = \frac{\mu_x - \mu_m}{\mu_M - \mu_m}$$

(3.11)

Before using these weights, we calculate the volatilities (v_m and v_M) and correlation (ρ_{Mm}) of the two funds:

$$v_m = \frac{1}{\sqrt{\overline{1}^{tr}\Omega^{-1}\overline{1}}}$$

$$v_M = \frac{\sqrt{\mu^{tr}\Omega^{-1}\mu}}{|\overline{1}^{tr}\Omega^{-1}\mu|}$$

$$\rho_{Mm} = \frac{|\overline{1}^{tr}\Omega^{-1}\mu|}{\sqrt{\overline{1}^{tr}\Omega^{-1}\overline{1}}}$$

Finally, the efficient frontier is generated by calculating the volatility of the optimal portfolio v_x as a function of the two funds volatilities (v_m and v_M), their correlation (ρ_{Mm}), and their weights (w_m and w_M):

$$v_x(\mu_x) = \frac{\sqrt{(\mu_M - \mu_x)^2 v_m^2 + 2\rho_{Mm}(\mu_M - \mu_x)(\mu_x - \mu_m)v_m v_M + (\mu_x - \mu_m)^2 v_M^2}}{\mu_M - \mu_m}$$

The efficient frontier is a hyperbola when plotted in an expected excess return/volatility diagram. As observed in the preceding equation, the efficient frontier is independent of utility; it reflects efficient combinations for all risk-averse investors. It is not, however, independent of beliefs: Any two investors with different anticipated return distributions will have different efficient frontiers.

Optimal Long-Only Portfolios

The optimization of long-only portfolios follows the same lines as those laid for the partially funded portfolios already discussed. Solutions require the introduction of additional constraints to ensure the nonnegativity of the allocations to all assets. More generally, it is common practice in portfolio-optimization problems to specify allocation restrictions among assets: minimum and maximum allowable allocations for each asset, constraints on aggregate weights to sets or families of assets, maximum leverage if we are considering partially funded portfolios, and so on. Although some of these cases have analytical solutions, as the complexity of the problem increases, it usually becomes necessary to rely on numerical techniques.

Illustration of Mean Variance Optimization

To illustrate this, we have constructed optimal portfolios using the Markowitz framework employing only historical covariance and average returns data between 1990 and 2009. We consider three specific cases in Figure 3.2:

- *With risk-free asset: partially funded, long-short positions.* In this case, the efficient frontier is a straight line passing through the origin (the risk-free asset) and the maximum Sharpe ratio portfolio. All risk/return combinations on this line are available given the theoretical assumptions we've used. However, the ideal portfolio on this line for any particularly investor will depend on the degree of risk aversion a.
- *Without risk-free asset: partially funded, long-short positions.* The efficient frontier is the concave line that passes through the maximum Sharpe ratio portfolio and the minimum variance portfolio.
- *Without risk-free asset and constrained: long only portfolio.* No borrowing is permitted, so the frontier is made up only of positive combinations of the asset classes. Since this is a constrained version of the preceding solution, some previously efficient portfolios now will be unattainable, and the frontier will lie below the unconstrained solution.

The precise solutions obtained for the efficient frontier depend not only on the availability of the risk-free asset and the constraints imposed but also on the multitude of assumptions that need to be made in determining the expected multivariate risk/return characteristics of the assets. In the figure, we simply assumed that the future risk, expected return, and correlations would be the same as in the past.

Future chapters will explore methods for establishing the most effective forecasts of future returns distributions at any point, but in what follows, we simply illustrate this by constructing an optimal portfolio with a different hypothesis, that is, with historical covariance and naive forward-looking expected returns. To establish these forward-looking expected returns, we assume that the historical data provide accurate assessments of future volatility, and we also assume a constant Sharpe ratio of 0.3 for all assets (so that all assets have the same ratio of expected excess returns to volatility). This allows us to infer the future

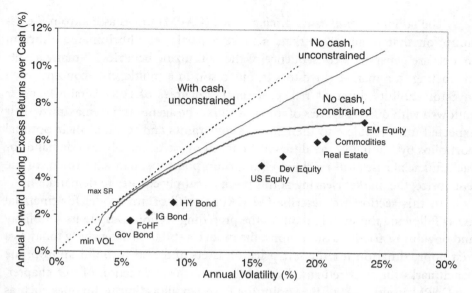

Figure 3.3 Optimal mean variance portfolios, assuming that Sharpe ratios define a good proxy for forward returns.

expected returns as 0.3 multiplied by the historical volatility. Again, we report in Figure 3.3 the three optimal situations as well as the two specific minimum volatility and maximum Sharpe ratio portfolios under these new assumptions. Note that the assets themselves all have the same annual volatility positions as in Figure 3.2 but that their expected excess returns have been adjusted so that they all fall on the straight line with the common Sharpe ratio of 0.3.

Capital Assets Pricing Model (CAPM): Equilibrium Pricing

In previous sections we analyzed a methodologic framework that allows investors to optimize their portfolios given their utility and risk preferences, on the one hand, and a statistical model for asset returns, on the other. However, the parameters in the asset return model were assumed to be externally given, that is, exogenous to the analysis. In this section, the loop will be closed, and the expected returns for the assets will emerge as the returns that price assets such that

- All investors maximize their utility subject to their budget constraints.
- Financial markets clear and achieve equilibrium.

The famous *capital assets pricing model* (CAPM) prices assets from the assumption that financial markets achieve a partial equilibrium. Equilibrium models are generally a consequence of the optimizing behavior of many agents interacting in a market (investors in our case). In a multiagent economy, each investor exhibits different risk preferences (degrees of risk aversion) and is endowed with different levels of initial wealth. The agents aim to maximize their expected utility subject to their budget constraints and to build their optimal portfolios by trading in the different financial markets. Supply and demand for each financial asset will reach an equilibrium point through adjustment of the asset price, the market clearing at this point as supply equates to demand.

In this section we describe the CAPM equilibrium model for financial assets following the steps laid out in the preceding section. Despite its simplicity and obvious restrictive assumptions, the model is still used extensively today as a first approximation for the fair price of assets and also to build appropriate benchmarks for asset returns. As we will see in the last section of this chapter, the CAPM is also the starting point for Bayesian allocation techniques such as the Black-Litterman approach.[6]

CAPM Assumptions

The CAPM relies on a set of somewhat idealized assumptions:

- First and most important, the CAPM assumes a population of rational investors, each described by the mean variance utility previously introduced.[7] However, each investor may exhibit a different risk tolerance a_i (i numbers investors from 1 to P).
- There are N risky financial assets, and these can be traded in their corresponding markets. The markets are ideal in the sense that there are no transactions costs.
- There is a risk-free asset, with equal lending and borrowing rates; that is, there are no borrowing spreads.
- Besides these, the CAPM assumes rational and homogeneous expectations from investors for expected returns, volatilities, and correlations for the different asset classes; that is, their *beliefs* about future returns are rational and identical. This means that there is a unique model for asset returns commonly used by all investors and whose parameters we aim to determine.

The CAPM has been extended in a few directions by lifting some of the preceding assumptions in an attempt to create a more realistic model. For instance, lack of transactions costs or zero borrowing spreads are not essential to the model. However, in this chapter we will restrict the analysis, keeping it within the previous set of assumptions.

Agents' Optimization Process

The first stage in finding an equilibrium model for financial assets is to establish the conditions that maximize the expected utility of all market participants subject to their budget constraints. This is the portfolio-optimization problem we have already addressed in preceding sections and solves the demand for financial assets. The solution previously obtained indicated that the optimal portfolio for each investor can be built from an adequate mix of two funds:

- The portfolio with maximum Sharpe ratio that contains exclusively risky assets (M with our notation):

$$x^M = \frac{\Omega^{-1}\mu}{\overline{1}^{tr}\Omega^{-1}\mu}$$

- The risk-free asset (or cash)

The optimal mix between the two portfolios is specific to each investor and depends on his risk-aversion parameter. The allocation to the M portfolio by investor i will be given by

$$w_M^{(i)} = \frac{\overline{1}^{tr}\Omega^{-1}\mu}{a_i}$$

whereas the allocation to the risk-free rate will be

$$w_C^{(i)} = 1 - w_M^{(i)} = 1 - \frac{\overline{1}^{tr}\Omega^{-1}\mu}{a_i}$$

The critical point is to realize that all participants ideally would hold a fraction of the same portfolio M, which we have not identified yet because we do not know the expected excess returns of assets μ.

Market Clearing and Equilibrium

Investors will trade in financial markets until supply equates demand and equilibrium is established in each market. The market-clearing conditions are set by aggregating the holdings of all investors in each specific asset and equating them to the value of the full market for this asset. Let us assume that when markets reach equilibrium,

- The market for the risky asset j has a total value of V_j, with j ranging from 1 to N. Let us define the market portfolio y as the vector with components

$$y_j = \frac{V_j}{\sum\limits_{k=1}^{N} V_k} = \frac{V_j}{V^R}$$

where we have defined V^R as the total value of the markets in risky portfolios.

- For the risk-free asset market, where investors lend or borrow at the risk-free rate, we can assume that the risk-free asset is not necessarily in zero supply because we are focusing on the balance sheets of private and institutional investors. Let us assume that the supply of the risk-free asset has a value of V^F in equilibrium.

If the investors participating in the markets have a distribution of wealth given by W_i, with i ranging from 1 to P (the number of investors), then we can aggregate their preferred portfolios as

$$\begin{bmatrix} \sum\limits_i W_i w_C^{(i)} \\ \sum\limits_i W_i w_M^{(i)} \end{bmatrix} = \begin{bmatrix} \sum\limits_i W_i \left(1 - \dfrac{\overline{1}^{tr} \Omega^{-1} \mu}{a_i} \right) \\ \sum\limits_i W_i \dfrac{1}{a_i} \Omega^{-1} \mu \end{bmatrix}$$

where the first row corresponds to the risk-free asset allocation and the vector below it to the allocation to risky assets.

To simplify the notation, let us define first the total wealth of investors W^T as $\sum_i W_i$ and an average risk aversion across investors as

$$\frac{1}{a^*} = \sum_{j=1}^{P} \frac{W_i}{W^T} \frac{1}{a_i}$$

The equilibrium conditions are now written by equating the demand for assets by investors to the actual supply value:

$$\begin{bmatrix} W^T \left(1 - \dfrac{\overline{1}^{tr} \Omega^{-1} \mu}{a^*} \right) \\ \dfrac{W^T}{a^*} \Omega^{-1} \mu \end{bmatrix} = \begin{bmatrix} V^F \\ V^R y \end{bmatrix}$$

By equating the portfolios for risky assets, we can readily observe that the market portfolio y should be equal to the portfolio x^M exhibiting the maximum Sharpe ratio. This means that every investor should hold part of her wealth in the market portfolio y ($= x^M$). The efficient frontier obtained by mixing the maximum Sharpe ratio portfolio x^M and the risk-free asset is, as discussed previously, a straight line called the *capital market line* (CML) for this reason. From this equality, we also find the famous CAPM pricing equation:

$$\mu = \frac{a^* V^R}{W^T} \Omega y \qquad (3.12)$$

The additional equation corresponding to clearing of the risk-free asset is redundant given the overall budget constraint for the total wealth of investors and the market value of financial assets:

$$W^T = V^R + V^C$$

Assuming zero net supply of the risk-free asset, the pricing equation simplifies to

$$\mu = a^* \Omega y \qquad (3.13)$$

where we observe that the excess returns demanded from risky assets increase with the average risk aversion for the investor population, with the risk of the assets, and with their proportion in the overall market portfolio. Notice that the actual risk-free rate is exogenous to this model. The excess returns derived from the CAPM formula usually are denominated as equilibrium excess returns because they stem from the assumption of markets being in equilibrium.

The expression for equilibrium returns so obtained permits us to find the optimal partially funded portfolio for an investor with risk aversion a_i. The allocation to risky assets x_i will be

$$x_i = \frac{a^*}{a_i} y$$

with the rest of the portfolio invested in the risk-free asset. We confirm that the investor holds his wealth optimally in a combination of the market portfolio and the risk-free asset.

Pricing with the CAPM: Security Market Line

The meaning of the previous CAPM pricing equation may be better understood if it is transformed into the more standard component-wise form. From the definition of the covariance matrix in terms of volatilities v_i and correlations ρ_{ij}, the expected excess return for asset i can be cast as

$$\mu_i = a^* \sum_j v_i v_j \rho_{i,j} y_j = a^* v_i v_{MK} \rho_{i,MK}$$

where v_{MK} is the volatility of the market portfolio and $\rho_{i,MK}$ is the correlation between asset i and the market. Knowledge of the average risk aversion a^* is equivalent to knowledge of the market risk premium μ_{MK}. Simplifying the last equation for the market yields

$$\mu_{MK} = a^* v_{MK} v_{MK} \rho_{MK,MK} = a^* v_{MK}^2 \tag{3.14}$$

For example. if μ_{MK} is 3 percent and v_{MK} is 10 percent. then a^* is about 3 if the risk-free asset is in zero supply. From the previous two equations we may rewrite the CAPM pricing equation as

$$\mu_i = \beta_i \mu_{MK} \tag{3.15}$$

where we have introduced the beta for asset i as

$$\beta_i = \frac{v_i}{v_{MK}} \rho_{i,MK} \tag{3.16}$$

Beta measures the systematic risk of a particular asset, that is, the risk related to its correlation with the market portfolio that cannot be diversified away:

- An asset completely uncorrelated with the market will exhibit a beta of 0, and the equilibrium excess return also will be 0.
- The market itself will have a beta of 1, which is considered the natural calibration point for all the assets.
- Assets with beta between 0 and 1 exhibit lower volatility than the market or maybe higher volatility but imperfect correlation with it.
- Assets with beta larger than 1 exhibit higher volatility than the market and usually a substantial correlation with it.

The representation of the assets' expected excess returns μ_i against their betas β_i is known as the *security market line* (SML) and should be a straight line with a slope equal to the market risk premium μ_{MK} within the CAPM pricing theory framework. If the expected excess return for an asset is above the SML, this asset is underpriced, and market forces will act to increase its price in line with the CAPM equilibrium value. Analogously, expected excess returns below the SML are an indication of overbought assets, priced above their equilibrium value.

CAPM and Arbitrage

The CAPM pricing methodology guarantees the absence of arbitrage opportunities between the asset classes. There may be redundant assets, but these will be fairly priced. Also, the market may be incomplete in the sense that only factors that exhibit correlation with the market, that is, are represented to some degree in the market of financial assets, will yield nonzero expected excess returns within the framework. Assume, for instance, a financial innovation uncorrelated with the market. Initially, its expected excess return will be zero, and only as its volume increases and becomes a sizable part of the capital markets will its equilibrium excess returns start to increase in value.

Case Study

Figure 3.4 presents the approximate empirical market weights of asset classes in the investment universe. From this, we can back out equilibrium returns by

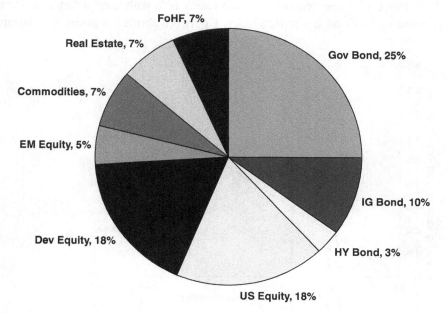

Figure 3.4 Market weights.

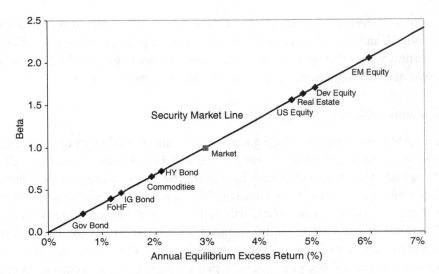

Figure 3.5 Security market line (SML) showing asset classes equilibrium excess returns given their beta to the market.

considering the market to be on the CML given its expected excess return arising from the average degree of risk aversion in the market.[8] Figure 3.5 shows how the equilibrium excess returns of all asset classes are determined, given the overall market's expected excess returns and each asset's beta with the market as a whole, by positioning them on the SML. Finally, Figure 3.6 shows the assets in volatility-

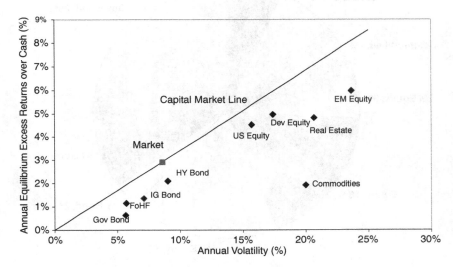

Figure 3.6 Equilibrium excess returns and capital market line (CML).

returns space: Their volatilities again are equal to the simple historical volatility, but expected excess returns all have been adjusted to their equilibrium levels.

The Black-Litterman Approach: A Bayesian Framework

Markowitz's portfolio-optimization methodology turns out to be extremely sensitive to the estimated value of the expected returns and covariance matrix for asset returns. Optimization methods generally will try to exploit as much as possible any errors in the estimated parameters to boost returns from quasi-arbitrage opportunities. In particular, the estimation of future expected returns usually is subject to great error (inefficiency) owing to the lack of history and the changing nature of the economic environment. Markowitz portfolios in fact are usually highly unrealistic portfolios with fairly extreme positions and are of little practical use. It was thought that the introduction of Bayesian techniques could help to ameliorate these problems.

In Bayesian techniques, the parameters to be estimated are assumed to themselves be random variables with a *prior* distribution, which reflects the possible distribution of values we would expect if we had no empirical or observed data to guide us, or *prior* to observing any data. Although the prior introduces a bias in the estimation process, it effectively limits the range of values that the data can take to ensure that the final distribution for the parameters is reasonable given our prior theoretical expectations; that is, it conforms to basic theoretical expectations.

The *posterior* (or final) distribution for the parameters is constructed by considering additional information from observations or, alternatively, further insights gained by the investor about the true distribution of the parameters. This additional information is blended with the prior distribution[9] to provide the posterior distribution combining both prior theoretical expectations and subsequent observations—from this we can infer the new moments of the distributions for the parameters sought.

Black and Litterman applied the spirit of the Bayesian approach to overcome many of the problems of the Markowitz approach. Their intuition was to use as prior for the distribution of asset returns the CAPM model introduced in the last section, that is, the expected excess returns derived from the *assumption* that the market portfolio is the optimal portfolio of risky assets (the one with maximum Sharpe ratio). This prior reflects fundamental expectations from a relevant theoretical framework and consequently assumes that investors are rational with homogeneous expectations and that the markets are information-efficient and in equilibrium.[10]

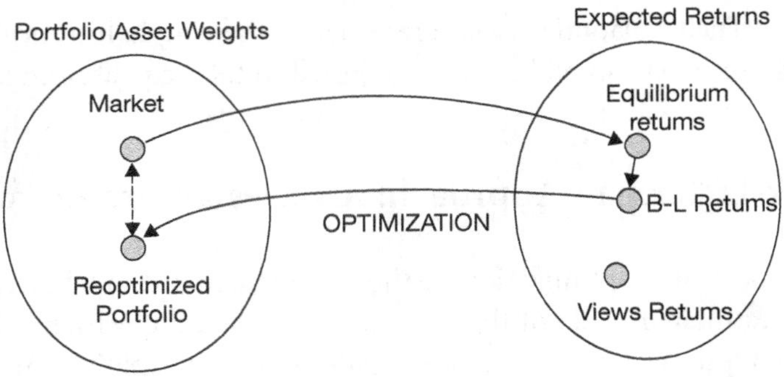

Figure 3.7 The Black-Litterman process. We extract equilibrium returns from the market (the CAPM approach) and then in the second step mix this prior (i.e., these equilibrium returns) with forward-looking views–based returns in order to form the posterior Black-Litterman returns from which we finally infer the reoptimized Black-Litterman portfolio.

In a second stage, the specific views of each investor (which can be regarded as additional information or further insight) are therefore blended with the prior to produce the posterior distribution for asset returns. This posterior model of asset returns is then used within the Markowitz optimization framework to construct the optimal portfolios for specific investors (Figure 3.7). This process will be described in more detail in the following sections.

Equilibrium Returns: The Prior Optimal Portfolio

The Black-Litterman approach starts by assuming that markets are in equilibrium and that the set of hypotheses behind the CAPM framework holds, so the prior model of excess returns is given by

$$r = \mu + \sigma W$$

where, as usual, we assume that the random variable W is Gaussian with zero mean and covariance Ω. As a consequence, the prior distribution of returns $f(r)$ implied by this model will be the normal distribution, characterized by the equation

$$f(r) = \frac{1}{\sqrt{(2\pi)^N |\Omega|}} \exp\left[-\frac{(r - \mu)^{tr} \Omega^{-1} (r - \mu)}{2} \right]$$

Using Markowitz at this stage, we would conclude that the prior optimal portfolio for an investor would be a mixture of the market portfolio and the risk-free rate in proportions depending on her risk aversion.

Views: Incorporating Additional Information

But let us now assume that the investor does not believe in the optimality of the prior portfolio because he may have superior information or models. The expected excess returns forecasted by him r_{for} could be modeled in terms of the true excess returns r plus an error in the forecast Z for the different states of the world ω at the next time period:

$$r_{for}(\omega) = r(\omega) + Z(\omega)$$

which we simplify into

$$r_{for} = r + Z$$

If our investor is a good forecaster, r_{for} will be close to r in every state of the world, and Z will be small. More generally, our investor may prefer to forecast linear combinations of returns v_{for}:

$$v_{for} = P \cdot r + Z$$

where the matrix P has a number of columns equal to the number of assets and a number of rows equal to the number of views. The second representation includes the first one when P is the identity matrix, so we will focus on this more general case.

Assuming that the random variable Z is also Gaussian with zero mean and covariance Σ, the conditional distribution $f(v_{for}|r)$ for the views v_{for} given returns r will be

$$f(v_{for}|r) = \frac{1}{\sqrt{(2\pi)^L|\Sigma|}} \exp\left[-\frac{(v_{for} - \mathrm{Pr})^{tr}\Sigma^{-1}(v_{for} - \mathrm{Pr})}{2} \right]$$

The covariance Σ can be interpreted as a measure of the confidence on the views or, alternatively, the investor's forecasting ability. We also will assume that the random variables W and Z are independent among themselves; that is, deviations of the realized returns from the equilibrium value are uncorrelated with the forecast errors.

Mixing Views with Equilibrium Returns: A Bayesian Framework

Once we have identified the prior distribution of returns $f(r)$ and the conditional distribution for the views given the returns $f(v_{for}|r)$, we will be in a position to use Bayes theorem to construct the posterior distribution for returns given the views $f(r|v_{\text{for}})$:

$$f(r|v_{\text{for}}) = \frac{f(v_{\text{for}}|r)f(r)}{f(v_{\text{for}})} = \frac{f(v_{\text{for}}|r)f(r)}{\int f(v_{\text{for}}|r)f(r)\, dr}$$

The posterior distribution is also a Gaussian distribution, and we will be interested mainly in the mean value of this distribution: the new posterior expected returns. By multiplying the two previously introduced density functions and grouping the terms in the exponent as a polynomial in r, we are able to identify the mean of the posterior distribution as

$$\tilde{\mu} = \left(\Omega^{-1} + P^{tr}\Sigma^{-1}P\right)^{-1}\left(\Omega^{-1}\mu + P^{tr}\Sigma^{-1}v_{\text{for}}\right)$$

which, after some manipulation, also can be expressed as

$$\tilde{\mu} = \mu + \Omega P^{tr}(P\Omega P^{tr} + \Sigma)^{-1}(v_{\text{for}} - P\mu) \qquad (3.17)$$

The last expression has very intuitive implications: The posterior expected excess returns are modified with respect to the prior equilibrium excess returns according to the significance of and the confidence in the investor's views. If the investor's views v_{for} agree with those implied by the equilibrium returns $P\mu$, then no correction to the equilibrium returns is required. On the other hand, if the views and priors are different, then the tilt of posterior returns with respect to equilibrium returns will be proportional to this difference of views $(v_{\text{for}} - P\mu)$ and further transformed by a matrix that depends on the volatility and correlation among assets (Ω) and the confidence in the views (Σ).

The Tilted Portfolio

Finally, once the posterior expected excess returns have been identified, the Markowitz optimization framework can be used to find their implications in terms of asset allocation. Focusing on the simple case where the portfolio includes the risk-free asset, the allocation to risky assets will be given by

$$\tilde{x} = \frac{1}{a}\Omega^{-1}\tilde{\mu}$$

The tilt in the portfolio (i.e., the tactical position) can be calculated as

$$\tilde{x} - x = \frac{1}{a}\Omega^{-1}(\tilde{\mu} - \mu) = \frac{1}{a}P^{tr}(P\Omega P^{tr} + \Sigma)^{-1}(v_{\text{for}} - P\mu) \qquad (3.18)$$

If we particularize for the case in which P is the identity matrix (i.e., we have views on individual assets), the tactical tilt can be simplified to

$$\tilde{x} - x = \frac{1}{a}(\Omega + \Sigma)^{-1}(v_{\text{for}} - \mu) \tag{3.19}$$

where the tilts are seen to depend on the difference between views and equilibrium returns, weighted by the confidence in the views and ultimately scaled by the risk aversion of the investor.

Illustrated Case Study

To illustrate the effects of such tilts to the portfolio, we briefly show two cases: the first where the investor has a defensive view relative to the equilibrium returns leading to a defensive portfolio tilt (Figure 3.8) and the second the adoption of more aggressive views (Figure 3.9).

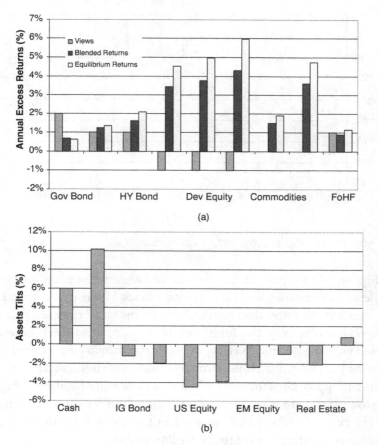

Figure 3.8 Constructing a Black-Litterman portfolio with defensive views.

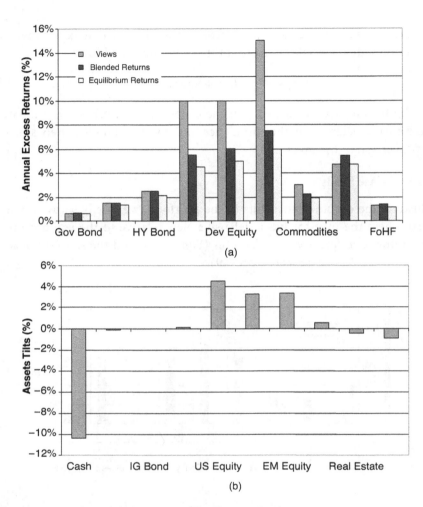

Figure 3.9 Constructing a Black-Litterman portfolio with aggressive views.

In Figure 3.8*a* we present the dislocation between the equilibrium returns and the view-based returns, leading to the new Black-Litterman returns. Here the views are substantially lower than equilibrium returns on all risky asset classes, and indeed expectations are negative for all equity. In turn, these Black-Litterman returns lead to weight adjustments (tilts) to the final portfolio (represented in Figure 3.8*b*), steering the optimal portfolio strongly toward cash and government bonds.

A similar approach is followed when views are more positive in Figure 3.9. The investor's views are much more positive on equities than the equilibrium returns (Figure 3.9*a*), which leads to a tilt in the optimal portfolio away from cash and toward equities relative to the CAPM solution.

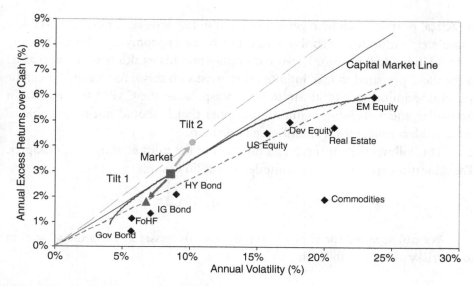

Figure 3.10 The impact of views on the CML.

Finally, we review how the Black-Litterman approach influences the efficient frontier. Looking at Figure 3.10, we observe that by imposing either defensive or aggressive views, we shift the CML slightly in each case relative to the
equilibrium solution. In the case of defensive views, the expected excess returns
of the risky assets are reduced relative to their equilibrium positions shown on
the diagram. This effectively lowers the efficient frontier and tilts the composition of the market portfolio toward less risky assets. This shifts it down and left
relative to the equilibrium market portfolio because it has both lower risk and
lower expected returns, entailing a lower Sharpe ratio. In turn, this means that
the CML lies below the original.

The opposite is true in the case of aggressive tilts. The composition of the
market portfolio shifts toward riskier assets because they offer relatively higher
expected returns for the same levels of expected volatility. This gives it a higher
Sharpe ratio and tilts the CML upward.

Appendix: Unfunded Portfolios

In this appendix we briefly outline the optimization process for *tactical* or *unfunded portfolios*, which do not require an initial investment and are created by
borrowing (or shorting) some securities to fund the purchase of other securities.

A tactical portfolio can be regarded as an infinitely leveraged portfolio. While a completely unfunded portfolio would not be an appropriate solution for any rational individual investor because it implies that his wealth is zero and that he is therefore prepared to take infinite relative risks on this zero wealth,[11] it can be a useful technical tool to illustrate certain aspects of the CAPM framework. In particular, the *no arbitrage* condition implies that it should not be possible to make riskless profits from an unfunded portfolio.

This follows the approach and notation of the third section of this chapter. The allocation vector x_T of an unfunded portfolio ensures

$$\bar{1}^{tr}x_T = 0$$

We can separate the allocation to the risk-free asset x_F from the allocation to the risky assets x as follows:

$$x_T = [x_F x]^{tr}$$

The expected returns for tactical or unfunded portfolios are calculated through very similar expressions to those of fully or partially funded portfolios, but the interpretation is slightly different. The concept of return is not appropriate for unfunded portfolios because their initial overall value is zero. The performance of tactical portfolios is measured in terms of the nominal profit or loss of the positions, that is, an absolute number rather than a relative return. However, we can assume that there is reference notional value (equal to 1) used to describe in relative terms both the portfolio allocation and the profit and loss of those positions. The expected profit and loss of the tactical portfolio with risky asset allocation $x (our reference is $1) will be

$$\mu_x = x^{tr}\mu \text{ dollars}$$

Notice that this is not an excess return now, but the profit or loss of the position. The volatility of the profit and loss simply is calculated as

$$v_x = \sqrt{x^{tr}\Omega x} \text{ dollars}$$

If the notional reference for our tactical positions was $1,000, then both the expected profit or loss and the volatility will scale by $1,000

For *tactical portfolios*, the corresponding measure to the Sharpe ratio is the *information ratio*, which measures the ratio between the expected value and the volatility of the tactical profit or loss.

$$\text{Information ratio} = \frac{\mu_x}{\nu_x} = \frac{x^{tr}\mu}{\sqrt{x^{tr}\Omega x}}$$

This is identical to the Sharpe ratio,

$$\text{Sharpe ratio} = \frac{\mu_x}{\nu_x} = \frac{x^{tr}\mu}{\sqrt{x^{tr}\Omega x}}$$

and it is worth understanding why this is so. The Sharpe ratio essentially measures the performance of a tactical portfolio built from the positions of the risky assets x, then taking a negative position in the risk-free asset so that the portfolio becomes unfunded. That is, the Sharpe ratio of a partially or fully funded portfolio is the same as the information ratio of a tactical portfolio with the same positions in the risky assets.

In particular, the optimal solution for a tactical portfolio that includes the risk-free asset is identical to the equivalent partially funded portfolio, the only difference being that the allocation to the risk-free asset becomes the negative of the total allocation to risky assets (to ensure the unfunded status). Consequently, the efficient frontier for tactical portfolios is also a straight line.

We can use tactical portfolios to provide a simple argument for the claim that the CAPM pricing methodology guarantees the absence of arbitrage opportunities. This starts with decomposition of the symmetric and positive semidefinite covariance matrix Ω in terms of its square-root matrix σ:

$$\Omega = \sigma\sigma^{tr}$$

The matrix σ is also symmetric, but we keep the transpose sign to give continuity with previous sections. We aim to show that any riskless tactical portfolio x (i.e., verifying that $x^{tr}\sigma = 0$) also should have a zero expected excess return $x^{tr}\mu = 0$. Since the CAPM expected excess return is given by $\mu = a^*\Omega y$, we easily prove

$$x^{tr}\mu = a^*x^{tr}\Omega y = a^*(x^{tr}\sigma)(\sigma^{tr}y) = 0$$

Thus the CAPM pricing framework verifies the absence of arbitrage.

Notes

1. And $\hat{r}_i(\omega) = \hat{r}_i$ for log returns.
2. There is a whole series of risk measures that aim to overcome some of the limitations of volatility as a risk measure. These measures generally focus on

downside risk rather than on the spread of the distribution and may be more accurate if the asset distribution exhibits tails (negative skewness and enhanced kurtosis). We do not delve into these here, though, because generally they are not used under the MPT framework.

3. We provide here only an outline of the justification for this approximation because a proof would require advanced mathematics for exact convergence properties:

$$
\log(1 + r_i) \approx r_i - \frac{1}{2}r_i^2 \approx \mu_i + \sum_j \sigma_{ij} W_j - \frac{1}{2}\sum_{j,k} \sigma_{ij}\sigma_{ik} W_j W_k
$$

$$
\approx \mu_i - \frac{1}{2}\sum_j \sigma_{ij}^2 + \sum_j \sigma_{ij} W_j
$$

4. See the beginning of Chapter 6 for a discussion of this point.
5. Notice too that there is an infinite number of portfolios on this straight line with the same Sharpe ratios—although they will not have the same expected utility for any given investor.
6. Black and Litterman (1992).
7. We can avoid placing this extreme restriction on investors' utility functions, but only if we make the alternative assumption that all asset returns are Gaussian. We shall return to this in more depth in future chapters.
8. The degree of risk aversion in the market is backed out using empirical analysis related to the equity risk premium averaged over long periods of time or anticipated in a forward-looking manner.
9. Through the ubiquitous Bayes theorem.
10. However, both these assumptions are to some degree questionable, as we explore in the rest of this book, and it is a common experience to see diverging opinions among investors about the expected performance of financial assets.
11. Investors with zero current financial wealth still may be able to invest rationally without taking infinite relative risks because total wealth also comprises the human capital asset of the net present value (NPV) of future savings.

Chapter 4

HOW WELL DOES MODERN PORTFOLIO THEORY WORK IN PRACTICE?

with Pierre Dangauthier and Prosper Dovonon

The mean variance portfolio construction methodology appeared to be a tremendous achievement for "modern finance." On the basis of rather stylized assumptions, it offered an elegant solution to the problem of constructing a portfolio that is optimal for each investor. As a model of investors' behavior, it managed to accommodate some well-known features, such as the intuitive appeal of diversification. As a normative theory (i.e., a description of what *should* be done), it influenced greatly the risk-management practices of portfolio managers.

However, the real investment world is not like a controlled lab experiment. As discussed in Chapter 1, market structure evolves over time because of volatility regimes, market cycles, and unexpected extreme events. This process of evolution sits uneasily with the two main assumptions that underpin mean variance portfolio optimization and thus modern portfolio theory (MPT) as a whole. These assumptions were stated by Markowitz in his seminal 1952 publication: "First, the investor must desire according to the [mean variance] maxim. Second, we must be able to arrive at a reasonable . . . probability belief on future performances of securities." These assumptions are open to challenge on a number of fronts.

In this chapter we review carefully how well MPT concepts work in practice. To do this, we first analyze the performance of such models very extensively under different periods, rebalancing frequencies, and so on. We then use various tests to investigate why mean variance fails to deliver investment outperformance. A particular problem, we argue, is MPT's belief in a stable diversification pattern among time series. In fact, as we demonstrate, the way the time series themselves are distributed leads to a misspecification of the satisfaction of the MPT investor, that is, of his utility function. We conclude by showing that the criticisms presented before are so fundamental that they affect not only the most simple version of the MPT but also more advanced implementations such as the Black-Litterman framework.

Analysis of the Performance of MPT

Presentation of the Data for Our Eight Asset Classes

In this chapter we consider a set of eight asset classes. We have computed the monthly arithmetic total return indices for government, corporate, and emerging-market bonds; developed- and emerging-market equities; commodities; property; and hedge funds from January 1990 to November 2009 (Table 4.1).

Note that we retain cash as a separate asset that is not integrated into portfolios because we treat all returns as excess returns over cash (i.e., total return – cash). Figure 4.1 illustrates the cumulative performance of the assets in the case of a buy-and-hold strategy from January 1990 to November 2009, and Table 4.2 gives a summary of their return distributions.

This data set gives us a wide diversity of asset classes, each with a different risk/return profile. We can see that from 1990 to November 2009, the best Sharpe ratios (excess returns divided by volatility) are exhibited by two quite different asset classes: hedge funds and government bonds. Hedge funds achieve a high Sharpe ratio thanks to their high average return, without the penalty of too much volatility, especially during the dot-com crisis; by contrast, government bonds have very low returns, but this is more than compensated for by their extremely low volatility.

The lowest Sharpe ratio was recorded by developed-market equities, where low returns were accompanied by high sensitivity to market cycles. By contrast, emerging-market equities managed to achieve a reasonable Sharpe ratio despite being the riskiest asset class during this period, thanks to high returns.

Table 4.1

Indices Used to Represent the Various Asset Classes

	Description	**Index**
EqDev	Developed-market equities ($US hedged)	MSCI World
EqEM	Emerging-market equities ($US hedged)	MSCI Emerging Markets
BondGov	Global government bonds ($US hedged)	Merrill Lynch Global Government Bond II
BondIGCredit	Global corporate bonds ($US hedged)	Merrill Lynch Global Broad Market Corporate
BondHYEM	Global high yield ($US hedged)	Barcap Global High Yield
Commodities	Commodities ($US hedged)	DJUBS-Future Commodities Index
HF	Hedge funds ($US hedged)	Tremont All Hedge FTSE
Property	Developed-market property ($US hedged)	EPRA Developed

Constructing the Mean Variance Model

We focus here on how people generally construct an optimal asset allocation according to the MPT framework. (See Chapter 3 for an extended discussion of this.) Given a set of assets, the mean variance algorithm recommends investing in the portfolio with minimum expected risk for a given expected return. Portfolio risk is measured by the dispersion of its future returns, as evaluated by the variance.

The key inputs to the mean variance optimization approach therefore are

- The expected variance-covariance matrix of asset returns, and
- The expected return of each asset considered for the portfolio

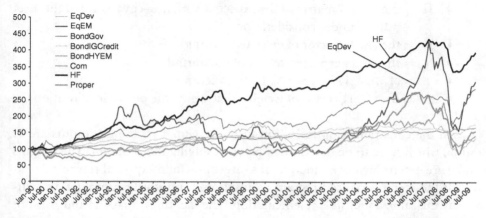

Figure 4.1 Cumulative performances of the monthly returns of nine asset classes (excess return over cash).

Table 4.2

Individual Performance of the Eight Time Series Sorted by Decreasing Sharpe Ratios (Data from January 1990 to November 2009)

	Annualized Average Excess Return, %	Annualized Volatility, %	Sharpe Ratio
HF	7.2	7.5	0.95
BondGov	2.7	3.2	0.83
BondIGCredit	3.0	4.4	0.67
Bond HYEM	5.8	10.2	0.57
EqEM	8.7	24.4	0.36
Property	4.1	19.1	0.21
Commodities	2.9	14.8	0.19
EqDev	2.7	15.5	0.17

As has been detailed already in Chapter 3, the mean variance optimization program is expressed as follows:

$$(M) : \begin{cases} \min_x x^{tr} \Omega x \\ x^{tr} \mu = \mu_p \\ x^{tr} \bar{1} = 1 \end{cases} \qquad (4.1)$$

where, with N being the number of assets,

- Ω = the (N, N) matrix of the expected-variance–covariance of the asset returns under consideration
- μ = the $(N, 1)$ vector of expected returns
- μ_p = the target expected return of the portfolio
- $\bar{1}$ = $(1, \ldots, 1)^{tr}$ = the $(N, 1)$ unit vector
- x = the $(N, 1)$ vector of weights that define the portfolio allocation

In the constrained optimization program (Eq. 4.1), the key inputs are Ω and μ, which have to be determined prior to solving the program. The weights x then are determined as a function of a target portfolio expected return μ_p.

If the mean variance program is simple and intuitively appealing, we cannot say the same about its implementation. The identification of Ω and μ is not trivial. In particular, the concepts of expected mean and variance are rather vague. This explains the emergence of a certain number of variants to the mean variance asset-allocation methodology. However, whatever variant is used, building our expected mean or variance requires forecasts, and the performance of the mean variance methodology is tied to the quality of these forecasts. Practically, for people who do not want to rely on purely subjective forecasts, we have identified two main schools of thought to estimate the two first moments (i.e., the mean and volatility characteristics of the distribution). We call them the *historical* and the *capital asset pricing model* (CAPM) *approaches* and review how they perform here.

The Historical Approach to Asset Allocation

This approach usually assumes that the time series of indices are stationary[1] in the long run around a drift. The existence of mean reversion forces is expected to bring these time series back close to this drift. The drift, which corresponds to the expected return vector μ, is commonly set to the historical average of the return realizations. Similarly, the expected covariance is set to the historical asset return variance.

Let us present a first example. We consider a portfolio of three assets: developed-market government bonds (BondGov), developed-market equity (EqDev), and emerging-market equity (EqEM) indices. For each of these indices, we consider the difference between the monthly total return index and cash. These excess return series start from February 2003 and go through to November 2007, resulting in a total of 58 monthly observations.

Looking at the performance statistics displayed in Table 4.3, we can see that this 58-month period corresponds to a period of growth in the equity market. Developed-market equities rose by 14.4 percent yearly, emerging-market equities by 30.0 percent, and government bonds by 0.75 percent. As expected, the risk, expressed as volatility, increases with returns.

We display in Figure 4.2 the allocations for five investors with a respective target return of $\mu_1 = 5$ percent, $\mu_2 = 10$ percent, $\mu_3 = 14.8$ percent, $\mu_4 = 20$ percent, and $\mu_5 = 30$ percent. The lower target return is obtained by the portfolio, which allocates a large weight to government bonds, a small weight to developed-market equities, and an even smaller weight to emerging-market equities. This portfolio also displays the smallest variance among the four portfolios that we consider (Table 4.4). As we notice from the figure, the higher the targeted return, the more weight the mean variance procedure allocates to the riskier assets. In the extreme case, the highest-return portfolio does not contain any government bonds at all.

Table 4.3

Performance Summary of Developed-Market Equities (EqDev), Emerging-Market Equities (EqEM), and Developed-Market Government Bonds (BondGov) between February 2003 and November 2007

Asset Series	Annualized Standard Deviation, %	Annualized Return, %	Cumulative Return over Full Period, %
EqDev	9.1	14.4	99.5
EqEM	17.3	30.0	319.4
BondGov	2.8	0.75	3.7

The value of the mean variance process is also evidenced in the comparison of portfolio 3 with developed-market equities. Both have a similar level of return, but the risk of portfolio 3, as measured by its standard deviation, is far smaller than the risk exhibited by the developed-market equity index on its

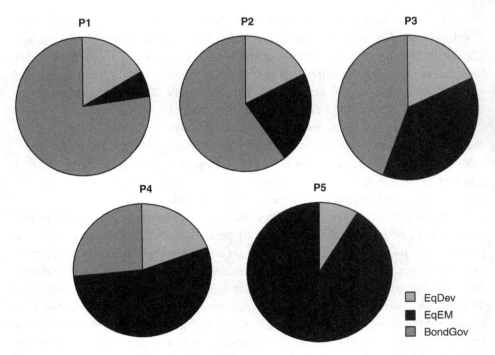

Figure 4.2 The five optimal portfolio allocations across developed-market equity (EqDev), emerging-market equity (EqEM), and developed-market government bonds (BondGov) using the historical approach.

Table 4.4

Volatility, Cumulative Performance, and Allocation of the Optimal Portfolios of Developed-Market Equity (EqDev), Emerging-Market Equity (EqEM), and Developed-Market Government Bonds (BondGov) Using the Historical Approach

Asset Series	Targeted Annualized Return, %	Annualized Standard Deviation, %	Cumulative Performance over the Full Period, %	Portfolio Weights, %		
				EqDev	EqEM	BondGov
Portfolio 1	5.0	3.1	27.0	16.9	6.0	77.1
Portfolio 2	10.0	5.2	60.8	17.8	21.9	60.3
Portfolio 3	14.8	7.8	100.5	18.7	37.0	44.2
Portfolio 4	20.0	10.7	154.0	19.7	53.6	26.7
Portfolio 5	30.0	16.4	293.5	9.0	91.0	0.0

own. This outlines the benefit of diversification. Picking the developed-market equity index alone looks riskier than diversifying across the asset classes to lower the risk while targeting the same level of return.

The CAPM Approach to Asset Allocation

As has been presented previously, the assumption of efficient markets means that all information already should be incorporated in the prices of indices. If we consider that the community of investors can be shrunk into a rational *representative investor* optimizing her portfolio in accordance with her risk aversion, then this portfolio (i.e., the market asset allocation) tells us something about the implicit assumptions of this representative investor concerning forward-looking asset returns. If we have knowledge of the relative weights of asset classes in market y, of the corresponding covariance matrix Ω, and of the risk premium a^* that the representative investor demands to move to risky assets, we then can back out these *equilibrium returns* μ^{eq}. Among practitioners, this methodology is often referred to as the *market-clearing approach*.

$$\mu^{eq} = a^*\Omega y \qquad (4.2)$$

We therefore have an alternative methodology with which to estimate the first moment (the expected return), although we have to stick with the historical approach to estimate the second moment. From there, we can rebuild the time series to align with the equilibrium returns and have a look at the performance of the corresponding portfolio optimization.

Measuring the Out-of-Sample Performance of the Historical and CAPM Approaches

In the preceding section, using two-moment estimation approaches, we described a simple mean variance optimization example. We showed how investors could reduce their risk by diversifying. This illustrative example was simplified in several ways:

- We worked with only three assets. In a more realistic asset-allocation setting, we typically would consider more indices.
- We optimized for target levels of expected return, therefore avoiding the introduction of a risk-aversion coefficient specific to the investor. In reality, the choice of a particular portfolio on the efficient frontier will depend on this subjective risk aversion of the investor, that is, his willingness to trade risk for return.
- The performance analysis was undertaken in sample.

This last point is the most important one. Reviewing performance *in-sample* is quite misleading in the sense that it corresponds to an optimization based on past information, which is in no manner informative for forward-looking performance. In this section we provide some evidence showing that simple mean variance portfolios in fact perform quite poorly in a more realistic *out-of-sample* configuration, whatever the estimation procedure is.

The Distinction Between In-Sample and Out-of Sample Analysis

Let us describe in more detail this distinction between an in-sample and an out-of-sample approach. An optimization is said to be in sample when portfolio construction and its performance evaluation are performed with the same data set. In the preceding case, we used data from the same time period to

1. Estimate the means and covariance matrix of the assets.
2. Compute the optimized portfolio and evaluate its resulting return and volatility.

This in-sample setting is fine for an illustration of a mean variance optimization, but it is not representative of what happens to a real investment strategy.

To obtain a better idea of the added value of a quantitative strategy such as a mean variance optimization, we instead need to perform an out-of-sample backtesting analysis. In order to do so, we divide our sample into two subperiods. The first data set, which is called *in-sample data, past data,* or *training data,* is used to fit the optimized asset allocation. In this case, fitting consists of estimating all the means, variances, and correlations of the assets and computing the optimal portfolio weights. The second data set, the *out-of-sample* or *test dataset,* is used to evaluate the performance of the portfolio in a new environment.

In other words, we take the viewpoint of an investor who currently stands at the cutoff date. She has a database of past financial history and no knowledge of the future. She will learn over time whether or not the allocation that she has retained will prove to be profitable.

To repeat, in-sample analysis is not a guarantee of future performance and can prove very misleading. This point is usually referred to as *overfitting* and means that the strategy is so well adjusted to a particular data set that it becomes too specific to be adaptable to slightly different data.

Historical Approach for a Given Investor with a Well-Identified Risk Profile

To assess the out-of-sample performance of a mean variance portfolio, we start by dividing the data set into two periods, with January 2002 arbitrarily chosen to be the cutoff date. We therefore stand in the position of a long-horizon investor who has access to the 1990–2001 data set and wants to derive an optimal mean variance portfolio in which to invest between 2002 and 2010. As we have seen previously, the investor has to provide to the mean variance optimizer two sets of parameters: expected returns and the covariance matrix for all assets. The best possible values would be the realized values between 2002 and 2010, but, of course, the investor does not have access to this future information. He can only rely on some kind of forward-looking views of what might happen in the future, from the perspective of January 2002. However, there always will be a discrepancy between these forecasts and what actually happens. This mismatch will lead to a decrease in performance.

In this instance, we consider a portfolio manager who does not have any subjective forecast about the future. This investor who does not have any explicit forecast still has to provide "expected" returns and a covariance matrix. One of the simplest options, quite common among real investors, is to suppose that in

Table 4.5

Individual Performances of Our Eight Asset Classes for the In-Sample Data Set, 1990–2001

	Annualized Average Excess Return, %	Annualized Volatility, %	Sharpe Ratio
HF	9.2	8.4	1.09
BondGov	2.9	3.3	0.89
BondIGCredit	3.3	4.0	0.83
BondHYEM	5.2	9.2	0.57
EqDev	2.6	14.6	0.18
EqEM	3.2	24.2	0.13
Property	0.7	17.0	0.04
Commodities	0.4	12.1	0.03

the future, assets will behave similarly to what they did in the past. Under this option, expected returns for 2002–2010 will equate to historical average returns over 1990–2001. Similarly, the expected covariance matrix between assets will be the empirical covariance matrix during 1990–2001. Another interpretation of this approach is to assume that the asset returns are drawn from a stationary multivariate distribution of which we estimate the first two moments. This estimation is quite crude because it does not try to correct any sampling bias and does not take into account the size of the data set.

Table 4.5 shows the empirical returns and variances of the asset classes as computed with the in-sample 1990–2001 data. We can see that even if individual figures are actually different from Table 4.4, the global risk/return profile of the assets is rather similar.

The investor favoring this historical approach now can run the mean variance optimization program. Let's assume that among all the portfolios on the efficient frontier, the investor ends up selecting the one displaying a 6 percent return. This optimal portfolio is composed of hedge funds (54 percent) and government bonds (45 percent), as represented in Figure 4.3. A striking feature of this optimized portfolio is its low diversification, which we will discuss later on in this chapter.

We now run this asset allocation on the 2002–2010 out-of-sample data set. We immediately notice that the target return is not reached out-of-sample, while being realized in-sample. Since the out-of-sample volatility is comparable with the in-sample volatility, the resulting Sharpe ratio becomes substantially lower. Table 4.6 presents the actual results.

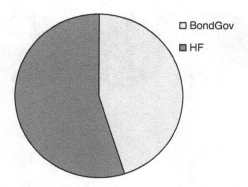

Figure 4.3 The in-sample optimal portfolio with a target 6 percent return is composed of 54 percent hedge funds and 45 percent government bonds.

This example suggests that a mean variance optimization approach based on historical estimates may not always fulfill its promises out of sample.

Historical Approach for Different Investor Risk Profiles

We now keep the previous settings but consider five different portfolios equally spaced on the efficient frontier, in sample. The composition of these portfolios is given in Figure 4.4, from the low-risk, low-return portfolio on the left to the riskier portfolio on the right. Again, we see that the diversification level among different assets is low, all portfolios being composed mainly of the highest Sharpe ratio assets: government bonds and hedge funds. We note that three of the asset classes are never included (i.e., EqDev, BondIGCredit, and EqEM).

We first report the cumulative out-of-sample performance in Figure 4.5. We choose to start from the arbitrary values of 100 and cumulate returns until January 2002. Then we reset all the performances to 100 in order to provide a fair comparison on the out-of-sample set.

Table 4.6

Poor Out-of-Sample Performance of the Optimized Portfolio Targeting 6 Percent Return

	In Sample	Out of Sample
Dates	1990–2001	2002–2010
Average return	6.0%	3.3%
Volatility	5.2%	4.9%
Sharpe ratio	1.15	0.68

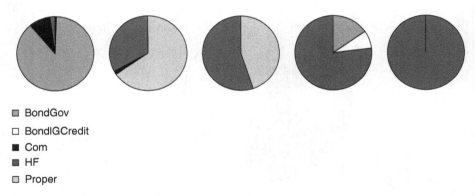

□ BondGov
□ BondIGCredit
■ Com
■ HF
□ Proper

Figure 4.4   Composition of five optimal portfolios on the in-sample (1990–2001) frontier.

In addition to the five curves for the five portfolios, we report the performances of a market-weighted benchmark portfolio[2] using a bold black line.

The results are summarized in Figure 4.6 in terms of standard deviation and return. The in-sample portfolios on the efficient frontier are represented by dots. The corresponding out-of-sample performance is represented by diamonds. In-sample mean variance portfolios perform well, with their performance exhibiting a fair risk/return tradeoff. Their rank ordering respects the logic of a risk/return tradeoff, with the more adventurous portfolios recording better performance. In addition, in-sample mean variance portfolios tend to outperform the equally weighted portfolio. Out of sample, the story looks different.

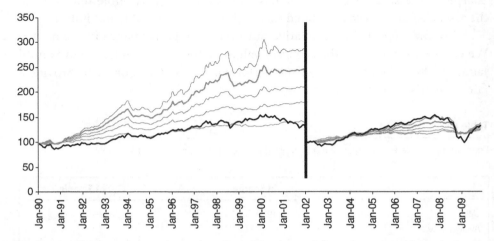

Figure 4.5   Discrepancy between in-sample and out-of-sample cumulative performances of five optimal portfolios.

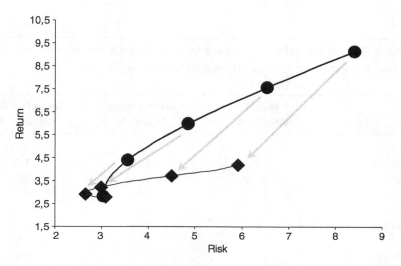

Figure 4.6   Out-of-sample portfolios are well below the efficient frontier (risk being equated to volatility).

Riskier portfolios do not always perform better than more conservative ones. None of the portfolios delivers its target return out of sample.

CAPM Approach for a Given Investor with a Well-Identified Risk Profile

In order to define the optimal asset allocation from January 2002 onward, investors will make their decisions based on the relative weights of the assets on the last day of 2001. Then they will back out the covariance matrix from the historical time series between 1990 and the end of 2001. Having observed that during the period, the risk premium demanded by investors was 4.5 percent, they will back out the *equilibrium returns* for all the time series, as given in Table 4.7.

With these new equilibrium returns and the aforementioned covariance matrix, the investor uses the mean variance procedure to back out the asset allocation corresponding to a 6 percent target return. This allocation serves as the basis for computing the performance of the portfolio between 2002 and 2010 (Table 4.8). In-sample and out-of-sample performance both look disappointing compared with the 6 percent target. The CAPM approach fails to deliver, as did the historical approach, out of sample.

Do the Cutoff Dates Matter?

One could argue that the preceding conclusions are sensitive to the choice of the data set and, in particular, to the cutoff date. To exclude this possibility, we

Table 4.7

Comparison of Historical Average Excess Returns with Excess Equilibrium Returns Inferred from Market Capitalization and the In-Sample Covariance Matrix at the End of December 2001

	Market Weights, %	Average Excess Returns, %	Excess Equilibrium Returns, %
EqDev	36	2.57	4.50
EqEM	5	2.62	5.72
BondGov	29	3.01	0.41
BondIGCredit	11	3.43	0.55
BondHYEM	2	5.23	1.96
Commodities	6	0.57	0.48
HF	3	9.14	1.54
Property	7	0.52	4.45

repeat the same experiment with varying definitions of the in-sample and out-of-sample periods for each possible cutoff date (any month from November 1990 to September 2008). As before, we impose a target return of 6 percent to the optimizer and study the out-of-sample mean return in the resulting portfolio. We obtain 217 values for the 217 different periods, which we report in Figure 4.7. The poor out-of-sample performance of the mean variance approach is confirmed for all periods. Interestingly, we notice a downward trend in the figure, suggesting that the longer the in-sample time series, the poorer is the out-of-sample performance. In Figure 4.8, the histogram of the out-of-sample performance confirms that the bulk of the distribution of returns is well below the desired 6 percent value.

So far we have looked at how mean variance portfolios tend to behave in stylized two-period settings. However, we also have to assess the performance of

Table 4.8

Out-of-Sample Performance of a Mean Variance Portfolio Based on Equilibrium Returns

	Targeted	In-Sample	Out-of-Sample
Dates		1990–2001	2002–2010
Average return	6.0%	2.7%	3.9%
Volatility		10.6%	13.4%
Sharpe ratio		0.26	0.29

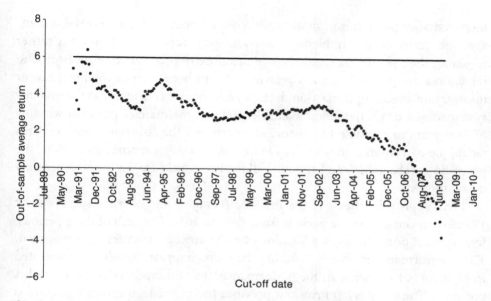

Figure 4.7   Out-of-sample mean variance performance for different specifications of the cutoff date, with a 6 percent target return.

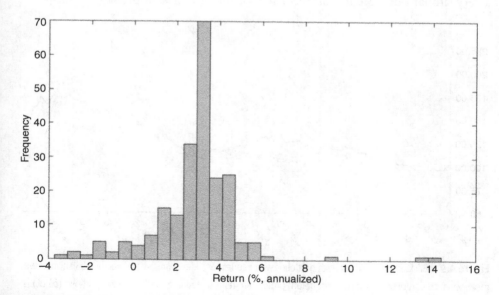

Figure 4.8   Histogram of out-of-sample performance.

mean variance portfolios in more realistic investment strategies. Portfolio managers generally do not implement buy-and-hold-forever strategies but rather
rebalance their portfolios regularly. We therefore now consider an investor who
rebalances her portfolio once a year in order to benefit from the most recent
information at each optimization date. In addition, we consider that the investor
systematically drops the oldest available data and maintains a constant window
of four years to estimate the historical return and the covariance matrix. This
technique corresponds to what is called a *sliding-window scheme*. Every year, the
portfolio is rebalanced, and the new allocation is held for 12 months before a
new optimization.

We apply this scheme to the 1990–2010 data set and obtain a succession of
17 one-year out-of-sample periods from 1993 to 2010. For each of these periods,
five optimal portfolio asset allocations on the efficient frontier are computed.
Their performance is observed during the following year. Results are presented
in Figure 4.9, together with the performance of a constantly rebalanced market
portfolio. The analysis confirms our previous findings: Mean variance portfolios
do not keep their promises. Only the least risky portfolio, composed mainly of
government bonds, competes in the long run with a market-weighted
benchmark.

This is true not only for the historical MV approach. We have implemented a similar sliding process using the CAPM framework, and it resulted in
a very similar outcome to that recorded for the historical approach.

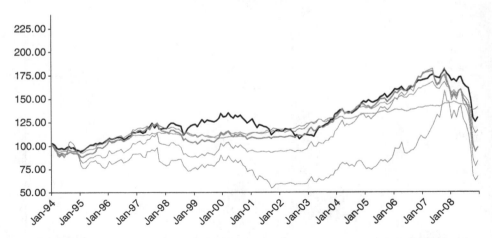

Figure 4.9 Backtesting mean variance portfolios with a four-year sliding window and yearly rebalancing. Five
mean variance portfolios with varying risk/return profiles are represented in gray. The market portfolio (*black*) is
compared with the mean variance portfolio with the same risk budget (*bold gray*).

Does the Breadth of the Investment Universe Matter?

Previous examples were based on a unique data set to improve the clarity of our presentation. However, these findings are not specific to this selected universe of indices. For example, DeMiguel, Garlappi, and Uppal (2009) show that the mean variance approach and some of its improvements cannot consistently outperform the equally weighted ($1/N$) naive portfolio. They undertake their experiment on seven empirical data sets corresponding to different equity industry sectors, different geographic indices, and different groupings of stocks.[3]

Why Does MPT Fail to Deliver?

There are several possible reasons for the lackluster performance of the mean variance approach—all stemming from the difficulty of accurately assessing the expected mean and variance of asset returns. In this section we therefore show that MPT fails to deliver out-of-sample performance because it does not capture the true dynamics of the data—whether the dynamics of each time series (their univariate behavior) or the joint dynamics of those series (their multivariate behavior). In addition, MPT ends up taking risks related to overconcentration.

An Analysis of the Univariate Dynamics of Time Series

As noted earlier, the difficulty of forecasting stock returns, backed by the efficient market hypothesis, has encouraged us to routinely feed the mean variance algorithm with historical averages and historical variance of asset returns. How good are these historical moments as proxies for the expected moments?

There are two aspects to this question. The first is related to the investment horizon and the second to the structure of the data themselves.

- Risky assets are known to display some common mean-reverting return patterns over long time horizons. But the required time needed to obtain a match between the historical average and the realized return could be long and is in any case unknown. Waiting for such a match to happen would not appear to be a normal investor strategy: Investors sometimes enter the market with a predefined time horizon, and there are opportunity costs to tying up capital while waiting for an indeterminate time for expected returns to be realized.
- The historical moments are only poor proxies for the expected moments, especially when looking at a short investment horizon. They are

obtained using past data over several years. To provide a practical idea of how this works, for a data set characterized by a weak time dependence and whose mean or variance is stable (so-called weakly dependent and stationary data), statistical textbooks suggest that at least 35 data points are necessary to obtain reasonably accurate estimates of these first two moments. Let us consider a short investment horizon and monthly observable data points. Several past years typically are required to estimate the parameters for the mean variance portfolio optimization routine. The economic reality at the start of this short investment horizon may be far off the historical mean and variance. This is a reason for the lackluster out-of-sample performance of the mean variance methodology.

This prompts us to further investigate what is truly going on with respect to the dynamics of the asset return time series using Monte Carlo simulations. The process consists of randomly generating data with distributional features similar to those of the real asset return series and pinpointing the specific features that are responsible for the poor out-of-sample performance.

We consider the asset return data set described at the start of this chapter. In the first instance, we simply run the mean variance procedure in sample and out of sample with a target expected return of 5 percent. The optimization algorithm is run on the first three-quarters of observations (in-sample) and evaluated on the remaining one-quarter of the data set corresponding to the last five years (out-of-sample). The mean variance optimal portfolio allocates 58.4 percent to government bonds, 1.8 percent to corporate bonds, 6.5 percent to commodities, 33.3 percent to hedge funds and nothing to the other asset classes. The evaluation of the out-of-sample performance of this portfolio shows an average yearly return of 1.5 percent, well below the targeted 5 percent level.

In a second step, we undertake four simulated experiments focusing chiefly on two features of the original data set: the asymmetries in the distribution of returns and the possible moment time-variations.

- The first experiment (iid Gaussian) considers pseudo–asset returns simulated independently from a multivariate Gaussian distribution with mean and variance set to match the estimated mean and variance of the real data.
- The second experiment (iid Skewed) considers pseudo–asset returns simulated independently from a skewed distribution displaying the same mean and variance as the original return series as well as the same skewness.

- The third experiment (iid Severely Skewed) is similar to the second experiment except that we amplify the asymmetries in the simulated data by 10 compared with the original return distributions. The purpose is to investigate to what extent large asymmetries and fat tails could affect the mean variance portfolio performance.
- The fourth experiment (deterministic Markov process [Det.MS]) also considers returns series independently simulated from a multivariate Gaussian distribution. The estimated mean and variance of this distribution, however, are updated every three years. The first 36 observations are generated using the mean and variance estimated from the first 36 actual observations. The following 36 are generated using the mean and variance estimated from the next 36 actual observations, and so on. As opposed to the preceding three experiments, Det.MS incorporates some of the variability in the mean and variance of the original data set.

In each experiment, the simulated sample length is similar to the original data set, and we consider 1,000 replications. We apply the mean variance techniques to each replication by selecting the portfolio using the first three-quarters of the simulated sample and then evaluating the out-of-sample performance on the remaining one-quarter.

Table 4.9 displays the results, that is, the average out-of-sample expected return and the standard deviation of the out-of-sample expected return for each experiment over the 1,000 replications. Let us remember that the target portfolio return is 5 percent and that we are attempting to understand why the true out-of-sample performance obtained is much lower than this. Looking at the first three experiments, we conclude that the assumption of *independent and*

Table 4.9

Simulated Out-of-Sample Performance

	Average of Out-of-Sample Simulated Means	Standard Deviation of Out-of-Sample Simulated Means
iid Gaussian	4.6%	2.3%
iid Skewed	4.7%	2.3%
iid Severely Skewed	4.6%	2.5%
Det.MS	2.3%	1.8%
Real data	1.5%	—

identically distributed (iid) returns, however skewed the distribution may be, fails to significantly alter the out-of-sample performance: The average out-of-sample expected returns, ranging from 4.6 to 4.7 percent, appear much closer to 5 percent than to the 1.5 percent obtained with the real data. These simplifying assumptions seem not to be the source of the poor out-of-sample performance.

The fourth Monte Carlo experiment mimics time variability by period, although within each period the simulated data remain independent and identically distributed (iid). Interestingly, in this case we are more successful. We observe in Table 4.9 that the average out-of-sample expected return obtained for this experiment is 2.3 percent, which is well below the targeted 5 percent. Thus the instability of the moments could be the main reason for the in-sample/out-of-sample discrepancies observed in the mean variance optimization process.

In order to confirm our finding, we turn to an empirical test[4] on the real data to evaluate the stability over time of the second moments of the eight time series in our data set. Table 4.10 shows the result of this test. We have less than 90 percent confidence that the variance is stable over time for four of our returns series. In addition, we can reject as having less than 95 percent confidence that the equally weighted portfolio (and three other asset classes) exhibits no substantial breaks in its variance.

We now have confirmation of the fact that a naive historical measure of moments, whether used directly or through the CAPM approach, is almost bound to lead to out-of-sample underperformance for structural reasons.

Table 4.10

Test of Stability of the Variance of Returns at a 90 Percent Confidence Level

	Stability	Test Statistic
EqDev	1	1.13
EqEM	1	0.91
BondGov	1	0.79
BondIGCredit	0	1.36
BondHYEM	1	1.18
Commodities	0	1.30
HF	0	1.36
Property	0	1.48
EWP	0	1.34

Note: 1 means a stability break and 0 means no stability break with a 90 percent confidence level. The critical values for the 90, 95, and 99 percent level tests are, respectively, below 1.22, 1.36, and 1.63 for a rejection (1) of no break. EWP = equally weighted portfolio.

1988	1989	1990	1991	1992	1993	1994	1995	1996	1997	1998	1999	2000	2001	2002	2003	2004	2005	2006	2007
Russell 2000 Value	S&P/Cit 500	LB Agg	Russell 2000 Growth	Russell 2000 Value	MSCI EAFE	MSCI EAFE	S&P/Cit 500 Growth	S&P/Cit 500 Growth	S&P/Cit 500	S&P/Cit 500 Growth	Russell 2000 Growth	Russell 2000 Value	Russell 2000 Value	LB Agg	Russell 2000 Growth	Russell 2000 Value	MSCI EAFE	MSCI EAFE	MSCI EAFE
29.47%	26.40%	8.96%	51.18%	29.15%	32.57%	7.78%	38.13%	23.97%	36.52%	42.16%	43.09%	22.83%	14.02%	10.26%	48.54%	22.25%	13.54%	26.34%	11.17%
MSCI EAFE	S&P 500	S&P/Cit 500 Growth	Russell 2000	Russell 2000	Russell 2000 Value	Russell 500 Growth	S&P 500	S&P 500	S&P 500	S&P 500	S&P/Cit 500 Growth	LB Agg	LB Agg	Russell 2000 Value	Russell 2000	MSCI EAFE	S&P/Cit 500	Russell 2000 Value	S&P/Cit 500
28.26%	31.69%	0.20%	46.05%	18.42%	23.86%	3.14%	37.58%	22.96%	33.36%	28.58%	28.25%	11.63%	8.43%	-11.43%	47.25%	20.25%	1.82%	23.48%	9.13%
Russell 2000	S&P/Cit 500	S&P 500	Russell 2000 Value	S&P/Cit 500 Value	Russell 2000	S&P 500	S&P/Cit 500 Value	S&P/Cit 500 Value	Russell 500 Value	MSCI EAFE	MSCI EAFE	MSCI EAFE	S&P/Cit 500	MSCI EAFE	Russell 2000	Russell 2000	S&P 500	S&P/Cit 500	Russell 2000 Growth
24.89%	26.13%	-3.11%	41.70%	10.52%	18.89%	1.32%	36.99%	22.00%	31.78%	20.00%	26.96%	6.08%	2.49%	-15.94%	46.03%	18.33%	4.91%	20.81%	7.05%
S&P/Cit 500 Value	Russell 2000 Growth	S&P/Cit 500 Value	S&P 500 Growth	Russell 2000 Growth	S&P/Cit 500 Value	S&P/Cit 500	Russell 2000 Growth	Russell 2000 Value	S&P/Cit 500	Russell 2000	Russell 2000	Russell 2000	Russell 2000 Growth	Russell 2000	S&P/Cit 500 Value	S&P/Cit 500 Value	Russell 2000 Value	Russell 2000	LB Agg
21.67%	20.16%	-6.85%	38.37%	7.77%	18.61%	-0.64%	31.04%	21.37%	29.98%	14.69%	21.26%	-3.02%	-9.23%	-20.48%	38.59%	15.71%	4.71%	18.37%	6.97%
Russell 2000 Growth	Russell 2000	Russell 2000 Growth	S&P 500	S&P 500	Russell 2000 Growth	Russell 2000	Russell 2000	Russell 2000	Russell 2000	LB Agg	Russell 2000	S&P/Cit 500 Value	S&P/Cit 500 Value	S&P/Cit 500 Value	S&P/Cit 500	Russell 2000 Growth	Russell 2000	S&P 500	S&P 500
20.38%	19.29%	-17.42%	30.47%	7.62%	13.37%	-1.55%	28.44%	19.53%	22.36%	8.70%	21.04%	-9.11%	-11.21%	-20.85%	31.79%	14.31%	4.55%	15.79%	5.49%
S&P 500	LB Agg	Russell 2000	S&P/Cit 500 Value	LB Agg	S&P 500	Russell 2000 Growth	Russell 2000 Growth	Russell 2000 Growth	Russell 2000 Growth	Russell 2000 Growth	LB Agg	MSCI EAFE	S&P 500	S&P 500	S&P 500	S&P 500	Russell 2000 Growth	Russell 2000 Growth	S&P/Cit 500 Value
16.61%	14.53%	-19.50%	22.58%	7.40%	10.08%	-1.81%	26.75%	11.32%	12.93%	1.23%	12.73%	-14.17%	-11.89%	-22.10%	28.68%	10.88%	4.15%	13.35%	1.99%
S&P/Cit 500 Growth	Russell 2000 Value	Russell 2000 Value	S&P 500	S&P/Cit 500 Growth	LB Agg	Russell 2000 Value	LB Agg	MSCI EAFE	LB Agg	Russell 2000	LB Agg	S&P/Cit 500 Growth	S&P/Cit 500 Growth	S&P/Cit 500 Growth	S&P/Cit 500 Growth	S&P/Cit 500 Growth	S&P/Cit 500 Growth	S&P/Cit 500 Growth	Russell 2000
11.95%	12.43%	-21.77%	16.00%	5.06%	9.75%	-2.44%	18.40%	6.05%	9.64%	-2.55%	-0.82%	-22.08%	-12.73%	-23.59%	25.66%	6.13%	4.00%	11.01%	-1.57%
LB Agg	MSCI EAFE	MSCI EAFE	MSCI EAFE	MSCI EAFE	S&P/Cit 500 Growth	LB Agg	MSCI EAFE	LB Agg	MSCI EAFE	Russell 2000 Value	Russell 2000 Value	Russell 2000 Growth	MSCI EAFE	Russell 2000 Growth	LB Agg	LB Agg	LB Agg	LB Agg	Russell 2000 Value
7.89%	10.53%	-23.45%	12.14%	-12.18%	1.68%	-2.92%	11.21%	3.64%	1.78%	-6.45%	-1.49%	-22.43%	-21.44%	-30.26%	4.10%	4.34%	2.43%	4.33%	-9.78%

Figure 4.10 The Callan Periodic Table of Investment Returns (annual returns for key indices, 1988–2007, ranked in order of performance).

In practice, market participants are fully aware of this already. For example, there is a well-known representation of the instability of asset returns that is quite widely used. The Callan Periodic Table of Investment Returns[5] (Figure 4.10) presents the rank-ordered performance of the main asset classes on a yearly basis using different color codes. As can be seen, there is no straightforward pattern.

An Analysis of the Multivariate Dynamics of Time Series

We now drill down into the dynamics of the correlation matrix of asset returns. The question is whether we can assume stability over time or whether—as in the case of mean and variance—we observe stability breaks. In this respect, we consider a new data set consisting of the daily returns of a set of equity and bond indices. Table 4.11 presents these indices.

Every day we estimate the correlation matrix related to these assets (relying on a 240-day sliding window) and then average these correlations to produce three values:

1. EqEq Corr, the average correlation across all equity indices
2. BondBond Corr, the average of correlations across bonds
3. EqBond Corr, the average of all equity/bond cross-correlations

The results are displayed in Figure 4.11.

This figure shows some interesting evidence. During crises, cross-equity index correlation rises. Meanwhile, the equity/bond cross-correlation turns

Table 4.11

Selected Daily Total Return Indices from February 1970 to December 2008

Equity Indices	Bond Indices
S&P 500 Composite	U.S. Benchmark 2 Years DS Govt.
FTSE 100	BD Benchmark 5 Years DS Govt.
DJ Euro STOXX 50	BD Benchmark 10 Years DS Govt.
AEX Index (AEX)	
Frank Russell 2000 (FRC)	
ASX 200	
TSX 60 Index	
Swiss Market	
TOPIX	

negative. Overall, correlations vary considerably during market cycles. No stability can be observed over time.

In addition to what we have discussed so far in this section, we need to mention a second problem related to the estimation of the correlation-covariance matrix. As discussed in Chapter 3 (Eq. 3.1), what matters when identifying the optimal mean variance weights is the inverse of the co-variance matrix

$$x = \frac{1}{a}\Omega^{-1}\mu$$

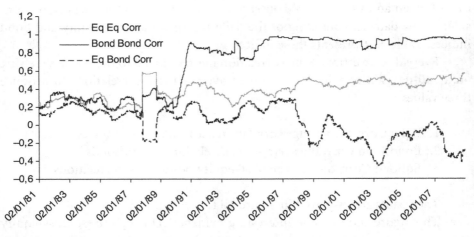

Figure 4.11   Rolling correlations over time for a set of equity and bond indices.

where x is the vector of asset-allocation weights, a is the risk-aversion parameter, μ is the vector of expected returns, and Ω is the covariance matrix.

When the data set contains highly correlated time series (e.g., U.S. large-cap equities, U.S. small-cap equities, and the Nasdaq), the matrix is poorly conditioned, and the inversion process is fairly unstable. This can mean that the recommend weights vary considerably.

As an illustration of this, let us consider two stylized cases. In these two cases, the vector of expected return for these three series is assumed to be (0.3 percent; 0.4 percent; 0.5 percent). Their variance is assumed to be similar.

In the first case, the correlation across all three assets is 0.9. The mean variance recommended weights are –200 percent, 30 percent, and 270 percent. In the second case, the correlation between assets 1 and 3 moves to 0.95. The new mean variance recommended weights change dramatically to –442 percent, –42 percent, and 500 percent.

What this shows is that a small alteration in one of the correlation estimates can lead to a massive but spurious change in the asset-allocation solution.

Why Mean Variance Fails to Deliver Diversification and Performance

In the two preceding sections, statistical tests have showed us that assets' return moments change over time. Therefore, naive attempts to form stable expectations from historical averages are unlikely to perform well.

One can propose two possible solutions to this issue. First, the problem would be solved if we had a perfect model of the dynamics of the moments of the assets. The alternative is to accept that since any forecast of the moments is likely to be uncertain, we therefore should quantify this uncertainty and use a portfolio-optimization procedure that is able to cope with such uncertainty. Concentrating on this latter option, we review here whether the mean variance approach does a good job in terms of fostering portfolio diversification.

The quick answer is that uncertainties about estimations are not properly taken into consideration by the mean variance approach. Even if investors were fully aware of such uncertainty, there would be no way to express it within the optimization process. The mean variance optimizer is deaf to any doubt and treats all inputs as perfect insights on future expected returns and the covariance matrix. Working on this basis, the optimizer outputs a concentrated solution that would be optimal in a perfect replica of the environment considered. As a consequence, typical mean variance portfolios look poorly diversified. Figure 4.12 illustrates the poor diversification of mean variance portfolios compared with a 1/N equally weighted portfolio or a portfolio with random weights.

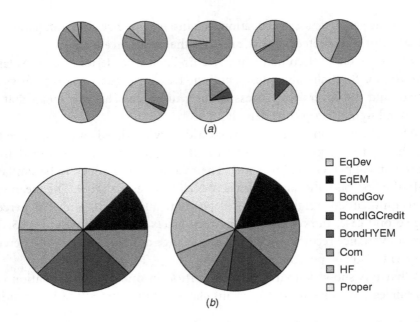

Figure 4.12 (*a*) None of the 10 mean variance portfolios on the efficient frontier uses more than three assets. (*b*) Weights in the 1/*N* (*left*) and a random portfolio (*right*) are well spread across all assets.

This goes back to the central problem that in a known future environment that perfectly mirrors the past, we merely have to pick the best assets in terms of risk/return tradeoff, taking into account their covariance. There is no need for us to consider assets that historically have delivered a poor expected return or a large variance. For instance, the efficient frontier presented in Figure 4.13 uses only three assets (*circled in black*). All others exhibit returns that are too low or volatility that is too high to be selected, even after taking into account their correlation properties.

To use a signal-processing analogy, we could say that the mean variance framework is a sensitive device: A slight variation in its inputs (moments) leads to a large difference in its outputs (weights). The efficient frontier and the weights will be very different if any one of the circled assets moves in Figure 4.13. If one moves far to the right, then another asset will come into play to define the frontier.

These input fluctuations in the optimization process lead deterministically to fluctuations in its output. Figure 4.14 presents a set of efficient frontiers recomputed every year with an identical-asset universe. It is quite clear that there is massive instability, which is not conducive to successful long-term buy-and-hold investment decisions.

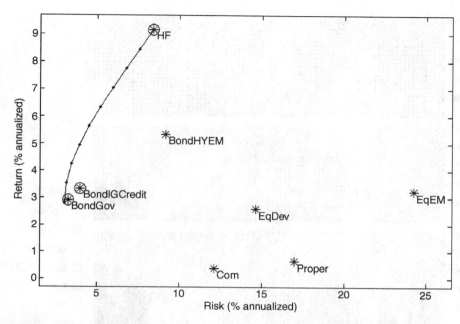

Figure 4.13 The efficient frontier for the period 1990–2002 is influenced by only three assets (*circled*).

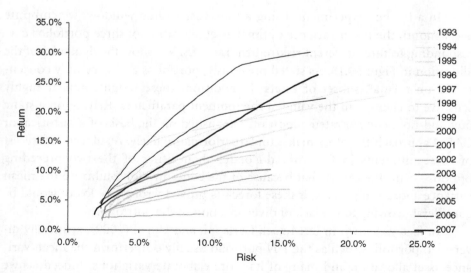

Figure 4.14 Annually calculated efficient frontiers based on a four-year sliding window.

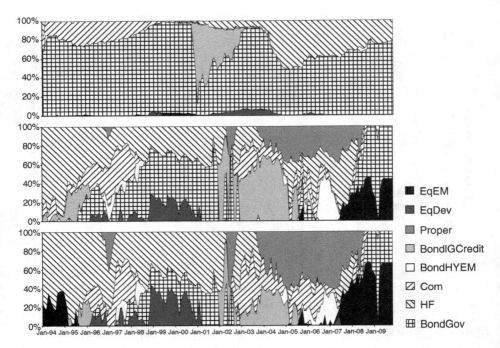

Figure 4.15 Evolution of the composition of mean variance portfolios. Three portfolios corresponding to three risk profiles are shown, from the least risky (*top*) to the most risky (*bottom*). Shading shows the proportions of the different assets composing each portfolio.

In a further experiment, using a four-year sliding window, we compute every month the mean variance optimal asset allocation of three portfolios corresponding to three different risk/return tradeoffs. We show the dynamics of the allocation in Figure 4.15. As stated previously, portfolios are excessively concentrated on a small subset of assets. In addition, these weights appear highly sensitive to changes in the value of the moment parameters. Relying on a static buy-and-hold concentrated allocation established on the basis of a historical or CAPM approach therefore makes underperformance likely. A subjective forecast of these moments in fact may do better than either of the two preceding options—with the caveat that because of the concentration built into the mean variance allocation process, if these forecasts proved wrong, the losses would be considerable owing to the lack of diversification in the portfolio.

In fact, as shown in DeMiguel, Garlappi, and Uppal (2009), artificially diversified portfolios such as the 1/N portfolio usually outperform the mean variance asset allocation and many of its more elaborate variations. Indeed, as we have seen, a mean variance portfolio is optimally balanced for an environment that no longer exists when the money is actually invested. Moreover, "brute force" diversification beats carefully optimized portfolios simply because it is robust to the market evolving in a different way to that expected. Diversification acts here therefore more as a safeguard against uncertainty than as an optimization device; it reflects a view that "because I know nothing about the future, I won't put blindly all my eggs in the same basket." This rationale for diversification was discussed by Warren Buffett at an investor meeting in 1996. As he put it, "Diversification is a protection against ignorance. It makes very little sense for those who know what they're doing."

When Markowitz introduced the mean variance approach, he was not particularly concerned about uncertainty. He was presenting a model that exploited optimal asset covariations to minimize risks. This was a tremendous intellectual achievement, but sadly enough, we have seen that the underlying assumption that we can get the relevant forecasts right is just too demanding.

From Mean Variance to MPT

In this section we move from the efficient frontier, which characterizes the full spectrum of optimal mean variance portfolios, to focus on the selection of the only optimal portfolio that matches the risk/satisfaction characteristics of the individual investor. In particular, we show here the link between the mean variance Markowitz framework with investor risk aversion and the implicit choice of a quadratic utility function for the investor.

New Light on the Rationale for a Quadratic Utility Function

The common paradigm of microeconomics is that a rational economic agent chooses the consumption and investment levels that maximize his satisfaction, as quantified by his so-called utility function. Utility functions have a predominant interest in microeconomic theory and are a major tool in describing the behavior of economic agents in general and consumers in particular. Chapter 2 has already described this in some detail.

We assume here that investors care about the expected utility of their terminal wealth and therefore have as a goal to make current choices with the aim of maximizing their expected utility function $EU(W)$, where U is the utility function of the economic agent.

Let us call W_0 the nonrandom initial wealth of the investor. His final wealth will be $W = (1 + x^{tr}r)W_0$, and in what follows, we simplify by normalizing such that $W_0 = 1$.

We make the reasonable assumption that $U(W)$ is smooth in a neighborhood of the expected terminal wealth EW and that all the moments of the random final wealth W are finite. A Taylor expansion of $U(W)$ in a neighborhood of EW gives

$$U(W) = U(EW) + U'(EW)(W - EW) + \frac{1}{2}U''(EW)(W - EW)^2$$
$$+ \sum_{j \geq 3} \frac{1}{j!}U^{(j)}(EW)(W - EW)^j \tag{4.3}$$

The expectation of utility becomes

$$E[U(W)] = U(EW) + \frac{1}{2}U''(EW)\sigma^2(W) + \sum_{j \geq 3} \frac{1}{j!}U^{(j)}(EW)m_j(W) \tag{4.4}$$

where $\sigma^2(W)$ stands for the variance of W and $m_j(W)$ stands for its centered moment of order j.

So far we have made no assumptions about the nature of the utility function associated with the investor, and from this expansion (Eq. 4.4), we can clearly observe that the expected utility is not only a function of the mean and the variance of W but also a function of all the higher centered moments of W.

Hence investors only have to care about the mean and the variance if the joint distribution or the asset return r is such that the higher-order centered moments of W are also a function of its mean and variance. A certain number of distributions, called *elliptical distributions*,[6] which include the Gaussian (normal) distribution,[7] satisfy this condition.

In order to be able to retain a quadratic utility function $U(z) = A + Bz + Cz^2$, as in the MPT framework presented in Chapter 3, at least one of the two following conditions must be true: Either investors are properly characterized by a quadratic utility function or the data are well described by an elliptical distribution (typically, but not exclusively, a multivariate Gaussian distribution). Since the first option has been clearly ruled out in Chapter 2, we must confirm that the second condition is true. If not, we have to reject the quadratic utility function that underpins MPT and turn instead to behavioral finance (or elsewhere) to find a utility function that is more suitable to investors.

In addition, it is worth noting in passing that if we cannot rely on elliptical distributions, we have a much deeper problem in the sense that the dependency structure across asset classes cannot be characterized by the covariance-correlation analysis because it requires recourse to higher moments too. Such a conclusion would therefore undermine the whole mean variance approach. As a result, in practice, the assumption that asset returns follow a joint Gaussian/ elliptical distribution is commonly accepted in the literature—but can it be proved? In practice, we will focus on Gaussianity, as other forms of elliptical distribution are easy to rule out in a similar manner.

Looking at the Univariate "Gaussianity" of Asset Returns

The question of whether or not asset returns are Gaussian has been intensively debated both by finance practitioners and by academic researchers. The consensus seems to be *not*. The main reason given for this is that asset returns exhibit large (positive or negative) values more frequently than can be accounted for in a Gaussian environment.

It is customary to refer to time series exhibiting extreme realizations more frequently than a Gaussian random variable would do as having *fat tails*. In this respect, we consider the series corresponding to daily return observations of the Standard & Poor's 500 Index (S&P 500) starting from January 1, 1980, through to December 31, 2008. Figure 4.15 shows the corresponding histograms, as well as the probability distribution of a Gaussian random variable with both mean and variance similar to that of the returns of S&P 500. We note a higher concentration of returns on the right and left extremes of the graph, beyond the boundaries of the Gaussian distribution.

The average daily return of the S&P 500 over the period is 0.028 percent with a standard deviation of 1.11 percent. In the case of a Gaussian distribution with these moments, only 1 percent of the time should the return stand outside the range [−2.84 percent; 2.88 percent]. In practice, the S&P 500 does so 2.1 percent of the time. Additional analysis reveals that the further we go into the tails, the stronger are the discrepancies between the two distributions. Returns should not get outside the [−3.40 percent; 3.45 percent] range on more than one day every 18 months; in fact, they do so on six days every 18 months.

Differences in the shape of the distributions in the figure are also noticeable. While the Gaussian distribution is symmetrical around the mean, the returns on the S&P 500 are negatively skewed. This adds to the departure from normality.

The fat-tail characteristics of a series are commonly evaluated by statistical measures known as the *kurtosis* and the *skewness*. Let the returns be y_i: $i = 1, \ldots, T$, where T is the sample size. The kurtosis and skewness are defined by

$$\text{Kurtosis} = \frac{\mu_4}{\mu_2^2}$$

$$\text{Skewness} = \frac{\mu_3}{\mu_2^{3/2}}$$

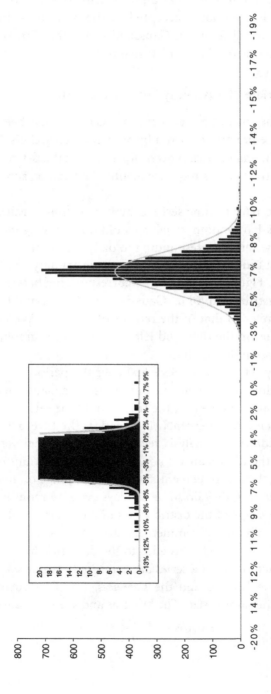

Figure 4.16 Histogram of daily total returns of the S&P 500 from January 1, 1980, through to December 31, 2008. The solid line represents the density of the normal distribution with the same mean and variance.

where the moments of order k are

$$\mu_k = \frac{1}{T}\sum_{t=1}^{T}(y_t - \bar{y})^k$$

and the first moment is

$$\bar{y} = \frac{1}{T}\sum_{t=1}^{T}y_t$$

Skewness and kurtosis are, respectively, the normalized third and fourth moments. Any normally distributed random variable will have a kurtosis of 3 and a skewness of 0. A kurtosis larger than 3 suggests thicker tails than the normal distribution, and such series are known as *leptokurtic*. A series with a negative skewness has a larger concentration of realizations below the mean than above the mean.

Table 4.12 presents the kurtosis and skewness of several daily asset index returns. As with the returns on the S&P 500, all start on January 1, 1980, and go through to December 31, 2008. The departure from normality seems clear. All the listed indices have kurtosis larger than 3, and 8 of the 12 asset index returns have skewness clearly different from 0.

Even though seemingly clear, our evidence against "Gaussianity" is so far only descriptive, and we need to know how significant these differences from the Gaussian characteristics are before drawing any clear conclusion. The assessment of a significant departure from normality can only be drawn from proper statistical tests.

There are several testing procedures available to test for the normality of samples. The most well known is probably the *Jarque-Bera test*, which checks how far the skewness and kurtosis of a sample jointly depart from those of a Gaussian random sample. We apply this test to the return series and report the results in Table 4.12. The normality hypothesis is strongly rejected at any reasonable level for all the series considered. We also have subjected the return data to another test for normality (the Meddahi and Bontemps test),[8] which better takes into account any time dependency of the data set.[9] The results are also presented in Table 4.12. The departure from "Gaussianity" is also confirmed by this test, although the evidence is less strong. We therefore can reject the Gaussian distribution of the returns confidently at any reasonable level of significance through this test, which accounts for serial dependences.

To conclude this discussion, we look at testing normality at lower frequency. Conventional wisdom suggests that *long-horizon returns smooth out short-term market noise and emotions.* We consider returns at lower frequencies, such as weekly, monthly, and quarterly. Table 4.13 shows the results of these tests.

Table 4.12

Skewness, Kurtosis, and Normality Tests of Daily Total Returns on Large Financial Indices

	Skewness	Kurtosis	Jarque-Bera test		Bontemps-Meddahi (BM) H(3-6) Test	
			Test Stat	*p* Value	Test Stat	*p* Value
S&P 500 Composite, price index	−0.71	30.02	231026.79	0.0000	12.51	0.014
FTSE 100, price index	−0.32	11.95	25396.19	0.000	12.74	0.013
DJ Euro STOXX 50, price index	0.03	11.86	24753.94	0.000	42.12	0.000
AEX Index (AEX), price index	−0.14	13.11	32248.73	0.000	38.78	0.000
Frank Russell 2000 (FRC), price index	−0.68	17.05	62849.40	0.000	14.27	0.006
S&P/ASX 200, price index	−2.06	52.58	780855.08	0.000	12.26	0.016
S&P/TSX 60 Index, price index	−0.60	15.98	53614.61	0.000	17.40	0.002
Swiss Market, price index	−0.48	15.71	51222.20	0.000	35.35	0.000
TOPIX, price index	0.07	18.17	72595.51	0.000	19.75	0.001
U.S. Benchmark 2-Year DS Govt. Index	0.36	15.63	50511.83	0.000	51.35	0.000
BD Benchmark 5-Year DS Govt. Index	−0.06	8.60	9900.68	0.000	75.22	0.000
BD Benchmark 10-Year DS Govt. Index	0.02	6.68	4263.91	0.000	77.34	0.000

The most noticeable point is that as we move to lower frequencies (i.e., longer time horizons), the evidence against "Gaussianity" seems to weaken. The evidence against normality is still strong for all the weekly returns except for the S&P 500, whose *p* value is large. As we move to monthly returns, the 5- and 10-year German government bonds no longer show evidence against "Gaussianity," whereas at a quarterly horizon three indices still reject normality at a 10 percent level.

Looking at the Multivariate "Gaussianity" of Asset Returns

Rejecting the univariate Gaussian distribution assumption for at least one series should be enough to reject the joint Gaussian distribution of asset returns.

Table 4.13

Normality Tests for Different Asset Return Frequencies

	Daily BM H(3–6)		Weekly BM H(3–6)		Monthly BM H(3–6)		Quarterly BM H(3–6)	
	Test	*p* Value	Test	*p* Value	Test	*p* Value	Test	*p* Value
S&P 500 Composite, price index	12.51	0.014	5.40	0.249	22.31	0.000	6.38	0.172
FTSE 100, price index	12.74	0.013	13.71	0.008	11.83	0.019	4.30	0.367
DJ Euro STOXX 50, price index	43.10	0.000	21.29	0.000	15.55	0.004	7.33	0.119
AEX Index (AEX), price index	38.78	0.000	26.46	0.000	15.85	0.003	8.89	0.064
Frank Russell 2000 (FRC), price index	14.27	0.006	16.64	0.002	23.12	0.000	5.56	0.235
S&P/ASX 200, price index	12.26	0.016	17.88	0.001	7.97	0.093	2.98	0.561
S&P/TSX 60 Index, price index	17.40	0.002	14.50	0.006	14.03	0.007	10.90	0.028
Swiss Market, price index	35.35	0.000	17.19	0.002	14.13	0.007	7.10	0.131
TOPIX, price index	19.75	0.001	17.39	0.002	12.48	0.014	1.81	0.770
U.S. Benchmark 2-Year DS Govt. Index	51.35	0.000	27.76	0.000	13.05	0.011	10.86	0.028
BD Benchmark 5-Year DS Govt. Index	75.22	0.000	27.30	0.000	4.32	0.364	3.45	0.485
BD Benchmark 10-Year DS Govt. Index	77.34	0.000	15.95	0.003	4.26	0.372	2.87	0.580

However, we apply a test of joint "Gaussianity" to the return series for which the Bontemps and Meddahi test fails to reject "Gaussianity" at a 1 percent level, namely, the S&P 500, FTSE 100, and ASX indices. The multivariate Gaussian test we use is the *omnibus test for normality* proposed by Doornik and Hansen (2008). From the results reported in Table 4.14, this test strongly rejects the joint normality of the S&P 500–FTSE 100–ASX. The

Table 4.14

Joint Normality Omnibus Test for Groups of Daily Asset Returns: Test of Doornik and Hansen (2008)

	Omnibus Test	
	Stat	*p* Value
S&P 500–FTSE 100–ASX	79994.00	0.000
All	193920.00	0.000

table also reports the results of the joint normality test for all the 12 index returns considered previously.[10]

Based on this analysis, we must reject the supposition that asset returns have a Gaussian distribution. As a consequence, we do not believe that the data justify the use of a quadratic utility function to define the satisfaction of the investor.

Conclusion

As the preceding analysis confirms, the two pillars of MPT—mean variance optimization and characterization of the investor through a quadratic utility function—look extremely shaky. Attempts to build on these foundations, such as the Black-Litterman model, have some advantages (notably, the incorporation of subjective forward views) but also carry the drawback of severe moments estimation in-sample overfitting. The incorporation of views is an improvement but still takes place within a mean variance environment. Such approaches generally also rely on inappropriate use of the quadratic utility functions. Thus, in conclusion, one should accept that there is no "quick fix" to MPT. Portfolio construction requires new approaches that need to acknowledge empirical evidence rather than rely wholly on a normative description of the world.

Notes

1. "In the mathematical sciences, a stationary process [or strict(ly) stationary process, or strong(ly) stationary process] is a stochastic process whose joint probability distribution does not change when shifted in time or space. As a result, parameters such as the mean and variance, if they exist, also do not change over time or position" (*Source*: Wikipedia).
2. It is based on the market capitalization of the different asset classes, as reported in the MSCI Global Capital Markets Portfolio.
3. Several additional previous pieces of work, such as Hodges and Brealey (1972), Michaud (1989), and Best and Grauer (1991), also discuss the difficulties of implementing mean variance portfolios successfully.
4. This CUMSUM test of stability of variance is described by Andreou and Ghysels (2002) and investigates whether the variance of a series is stable over time.

5. www.callan.com/research/periodic/files/Pertbl.pdf.
6. Elliptical distributions also include the multivariate Student's t distributions.
7. If it is Gaussian with variance σ^2, then $E(W - EW)^{2j+1} = 0$ and $E(W - EW)^{2j} = [(2j)!/2^j j!]\sigma^{2j}$, for $j \geq 1$.
8. We need to be careful when interpreting the results of the Jarque-Bera test. The conditions under which this test is derived require the sample studied to be random. Clearly, this is not the case for time series in general and asset returns in particular, and the same is true for asset index returns. Even though they do not exhibit strong linear dependency, they do exhibit strong nonlinear dependencies. The most known is the so-called GARCH effect, according to which large returns are followed by large returns of either sign. In this context, a statistical test constructed for independent data or random samples, if applied, has to be read with caution. There is clearly a risk that clusters of large realizations amplify arbitrarily the test statistic and lead us to reject the hypothesis of a Gaussian distribution.
9. The existing tests include the joint skewness and kurtosis test of Bai and Ng (2005) and its extension proposed by Bontemps and Meddahi (2005). We apply the test of Bontemps and Meddahi to the returns under consideration.
10. Even though the conclusions of the omnibus test are as expected, it is worthwhile to recall that this test is also derived under the condition that the sample is random. As we saw with the univariate tests case, the omnibus test may thus inflate the evidence against the joint normality. A joint normality test for time-dependent data should therefore be preferred to validate this result, but to the best of our knowledge, such a test does not exist in the literature.

Chapter 5

"BEHAVIORALIZING" RISK/ RETURN OPTIMIZATION

with Shweta Agarwal

In this chapter we focus on the identification of stable, reasonable, long-term individual preferences that can provide a foundation for determining the optimal long-term risk/return tradeoff for each individual. It is only by defining what truly makes a difference to investors that we can determine what portfolio would best achieve this.

In the first part of this book we arrived at a number of observations that can help us to guide this effort:

- It is important to start from the preferences of individuals because there is no direct link between aggregate market conditions and individual preferences—investors can be very different from each other, and as a result, optimal portfolios can also differ considerably.
- It is important to take into account all features of individuals' preferences, but the optimal portfolio should not simply replicate decision-making biases, errors, and irrationalities.
- We know that asset classes are not, in general, normally distributed, so in trading off risk and return, we need to account very clearly and rigorously for what risk truly means to investors and not ignore asymmetries and fat tails in the returns distributions.

As a result of this, our ambition is to go beyond the Modern Portfolio Theory (MPT) paradigm and account for observations and insights from behavioral science. In doing so, we show that we can deliver a modeling framework that is very close to MPT in spirit but nonetheless differs in one major area: The risk/return framework is no longer fully objective. That is, it does not arrive at the same market portfolio for all investors irrespective of their own preferences. In one respect this has always been the case because any two individuals with different beliefs about the future will have different subjective distributions of future outcomes as an input into the optimization process. However, in our framework, risk itself has become subjective, but in a much deeper sense than investors merely having their own beliefs about future returns: Two individuals may have different subjective perceptions of the overall risk of an investment while still agreeing completely on the shape of the returns distribution.

In this chapter we attempt to disentangle the preferences of individuals from the behavior of asset classes. We focus here specifically on the long-term rational preferences of individuals and how this solution compares with the traditional MPT model. In Chapter 6 we will explore how to generate a forward-looking distribution across the range of asset classes that forms the input to the utility function optimization of these preferences. Chapter 7 will describe how these two elements—individual preferences and the anticipated returns distribution—can be used together to arrive at an optimal portfolio.

An important initial caveat is that in this chapter we will be concerned only with determining the optimal single-period optimization, not with the dynamics of rebalancing programs along the way. Rebalancing to correct the natural drift in the portfolio makeup and to reflect changes in information along the journey is crucial to good long-term performance and is dealt with in Chapter 6. Here we simply want to understand what the optimal portfolio mix is for any individual to suit his long-term, rational preferences when faced with any particular anticipated distribution of returns across the available assets at any given time horizon. The fact that this solution is applicable to any time horizon will be crucial when we incorporate the possibility of dynamic rebalancing in Chapter 6.

We will also be concerned here exclusively with the rational normative solution. We have already seen how our short-term selves may lead us to behavioral deviations from our rational long-term preferences—how we incorporate this knowledge will be a key part of Chapter 8. Here we assume, like MPT, that we can easily overcome such behavioral proclivities and focus on developing the revised normative solution, that is, what we would do if we were able to optimize solely our long-term preferences without any interference from our short-term emotional/behavioral selves.

Isolation of Long-Term Stable Investment Preferences

The last 60 years of research into behavioral science and decision making have made it clear that people simply do not conform to the simple quadratic utility function assumed by Markowitz. Human attitudes toward risk are more complex, and we cannot assume that people are concerned solely with the mean and variance of distributions of future returns.

In fact, as we saw in Chapter 2, people cannot even be assumed to follow the broader model of expected utility theory (EUT), often taken as the standard of rationality applied to decision making. Instead, in making decisions we all exhibit various deviations from EUT regardless of what specific utility function we try to use to model decisions. In part, this is so because we are humans rather than robots or computers—and as such, we are not particularly good at probabilistic reasoning. When making decisions, we instead often rely on swift rules of thumb to speed up our decision making and are also subject to biases in the way we perceive the world. And we make mistakes along the way.

However, our deviations from EUT are partly because EUT provides only a very narrow definition of what it means to be "rational." It is highly dependent on people having a complete and coherent ordering of their preferences over all possible options available to them. In reality, as we saw in Chapter 2, people seem to use two distinct systems of reasoning when making decisions: a more rational, considered decision-making system and a faster, more intuitive and emotional decision-making system. At times, these can conflict, which throws the tidy ordering of options required by EUT into disarray. The ordering of our rational preferences for long-term outcomes is not necessarily the same ordering that represents which options will make us emotionally comfortable over the journey. When we have conflicting preferences such as this, EUT cannot provide us with a rational solution.

Am I more concerned with achieving the best long-term outcomes, or am I more concerned by having a stress-free journey? When investing, both these objectives may be important. A rational focus on long-term objectives is essential if investing is going to be successful in achieving the best possible long-term risk/return tradeoff. However, unless investors are comfortable along the journey, they are unlikely to stick with the portfolio that gives them the best long-term potential. Because of this, the "rational" portfolio for each of us is therefore not necessarily the one with the best long-term risk/return tradeoff. Instead, the rational portfolio is the one that gives us a good chance of actually achieving an outcome as close to this as possible. In addition to optimizing long-term utility, we also need to reduce the likelihood of our emotional intervention along the way, and this protection may come at a cost. To put it bluntly, as investors, we need to account for our own emotional responses and human fallibility.

What Should Be Left Out of the Rational Utility Function?

When thinking about all the factors that influence people's financial decisions, which should we consider when optimizing a portfolio? The preceding discussion leads to three categories of factors that influence our actual daily decisions. The first consists of errors and biases in decision making that we should seek to eliminate; the second consists of factors that may be inconsistent with, or harmful to, our long-run preferences but which can increase our comfort with the investment journey—we should make sure that we consider these preferences because ignoring them could mean we fail to stick with the rational long-run portfolio, but they should not be part of core long-term preferences—and finally, there are stable, rational preferences for outcomes in the long run that must form the core of any portfolio optimization theory. Let's examine each in turn.

Errors, Biases, and Heuristics

The behavioral literature is full of experimental demonstrations of errors, biases, and deviations from EUT that are inconsistent with rational approaches to our goals (some of which were set out in Chapter 2). Some of these arise from the conflict between short- and long-run preferences, but some are harmful regardless of which preferences we're considering. These biases harm our ability either to achieve our long-term investment goals or to provide the short-term emotional composure that is so essential to successful investing.

In this category we might consider actions that are inconsistent with each other, such as simultaneously choosing options that offset each other; pure framing effects, where one makes different choices in situations where the options are presented differently even though the actual outcomes are identical; and any of the effects of probability distortions on decision making, which should also be eliminated from rational portfolio optimization—regardless of preferences, if we distort probabilities when seeking to satisfy them, we are necessarily less likely to do so.

Including such errors, biases, and heuristics in a model of decision making may help to *explain* people's decisions better but does investors no favors if included in portfolio-optimization techniques. They simply replicate the natural errors that we'd rather not make and should be excluded from any portfolio-optimization model. Being particularly prone to some behavioral bias results in irrational decisions and in the long run will result in poorer financial performance.

Effects Related to Short-Term Behavioral Preferences

In the second category are some common behavioral effects that, while not consistent with rational long-term preferences, are nonetheless a true description of preferences in the shorter term. Incorporating these when building an optimal portfolio may result in slightly worse expected performance from the perspective of the fully rational long-term investor but may genuinely help to make investors more satisfied over the investment journey and, crucially, may actually result in better performance owing to greater emotional comfort with the journey and thus less emotionally driven decision making along the way.

For example, many behavioral influences on our decision making are due to reference dependence—our tendency to evaluate outcomes relative to our current situation (see Chapter 2). This reliance on a current reference point to evaluate potential outcomes of any decision is responsible for many of the effects encoded in well-used behavioral models of decision making, such as Daniel Kahneman and Amos Tversky's prospect theory.[1] For example, the notion of *loss aversion* is a frequent component of any behavioral approach to decision making and depends heavily on the decision maker's current reference point.

There is little doubt that such reference-dependent behavioral effects genuinely affect our experience of outcomes and so should be included in any model that attempts to optimally satisfy short-term preferences. The problem with this category for investing is that the reference point itself is inherently unstable. In 20 years' time, our wealth level, and thus our reference point, may be very different from what it is today. Therefore, if we allow loss aversion to feature in the construction of our rational long-term portfolio, we are reflecting our emotional responses to losses from where we are today, which may be quite irrelevant to how we feel about our portfolio outcomes in 20 years. Our approach is to exclude preferences in this category from consideration when constructing a purely rational long-term portfolio. We will, however, find these preferences essential when implementing this portfolio and will return to these important considerations in Chapter 8.

Long-Term Stable Preferences

This category contains only those preferences a completely rational individual following EUT would wish to fulfill in the long term. Markowitz's use of

quadratic utility was an attempt to specify preferences for this category—
rational preferences for risk and return that obeyed all the principles of EUT. As
discussed in Chapter 2, it is clear that quadratic utility does not provide an adequate description of such preferences. Nonetheless, superrational investors who
did not face any risk of short-term emotional responses to the investment journey presumably would wish to follow EUT, but to do so using a different utility
function that accurately represented their long-term preferences for risk and
reward. We shall develop the model for this investor in this chapter.

No matter how people actually make decisions, the point of portfolio optimization is to help them to be better investors, so we should seek to "clean"
their actual decision making of errors and biases (those in the first category
above). And, with the advent of behavioral finance and our ever-increasing
knowledge of the importance of emotional factors in investing, we can now see
the importance of dealing with and filtering short-term behavioral preferences,
as discussed in the second category above.

It is thus desirable to have a pure model against which our more behavioral
tendencies can be judged. Such a model would provide us with a prescription for
how we should all invest if we were not plagued by short-term emotional biases
and would provide us with the best-case risk/return tradeoff.

The rest of this chapter will develop this touchstone model for these super-
human investors who consider only their stable long-term preferences, thus
describing a more reasonable *Homo economicus* than assumed by Markowitz.

Defining the Inputs to the Utility Function

The long-term investor would wish to ensure that the utility function used represented only genuine, stable long-term preferences. To construct a portfolio
that reflects a 20-year-plus investment horizon, we might want to reflect our
short-term tactical perspective on the market and our forecast of the returns distribution, but short-term perspectives should not be allowed to enter the utility
function that we use to evaluate this distribution. We would want to exclude any
influences of our current emotional responses to short-term market movements.
We would also wish to exclude all the second-category behavioral influences on
our decision making that are determined narrowly by our current reference point.

Utility of What?

Traditional economic analysis tends to use *total wealth levels* as inputs into the
utility function, so the status quo is expressed as the number of dollars that the

investor currently owns. Alternatively, we can represent the outcomes of investments in terms of *percentage returns on initial wealth*. This latter fits much better with the strong finding from behavioral economics that people attribute utility not to changes in absolute levels but to changes from a starting status quo or *reference point*: Losses should have negative utility and gains positive utility. Using returns, rather than absolute changes, means that we can represent every investment consistently for all investors—much easier than always having to convert those into dollar amounts for investors with different starting wealth amounts.

Looking at returns, we wish to be able to examine returns at any time interval because different investments may mature at different times. To ensure comparability of final returns at different time horizons, and to escape the problem of different compounding frequencies, it makes sense to use continuously compounded returns:

$$r = \ln\left(\frac{w_t}{w_0}\right)$$

where w_0 is the initial wealth level and w_t is the final wealth level achieved.[2] If required, it is always possible to translate from returns to wealth levels using $w_t = w_0 e^r$. For any investor, a utility function expressing the strength of preference for log returns from the initial wealth level has an equivalent utility function that expresses the strength of preference for levels of wealth.

Expressing the utility of log returns on initial wealth has a number of implications for the utility function used: It must reflect rational responses to long-term stable preferences for returns on initial wealth, and it needs to be calibrated on returns over total wealth rather than on investments that are insignificant relative to the total wealth of the investor. This is important because the utility function and the degree of risk aversion appropriate to a smaller component of wealth may not be the same as those expressed over total wealth. For example, people may be quite rationally prepared to take larger risks (or even be risk-seeking) for a small portion of their wealth, but applying these small-scale preferences to total wealth could be disastrous.[3]

Desired Characteristics of the Long-Term Utility Function

We turn now to the problem of defining a suitable utility function to express rational long-term preferences for real, post-tax, log net returns over an investor's total investment portfolio. One of the great advantages of EUT is its tremendous flexibility to express different sets of preferences while still remaining true to strong principles of rationality. However, this flexibility also means that we have to be precise about what constitutes "reasonable" and stable preferences for the long-term investor if we want it to be usable for portfolio theory. Put simply, there is a large range of different utility functions that satisfy the formal requirements of EUT but which don't provide particularly good descriptions of investors' preferences. We have to ask ourselves what characteristics these rational long-term preferences should have in order to narrow the choice down to a single utility function.

In Chapter 2 we described in detail the three requirements for a rational long-term utility function. In summary, they are that more utility is always preferred to less, that investors should be averse to risk, and that there should be no sudden jumps in utility for only small increases in return. A plethora of possible utility functions satisfy these three requirements. But we need a further requirement for rational preferences to constrain the set down to a specific functional form.

A utility function that is risk-averse, our second condition, is described as concave (from the shape of the curve). However, different functions have different implications for how risk attitudes change across the range of returns. We would expect to see the risk aversion decrease in absolute terms as wealth increases, known as *decreasing absolute risk aversion* (DARA). This implies, quite reasonably, that an investor would be happier gambling with $100 of his money if he were a millionaire than if he were impoverished. If a utility function failed to satisfy DARA, then an investor would be equally worried about the $100 regardless of his wealth, so exhibiting constant absolute risk aversion. In an even more extreme, and implausible, case, an investor would become *more* worried about gambling a given fixed amount as he got wealthier, so displaying increasing absolute risk aversion (which is a feature of the quadratic utility function).

DARA puts further restrictions on the possible functional forms of concave utility functions, but it still leaves room for multiple specifications. It is interesting to examine attitudes toward relative risks, or risks involving returns on current wealth. Will an investor have the same attitudes toward investing a given *proportion*, say, 10 percent, of his wealth if his overall level of wealth changes? As noted earlier, it is highly intuitive that investing $100 (a constant amount) should become of less concern as an investor's wealth increases, but there is no clear intuition of how an investor's attitude toward investing 10 percent of his wealth (i.e., a constant percentage) should change as he becomes wealthier or poorer. If investors have completely consistent attitudes toward risk over all possible wealth levels, then their willingness to risk a given percentage of their wealth would be the same regardless of the starting point. This is a common assumption in economics known as *constant relative risk aversion* (CRRA).

Put succinctly, absolute risk aversion shows our risk attitudes toward given *amounts* of money, whereas relative risk aversion shows our attitudes toward given *percentages* of money. We would expect individuals to be happier taking risks with a given absolute amount of money as they get wealthier but have no good reason to expect them to be necessarily more or less happy to take risks with a given percentage of their total wealth as they get wealthier.

Many people have found CRRA to be a very appealing assumption to make when considering risk attitudes because there does not seem to be any particularly strong reason to suppose that attitudes toward risks concerning proportions of wealth should be either increasing or decreasing over different possible future wealth levels. Some empirical evidence suggests that CRRA is approximately true on average through the population as a whole. Indeed, over the preceding centuries, there have been dramatic changes in per capita wealth and consumption, but average interest rates (the price investors are willing to pay for risk on average) show no pattern of response to these shifts, indicating CRRA on average. However, while CRRA may be approximately right on average, we observe a wide range of behaviors. Some people, on becoming wealthy, take the attitude that now they can afford to take greater risks because they are much further from having to worry about basic necessities. Others, though, take quite the opposite view when they've made their fortune. Now that they are comfortably off, why would they need to take any further risks to become yet wealthier still? The truth is that people are indeed different and that we have few grounds on which to predict how any given individual's risk attitudes will change in the future.

By making the assumption of CRRA, we are therefore deliberately remaining agnostic about how the risk attitudes of individual investors will change in the future and are also admitting that we should not be trying to second-guess this effect through the use of reference-dependent effects over the long term. As situations change, we can periodically elicit new preferences over real returns from the current wealth position and reposition the portfolio accordingly. At any point, however, we work solely with what we know, that is, current preferences for real returns, and not with guesses.

Having established that in a great number of respects it is desirable for a rational long-term investor to describe preferences for future outcomes using a CRRA utility function, we are in a position to narrow down our possible replacement for quadratic utility to a single functional form.

The *only* functional forms that satisfy CRRA when relative log returns are used are the exponential functions, which we can represent mathematically as

$$u(r) = 1 - e^{-2r/T}$$

where r is the log return, and T is a parameter reflecting the degree of rational risk tolerance specific to the investor. This function satisfies the basic characteristics we want: It's smoothly increasing and everywhere concave and thus risk-averse; it also passes through the origin, so a return of zero has zero utility.[4] This function also exhibits DARA—as do all CRRA functions—because investors who remain equally averse to gambles over percentages of their wealth as they get wealthier will necessarily become less concerned about gambles over fixed amounts. We can see these points by examining the Pratt-Arrow coefficients of risk aversion, which measure the curvature of the utility function for each wealth level x.

The coefficient of absolute risk aversion is usually applied to wealth levels, so in the case of relative inputs, it becomes a coefficient of relative risk aversion instead:

$$-\frac{u''(r)}{u'(r)} = -\frac{-\frac{4}{T^2}e^{-2r/T}}{\frac{2}{T}e^{-2r/T}} = \frac{2}{T}$$

which shows that risk aversion to gambles involving log returns depends only on the degree of risk tolerance T and not at all on the level of returns themselves. Thus risk attitudes are constant throughout the full range of possible returns.

Figure 5.1 shows the exponential function for three different values of T, which we may take to reflect values approximately appropriate for low-, medium-, and high-risk-tolerant investors, respectively. We shall return to the challenge of establishing estimates for these parameters later. As already mentioned, the functions are globally concave, and the utility of zero returns is fixed at zero. This, in turn, implies that the real risk-free rate generates positive utility—so for an investment to be accepted in preference to holding the risk-free asset, expected utility would have to exceed this risk-free utility. The lower one's risk tolerance, the faster one's utility decreases for losses, and the more one is concerned about ensuring gains. Notice too that the utility function, which is exponentially decreasing for losses, places considerable emphasis on avoiding outcomes in the far left tail. In addition to being risk-averse, the function exhibits both a preference for positively skewed investments and an aversion to

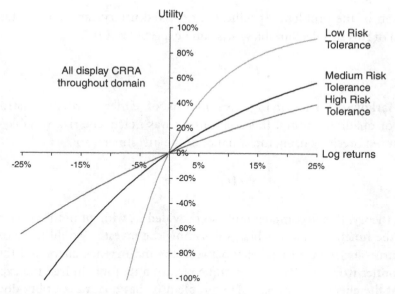

Figure 5.1   Returns versus utility for three levels of risk tolerance.

investments with fat tails. Thus, crucially, this utility function discerns between differently shaped distributions even if they have the same expected returns and standard deviation. This will be very important in defining what risk means to our rational long-term investor in the next section.

Desired Criteria for the Behavioral Risk Measure

It would be possible to stop at this point. By defining the rational utility function, it becomes possible to determine the expected utility for any investment and thus to find the optimal portfolio. However, there is value to going further. Expected utility values are not particularly meaningful or interpretable, so translating expected utility into a tradeoff between more easily understood measures of risk and expected return contributes a great deal to the framework's usability. This decomposition into risk and return also permits the graphic display of an efficient frontier showing the available combinations from any set of assets that dominate all the others.

Limitations of the MPT Indifference Curve

Markowitz's essential insight was this: We can decompose expected utility into two distinct components and thus greatly simplify both the computation and exposition of the problem. Specifically, expected utility can be rewritten as a function of two simpler variables—risk and expected return[5]:

$$E[u(r)] = f(\bar{r}, \text{risk})$$

With Markowitz's simplifying assumptions of either normally distributed returns or quadratic utility, this relationship was exact: The risk variable could be measured precisely using the variance of the investment, so

$$E[u(r)] = f(\bar{r}, \sigma^2)$$

In theory, this decomposition also provided us with an indifference curve, that is, the function f itself, which shows how the investor would trade off risk and return. The point of tangency between the indifference curve and the efficient frontier would pick out the unique portfolio that maximized the expected utility of the client (Figure 5.2). The problem is that quadratic utility does not provide a particularly useful tradeoff function. Its unsuitability also makes it impossible to calibrate to different degrees of risk tolerance meaningfully. Thus, in most of the applications of mean variance portfolio theory, the role of the indifference curve in picking the optimal portfolio for an individual investor has largely been forgotten.

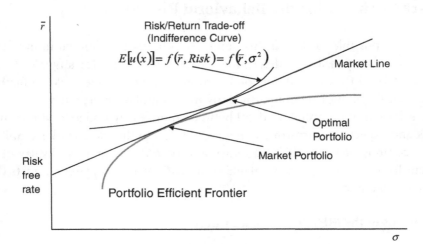

Figure 5.2 Using the indifference curve to define an optimal portfolio.

Tailoring a Subjective Measure of Risk

If we drop these assumptions in favor of a more realistic set of return distributions and also use a rational utility function that is exponential rather than quadratic, then Markowitz's handy assumption that risk is identical to variance is no longer plausible. Now, the higher moments do affect utility. It turns out, however, that while using a rational exponential utility function, it is possible to redefine the risk component by capturing all the moments of the return distributions other than the mean into a single risk measure such that the useful decomposition of expected utility still holds.

Furthermore, this behavioral risk measure gives us much greater insights into the concept of risk as it pertains to a rational decision maker. It will reflect the notion that risk is inherently subjective and not just because people can disagree among themselves on the future distribution of outcomes. Something can be risky only if it is risky for someone, because the variability in outcomes matters for someone. The degree to which outcomes matter to each investor is reflected in the utility function. However, different individuals have different degrees of risk tolerance and therefore different utility functions, so it follows that they may attribute different amounts of risk to the same investment.

It is worth spending a bit of time on this notion of subjective risk, if only to dispel any worries that it might prove to be a weakness compared with the traditional model. The first thing to notice is that traditional MPT is, in theory, also subjective—it is also about maximizing utility—and in doing so, each investor should trade off mean and variance in a way that is subjectively appropriate to them. Investors were assumed to have a subjective preference for trading off mean returns against the variance of returns, but each of these components could be defined objectively. The problem with this is that the assumption of quadratic utility means that we ignore the fact that investors also have to express preferences for more than just the trading of mean and variance in any world where returns are not normally distributed. If we want to maintain objective measures of all the components that investors' preferences are trading off, then it would be possible to do so—we could measure each moment of the distribution objectively but would then have to define a tradeoff function that requires many more than two dimensions. Instead of just a two-dimensional tradeoff between variance and return, we would have an indifference curve in multiple dimensions, trading off the different moments—mean, variance, skewness, kurtosis, and so on—so expected utility would be a function of all moments:

$$E[u(X)] = f(m_1, m_2, \ldots, m_n)$$

Thus, on the one extreme, we can choose to optimize a single number—expected utility, which is an entirely subjective value. Or we can choose objectivity, but at the cost of introducing an indifference curve trading off objective values in a highly complex multidimensional space.

The Merits of Retaining a Tradeoff Between Risk and Return

There is, however, genuine value to the conventional move to a tradeoff between two dimensions. Trading off risk and return is much more intuitive and easy to grasp than simply maximizing expected utility, a value that doesn't refer to any identifiable features of the portfolio distribution. It is also more intuitive than a simultaneous tradeoff between all moments of a distribution. The compromise we need to make to get back to a two-dimensional tradeoff is that all these higher moments need to somehow be collapsed into one or the other of the two dimensions. Expected return is a feature that all investors care about; risk is another. But there is nothing requiring risk to be only variance. In fact, by adjusting our risk measure to include the investor's preferences for all the higher moments, we can retain a tradeoff between just two features of the distribution—expected returns and risk—so that

$$E[u(x)] = f(\bar{r}, \text{risk})$$

The cost is that our measure of risk needs to be subjective because any two investors with different utility functions will be affected differently by skewness or kurtosis, and this means that for each, the perceived risk of the distribution will be different (unless the distribution is elliptical).

The second additional benefit is that because the exponential utility function is a reasonably straightforward reflection of rational preferences, it can be calibrated sensibly by assigning values to the risk-tolerance parameter of different individuals. Thus the indifference curve can once again become a useful tool in picking out the optimal portfolio from those on the efficient frontier.

Criteria for the Risk Measure

So how do we derive a risk measure that permits the decomposition of our rational exponential utility function into a tradeoff between risk and return? Actually, there are a number of potential risk measures that will do the job. It depends on what characteristics we wish to have included in the risk measure and which in the indifference curve. Because the utility function is fixed and expected returns are fixed, we have two unknown quantities in the decomposition equation:

$$E[u(r)] = f(\bar{r}, \text{risk})$$

First, our definition of behavioral risk, and second the tradeoff function f that defines indifference between various combinations of risk and return. They must together ensure that the right-hand side of the equation equals our chosen form of expected exponential utility for the left-hand side. Thus the specific choices we make for the risk measure will fix the form of the tradeoff function, and vice versa. To some extent, it is a matter of choice and convenience how we divide up the work between a risk measure and a risk/return tradeoff function, but only certain divisions will make intuitive sense and combine in the right way to equate to expected exponential utility. Because users of the existing mean variance framework are more familiar with the risk measure than with the tradeoff function, it will make sense to find a measure of risk that is intuitive and intelligible and then subsequently to derive the function that defines how a rational investor will trade off expected returns and this new behavioral measure of risk.

As we did when narrowing options down to a single functional form for the utility function, we can state a number of characteristics that it would be desirable for our risk measure to have and thereby narrow down our options for the risk measure to one that is intuitive, plausible, and easy to use. Along the way we can discard a number of commonly used risk measures that do not meet these criteria.

1. *A risk measure should display downside orientation.* Risk is related to the chance of something bad happening, so any measure that has better than expected outcomes adding to an investment's risk should be excluded. This excludes variance from the outset.
2. *Any investments that are entirely risk-free (i.e., their outcome is certain) should have a risk score of zero.* Variance passes this test, but some other risk measures fail. Value at risk (VaR), for instance, assigns a nonzero value even to certain outcomes.
3. *A rational investor should be concerned with the shape of the entire returns distribution, not just the shape at certain arbitrarily chosen points.* Any risk measure that ignores the shape of the returns distribution for any arbitrarily chosen part of the full range of possible returns should be ignored.[6]
4. *The risk measure should be independent of expected returns.* The whole point of decomposing the expected utility for our purposes is to

separate risk and return. Any risk measure that fails to do this will not be useful for this purpose. Risk measures may be broadly categorized into two classes: *deviation risk measures* and *generalized risk measures*. Deviation risk measures, of which variance is an example, are independent of expected returns: When the whole distribution of returns is shifted up or down, expected returns will change, but the risk measure remains constant. It represents deviations from the mean value. By contrast, generalized risk measures argue that when the whole distribution is shifted up, the risk to the investor must decrease. VaR is such a measure—add a constant amount to every possible return in the distribution, and the VaR will decrease. This principle is quite reasonable, and there is a valuable place for both types of risk measures. For our purposes, however, we deliberately want to separate risk and return, so only deviation measures will do.[7] Note that a generalized risk measure will always fail on our second criterion as well.

Deriving the Behavioral Risk Measure

Extracting the Risk Measure from the Expected Utility

Let's begin with expected utility[8]:

$$E[u(r)] = E(1 - e^{-(2/T)r})$$
$$= 1 - E(e^{-(2/T)r})$$

In order to separate risk from expected returns, we can both add and subtract expected returns in the utility formula and then split the expectation into two parts, one containing only the mean return and the other containing only deviations from this return:

$$E[u(r)] = 1 - E(e^{-(2/T)(r-\bar{r}+\bar{r})})$$
$$= 1 - E(e^{(2/T)[-\bar{r}+(\bar{r}-r)]})$$
$$= 1 - E(e^{-(2/T)\bar{r}}e^{(2/T)(\bar{r}-r)})$$
$$= 1 - E(e^{-(2/T)\bar{r}})E(e^{(2/T)(\bar{r}-r)})$$
$$= 1 - e^{-(2/T)\bar{r}}E(e^{(2/T)(\bar{r}-r)})$$

Next, we replace the component containing the expectation of deviations from the mean return with some placeholder for the risk measure, which we call

R, for risk.[9] This means defining R such that

$$e^{(2/T)R} = E\left(e^{(2/T)(\bar{r}-r)}\right)$$

and then substituting back in so that

$$E[u(r)] = 1 - e^{-(2/T)\bar{r}}e^{(2/T)R}$$
$$= 1 - e^{-(2/T)(\bar{r}-R)}$$
$$= f(\bar{r}, R)$$

In doing this, we have expressed expected utility as a function that trades off risk and expected return. All variation of the returns distribution is completely captured within the risk measure R. And we can also solve the substitution to arrive at the precise formula for the risk measure:

$$e^{(2/T)R} = E\left(e^{(2/T)(\bar{r}-r)}\right)$$
$$\frac{2}{T}R = \ln E\left(e^{(2/T)(\bar{r}-r)}\right)$$
$$R = \frac{T}{2}\ln E\left(e^{(2/T)(\bar{r}-r)}\right)$$

At this point, both the tradeoff function and the risk measure may appear complicated, but as we shall see, they can both be interpreted accurately in much simpler ways.

Before going there, however, we will add in one more desired feature for the risk measure to refine it further. It turns out[10] that for distributions of log returns that are normally distributed, the risk measure has a particularly simple form:

$$R = \frac{\sigma^2}{T}$$

It would perhaps suffice to observe this pleasing fact and move on, but in deciding how to divide the work between the risk measure and the risk/expected return tradeoff function, this presents us with an opportunity. Slightly altering the behavioral risk measure by multiplying it by the risk tolerance parameter T means that any investments with normally distributed log returns will have exactly the same risk as in the traditional mean variance framework, namely, variance. This in one stroke has the desirable effect of making the Markowitz framework a special case of the behaviorally motivated model when log returns are normal. Thus, if we define the new risk measure as $R \times T$ and denote it symbolically by σ_B^2, or behavioral variance, then we can adjust the preceding equations such that $RT = \sigma_B^2$, and risk can be defined as

$$\sigma_B^2 = \frac{T^2}{2} \ln E\left(e^{(2/T)(\bar{r}-r)}\right)$$

The tradeoff between risk and return is now given by

$$E[u(r)] = f\left(\bar{r}, \sigma_B^2\right) = 1 - e^{-(2/T)\left[\bar{r}-(\sigma_B^2/T)\right]}$$

By maximizing expected utility, we also arrive at the optimal combination of expected return and behavioral variance for each investor. Indeed, maximizing this equation is equivalent to maximizing just the expression within the brackets in the exponent, $\bar{r} - (\sigma_B^2/T)$, that is, maximizing expected returns after subtracting an amount that accounts for the subjective effect of risk on that investor.

An Intuitive Explanation of Behavioral Risk

Here, we begin to see that using the exponential utility function with log returns is closely analogous to relying on the traditional mean variance framework, but with risk measured using behavioral variance. The risk/return tradeoff is precisely defined, and as long as T is estimated to accurately describe the investor's degree of risk tolerance over log returns on his overall wealth, the resulting model is both familiar and broader, being both rational and behavioral.

By using a Taylor expansion of σ_B^2, we can see in more detail what the behavioral risk measure is doing and why it serves the dual function of being close in spirit to variance while incorporating broader and more realistic attitudes toward risk at the same time. The expansion results in the following approximation for behavioral risk:

$$\sigma_B^2 \approx \sigma^2 \left(1 - \frac{2\sigma}{3T}\text{skew} + \frac{\sigma^2}{3T^2}\text{kurtosis}\right)$$

For normal distributions, which have zero skewness or kurtosis,[11] behavioral risk is simply equal to variance. However, for nonnormal distributions, behavioral risk adjusts the variance to account for the higher moments of the distributions: For positively skewed distributions, the risk to the investors is actually overstated by the distribution's variance, and the preceding approximation shows how the behavioral risk is decreased; for distributions with fat tails, however, the true risk is understated by variance, and the approximation demonstrates the degree to which variance is increased to arrive at behavioral variance. The effects of these higher moments are smaller for investors with higher risk tolerance (i.e., higher values of T).

This decomposition is only an approximation because the exact formula for σ_B^2 adjusts not only for skewness and kurtosis but also for all higher moments of the distribution simultaneously.

Before examining the tradeoff between risk and expected return implied by the preceding equation, however, there is one very important difference to note between behavioral variance and standard variance: Behavioral variance is inherently subjective. You can see from the equation

$$\sigma_B^2 = \frac{T^2}{2} \ln E\left(e^{(2/T)(\bar{r}-r)} \right)$$

that the individual investor's degree of risk tolerance T finds its way directly into the risk measure. Examining the approximation shows us that, again, this only makes a difference for nonnormally distributed investments. Where mean and variance do not fully describe the distribution, rational investors must have preferences for other aspects of the shape of the distribution. Given that expected utility fully describes the rational investor's preferences, these must be reflected in the components of the decomposition into preferences trading off risk and expected return. And since expected utility has only a single parameter for risk tolerance, differences between investors' preferences for higher moments necessarily involve understanding their risk tolerance. The higher the risk tolerance, the less the individual cares about the effect of the higher moments of the distribution, and the less these contribute to overall risk. For highly risk-averse investors, on the other hand, skewness and fat tails will make a big difference to the riskiness of the investment.

While this subjectivity of the risk measure adds to the complexity of the model, it also adds to its accuracy and ability to cover the full range of investments. When asset distributions are complex, we should also expect investors to have different preferences not only for variance versus expected return but also for skewness and kurtosis, as well as for the infinite higher moments of the distributions.[12]

Demonstrating the Behavioral Risk Measure

Let us examine this behavioral risk measure on some real asset data to make it clear what is going on here. To do this, we use the same nine asset classes that

Table 5.1

Moments of the Nine Asset Classes Estimated from 1990

	Cash	Gov Bond	IG Bond	HY Bond	Dev Equity	EM Equity	Commodities	Real Estate	Hedge Funds
Mean	3.7%	6.7%	7.4%	8.7%	4.5%	10.2%	4.0%	11.9%	11.3%
Variance	0.0%	0.2%	0.3%	0.8%	3.2%	6.2%	4.8%	4.5%	0.5%
Skewness	-0.2	-0.3	-1.1	-1.6	-0.7	-1.1	-0.5	-1.6	-0.9
Kurtosis	-0.8	1.0	5.7	11.7	1.9	3.3	3.1	10.6	3.1

we've already explored in somewhat different contexts in earlier chapters. We use the historical data from January 1990 onward (the earliest point for which we have data on all the indices) without any attempt to adjust these to account for idiosyncrasies of the period. The purpose of data use in this chapter is to illustrate the risk/return framework arising from use of the exponential CRRA utility function for any possible returns distribution and is not concerned with establishing accurate distributions of future returns—this will be addressed in Chapter 6.

Table 5.1 shows that aside from the mean and variance, all assets have negative skewness (with cash and government bonds very close to zero), and all assets except for cash have positive kurtosis, or fat tails. This should mean, according to the approximation given earlier, that variance understates the true risk in most cases. It is particularly true of high-yield and emerging-market bonds and real estate. Figure 5.3 shows the traditional risk/return framework of Markowitz, where risk is taken to be standard deviation.

Let us see how the higher moments affect the adjusted (behavioral) standard deviation for each of three possible investors: one with relatively high risk tolerance ($T = 1.5$), one with moderate risk tolerance ($T = 1$), and one with relatively high risk aversion ($T = 0.5$). The adjusted behavioral standard deviations for each of these are shown in Table 5.2 along with the objective standard deviations.

There are a number of interesting things to note about this table:

1. For many asset classes, particularly those that have low variability, the adjustment for higher moments makes little or no appreciable difference. This includes cash, all bonds, and, interestingly, hedge funds. This is not surprising when we look at the Taylor expansion

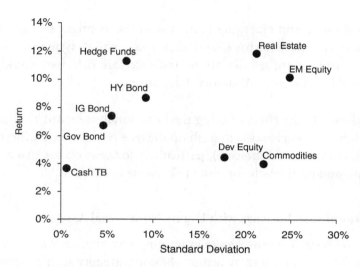

Figure 5.3 Positioning of the nine asset classes in mean variance space.

approximation,

$$\sigma_B^2 \approx \sigma^2 \left(1 - \frac{2\sigma}{3T} \text{skew} + \frac{\sigma^2}{3T^2} \text{kurtosis} \right)$$

where we see that the higher moments will make a greater difference for investments that already have high volatility.

2. Of the remainder, standard deviation always somewhat underestimates true risk for all three levels of risk tolerance.

Table 5.2

Standard Deviation versus Behavioral Standard Deviation for Investors with High, Medium, and Low Risk Tolerance

	Cash	Gov Bond	IG Bond	HY Bond	Dev Equity	EM Equity	Commodities	Real Estate	Hedge Funds
Standard deviation	0.6%	4.6%	5.4%	9.1%	17.8%	24.9%	22.0%	21.2%	7.1%
Behavioral standard deviation ($T = 0.5$)	0.6%	4.6%	5.5%	9.4%	18.2%	26.4%	22.6%	23.2%	7.1%
Behavioral standard deviation ($T = 1$)	0.6%	4.6%	5.5%	9.3%	18.0%	25.5%	22.2%	22.0%	7.1%
Behavioral standard deviation ($T = 1.5$)	0.6%	4.6%	5.4%	9.2%	17.9%	25.3%	22.1%	21.7%	7.1%

3. Real estate and emerging-market equities, as might be expected from their variance, kurtosis, and skewness, exhibit systematically higher behavioral standard deviations and therefore risk than would be indicated by conventional standard deviations.

Thus, overall, the effect of using the behaviorally adjusted risk measure at the level of these asset classes is to push up the true risk somewhat (beyond what standard deviation would indicate), particularly for asset classes that are already more risky—and particularly for more risk-averse individuals.

The Behavioral Risk Measure with Highly Nonnormal Assets

So far we have restricted ourselves to examining very high-level asset classes that, despite the fact that they display features of nonnormality such as skewness and fat tails, nonetheless are fairly normally distributed compared with some investments that are available—in particular, derivatives and structured products frequently have return distributions that are extraordinarily nonnormal despite often being based on the very indices that we have examined already.

In this section, therefore, we will examine briefly the effect of combining one of the preceding indices with a simple put option at various strike prices. This has the effect of creating a floor at the strike price so that the investor is fully exposed to the underlying index above this point but doesn't lose any more if the price drops below this level. Figure 5.4 shows a diagram of this with the strike set at –30 percent.[13]

To illustrate, we will pick a single index from the preceding nine—in this case the emerging-market equities index because it has the highest variance and thus will make the differences more readily visible. However, because over short time horizons the index will seldom make shifts large enough to cross the strike barriers, we will need to amend the data to look at a longer horizon. Here we use annualized three-year returns, thus assuming that we determine the effect of the floor on the returns distribution at the three-year point. At the same time, this will allow us to show how the framework also can deal with differences in the time horizon of the underlying.

First, note in Table 5.3 that, although we have used exactly the same data series as for the earlier tables with all nine asset classes, changing the horizon to three years (i.e., using a rolling window of three-year returns) has altered the moment statistics of the underlying emerging-market equity index somewhat. In order, these were 10.2 percent, 6.2 percent, –1.1, and 3.3. The mean has decreased slightly, but this is largely due to the effect of losing the first three

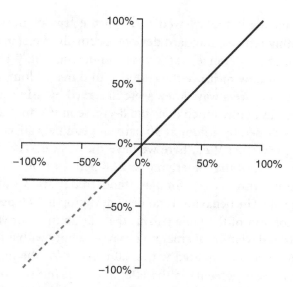

Figure 5.4   Payoff functions of the underlying index (*black*) and an index with a floor at –30 percent (*dashed*).

years of data, variance is very similar, but the negative skewness and heavy positive kurtosis have changed dramatically when we look at the longer time horizon. In fact, both are now close to zero, with kurtosis even slightly negative. As expected, by placing a floor on the index, we increase expected returns and reduce variance—with the effect being stronger the higher the floor (which thus adds more protection). A floor at –50 percent has barely any effect on the four moments because the index will seldom breach this in any given three-year period. The kurtosis is relatively unaffected by the derivative, but skewness gets considerably more positive for a high degree of downside protection.

Table 5.3

Moments of EM Equity and EM Equity with Five Different Floor Levels Estimated from 1990

	Underlying (EM Equity)	Derivative Floor (–10%)	Derivative Floor (–20%)	Derivative Floor (–30%)	Derivative Floor (–40%)	Derivative Floor (–50%)
Mean	9.4%	10.7%	10.1%	9.7%	9.5%	9.4%
Variance	6.4%	5.1%	5.7%	6.0%	6.3%	6.4%
Skewness	0.2	0.5	0.4	0.3	0.2	0.2
Kurtosis	–1.0	–1.1	–1.2	–1.2	–1.1	–1.1

What this means is that viewed through the lens of three-year returns rather than monthly returns, standard deviation actually overstates true risk (for all three levels of risk tolerance) rather than understates it.[14] However, more importantly, we can now measure the true risk to different long-term investors of synthetic assets that we always knew were ill served by using standard deviation as a risk measure. How much does the decrease in variance and increase in positive skewness caused by a floor at 90 percent genuinely affect the risk of the investment to an investor? Well, here we have the answer. The floor decreases the standard deviation of the underlying to 22.6 percent from 25.4 percent. For an average investor (with $T = 1$), though, standard deviation was already over-representing the risk: The behavioral standard deviation is 24.0 percent. Looking down the third column of the table tells us that for an investor with $T = 1$, the behavioral standard deviation of emerging-market equity with a floor at 90 percent is only 20.6 percent compared with 24.0 percent for the underlying. Built into this number (20.6 percent) is the effect *for that investor* of not only the skewness and kurtosis of the underlying distribution but also of the distortion to the returns distribution introduced by the floor on *all higher moments of the distribution.* This allows us to determine an accurate risk value for any shaped distribution once we have fixed the risk tolerance *T* of the investor.

As before, we observe in Table 5.4 that the lower the risk tolerance (the higher the value of *T*), the less true risk is influenced by the higher moments. And the lower the floor, the more the distribution comes to resemble that of the underlying.

Table 5.4

Standard Deviation versus Behavioral Standard Deviation for Investors with High, Medium, and Low Risk Tolerance

3-Year Annualized Returns	Underlying (EM Equity)	Derivative Floor (−10%)	Derivative Floor (−20%)	Derivative Floor (−30%)	Derivative Floor (−40%)	Derivative Floor (−50%)
Standard deviation	25.4%	22.6%	23.8%	24.6%	25.0%	25.3%
Behavioral standard deviation ($T = 0.5$)	22.2%	18.6%	19.8%	20.8%	21.5%	22.0%
Behavioral standard deviation ($T = 1$)	24.0%	20.6%	21.9%	22.9%	23.5%	23.9%
Behavioral standard deviation ($T = 1.5$)	24.6%	21.3%	22.6%	23.5%	24.1%	24.4%

Desirability: Trading Off Risk and Expected Return

Having defined firm measures for both risk and expected return, we can now examine how a rational long-term investor would trade these off. The tradeoff function was derived earlier:

$$E[u(r)] = f(\bar{r}, \sigma_B^2) = 1 - e^{-(2/T)[\bar{r}-(\sigma_B^2/T)]}$$

This could be used to define the indifference curve in expected return and risk space and therefore for picking out the portfolio that traded these off optimally to maximize expected utility for an investor of a given risk tolerance. However, expected utility is not a particularly intuitive measure to work with (what does it mean to say an investment has an expected utility of x?), and the tradeoff is that a term embedded in an exponential function is not easy to visualize or work with either. What we seek instead is a unique indicator of an investor's preference for all possible portfolios (or investments) that is expressed in meaningful measurement units.

To simplify the story, we can ask a more meaningful and direct question: What is the additional amount of risk-free return that would make the investor indifferent between holding this investment and investing at the risk-free rate? If the investor prefers the risk/return tradeoff to risk-free returns, then this amount will be positive—the risk-free rate would need to be higher to make me indifferent between this desirable (for me) investment and not taking any risk at all. Let's call this amount of extra returns the *desirability* of the investment. The expected utility of the risk-free investment is given by

$$E[u(r_f)] = f(r_f, 0) = 1 - e^{-(2/T)r_f}$$

The desirability of any investment is the amount D that should be used to boost the utility of the risk-free investment to make the investor indifferent between investing or not investing in any particular asset:

$$f(r_f + D, 0) = 1 - e^{-(2/T)(r_f+D)}$$

Thus, for any risky investment, its desirability is the value of D that makes the risk-free asset equal in expected utility to that of the investment itself:

$$f(r_f + D, 0) = f(\bar{r}, \sigma_B^2)$$

Thus the desirability is the solution to

$$1 - e^{-(2/T)(r_f+D)} = 1 - e^{-(2/T)[\bar{r}-(\sigma_B^2/T)]}$$

which, after simplifying, becomes

$$D = (\bar{r} - r_f) - \frac{\sigma_B^2}{T}$$

That is, the desirability of any investment can be simply stated as the expected excess return over the risk-free rate less a term that represents the compensation that the investor requires to take the risk. Importantly, there is a one-to-one relationship between the expected utility of an investment and desirability: The higher the expected utility, the higher is the desirability. This means that by maximizing desirability, one is also maximizing expected utility—but desirability has the advantage of being measured in units that are both familiar and intuitive: It is measured as a rate of return. In fact, all the terms in this equation are rates of return.

Total expected return may thus be decomposed into three distinct components: (1) the return that all investors should get for holding the risk-free asset r_f, (2) the return that an investor with a specific risk tolerance requires as compensation for taking on the risk of the investment σ_B^2/T, and (3) desirability, the additional amount of return that is pure marginal (we could say psychological) profit because all risks already have been compensated for.

An investment that has zero desirability, by definition, will have only just sufficient expected returns to compensate for its behavioral (subjective) risk, and the investor will be indifferent to investing in it or holding the risk-free investment. Any investment with negative desirability will not compensate for its risk and will be rejected by the investor.

Risk versus Return: A Graphic Representation

One advantage of adhering to Markowitz's decomposition approach is the mathematical simplicity of the preceding risk versus expected return tradeoff. But a further advantage is that in using tradeoffs between just two entities, risk and expected return, we can represent the whole framework graphically on a simple two-dimensional diagram that is analogous to the mean variance diagram that we have all become so accustomed to. In Figure 5.5 we show how all the preceding components for any investment may be represented in the graphic space of expected return and behavioral risk.

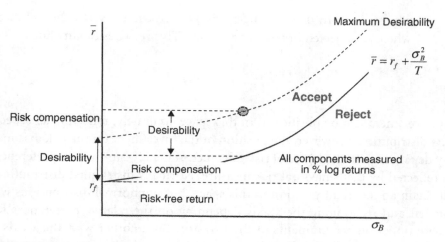

Figure 5.5 Representing our investment components in terms of return versus behavioral risk.

A number of points bear some emphasis in relation to this figure:

1. We have chosen to let the x (risk) axis of the graphic be defined in terms of behavioral standard deviation rather than behavioral variance. It is common in conventional risk/return diagrams for the risk axis to represent standard deviation instead of variance despite the fact that the Markowitz model is a mean variance model—it is much more natural to speak of the standard deviation (or volatility) of an investment than its variance because standard deviation is in the same units as returns. This concession doesn't change the model at all, and the decomposition of total returns that is an essential benefit of the exponential utility approach can be fully represented on the y axis.

2. The total expected return of the investment is made up of (a) risk-free return, (b) compensation for risk, and (c) desirability. All are measurable in terms of percentage log returns:

$$\bar{r} = r_f + \frac{\sigma_B^2}{T} + D$$

3. The desirability equation

$$D = (\bar{r} - r_f) - \frac{\sigma_B^2}{T}$$

is the indifference curve in this space. However, by setting $D = 0$, we may divide the whole space into combinations of behavioral risk and expected return that are preferred to the risk-free investment and those which are rejected in favor of zero risk. This zero desirability line is

$$\bar{r} = r_f + \frac{\sigma_B^2}{T}$$

Any investment can be positioned in this space accurately, reflecting all aspects of its distribution. However, the position of the investment on the risk axis may vary depending on the degree of risk tolerance of the investor, whose preferences are reflected by the behavioral risk measure. Normally distributed distributions will retain an invariant position in this space, but nonnormal distributions will shift left and right along the x axis depending on the relative preferences for distributional higher moments of the investor. Put another way, the x axis is specific to a particular level of risk tolerance. In particular, positive skewness will cause the investment to have lower behavioral risk than reflected by its variance, and fat tails will cause it to have higher behavioral risk (Figure 5.6). Both of these effects will be exacerbated for individuals with low risk tolerance.

Similarly, the shape of the indifference curve, which determines the desirability of the investment, is governed by the degree of risk tolerance. Figure 5.7 shows how for any given normally distributed investment, desirability will differ depending on the risk tolerance of the investor. If, in addition, the returns distribution is nonnormal, then the investment itself may shift left or right along the risk dimension as the degree of risk tolerance changes.

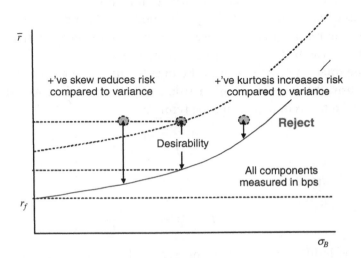

Figure 5.6 How skewness and kurtosis alter the relationship between risk and variance.

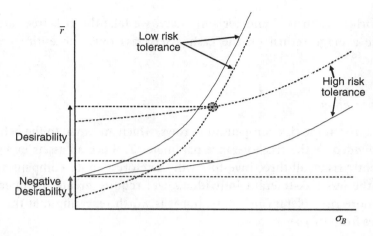

Figure 5.7 How investment desirability varies depending on the risk tolerance of the investor.

Risk Compensation and Desirability for Each of the Nine Asset Classes

Each asset will have a total expected return that can be decomposed into (1) risk-free return, (2) compensation for risk, and (3) the residual desirability of the investment. Examining each of the nine asset classes through this framework gives Table 5.5. As before, we look only at historical data before any adjustment

Table 5.5

Decomposing Total Returns into the Three Categories Presented Earlier

	Cash	Gov Bond	IG Bond	HY Bond	Dev Equity	EM Equity	Commodities	Real Estate	Hedge Funds
Return	3.7%	6.7%	7.4%	8.7%	4.5%	10.2%	4.0%	11.9%	11.3%
Risk-free rate	3.7%	3.7%	3.7%	3.7%	3.7%	3.7%	3.7%	3.7%	3.7%
Risk compensation ($T = 0.5$)	0.0%	0.4%	0.6%	1.8%	6.7%	14.0%	10.2%	10.7%	1.0%
Risk compensation ($T = 1$)	0.0%	0.2%	0.3%	0.9%	3.2%	6.5%	4.9%	4.8%	0.5%
Risk compensation ($T = 1.5$)	0.0%	0.1%	0.2%	0.6%	2.1%	4.3%	3.3%	3.1%	0.3%
Desirability ($T = 0.5$)	0.0%	2.7%	3.2%	3.3%	−5.8%	−7.4%	−9.9%	−2.5%	6.6%
Desirability ($T = 1$)	0.0%	2.9%	3.5%	4.2%	−2.4%	0.0%	−4.6%	3.4%	7.1%
Desirability ($T = 1.5$)	0.0%	2.9%	3.6%	4.5%	−1.3%	2.3%	−2.9%	5.1%	7.3%
Sharpe ratio	−	0.67	0.70	0.55	0.05	0.26	0.02	0.39	1.08

for equilibrium returns,[15] and for simplicity, we take the risk-free rate to be the simple average return on the cash asset class over the entire period— 3.7 percent.[16]

Risk Compensation

Let us look first at the risk compensation rows, which are equal to the behavioral variance divided by the risk tolerance parameter T. Since all assets except cash are inherently risky, all three investors will therefore require compensation. In all cases, the less risk-tolerant individuals will require greater compensation than the more risk-tolerant investors, but it is worth repeating that this difference comes from two separate effects:

1. As we saw earlier, the risk itself for many assets is slightly higher for low-risk-tolerant individuals because they place greater emphasis on skewness and kurtosis than more-risk-tolerant individuals.
2. The larger effect is that of dividing the behavioral variance by T. For our three levels of risk tolerance, this difference can be quite substantial. The most risk tolerant of our three levels requires compensation for taking on risks equal to only two-thirds of the behavioral variance. The least risk tolerant, with $T = 0.5$, requires compensation equal to twice the behavioral variance.

This difference can be substantial in terms of the annual returns required to compensate different investors for the risks. For example, the annual compensation required for an investor to hold 100 percent emerging-market equity is 4.3 percent for the most risk-tolerant investor with $T = 1.5$, 6.5 percent for those with average risk tolerance ($T = 1$), and up to 14.0 percent for the least risk-tolerant investors ($T = 0.5$). Despite the two effects and the possible magnitude of the differences, with a single exception, the asset classes all have the same rank order for any single investor. The exception is that commodities are slightly more risky than real estate for all investors except the one with the lowest risk tolerance, for whom real estate requires greater compensation. This is so because real estate has slightly lower volatility (6.1 percent as opposed to 6.3 percent) but higher kurtosis and negative skew—for the investor with the lowest risk tolerance, the effects of these higher moments come to dominate the slightly lower variance.

In Figure 5.8 we show all nine asset classes in the risk/return space for each of the three investors in turn, together with the zero desirability line, which divides the whole space into risk/return combinations that are either accepted

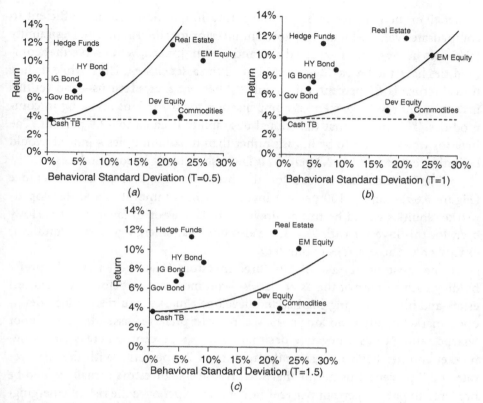

Figure 5.8 Retrospective accept (above zero desirability curve) or reject (below zero desirability curve) decisions for investors with (*a*) high, (*b*) medium, and (*c*) low risk aversion.

or rejected. We can make out graphically the *risk compensation*—it is the vertical distance below each asset from the risk-free rate to the zero desirability line. The vertical distance above this line to the investment itself (or below in the case of assets that are rejected) is the desirability, in annual percentage points, of the investment to that investor.

Desirability

Recall that desirability is the amount of total returns left after the compensation required to accept the risk of the investment or portfolio. For the most risk-tolerant individual (Figure 5.8*c*), desirability for most asset classes is positive—this investor would prefer to hold 100 percent of total wealth in any of these asset classes to merely earning the risk-free rate. The exceptions are developed-market equity and commodities, both of which achieved total returns not much higher than the risk-free rate over the period in question and not sufficient to compensate even the highly risk-tolerant investor for the risks taken. Desirability takes into account both expected risk and return. Indeed, we observe that commodities have the lowest Sharpe ratio of all the asset classes. Thus, while its historical return is 4.0 percent, this is only 0.3 percent excess returns—and yet this investor requires 3.3 percent as compensation for the risk of investing in commodities. This means that the annual desirability is equal to −2.9 percent. The investor would prefer to be in cash rather than in commodities—indeed, would be indifferent to earning 2.9 percent *below* cash or being in commodities.

This is also almost true for the investor with average risk tolerance (Figure 5.8*b*)—only a 100 percent investment in commodities and developed-market equities would be turned down by this investor in favor of cash. However, for this investor with $T = 1$, we also find that emerging-market equities is exactly on the accept/reject boundary.

The most risk averse of our three investors (Figure 5.8*a*) would prefer holding cash to four of the asset classes—commodities, as before, but also real estate and both emerging-market and developed-market equities. In fact, developed-market equity is no longer the second least preferred asset despite its poor Sharpe ratio: It has a negative desirability of 5.8 percent, whereas emerging-market equities have a negative desirability of 7.4 percent. With the risk-free rate at 3.7 percent, this means that such risk-averse investors actually would be prepared to pay 3.7 percent per year rather than experience the risk of emerging-market equities, for which the risk compensation is 14.0 percent.

Risk-Adjusted Performance and the Sharpe Ratio

Measuring performance raises an interesting discussion about the frequent and common use of the Sharpe ratio as a measure of risk-adjusted performance, in which function it is questionable. Assuming exponential utility as we have, the true measure of risk-adjusted returns becomes desirability because equivalent desirability means equivalent expected utility. If the Sharpe ratio were a good measure, then any two assets that have the same ratio of excess returns to volatility would be equivalent in terms of their risk-adjusted performance. For example, consider two assets, one with excess returns of 0.6 percent and standard deviation of 1.5 percent and the other with excess returns of 6 percent and standard deviation of 15 percent. Both have a Sharpe ratio of 0.4 and thus should be equivalent in terms of risk-adjusted performance. And yet, from the desirability equation, we can see that investors do not trade off risk and return as a ratio but linearly (after accounting for risk tolerance). These two investments will have the same level of desirability for one specific value of T,[17] and in general, any two investments with the same Sharpe ratio but different levels of risk and return will have quite different levels of desirability for any investor.

Examining our nine asset classes, we can see that hedge funds always have the highest desirability for all three investors, as well as the highest Sharpe ratio, and commodities have both the lowest Sharpe ratio and the lowest desirability for all three levels of risk tolerance. However, these are more the exception than the rule. For example, real estate has a substantially lower Sharpe ratio (0.4) than investment-grade credit, and the most risk-averse investor of the three does indeed substantially prefer the latter. For the other two investors, though, real estate is considerably preferable. We simply cannot infer whether one asset is a better combination of risk and return simply by using a Sharpe ratio. Figure 5.9 shows this graphically. All points on the straight line have the same Sharpe ratio, and yet those in the middle lie well above the indifference curve, indicating that they have greater risk-adjusted performance than those below the indifference curve. At the two points where the indifference curve crosses the Sharpe ratio line, the two risk/return combinations with this Sharpe ratio are equivalent, but in general, the Sharpe ratio tends to privilege investments with either high or low risk relative to those intermediate in risk, which will actually have much better risk-adjusted performance.

Desirability for Highly Nonnormal Assets

The beauty of this framework is that it applies with perfect consistency to both well-behaved indices and assets that typically cannot be evaluated within the

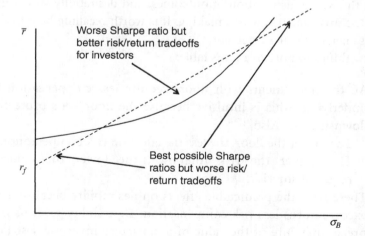

Figure 5.9 Sharpe ratio and optimal investing.

Table 5.6

Decomposition of Total Returns for Derivative Assets on Emerging Markets Equities Underlying

	Underlying EM Equity	Derivative Floor (−10%)	Derivative Floor (−20%)	Derivative Floor (−30%)	Derivative Floor (−40%)	Derivative Floor (−50%)
Excess returns	5.7%	7.0%	6.4%	6.0%	5.8%	5.7%
Risk compensation ($T = 0.5$)	9.9%	6.9%	7.9%	8.7%	9.3%	9.7%
Risk compensation ($T = 1$)	5.8%	4.3%	4.8%	5.2%	5.5%	5.7%
Risk compensation ($T = 1.5$)	4.0%	3.0%	3.4%	3.7%	3.9%	4.0%
Desirability ($T = 0.5$)	−4.2%	0.1%	−1.5%	−2.7%	−3.4%	−4.0%
Desirability ($T = 1$)	−0.1%	2.7%	1.6%	0.8%	0.3%	0.0%
Desirability ($T = 1.5$)	1.7%	3.9%	3.0%	2.3%	2.0%	1.8%

standard MPT framework. How do we assess derivatives, structured products, and even debt instruments? With a mean variance framework, we simply cannot. Typically, the industry has reached for alternative risk measures, such as value at risk (VaR), to overcome this problem to some degree—but these have equally unreasonable implications for the preferences of the investor who uses them as quadratic utility does, if not more so.

Once we have fixed the value of the risk-tolerance parameter T appropriate to the investor, our behavioral risk measure and the desirability measure can consistently evaluate and compare the complete risk/return tradeoff for any distribution (Table 5.6). The risk compensation captures the total cost to the investor of accepting the whole distribution of outcomes, and desirability shows the degree to which the investment is worth making. It is worth recalling here that the risk-free rate is an additional 3.7 percent.

A few things to note from this table:

- All the investments with floors require less compensation than the underlying—this is intuitive because the floor adds protection from downside risk. Also,
  o The higher the floor, the less the effect on risk compensation.
  o The higher the risk tolerance, the lower the compensation required for risk.
- These have the predictable effects on desirability because it is simply excess returns less risk compensation. Desirability gives us not only a precise measure of the value of a particular investment structure but also a clear signal of whether to buy it or not. Thus,

- ○ The only one of the preceding investments that a risk-averse ($T = 0.5$) investor would put his whole wealth in would be the one with a floor at 90 percent. All others, including the underlying, bring negative desirability.
- ○ An investor with $T = 1$ would invest in all the derivative structures (with indifference in the case of a 50 percent floor) but not the underlying.
- ○ The highly risk tolerant investor would invest in all the assets.

We have not tried here to include the cost of the downside protection: This will fluctuate from moment to moment in the market, so it is difficult to generalize about it. However, what we do know is that protection is more expensive the earlier it kicks in, so each investor could use his own current schedule of fees and costs to figure out both the most appropriate level of protection and the optimal combination of assets.

Figure 5.10 shows the risk/return tradeoff and the accept/reject curve for the investor with low risk tolerance ($T = 0.5$). On this chart you can see not only the position of each of these potential investments if we use traditional standard deviation to measure the risk but also the true risk to the investor with $T = 0.5$ and, even more important, the effect of downside protection on the risk/

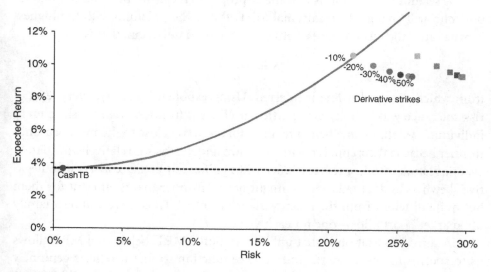

Figure 5.10 Points represent different strikes (floors) for derivatives on Emerging Markets equities index. Squares show normal standard deviation and circles the equivalent behavioral standard deviation.

return tradeoff for this investor: Every derivative structure reduces risk relative to its standard deviation, but only the 90 percent floor is sufficient to make the underlying sufficiently desirable to an investor with low risk tolerance.

We stress that this analysis can be applied to *any* distribution of returns outcomes, no matter how complex and no matter what the fees and costs involved (as long as these are accurately subtracted from expected returns): With good inputs, this methodology will always provide a solid comparative evaluation of any returns distribution for any degree of long-run risk tolerance. And the more nonnormal the distribution, the more it is likely to deviate from the risk assessment provided by standard deviation.

Implications for Portfolio Optimization

So far we have discussed the risk/return assessment at the single asset class level. We would like to understand here the consequences at the portfolio construction level. The move from mean variance to mean behavioral variance has a number of implications for finding the optimal portfolio for a given investor. The first implication is, as we have seen, that the traditional "efficient frontier" is inefficient. Since we measure risk using a behavioral risk measure, then the true efficient frontier will reflect the maximum expected returns attainable for each level of behavioral risk.

A second implication is that the appropriate means to pick out the market portfolio will change. In traditional MPT, this is the portfolio with the highest Sharpe ratio, the ratio of excess returns to standard deviation, that is,

$$S = \frac{\bar{r} - r_f}{\sigma}$$

from which the market line is inferred. Using exponential utility, every level of risk tolerance will have its own particular efficient frontier. Highly risk-tolerant individuals will have an efficient frontier that is pretty close to the mean variance frontier because their concern with skewness and kurtosis is relatively low. However, investors with low risk tolerance will significantly penalize assets with negative skewness and fat tails and so might have a frontier that is efficient for them but quite different from the mean variance frontier. Thus there will be a family of "market" portfolios—one for each value of T.

A third implication is that unlike traditional MPT, behavioral MPT allows us to specify and estimate the indifference function so that it reflects genuinely reasonable assumptions about long-term preferences for returns. This means that we can go much further than simply picking off portfolios on the efficient frontier that "seem" right for investors with different degrees of risk tolerance. The indifference curve allows us to determine precisely which portfolio is most appropriate for each type of investor. It also enables us to give precise values to the benefits that each portfolio provides through the risk compensation and desirability values. Thus not only could we establish what the most beneficial available risk/return tradeoff is, but we also could determine with accuracy how much better it is, measured by percentage returns, than the mean variance solution or any other portfolio. These values also mean that we no longer have to use the Sharpe ratio (a measure of excess return versus risk) to evaluate how good portfolios or investments are.

In Chapter 7 we will combine the insights from behavioral science described in this chapter with the progress made in the techniques related to portfolio construction.

Estimating the Risk-Tolerance Parameter T

Establishing the value of T can make a difference both to the actual risk σ_B^2 of the investment and, more strongly, to the compensation that the investor demands to hold this risk σ_B^2/T and thus to the risk-adjusted desirability of the investment. This makes it very important to get the value of T as correct as possible for each investor. However, this is not necessarily a simple matter.

We have seen in Chapter 2 that investors are subject to all manner of biases and that the preferences of our short-term selves can often come to dominate our rational long-term preferences for risk and return. And yet, when calibrating T, we want to be sure that the value we select captures only the stable long-term risk/return preferences and is not polluted by short-term responses. We also need to ensure that T is estimated to determine the appropriate risk/return tradeoffs for total wealth and not the degree of risk aversion that individuals might display over much smaller gambles.

All these points are unfortunate in the sense that we cannot simply rely on elicitations of T that come from laboratory gambles or observed choices in questionnaires. The finding of the descriptive literature is precisely that such protocols lead to choices that display the sort of behavioral features from which we wish to abstract, such as short-term reference dependence, loss aversion, risk-seeking for losses, probability distortion, and framing. Reliance on such choice experiments could result in values of T that, depending on the specific questions asked, are wildly too low (because people focus myopically on short-term proportion of losses or observe small gambles only in isolation, leading them to dramatically overstate risk aversion relative to what would be appropriate for long-term total wealth decisions) or perhaps in some cases wildly too high (people are risk-seeking for losses owing to behavioral framing effects, which increases the observed willingness to take risks). Instead, we have to turn to other methodologies to obtain values of T that are *cleaned* of these short-term, small-scale, and behavioral contaminants to the extent possible.

Because we're trying to extract an unobservable abstract notion of pure long-term total-wealth risk aversion, this will always be something of a mix of art and science. However, there are some pointers to help us on our way. First, although we don't want to rely too heavily on notions of market equilibrium and efficiency, we can look to see what sort of average value for T is implied by the overall market. By examining a portfolio of traditional asset classes that are reasonably well distributed, we can see what value of T would make these portfolios optimal while abstracting from the difference between variance and behavioral variance.

For any investor, the optimal portfolio will be the one where the indifference curve is tangential to the efficient frontier at that point. Thus, taking the first derivative of the indifference curve,

$$\bar{r} = r_f + \frac{\sigma^2}{T} + D$$

with regard to standard deviation gives

$$\bar{r}' = 2\frac{\sigma}{T}$$

Assuming that we have chosen a portfolio that is close to efficient, the efficient frontier is approximately the straight line connecting this portfolio to the risk-free rate[18] $\bar{r} = r_f + S\sigma$, where S is the Sharpe ratio of our chosen portfolio. Taking the first derivative of this gives $\bar{r}' = S$. Equating these two lines gives us the conditions for tangency:

$$S = 2\frac{\sigma}{T} \quad \text{or} \quad T = 2\frac{\sigma}{S}$$

The further up the straight line we go, the higher is the level of risk tolerance required to make that point optimal. The higher the Sharpe ratio of the optimal portfolio, the lower is the risk tolerance required to make each point on the line optimal.

For simplicity, let us examine a traditional "balanced" portfolio, close to the market portfolio, that might be argued to be close to optimal for an average investor (or at least is frequently sold as such in the industry) of 50 percent developed-market equity and 50 percent investment-grade bonds. In equilibrium, this may have an expected excess return of around 3.5 percent. Let's also consider that the combined portfolio has a standard deviation of 10 percent and is sufficiently normally distributed not to cause us to worry about the differences between variance and behavioral risk. This portfolio has a Sharpe ratio of 0.35 and would be the point of tangency, and thus, according to the preceding formula, would have the optimal portfolio risk-tolerance value of $T = 0.57$. Of course, it's unlikely that this simple portfolio is truly on the efficient frontier, so to account for this, let's see what happens to the inferred level of risk tolerance if we have a portfolio with the same risk level but expected excess returns of 4 percent. The inferred value of T decreases to $T = 0.5$. On the other hand, it's also likely that variance is somewhat understating the true risk, so let's increase the risk to 11 percent behavioral standard deviation from 10 percent—keeping excess returns at 4 percent, the inferred risk tolerance is $T = 0.61$. Increasing the risk to 11 percent without increasing the expected returns gives $T = 0.69$. Thus this rather unscientific exploration gives us a range of T from basic assumptions about simple diversified portfolios in the market for the average investor from 0.5 to 0.7.

This is closest to the lowest of the three values for T that we have used throughout this chapter. This is so partly because we chose those three values of 0.5, 1, and 1.5 purely for convenience of illustration and the fact that they were in the right ballpark. In addition, however, the whole notion of myopia and narrow framing that we explored in Chapter 2 would tend to indicate that the sort of risks that the average investor is likely to take with his total investments in the financial markets is substantially under that which would be optimal from the perspective of his long-term rational self. Myopic loss aversion causes investors to exaggerate the true long-term risks, and thus the level of risk tolerance observed from their market behavior is likely to be somewhat lower than that appropriate to their long-term risk/return preferences. Thus, in searching for cleaned preferences, we should seek to increase the values of T we observe in the markets to account for this myopia, which would argue for risk tolerance for the average investor being somewhat above $T = 0.6$.

It is also clear that there are investors who are far less inclined to take risks than this, who are quite happy to maintain a portfolio of predominantly cash and are not prepared to stomach annual volatility of more than, say, 3 or 4 percent. Again, assuming a normally distributed world, an investor for whom a portfolio with annualized volatility of 3 percent and excess returns of only 1.1 percent was optimal (thus maintaining the Sharpe ratio of 0.35 from earlier, but with far more cash mixed in) would have risk tolerance of approximately $T = 0.16$.

And there are some who are far more prepared to take risks: Someone who found an annual volatility on his total wealth equal to that of our riskiest asset class (emerging-market equities) to be optimal would, with the same Sharpe ratio, expect substantial excess returns of 8.8 percent per year. This is much more risk-taking than the average investor but not beyond the realm of some of the more extreme risk-takers in financial markets. This investor would have $T = 1.42$.

In addition to thinking about optimal tradeoffs between risk and return for different investors, which always requires us to think about the possible location of the efficient frontier, we can take a different approach. Let's turn our attention briefly to what risk/return tradeoffs are considered to be acceptable to investors with different levels of T. These can be determined easily by the lines of zero desirability or the risk compensation lines we have already used. These can be seen in Figure 5.11 for each of $T = 0.25$, 0.5, 1, and 1.5 along with a straight line reflecting approximately the risk/return combinations of a log-normally distributed market portfolio with a Sharpe ratio of 0.35 and the risk-free asset. We can ask ourselves, when thinking about acceptance boundaries for log-normally distributed investments over total wealth, whether these seem reasonable or are highly unreasonable.

Take, for example, a log-normal investment with an annualized standard deviation of 5 percent: These curves imply that our example low-risk investor

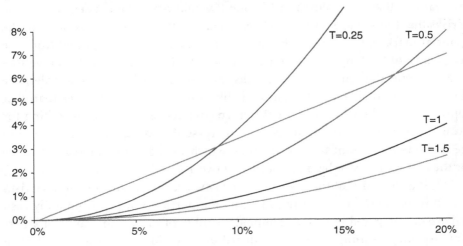

Figure 5.11 Risk compensation lines (for T=0.25, 0.5, 1, and 1.5) in the volatility return space (highest curvature = highest risk aversion, i.e., $T = 1.5$).

($T = 0.5$) would not be prepared to accept this over total wealth for an expected excess return of less than 0.5 percent. The more extreme risk-averse investor ($T = 0.25$) requires 1 percent. For more risk-tolerant investors, on the other hand, this level of risk is paltry. They'd still want to see positive returns, but the $T = 1$ investor would take the risk for an expected excess return of 25 basis points and the high-risk-tolerant investor for only 17 basis points. It is very important to emphasize that this is not *desired* return—all investors should be able to do much better by combining assets efficiently—this is the *minimum* acceptable return for each level of risk.

Take, instead, an annual volatility of 10 percent—in line with many mixed portfolios of stocks and bonds available in the market. The investor with high risk tolerance ($T = 1.5$) would require expected excess returns of only 0.67 percent to take this risk, the investor with moderate risk tolerance would require 1 percent, and the investor with low risk tolerance ($T = 0.5$) would require 2 percent. All these nonetheless are comfortably below the 3.5 percent we'd anticipate for a portfolio of this level of risk with a Sharpe ratio of 0.35. A highly risk-averse investor with $T = 0.25$, on the other hand, would require a full 4 percent expected excess returns even to accept this diversified optimal portfolio and thus would remain in cash. Although we are arguing here from intuitions about what is acceptable for long-term investors after cleaning preferences from short-term behavioral concerns, and it is therefore difficult to say with certainty where the dividing lines are, it nonetheless seems pretty reasonable to say that the average investor should be able to relatively easily accept a risk/return profile over the long term that fairly closely approximates the market portfolio. In addition, the range of T that we use should be broad enough that sufficiently risk-averse investors do turn down this investment (here investors with $T < 0.3$).

We can also see from these curves the location of the optimal points on the straight Sharpe ratio line—this is where, for each risk compensation line, the gap between the risk compensation and the straight line is the greatest (i.e., desirability is greatest). Rearranging $T = 2\sigma/S$ from earlier (the equation for optimality) to solve for risk, we get $\sigma = ST/2$. For our example Sharpe ratio of 0.35 and $T = 0.25$, the optimal amount of risk is to have

$$\sigma = \frac{0.35 \times 0.25}{2} = 4.4\%$$

For $T = 0.5$, it is 8.8 percent; for $T = 1$, $\sigma = 17.5$ percent, which is at about the long-run volatility level for a portfolio comprising 100 percent of the developed-market equity index (although the optimal portfolio would need to be a diversified combination of this and other asset classes because, historically, developed-market equities have only managed a Sharpe ratio of 0.23). A highly risk-tolerant investor with $T = 1.5$ would have an optimal portfolio at $\sigma = 26.3$ percent and so would need to use leverage to get near the optimal long-run portfolio.[19] We also should be aware that 0.35 may overstate the long-term risk premium available on a market portfolio: With a Sharpe of 0.3 rather than 0.35, these two investors with higher risk tolerance would have optimal levels of volatility that are slightly lower, at 15 and 22.5 percent, respectively.

Thus, although these data are open to discussion and interpretation, it would appear that the investor with average risk tolerance should have a level of risk tolerance of between $T = 0.75$ and $T = 1$ depending on how much you think that observed levels of risk-taking in the markets are too low owing to the effects of myopia and behavioral loss aversion. In addition, at the low end human risk tolerance would appear to have reasonable values of $T = 0.25$ to 0.3. At the high end, although there are always exceptions (that is, people who appear to take on massive risks with total wealth), when we consider that this is risk-taking with total wealth, values above $T = 1.5$ would seem quite extreme.

Notes

1. Kahneman and Tversky (1979); Tversky and Kahneman (1992).
2. People get utility from the outcomes they receive, so to determine the expected utility of an investment accurately for a particular investor, we should also be careful to consider the roles of costs, fees, and taxes in determining the final return received. All returns used as inputs into the function should be net of costs and post-tax. And although in the short term the natural psychological response will be to the nominal value of returns, the rational long-run investor would wish to invest to achieve real gains in spending power, so we should use real rather than nominal returns. However, since many of these adjustments are specific to the investor and simply require transformations of the input data rather than changes to the fundamental mechanics of the model itself, we shall largely put these considerations to one side in this chapter.
3. Indeed, Rabin (2000) shows that the typical level of risk aversion observed in experimental attempts to calibrate utility functions using small amounts actually implies ludicrously high levels of risk aversion for large gambles. We have to ensure that the function is calibrated to the decision problem, and for rational portfolio theory, this implies taking as broad a view as possible.

4. Those familiar with the functional forms used for utility functions in economics may be used to the exponential function being presented as the form representing *constant absolute risk aversion* (CARA) rather than *constant relative risk aversion* (CRRA)—but this is when wealth levels are used as the inputs to the utility function. Here, the inputs to the function, log returns, are themselves already relative, so a function that leads to CARA when absolute inputs are used naturally leads instead to CRRA when relative inputs are used.

5. Where $\bar{r}$ is the expected return.

6. A risk measure that does not meet this criterion again is VaR, which measures risk by determining the single point at which, for instance, for 95 percent VaR, 5 percent of potential outcomes are worse than that point. VaR ignores the shape of the distribution above this point, and, more crucially, it ignores the shape of the left tail below this point. It is concerned solely with the point that divides the probability distribution 5/95. Thus two different investments, both of which have a 5 percent chance of losing more than 10 percent, would both have a VaR of -10 percent. However, one of them may have a floor at −11 percent, whereas the other may have a very long tail with a significant chance of losing everything. VaR cannot discriminate between them, but a rational investor certainly should. A further problem with VaR is the arbitrary nature of the point chosen; 90, 95, and 99 percent VaRs are used frequently, but there is no particular reason why any particular point should be chosen in preference to any other. Other potential risk measures such as conditional value at risk and expected loss suffer from the same problem.

7. In fact, if we were looking for a good generalized risk measure, we already have one. The negative of expected utility is a generalized risk measure. It reflects the complete risk attitudes of the investor, it is downside oriented, it considers the entire distribution of returns, and it increases if the distribution is shifted upward. What we are seeking here is a corresponding deviation risk measure that permits complete independence of risk and expected return.

8. This derivation has been adapted from Bell (1995).

9. At this point, a number of possible choices can be made. For example, we could simply fix R to be the expectation in the preceding equation,

$$R = E\left(e^{(2/T)(\bar{r}-r)}\right)$$

and therefore arrive at

$$f(\bar{r}, R) = 1 - Re^{-(2/T)\bar{r}}$$

However, this makes the tradeoff between risk and expected returns extremely complicated because expected returns are in an exponent, whereas risk is not.

10. Bell (1995).

11. We use normalized kurtosis in this equation, subtracting 3 from kurtosis such that a normal distribution will have zero kurtosis.

12. Although the impact of higher moments diminishes rapidly.

13. We abstract here from issues of the cost of purchasing the put in order to simplify the illustration.

14. This ignores the autocorrelation bias introduced by using a rolling (overlapping) time series rather than nonoverlapping returns calculations. However, this can be corrected for, and the main point stands: If your observation horizon and rebalancing period do not match, you could be misspecifying the risk inherent in your portfolio.

15. Thus, for example, hedge funds stand out as having uncharacteristically high returns on this index relative to their level of risk—this could be due to particular biases in the index or of the period during which the data are recorded.

16. This ignores some small fluctuations, and therefore risk, in the cash data. However, the framework may easily be adapted to incorporate alternative estimates of both the risk-free rate and the expected returns of any of the asset classes.

17. For $T = 0.4125$ to be precise.

18. This is not quite true when log returns are used—the line that blends the portfolio with the highest Sharpe slope with cash is in fact slightly concave. See Campbell and Viceira (2002, p. 28) for the details.

19. This assumes that a Sharpe ratio of 0.35 is still available at such high risk levels, which relies on the assumption of costless leverage. The cost of borrowing would reduce the risk level of the optimal portfolio.

Chapter 6

REPRESENTING ASSET RETURN DYNAMICS IN AN UNCERTAIN ENVIRONMENT

W e now focus on creating a more effective way of describing the dynamics of asset returns. This chapter is about how to approach the dynamics of future asset returns and their comovement, that is, their dependency structure. It is not about determining the portfolio with the optimal risk/return tradeoff because we will approach this topic in Chapter 7, where we'll apply portfolio optimization and risk-management procedures to these assessed distributions. At this point we consciously assume Gaussian return distributions and use mean return and volatility to measure risk-adjusted performance—we do not yet rely on tail risk measures.[1] We are conscious of the limits of this approach, but these will be mitigated in due time in Chapter 7.

A Conceptual Elaboration of the Dynamics of Asset Returns

In this section we focus on establishing a simple and coherent framework to describe the dynamics of asset prices in an uncertain environment. In order to do so, we break down the analysis into three steps:

1. Articulation of the dependency structure of the assets in a portfolio and a review of the volatility of each asset class

2. The role played by single-asset-class forecasts in portfolio construction
3. Aggregation of the two preceding steps to represent the dynamics of assets in a portfolio

In Chapter 1 we examined the structural mid-/long-term trends that affect the global economy. Some of these trends lead to movement and comovement stability, some less so, but overall, they affect the dynamics of assets in complex ways. Table 6.1 lists a few of these trends that have now been in play for some time.

The likely results of these structural mid-/long-term trends look complex, sometimes contradictory, and unstable. They cannot be ignored, however, in the way we represent the dynamics of asset prices. Instead, they imply that we need a solution that is both robust and adaptable. We need a robust solution because we do not want a solution that is optimal under one scenario only. Adaptability

Table 6.1

Long-term Trends and Their Impact on the Dynamics of Asset Classes

	Impact on Individual Asset Classes	Impact on the Joint Dynamics of Asset Returns
Aging/increased healthcare costs/tensions on pensions	Changes demand mix for assets; increases aversion to risky assets	Creates noise, i.e., an increasing dislocation between gross domestic product (GDP) growth and the valuation of risky assets
High debt levels (public and private)	Magnifies the risk of risky assets	Increases the instability of patterns across asset classes through increasingly volatile sentiment
Growing role of states	Has a negative impact on risky assets, burdened by taxes; drains savings; increased control on the yield curve	Artificially constrains the relationship across asset classes; favors equity/bond diversification when Keynesian policy mix used, as long as sovereign counterparty risk remains under control
Unstable monetary environment/liquidity conditions	Increases volatility	Reduces the role of diversification because it tends to favor asset bubbles running across risky assets
Globalization	Favors growth and thereby risky assets	Reduces the role of diversification owing to higher economic integration
Innovation	Favors risky assets	Increases the profitability of risky assets over low-risk assets
Emergence of developing economies	Favors risky assets in particular but not only in developing economies	Reduces the gap between emerging- and developed-market dynamics

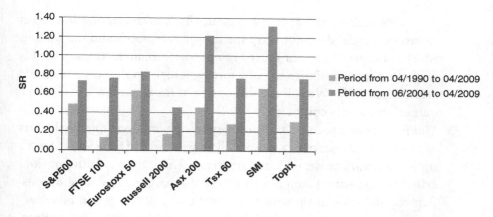

Figure 6.1 Momentum as a short-term pattern that affects asset return performance. The bars reflect the Sharpe ratio of a strategy that is long or short depending on the sign of the moving average of the previous 13 months.

is needed because any attempt to look for "all-weather" rules of asset management is likely to end in failure.

In addition, as we showed in Chapter 1, the adaptability requirement has its own consequences; for example, it requires us to be sensitive to the investment time frame. Short-term patterns can play a role in the dynamics of assets. As a reminder of this we present Figure 6.1, which gives a sense of the positive performance contribution that can be extracted from momentum.[2]

Bearing this complexity and these different time horizons in mind, we now review and discuss the options we have available to us to account for the joint movement of the asset classes. We will then review the modeling options for the dynamics of single asset classes.

The Dependency Structure Across Assets and the Volatility in a Portfolio: Options and Discussion

Portfolio construction is difficult without defining a dependency structure. We can characterize the main options as follows:

1. *Multivariate option 1 – Unknown pattern.* Establish a knowledge-fee naive rule, such as weighting equally all asset classes[3] or weighting them equally on a volatility-adjusted basis.[4] This kind of rule implies a similar pattern of dependency across all asset classes.

This multivariate option 1 is clearly light in conception but rather robust because it does not carry the risk of overspecification in sample, which translates into poor out-of-sample performance. Its main quality is, above all, to minimize risks by forcing a high level of diversification into the portfolio. We will use this option as the benchmark over which outperformance is compared.

2. *Multivariate option 2 – Through-the-cycle stability.* Examine the history of these asset classes over a reasonably long period of time and extract a static multivariate dependency structure. Different modeling options exist, starting with a simple correlation matrix (i.e., assuming a Gaussian copula), to end up with more exotic copulas[5] that can better account for the existence of fat tails in the multivariate distribution. According to our analyses in Chapters 1 and 4, though, there is no such stable through-the-cycle static dependency pattern to be observed over time. This lies at the heart of our rejection of modern portfolio theory (MPT) and its refinements.

3. *Multivariate option 3 – Regime-switching stylized dynamics.* Estimate the stylized joint dynamics of past data to account for the major changes in dependency patterns (typically using regime-switching models). The focus of this approach is really to extract the gist of the impact of these mid-/long-term trends on the changes in asset comovement patterns.

This option is intellectually attractive. In essence, it accounts for the fact that different periods of time correspond to different patterns, for example, stressed periods during which all risky asset classes seem to be highly correlated and other periods during which they behave more independently. From a mathematical perspective, this enables us to describe a complex joint distribution of return outcomes as the mixture, that is, a time-varying probability distribution, of much more simple return distributions representative of each underlying regime. In doing so, we are able to account for a complex dependency structure while providing a practical way to solve well-understood covariance problems.

In this chapter we will use this setup and discuss its strengths and weaknesses. Intuitively, however, we already see two difficult issues with such a modeling framework. The first is that although it is demonstrated that each asset class can be better modeled by considering multiple regimes than through a single-regime approach, it is not clear that there is a simple joint overall dynamic of these regimes for asset classes when considered all together. For example, equities and real estate may not change regime at the same time. This situation rapidly leads to an increase in the required number of regimes, that is, to a higher degree of complexity, in order to represent reality appropriately. This brings us to the second potential problem. An increase in the number of regimes represents an issue in the sense that the estimation process for the various parameters in each regime typically rapidly becomes very cumbersome and therefore imprecise and unreliable.

4. *Multivariate option 4 – Time-adaptive dependency.* This corresponds to a correlation matrix estimated dynamically on the basis of the most recent short-term information. This approach acknowledges that market and macroeconomic conditions influence the dynamics of assets in a way that is difficult to account for using a stable long-term perspective but takes advantage of the stickiness of these patterns over relatively short periods of time.

Multivariate option 4 is easy and quick to estimate. Because we consider asset returns over short periods of time (i.e., most of the time, all assets will be within a given regime), dependency can easily be simplified and approximated with a covariance matrix related to empirical distributions that can be fitted to Gaussian laws or to Student's *t* laws that can cope with fat tails. The main reason for this is again to simplify the overall unknown complex joint distribution of returns over time into much simpler time-varying joint distributions considered over shorter periods of time. By so doing, we translate a complex static dependency problem into a more tractable dynamic covariance problem. The main drawback with this approach is that it implies that the asset-allocation weights should be revised frequently and somewhat dramatically. A way to mitigate this issue could be to account for the existence of some noise in the estimation process in such a way that it smoothes the extent of the changes in the allocation. We also need to consider the frequency of the estimation process as a tradeoff between optimal performance and practical implementation constraints.

The Role of Single-Asset Forecasts in the Portfolio Construction Process

The objective of portfolio construction is to target optimal combinations of expected returns and a risk budget. These expected returns will ultimately come from the performance of each of the asset classes held in the portfolio. Reverting to Table 6.1, it is quite clear that establishing a sound forward-looking view on each asset class is challenging, although it is the only way to outperform markets.

We can identify three sources to inform us and identify enhanced expected returns:

1. *Historical returns.* This source estimates returns based on long time series and assumes that these historical averages are a fair estimate for future performance. However, the empirical work in Chapter 4 showed us the poor forward-looking information content such returns display and the poor performance results to which they lead.

2. *Equilibrium returns.* This source assumes that, in an efficient-market environment, we can rely on a representative investor holding the "market." From this view, and relying on both the risk aversion of this representative investor and an adequate covariance matrix across asset classes, we can back out the implied equilibrium returns that the market-derived asset allocation assumes.

   This second forecasting source of expected return is subject to many estimation shortfalls. Because of this, the estimation of a meaningful covariance matrix is not easy, and the estimation of a sensible risk-aversion parameter is hard. In Chapter 4 we observed that these equilibrium returns did not lead to much performance improvement from a forward-looking perspective. We think, however, that it might be premature to completely completely rule out upfront this source as an anchor around which to blend factor forecasts.

3. *Factors and views.* Different types of econometric factors or forward-looking subjective views can be used to improve our assessment of future expected returns—some based on mid-/long-term macroeconomic assessments and some based on more short-term market data, either systematic such as momentum and mean reversion or nonsystematic, based on tactical market views.[6]

Defining the Most Relevant Combinations of Multivariate Options and Forecasting Sources

We now need to consider how to better understand the dependency structure. We then will have the choice of whether or not to complement the approach with single-asset forecasts.

We therefore structure this chapter as follows:

- We first empirically confirm that asset classes are well described by regimes and show the performance differential of a two-regime model over a one-regime model for a simple portfolio containing three assets: equities, bonds, and cash. This provides a good opportunity for us to describe the mechanics of a regime-switching model and its implementation.

- In a second section we perform a comparative analysis of different performance analyses using different portfolio methodologies, different portfolio compositions, and different rebalancing frequencies. We draw conclusions from this analysis, and this leads us to the selection of our preferred multivariate option.

- In a third section we present methodologic principles related to the identification of factors. We discuss the respective value of forecasting the expected return, its direction, or its magnitude. We then briefly discuss the incorporation of these factors, based on the confidence we have in them, in the approach in a Black-Litterman spirit.

Empirical Portfolio Construction

The Regime-Switching Framework

A regime-switching model assumes the existence of different states of the world. These states of the world are discrete, and they are not directly observable through a clear, recognizable variable. They are characterized by a *hidden variable* that we call s_t. Assuming that this framework is a fair representation of reality, the questions we are left with relate to identification of the state of the world we are currently in, as well as to an understanding of the dynamics that will enable us to define the most probable state over the next period. Regarding this latter point, regime-switching models typically rely on a simplification: Knowledge of the state we are in today is sufficient to anticipate the state we should be in tomorrow. Moreover, this simplification is extended forward in the sense that we generally assume this rule to be stable over time (the transition rule is often set as time-independent[7]). The more scientific terminology used to describe this multiperiod framework is to say that the hidden variable s_t characterizing the state dynamics follows a *first-order Markov process*.

Let us consider a time series of asset returns r_t. Starting with the simplest specification, we can describe it, as in Chapter 3, as a time-independent mean μ complemented by a random innovation term σW_t, with W_t being normally distributed $N(0, 1)$:

$$r_t = \mu + \sigma W_t \tag{6.1}$$

With a regime-switching approach, we increase the degrees of freedom in Eq. (6.1) by allowing both the intercept and the standard deviation terms to be regime-dependent. Naming the regime we are in by the superscript $s = \{1, 2, 3, \dots\}$, we now can write the asset return as

$$r_t^s = \mu^s + \sigma^s W_t \tag{6.2}$$

In a further level of refinement, we can introduce a factor that can explain some of the asset returns in a forward-looking manner (e.g., the performance of the market as a whole). Let us call this factor x_{t-1} and β the time-independent weight (also called *factor loading* on this factor). We can then rewrite Eq. (6.1) as

$$r_t = \mu + \beta x_{t-1} + \sigma W_t \tag{6.3}$$

Translating Eq. (6.3) in a regime-switching framework, we now allow the factor loading to be regime-dependent. The generic equation to account for the dynamics of the asset returns under a regime-switching framework now becomes

$$r_t^s = \mu^s + \beta^s x_{t-1} + \sigma^s W_t \tag{6.4}$$

This means that in each regime, Eq. (6.4) is written

1. Regime 1: $r_t^1 = \mu^1 + \beta^1 x_{t-1} + \sigma^1 W_t$
2. Regime 2: $r_t^2 = \mu^2 + \beta^2 x_{t-1} + \sigma^2 W_t$

Figure 6.2 summarizes the dynamics of a regime-switching model, where identification of the state we are in, as well as the previous period factor score, enables us to fully characterize the asset returns.

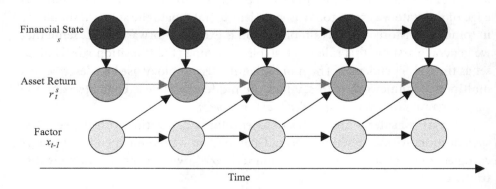

Figure 6.2   Graphic representation of a regime-switching model.

As can be seen, each regime s requires the estimation of three parameters (μ^s, β^s, and σ^s), in addition to the transition matrix,[8] which, over time t, drives the state dynamics from one regime to the other.

We now have a generic presentation of the regime-switching model for one asset class. We could easily expand the framework to a set of asset returns by rewriting the same equations as earlier using a vector notation instead of a scalar notation and a covariance matrix instead of volatility.

The two questions we need to ask ourselves are

- What is the best way to estimate all the parameters we have identified?
- Is this representation relevant to the description of the dynamics of asset returns?

Focusing on the first question, estimation of the regime-switching parameters is carried out using the expectation-maximization (EM) algorithm. The traditional way to estimate parameters in a model is to maximize a likelihood function using a numerical optimization process. The challenge here is to reach the optimum in a computationally efficient way. Rather than exploring the full parameter space, the EM algorithm introduced by Hamilton (1989) approaches the optimum in an iterative way through a two-step mechanism. First, during the expectation phase, it estimates the best-fitted dynamics for the different hidden states (which means estimating the transition matrix) while relying on the previous best fit for the other return-related parameters. In a second step, called *maximization*, it relies on the previously estimated hidden-state parameters to reestimate the optimum related to the return parameters. Through such an iterative process, a convergence to a maximum is quickly obtained.[9]

Regarding the second question, the good news is that there exists a test that enables us to assess whether a better representation of the dynamics of an asset return time series can be found using multiple regimes rather than assuming only one regime. This test, the *likelihood-ratio test*, is based on a comparison between the fitted log-likelihood values under the different hypotheses (actually, its difference across these different hypotheses). For example, the reference *null* hypothesis could be the existence of one regime only, and the competing alternative hypothesis the existence of two regimes.

With this specification, using a large set of artificially generated asset return series built with one regime only, we can compute the distribution of the log-likelihood difference values corresponding to the null hypothesis. In a second stage, we can compute the log likelihood using the asset return data we want to test. If this latter result cannot find its place within the distribution of values

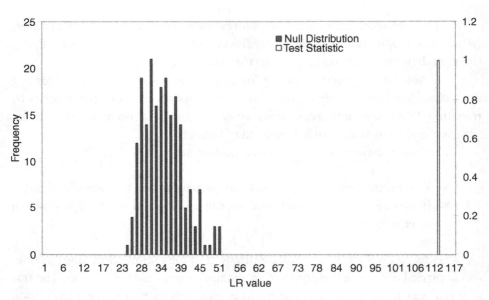

Figure 6.3 The distribution of the log-likelihood difference values corresponding to the null hypothesis.

corresponding to the null hypothesis, then the null should be rejected. This would mean that a two-regime framework outperforms a one-regime framework in its description of the dynamics of the tested time series. Figure 6.3 presents a graphic representation of the test in a case where the null is rejected. Since the test statistic clearly is outside the null distribution, we can reject the null hypothesis, in this case based on the existence of only one regime. The distance between the two hypotheses is very large compared with the standard deviation of the null distribution, so it can be rejected with a high significance level. Applied to all asset classes, the test supports generally the existence of multiple regimes.

At this stage, we consider a simplified example with three assets in the portfolio (equity [Standard & Poor's 500 Index], bonds [ML Global Sovereign Bond Index II], and cash [$US London Interbank Offered Rate 3 months]). The data have monthly frequency between January 31, 1989, and November 30, 2007 (227 points).

When estimated with one regime over the full period, the monthly expected excess returns over cash for equities and bonds are $\mu = (0.95\%\quad 0.18\%)$, and the monthly covariance matrix is

$$\Omega = \begin{pmatrix} 0.0014 & 0.00010 \\ 0.00010 & 8.58E-05 \end{pmatrix}$$

When estimated over two regimes the expected excess returns in both regimes are

$$\mu^1 = (1.07\% \quad 0.14\%)$$
$$\mu^2 = (-1.4\% \quad 0.39\%)$$

The monthly covariance matrices corresponding to the two states are

$$\Omega^1 = \begin{pmatrix} 0.00111 & 0.000122 \\ 0.000122 & 8.75E-05 \end{pmatrix}$$

$$\Omega^2 = \begin{pmatrix} 0.00298 & -0.00026 \\ -0.00026 & 5.88E-05 \end{pmatrix}$$

And the transition matrix from state to state is

$$T = \begin{pmatrix} 0.986 & 0.0135 \\ 0.0585 & 0.941 \end{pmatrix}$$

The first regime is typical of a bull market, where the average equity return is positive, its volatility low, and the correlation with bonds positive, whereas the second regime can be associated with a bear market, where the average equity return is negative, its volatility is higher, and the correlation between equities and bonds is expected to turn negative. The transition matrix exhibits a high persistence level to remain within the previous state, with a higher probability to remain in the bull market (98 percent) than in the bear market (94 percent).

We now want to estimate the regime-switching parameters, rebalance the portfolio, and measure its performance using a clean out-of-sample approach. In order to do so, we consider an expanding-window approach presented in Figure 6.4. Here, the dynamics of the asset return time series are generated to anticipate the distribution at time $t + 1$ based on modeling of the dynamics of

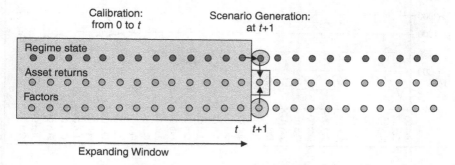

Figure 6.4 An expanding-window approach to estimating regime-switching, rebalancing, and performance measurement.

regimes and realization of the factor at the previous period without having knowledge of what will really take place at time $t + 1$.

The minimum length of the expanding window we consider is 10 years. We therefore start backing out the recommended monthly asset-allocation weights starting in June 1998. The model is estimated assuming no factor, that is, with an intercept and a covariance matrix, susceptible to switching. We perform the same exercise with a one-regime and a two-regime approach.

Starting with the one-regime approach, we display, in Figure 6.5, the monthly evolution of the weights in the three asset classes and the cumulative excess return over cash over the period.

The performance statistics of the portfolio over the period are summarized in Table 6.4.[10]

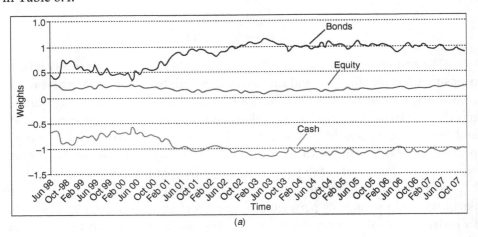

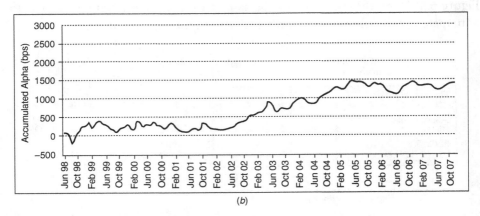

Figure 6.5 (a) The evolution between June 1998 and October 2007 of the weights in the three asset classes (one regime). (b) The cumulative excess return over cash during the same period.

Table 6.4

Performance Statistics over the Full June 1998–October 2007 Period

	Results
Excess return over cash (annual)	1.43%
Volatility (annual)	3.21%
Sharpe ratio	0.45
Desirability ($T = 0.5$)	1.22%
Desirability ($T = 1$)	1.33%
Desirability ($T=1.5$)	1.36%

Moving to the two-regime approach, we perform the same exercise. Figure 6.6 presents quite different results.

The performance statistics of the portfolio over the period are summarized in Table 6.5.

The performance of the model incorporating a regime-switching framework looks superior from both a return and a volatility perspective, as well as from the perspective of our three investors with very different degrees of risk tolerance. One of the points worth further investigation is to understand whether changes in regime are frequent or rather infrequent. In Figure 6.7 we show two lines; one corresponds to the performance of a static portfolio created in 1991 until the beginning of 2009, and the second represents what we call the *smoothed probability* of being in the first regime. The smoothed probability corresponds to a representation of the path followed by the model a posteriori. The interesting point is that we observe resilience in regimes. Once a given regime is in place, it will stay *as is* for a period of time typically between two and five years. This point is very important because it validates the fact that there is a structure—a pattern—in the dynamics of time series that is yet to be discovered. In addition, the regime-based stylized binary structure showing that we are either in one regime or in another is truly groundbreaking because it implies that conditional on knowledge of the regime we are in, we can consider the distribution of asset returns to be well behaved, that is, normally distributed.

Regime-switching models rely on a multiasset dependency pattern called a *Gaussian mixture copula*. In other words, such a model assumes that the complex distribution of the asset returns, including fat tails, skewness, and so on, can be represented using a mixture of simple underlying Gaussian distributions, as is represented graphically in Figure 6.8 in the simple case of one asset class

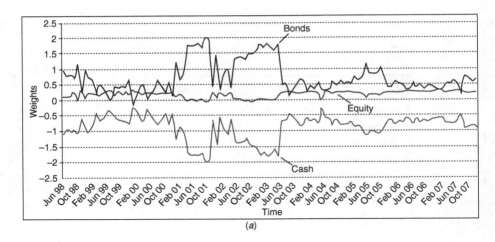

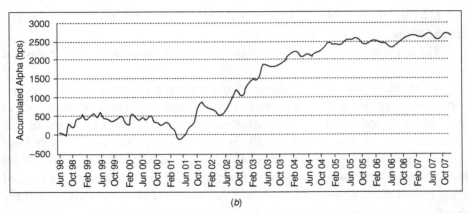

Figure 6.6 (*a*) Evolution of the weights in the three asset classes between June 1998 and October 2007 (two regimes). (*b*) Cumulative excess return over cash during the same period.

Table 6.5

Performance Statistics over the Full June 1998–October 2007 Period

	Results
Excess return over cash (annual)	2.82%
Volatility (annual)	3.97%
Sharpe ratio	0.71
Desirability ($T = 0.5$)	2.50%
Desirability ($T = 1$)	2.66%
Desirability ($T = 1.5$)	2.71%

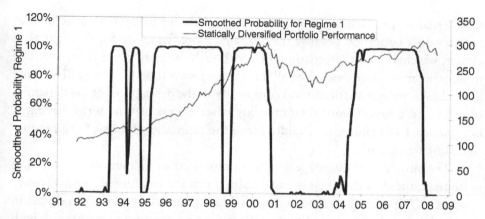

Figure 6.7 Focusing on the frequency of shift from one regime to another.

only and two regimes. Each of these Gaussian distributions, characterized by a specific mean and variance, corresponds to one of the regimes.

What this means overall is that by considering homogeneous periods of time, defined by one regime, we can assume a traditional mean variance characterization/optimization with clearly defined mean and variance parameters, but as soon as we move to another regime, we need to shift to another mean variance characterization/optimization with other parameters.

Guidolin and Timmermann (2007) have found that when considering different stock and bond asset classes, four regimes are needed to characterize precisely the dynamics of assets. On our side, we have found similarly that the more asset classes we add to a portfolio, the more difficult it becomes to account for

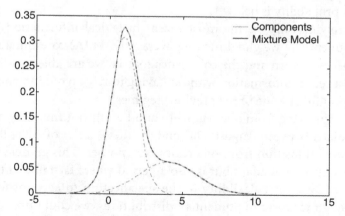

Figure 6.8 A regime-switching model is powered by a Gaussian mixture copula model.

their dynamics, relying on two regimes only. We have found that three or four regimes do a better job because they provide more flexibility for different asset classes, which are not perfectly in synch with each other, to move from one state to another more independently. What it boils down to is that by adding more asset classes, we automatically add complexity to the description of the dynamics of assets. Because we work with monthly observations of time series having at best 30 years of history, we rapidly reach the estimation limits of the regime-switching framework.

The situation at this stage can be summarized as follows: We have found patterns in the data that enable us to outperform the traditional mean variance approach. The overall stylized regime-switching model we have introduced in this section has demonstrated that it offers a sound conceptual framework with which to work; that is, it shows that a mean variance framework can work only when its parameter estimation is conditioned by the regime we are in. However, we do not have sufficient breadth of available data series to help us fully specify such a regime-switching model, and if we keep its parameterization to, for instance, a simple two-regime model, because of data-availability constraints, we are bound to underperform with respect to our potential. We know that multiple regimes exist, but we are not capable of describing them accurately. What should we do?

From here, though, we can see a potential opening:

- By frequently reestimating the mean variance parameters corresponding to a portfolio of assets, say, every month, we are very likely to be and remain in just one of the unknown regimes. There is in addition a high probability that it corresponds to that of the last period, although this probability is below 1.
- By relying only on the most recent historical information, using an exponentially weighted moving average (EWMA) to estimate both the expected return and the covariance matrix, we are able to adjust to the most recent information without having to rely on old information corresponding to one of the previous regimes.
- When moving from one regime to another, the journey may not be immediate. Between August 2007 and the first quarter of 2008, there was a gradual transition from one regime to another. This gradual transition gives us time to adapt but is also a period where fat-tail events can take place. By adding flexibility in the specification to account for fat tails through recourse to Student's t distributions, we could improve our fit of the dynamics of the assets during periods of regime shifts.[11] The nice

feature here is that because we are relying on an approach that already accounts for a shifting mean vector of returns, as can be seen in Figure 6.7, the skewness of the distribution is already taken care of. We can therefore focus on the kurtosis. In Figure 6.7 we show visually why a static asset allocation relying on a through-the-cycle estimate of the covariance matrix and the expected returns vector is bound to capture effectively the state corresponding to growth, which typically happens 70 to 80 percent of the time, but will underestimate the effects of the recessionary state, leading to a heavily skewed distribution.

• By smoothing the associated estimation noise through addition of some transactions costs, we should be in a position to remove the spurious rotation between highly correlated assets that might be suggested by the mean variance optimization process.

In Figure 6.10, we describe graphically the process we will test from now on. In order to allow for the existence of some regimes we do not know exist, rather than trying to specify them, we slice time in monthly periods for which we estimate the expected return and the covariance matrix using a time-decaying estimation technique. Within each of these periods, we perform a mean variance optimization of the portfolio. In the next section we will assess this

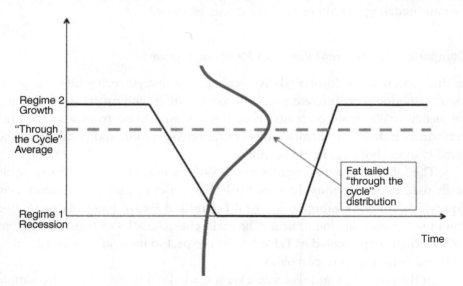

Figure 6.9 The recourse to data averaging in the traditional mean variance optimization process leads to an underestimation of recessionary states and therefore to durable risk spikes leading to a portfolio return distribution skewed on the loss side.

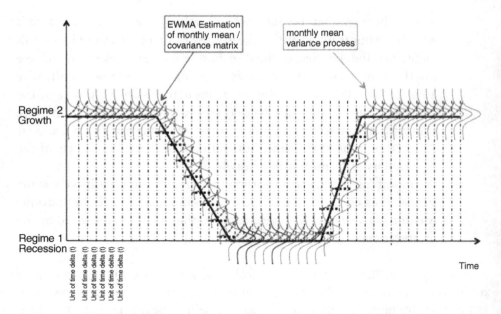

Figure 6.10   Slicing time in monthly subperiods in order to adjust to the existence of unknown regimes.

hypothesis empirically by performing a systematic comparative test across the various modeling techniques we have discussed so far.

Comparing the Different Portfolio Modeling Options

In this section we perform a relative performance analysis using different portfolio methodologies, different portfolio compositions, and different rebalancing frequencies. We analyze results from three perspectives: from a risk/return performance standpoint, from a diversification viewpoint, and considering the stability of the holdings in the portfolio.

The full universe we consider consists of the nine asset classes we have already used in the previous chapters: CashTB, GovBond, IGBond, HYBond, Dev Equity, EM Equity, Commodities, Real Estate, and Hedge Funds. For each, we compute the monthly log returns. The main characteristics of these series from 1990 to 2010 are presented in Table 6.6 with respect to mean and variance and in Table 6.7 with respect to correlation.

In the remainder of this section we will use 1990 to 2000 as the in-sample period and 2001 to 2010 as the out-of-sample period. We consider the two portfolios presented in Table 6.8. It is worth noticing that the first portfolio does not include alternative assets, in particular, hedge funds, unlike the second portfolio.

Table 6.6

Description of the Universe of Asset Returns Considered in this Section (Mean Return and Volatility) Over the Period 1990–2010

Total (log) returns	CashTB	Gov Bond	IG Bond	HY Bond	Dev Equity	EM Equity	Commodities	Real Estate	Hedge Funds	US Equity	FoHF
Annualized Mean	0,0%	6,8%	7,5%	8,7%	4,5%	10,2%	4,0%	11,9%	11,3%	7,98%	7,71%
Monthly return	0,30%	0,56%	0,62%	0,72%	0,38%	0,85%	0,34%	0,99%	0,94%	0,66%	0,64%
Equ Monthly Return	0,30%	0,56%	0,62%	0,72%	0,38%	0,85%	0,34%	0,99%	0,94%	0,66%	0,64%
Equ ann return	3,67%	6,77%	7,47%	8,73%	4,54%	10,23%	4,04%	11,93%	11,34%	7,98%	7,71%
Annualized stdev	0,6%	4,6%	5,4%	9,1%	17,8%	24,9%	22,0%	21,3%	7,1%	15,46%	5,95%
Rank	11	10	9	6	4	1	2	3	7	5	8
Excess Return	0,00%	6,77%	7,47%	8,73%	4,54%	10,23%	4,04%	11,93%	11,34%	7,98%	7,71%
Sharpe	-	1,47	1,37	0,95	0,25	0,41	0,18	0,56	1,60	0,52	1,30
Annualized Variance	0,0%	0,2%	0,3%	0,8%	3,2%	6,2%	4,9%	4,5%	0,5%	0,30	0
Equil T		0	0,04	0,10	0,70	0,61	1,20	0,38	0,04	0,30	0,05
stdev	0,17%	1,33%	1,57%	2,63%	5,14%	7,17%	6,34%	6,13%	2,04%	4,45%	1,71%
Variance	0,000%	0,018%	0,025%	0,069%	0,264%	0,515%	0,403%	0,375%	0,042%	0,198%	0,029%
Skewness	- 0,2	0,3	1,1	- 1,6	0,7	1,1	0,5	1,6	0,9	- 0,8	0,9
Kurtosis	- 0,8	1,0	5,7	11,7	1,9	3,3	3,1	10,6	3,1	1,5	4,5
Prob (rt<0)	0,00%	29,7%	29,3%	26,1%	41,0%	37,3%	44,6%	35,7%	28,1%	36,9%	28,5%

Table 6.7

Average Correlation Structure Across the Asset Returns Between 1990 and 2010

Cash TB	1.00	0.08	0.00	−0.07	−0.05	−0.09	0.07	−0.01	0.09	0.07
Gov bond	0.08	1.00	0.71	−0.03	−0.06	−0.16	−0.10	0.01	−0.09	−0.03
IG bond	0.00	0.71	1.00	0.55	0.32	0.24	0.15	0.33	0.31	0.32
HY bond	−0.07	−0.03	0.55	1.00	0.57	0.60	0.21	0.59	0.64	0.60
Dev equity	−0.05	−0.06	0.32	0.57	1.00	0.74	0.25	0.51	0.69	0.75
EM equity	−0.09	−0.16	0.24	0.60	0.74	1.00	0.24	0.46	0.80	0.70
Commodities	0.07	−0.06	0.15	0.21	0.25	0.24	1.00	0.17	0.30	0.15
Real estate	−0.01	0.01	0.33	0.59	0.51	0.46	0.17	1.00	0.47	0.58
Hedge funds	0.09	−0.09	0.31	0.64	0.69	0.80	0.30	0.47	1.00	0.74
US equity	0.07	−0.03	0.32	0.60	0.75	0.70	0.15	0.58	0.74	1.00

We consider two rebalancing frequencies (monthly and annually) and focus on the four different portfolio methodologies described in Table 6.9.

In all four methodologies, it is important to notice that there is no forward-looking forecasting of returns. We are looking purely at different backward estimation techniques of the return and of the covariance matrix. In terms of risk budget, in all approaches we target a volatility level of 8 percent.[13] All the reported results correspond to out-of-sample performance. We are now in a

Table 6.8

The Two Portfolios Used in This Section

	Portfolio 1 (Four Assets)	**Portfolio 2 (Nine Assets)**
Composition of each portfolio	Equity/bonds–United States • U.S. equity • U.S. T-bills (cash) • U.S. corporate bonds • U.S. high-yield bonds	Equity/bonds–global • Developed-market equity • Emerging-market equity • U.S. T-bills • U.S. government bonds • U.S. corporate bonds • U.S. high-yield bonds • Commodities • Real estate • Hedge funds

Table 6.9

A Summary of the Various Methodologies Used, Split into Four Families

Family	Methodology	Description	Rebalancing Frequency
Standard: Mean variance	Methodology 1	Historical mean variance	Annual reestimation using a 10-year sliding window
Adaptive standard: EWMA yearly	Methodology 2	Historical mean variance with a covariance matrix estimated using an EWMA methodology	Annual reestimation using a 10-year sliding window (decay factor $\lambda = 0.85$)[12]
Dynamic: EWMA monthly	Methodology 3	Exponentially weighted moving average for estimation of both the expected return and of the covariance matrix	Monthly reestimation using a 10-year sliding window (decay factor $\lambda = 0.85$)
Benchmark: Equally weighted	Methodology 4	Naive equally weighted (1/N)	Annual rebalancing

EWMA = exponentially weighted moving average.

position to review the results related to the competing methodologies on the basis of four criteria. We will do so for each of the two portfolios:

1. *Risk control.* This covers two aspects. The first relates to portfolio volatility (expected versus realized), and the second corresponds to an assessment of tail risk proxied by the maximum monthly loss.
2. *Performance.* Annual returns and average Sharpe ratio[14] over the full out-of-sample period. The higher the Sharpe ratio, the better.
3. *Stability/turnover in the portfolio.* Average percentage of the portfolio modified from one period to another. The lower the number, the better.
4. *Diversification.* An indicator of the independent assets in the portfolio once correlation is taken into account.[15] The higher the number, the better.

The Case of Portfolio 1 (Four Asset Classes)

Risk Control

In Figure 6.11 we compare for each of the four methodologies between 2001 and 2010 the ex post one-year observed volatility in the portfolio with the ex ante targeted 8 percent volatility. As can be seen, the three annually rebalanced

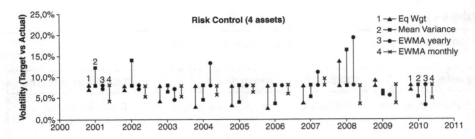

Figure 6.11 Realized portfolio volatility deviation versus the 8 percent target.

strategies (mean variance, EWMA annual, and equally weighted) exhibit higher deviations from the target.

In Figure 6.12 we report the maximum monthly loss every year. As can be seen, the monthly strategy does curb the drawdown during recessionary periods.

Performance

In the first instance, in Figure 6.13 we present the annual excess log return of the year for each of the four methodologies. As can be seen, from a return perspective, the two EWMA techniques seem to outperform the other two methodologies.

In Figure 6.14 we report the full-period Sharpe ratio. When taking into account risk, it becomes clearer that the EWMA monthly outperforms the others. Note that the annual optimized mean variance underperforms the equally weighted portfolio.[16]

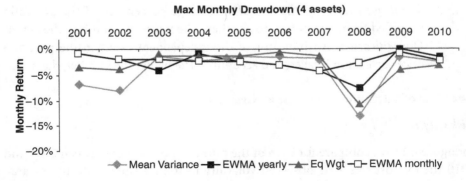

Figure 6.12 Comparison of the drawdowns across methodologies.

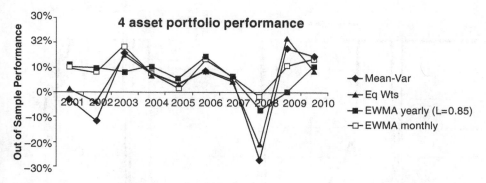

Figure 6.13 Comparison of the yearly excess log returns across methodologies.

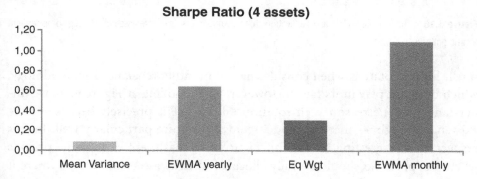

Figure 6.14 Comparison of the out-of-sample Sharpe ratios over the 2001–2010 period.

Stability/Turnover

In this subsection we look both at the year-on-year rotation of the assets (Figure 6.15) and at the shift from risky assets to nonrisky assets when looking at the monthly rebalanced methodology (Figure 6.16). Obviously, we observe

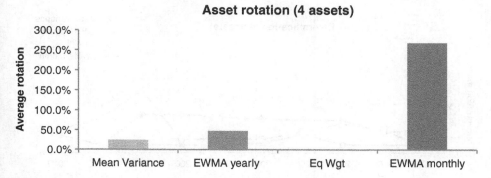

Figure 6.15 Comparison of the year-on-year asset rotation over the 2001–2010 period.

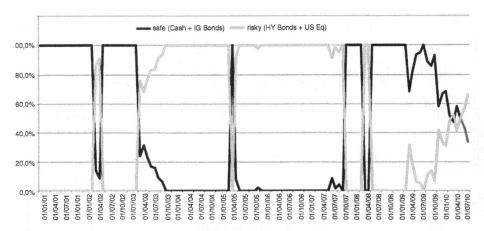

Figure 6.16 The four asset class asset-allocation shifts from risky assets to safe assets displaying some resilient regime patterns.

much higher rotation when considering the monthly rebalanced methodology, which does not play in its favor. However, when looking at Figure 6.16, we understand that the reason such rotation takes place is precisely because of the existence of regimes that the model seems to capture particularly well. In this respect, it is interesting to note on Figure 6.16 that there exist stable periods where the portfolio should be fully allocated to risky assets and others where it should not.

Diversification

We now look at the level of diversification obtained with each of these methodologies after accounting for the fact that the asset classes can be heavily correlated. In Figure 6.17 we provide an indicator of diversification. There are two

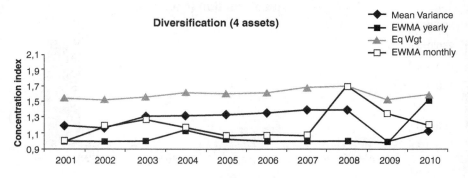

Figure 6.17 A comparison of diversification patterns associated with the four methods.

observations: Only in the case of an equally weighted portfolio does diversification remain high across all periods. Interestingly, when diversification is most needed, that is, during crisis periods, the monthly rebalanced methodology seems to offer enhanced diversification but concentrates risk during benign periods. The mean variance approach leads to the opposite result.

The Case of Portfolio 2 (Nine Asset Classes)

In this case, we incorporate asset classes known for their nonnormal distribution and, in particular, fat tails. We go through the same process and analyze performance according to the four characteristics we used in the preceding section.

Risk Control

In Figure 6.18 we compare for each of the four methodologies, between 2001 and 2010, the ex post one-year observed volatility in the portfolio with the ex ante targeted 8 percent volatility. As can be seen, the three annually rebalanced strategies (mean variance, EWMA yearly, and equally weighted) exhibit high deviations, higher than in the case of four asset classes.

In Figure 6.19 we report the maximum monthly loss every year. As can be seen, losses can be more extreme than in the case of four asset classes. The monthly strategy does curb the drawdown during recessionary periods.

Performance

In the first instance, in Figure 6.20 we present the annual excess log return of the year each year for each of the four methodologies. As can be seen, from a return

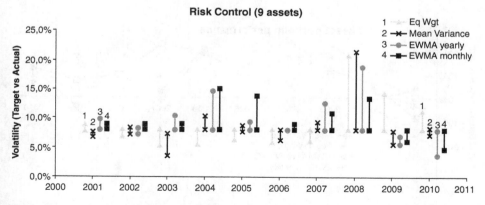

Figure 6.18 Realized portfolio volatility versus the 8 percent target.

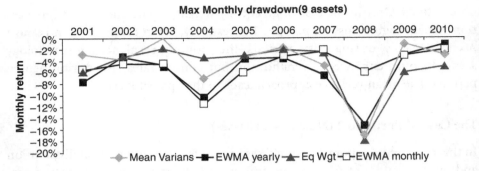

Figure 6.19 Comparison of the drawdowns across methodologies.

perspective, the monthly EWMA technique now appears to be the best-performing technique, with a very positive return in 2008. Note, however, that it failed to capture the full benefit of the 2009 recovery.

In Figure 6.21 we report the full-period Sharpe ratio, which shows that the EWMA monthly outperforms after we account for risk in this manner.[17] Note that the increase in the number of asset classes benefits the static methodologies more than it does the dynamic one. One of the likely reasons for this is that if we are using asset classes that are far from normally distributed, we should not use volatility as a risk indicator to make asset-allocation decisions. In this respect, the risk measures defined in Chapter 5 should greatly help to enhance performance. This will be the focus of Chapter 7.

Stability/Turnover

In this subsection we look again both at the year-on-year rotation of the assets (Figure 6.22) and at the shift from risky assets to nonrisky assets when looking at

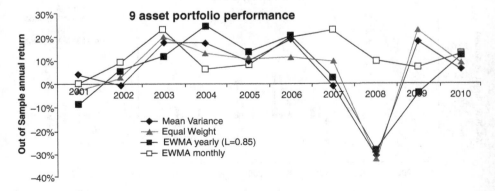

Figure 6.20 Comparison of the yearly excess log returns across methodologies.

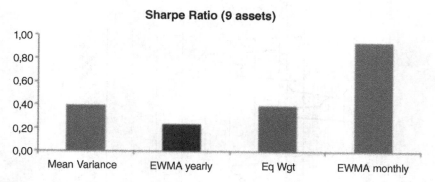

Figure 6.21 Comparison of the out-of-sample Sharpe ratios over the 2001–2010 period.

the monthly rebalanced methodology (Figure 6.23). However, when looking at Figure 6.23, we understand that the reason such rotation takes place is precisely because of the existence of regimes that the model seems to capture particularly well. In this respect, it is interesting to note in Figure 6.22 that there seem to be three different regimes: risk fully on, risk half on, and risk off.

Diversification

By increasing the number of asset classes, we do not seem to increase diversification very substantially, and EWMA monthly almost always outperforms the other more statically rebalanced optimized portfolios (Figure 6.24).

This experiment very strongly supports the adoption of a monthly rebalancing of the portfolio in order to obtain higher performance (a Sharpe ratio of 1 or above without any factor-related forecast of the returns is a surprise) and to curb risks (in the sense that both volatility and tail risk are reduced as expected). And lastly, this empirical analysis demonstrates the existence of stable regimes

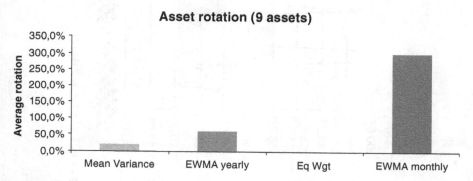

Figure 6.22 Comparison of the year-on-year asset rotation over the 2001–2010 period.

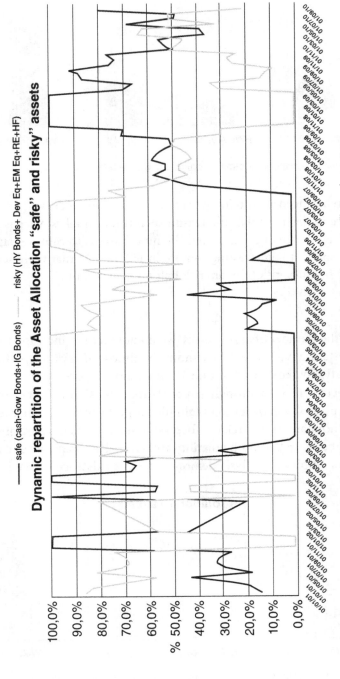

Figure 6.23 The nine asset class asset allocation is shifting from risky assets to safe assets, displaying some resilient regime patterns.

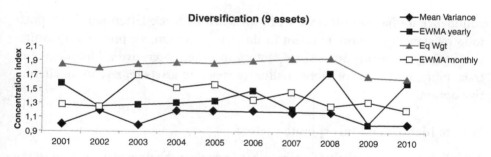

Figure 6.24 A comparison of diversification patterns associated with the four methods.

over periods of time as initially anticipated. A last point worth emphasizing is that a lot of attention has been put on diversification, hence the incorporation of a variety of new asset classes in asset allocations, which may not add a great deal to overall performance but certainly reduces tail risk.

Regarding transactions costs, there are two aspects to consider. The first is the nature of the instrument we use to implement the asset allocation, and the second relates to the pricing gap between the theoretical index on which we perform the asset allocation and the proxy we use to invest in. Typically, there are two options to consider: investing either through real assets (e.g., exchange-traded funds [ETFs] or a basket replicating each index) or, alternatively, in futures. In the first case, transactions costs will be higher, but in the second case, negative effects such as the impact of the *roll* and the slippage between the decision time and the investment time can have a significant impact on performance. Overall, in the two cases we have found that the cost of a monthly rebalancing ultimately is quite similar and typically represents a toll of 0.1 point in the Sharpe ratio.[18] Obviously, buy-and-hold instruments such as mutual funds and hedge funds do not lend themselves easily to frequent rebalancing, and rebalancing would entail much higher transactions costs. In general, more frequent rebalancing of the portfolio seems to pay for itself easily.

We could well stop the chapter here, considering that the degree of profitability of the strategy, that is, taking advantage of our understanding of the joint dynamics of the assets, is sufficiently high for our needs. In the next section, though, we look at potential ways to enhance this effort further by focusing more specifically on the dynamics of the assets when considered separately. In a sense, the attempt of this next section is to mirror the evolution from mean variance optimization to the Black-Litterman framework to incorporate forward views on asset classes. Similarly, we move here from a monthly EWMA mean variance optimization to a framework that uses quantitative factors to allow us to incorporate views on individual asset classes, taking into consideration the confidence we have in these views, in the spirit of Black-Litterman. Since portfolio rebalancing is more frequent in the new paradigm, we present a quantitative process to incorporate these factors in order to ensure a high degree of tractability. Direct use of more qualitative views on assets represents an alternative option.

How to Identify and Incorporate Factors

The idea of using predictive factors to better explain the unexplained, that is, the innovation term in asset return Eq. (6.1), has attracted some attention in the context of the capital assets pricing model (CAPM) framework. Fama and French (1992, 1993, 1995, 1996) have popularized in particular two such factors in addition to the market excess return dynamics: a value versus growth–related factor, *high-book-to-market minus low-book-to-market* (HML), and a size premium factor, *small firms minus big firms* (SMB). The factor-based approach already had some credentials in the sphere of technical analysis, and Carhart (1997) and Jegadeesh and Titman (1993, 2001) introduced an additional momentum factor in the expanded Fama-French three-factor model.

What is interesting is that everyone now seems to agree on the value provided by factors carrying some predictive power. The idea that no such factor exists in an environment dominated by the efficient market hypothesis is no longer credible. The techniques of this section require more than public knowledge and constitute the competitive advantage of fund/hedge fund managers. We describe briefly some core findings here.

Let us restate Eq. (6.3), where x_{t-1} corresponds to a predictive factor considered at the previous period:

$$r_t = \mu + \beta x_{t-1} + \sigma W_t$$

The questions we need to ask ourselves are how to categorize and identify the factors, how to assess their predictive power and to blend them together, how to account for them in forecasting the expected asset return, and how a model incorporating factors typically outperforms a model that does not.

The Number of Time Series to Potentially Consider as Factors Can Be Overwhelmingly Large

In terms of classification, in order to keep things simple, we can split factors into two categories:

- Macroeconomic/financial factors
- Technical factors

Table 6.10

Creating a Universe of Eligible Factors

	Macroeconomic/Financial Factors	**Technical Factors**
Raw information	• Microeconomics factors (e.g., railway freight, car matriculations, new houses, etc.) • Macroeconomic factors (e.g., gross domestic product, consumer price index, monetary, unemployment, etc.) • Survey factors (ISM, etc.) • Financial factors (company size, dividend yields, price to book ratio, earnings surprises, volatility, etc.)	• Moving averages (momentum) • Autoregressive moving average (ARMA) • Mean reversal triggers • Trading volumes
Transformed information	• First difference stationarity transformation • Lagged • Squared • Ratio of factors	• Cointegration residuals • Generalized autoregressive conditional heteroskedasticity (GARCH) models
Processed information	• Dynamic factors (e.g., Kalman filter)	• Wavelet decomposition • Multifractal filtering

We can complement this classification with the degree of transformation/ filtering that is performed on the raw data.

Table 6.10 summarizes the usual filtering and technical transformations that can be applied to the data to transform them into factors. As is easy to understand, the major risk we face is being swamped by the number of candidates to assess. To give a practical example, collecting such data from Datastream on different geographies could give us up to 800 time series. After some transformation, the number of factors to investigate could easily jump to above 5,000. Obviously, many of these factors will not be retained because they do not make economic sense and could lead to spurious forecasting power, but there is a need for a methodology to identify and select the most meaningful factors.

Identifying the Predictive Power of Factors and Blending Them Together

The traditional method used to incorporate factors in forecasting asset returns often has been linear regression. There is a reasonably large body of literature on the estimation of such regressions using ordinary least squares (OLS) methods.

In practice, we have observed that such approaches tend to lead to suboptimal results. Practitioners resorting to linear regressions are too ambitious, trying to get two things right at the same time:

- The direction of the asset return over the next period
- The magnitude of the asset return over the next period

The interesting point is that with respect to identifying direction, the most advanced modeling techniques tend to differ from linear regressions. The goal to achieve is to anticipate a binary result (positive/negative) from a set of observable continuous data. This is precisely a machine-learning/Bayesian problem. The toolbox of machine learning is very broad, encompassing logistic regressions, support vector machine, and so on. For a brief description of some of the techniques used in this field, see Appendix 6B. Overall, instead of trying to guess the value of the asset return series over the next period, we are more modestly trying to define the probability of these series being positive over the same period, conditional on factors we can observe.

Let us take the case of a simple logistic regression, in which the probability model can be written as

$$P_{x_{t-1}}(r_t > 0) = \frac{1}{1 + \exp(-\delta_0 - \delta_1 x_{t-1})}$$

where the terms $\{\delta_0, \delta_1\}$ are estimated on an in-sample data set. In turn, we can use direction forecasting as a factor and incorporate it into Eq. (6.3):

$$r_t = \mu + \beta P_{x_{t-1}}(r_t > 0) + \sigma W_t \tag{6.5}$$

Through extensive data analysis, we have empirically observed two phenomena:

1. Trying to extract the direction from binary classification techniques usually leads to a strong result, stronger than when extracting it from linear regressions.
2. Direction forecasting matters much more than magnitude forecasting, and introducing a sign factor in the asset return equation is the core contributor to performance.

The first observation is easy to understand because, when considering linear regressions, there are competing direction/magnitude optimization targets where, as in a machine learning framework, forecasting accuracy is purely focused on getting the sign of the asset return right, possibly using advanced nonlinear techniques.

Regarding the second observation, the intuition is that magnitude forecasting is of primary interest where the objective is to forecast volatility (the second moment), whereas in our case, we are focused on asset returns and on their sign (the first moment). In addition, factors related to magnitude forecasting can prove fairly difficult to estimate in practice because it is hard to distinguish the contribution of the factor itself from that of the intercept and that of the innovation residual term. This is particularly relevant because we have spotted in a previous section of this chapter that, in the context of a regime-switching model, we can no longer consider the covariance of the intercept as equal to zero or likewise the innovation covariance term $\sigma^s \sigma^{s^{tr}}$ as time-independent. The estimation process of the magnitude therefore is bound to be rather noisy.

$$\text{cov}(r_t, r_t) = \text{cov}(\mu^s, \mu^s) + \beta^s \text{cov}(x_{t-1}, x_{t-1}) \beta^{s^{tr}} + \sigma^s \sigma^{s^{tr}} \tag{6.6}$$

A further topic is the number of factors we should add together to create an optimal aggregated factor. There are three aspects to this topic: The first relates to how to identify individual factors, the second to how to move from the selection of one optimal factor to the selection of an optimal combination of factors, and the third relates to the maximum number of raw factors that can be incorporated into the aggregate factor without weakening its robustness out of sample. Let us take these in turn:

1. How should one select an individual factor? The academic literature and empirical evidence have shown us that there are very few factors that consistently display stable, meaningful predictive power over time. For instance, some financial factors, such as those derived from earnings, will perform reasonably well during growth periods and less so during recessionary periods. Momentum is another good example because it works well within regimes but does a terrible job across regimes. Typically, we have found that less than 2 percent of the universe of factors may exhibit meaningful statistical significance over periods of five years. The question then becomes how to either identify the right factors independent of the idiosyncrasies of the in-sample data set on which they are assessed or be able to use the factors conditionally on the periods where they exhibit predictive power.[19] Many practitioners have moved to the dynamic use of factors relying on time-varying

adaptive regressions using techniques such as the Kalman filter, which relies on the assumption that the weights on the factors should be time-varying, as briefly described in Eq. (6.7):

$$r_t = \beta_t^0 + \beta_t^1 x_{t-1} + \varepsilon_t$$
$$\beta_t = \beta_{t-1} + \nu_t \tag{6.7}$$

2. With respect to the second aspect, the challenge we face is that there is no defined methodology that would enable us to reach a unique optimal combination of factors. The problem is that what matters when grouping several factors is not their predictive power when considered individually, but their marginal predictive power on top of the previously selected factors. In other words, assuming that we have at hand 1,000 factors, the only way to identify with certainty the optimal triplet combination in sample is to go for a brute-force approach and test close to 10^9 combinations. Assuming a repeated selection process on sliding windows, the process rapidly becomes almost intractable. In order to make the optimization process less time-consuming, different algorithms are presented in the literature, such as the greedy algorithm,[20] the least angle regression (LARS),[21] and the least absolute shrinkage and selection operator algorithm (LASSO).[22] They are all valuable, but in our experience, there is no one technique that always performs better than any other, and results largely depend on the data set. In addition, as in the case of portfolio optimization, we can be better served by relying on a simple factor-averaging approach that will be more robust out of sample rather than being penalized by an overfitted in-sample optimization.

3. Concerning the last aspect, there is a broad consensus that factor parsimony is critical. In order to keep the situation under control, a penalty term weighs in as the number of factors increases. A short presentation of some of the techniques is given in Appendix 6B. In practice, three to four factors will represent an upper limit.

Incorporating Factors to Forecast Asset Returns

In the Black-Litterman model, forward views on asset classes typically are incorporated into the model with weights that correspond to the confidence level we have in them. In the preceding paragraphs we have focused so far on a quantitative means with which to consider such views, calling them *factors*. We have shown different steps leading to the generation of an aggregated factor corresponding to each asset return. It would be naive to allocate to this aggregated factor a static factor loading because there are some periods where it will have more predictive power than others. Time-varying confidence should mean a time-varying weight. Among the different options that exist to define this weight, the most straightforward way to proceed is to use the rolling correlation between the period t asset return to be predicted and the period $t-1$ aggregated factor. By doing so, we resort to a time-adaptive approach.

Additional Considerations

At this stage, there remain three questions worth answering:

1. Is there a place for short-term tactical qualitative views in such models? The answer is a straightforward yes because we can move from a more frequently reestimated mean variance model to a more frequently reestimated Black-Litterman model to incorporate qualitative views.

2. How should we take advantage of the long-term strategic views that we might have on some asset classes? There are two options to consider here:

   a. If we are able to practically rebalance the portfolio every month, the short-term parameters we have to estimate naturally will take into account the longer-term views we might have. In addition, by keeping the long-term expectations in mind, we can either tilt the short-term views toward them or create alternative scenarios for the purpose of testing the robustness of the resulting asset allocation.

   b. Alternatively, if there is a requirement to keep the portfolios relatively stable over time, we may think of the dependency structure as a blend between a stable, long-term view–driven covariance matrix and the shorter-term estimated covariance matrix.

3. What type of distribution should we consider for the residuals? So far in this chapter we have considered Gaussian correlated residuals in practice. We have also discussed whether the skewness of the distribution of innovation terms was something we should spend time on, and we intuitively concluded in the negative (this point is empirically verified in the appendix of Chapter 7). Therefore, we should focus on fat tails, and the distribution that enables us to account for fat tails while remaining in the elliptical world where we can keep correlation matrices as a sound way to account for dependency is the Student's t law.

Conclusion

By moving from a static asset-allocation process to a dynamic one, we have acknowledged the fact that the world is changing and that, as a result, stable relationships or laws of nature need to give way to more modest conditional relationships depending on the economic states of the world. Even without any specific forecast, we have seen that a more thorough understanding of these conditionalities translates into a more refined understanding of the dynamics of the distribution of the assets. This newly gained understanding translates, in turn, into a performance greater than many asset managers are able to exhibit in real life. If, in addition, the asset manager is able, through a qualitative or a quantitative process, to add forward-looking views, then performance can be increased further.

The last point to mention is that a highly diversified portfolio across many different asset classes may not bring as much diversification benefit as intuitively thought (as we observed when moving from four to nine assets). It may, however, increase tail risks in the portfolio in extreme financial conditions, and these risks are typically not well captured using volatility. This means that we need the more active tactical rebalancing approach described in this chapter to genuinely reduce risk, and it creates a good opportunity to use the risk measures developed in Chapter 5 designed to support diversified and fat-tailed portfolios. Chapter 7 will address this issue.

Appendix A

SINGLE-PERIOD VERSUS MULTIPERIOD MODELS

Based on the review undertaken in Chapter 1, our representation of asset classes remains based on market indices. The CAPM has indeed made it possible for us to use geographic/sectoral indices as a reasonable representation of the dynamics of each corresponding market, also referred to as its *beta*.

In this chapter we have made the decision to resort to a single-period approach rather than to a multiperiod one. We have given a lot of thought to this problem, conducted empirical tests, and compared results, and we have found that there is good reason to do so. Empirical evidence has taught us that a single-period model can be seen as the single-step decomposition of a multiperiod approach conditioned by the most recent information. On the contrary, a fully specified upfront multiperiod model is more complex and carries the major drawback of being conditioned only by the information available at the beginning of the first period. It therefore quickly becomes more imprecise as errors accumulate and propagate over time. However, this choice needs to be reviewed carefully because it is related to the point discussed in the financial literature under the title of "Myopic Portfolio Choice."[23]

As has been shown in Chapter 4, we cannot rely on the hypothesis that time series of asset returns are independent and identically distributed (iid). For a long-term investor, this means that because there is time dependency embedded in financial series, we cannot consider that rolling repeatedly independent short-term portfolio allocation decisions over a long-term horizon will be equivalent to making one long-term portfolio asset allocation over the same horizon.[24] The question, then, is: Will repeated independent allocation decisions be less optimal, as the word *myopic* suggests? The main criticism of frequent rebalancing usually refers to the behavior of equity volatility. By rebalancing frequently, we tend to in practice assume iid time series; that is, in the mean variance framework, we implicitly consider that volatility is ever increasing with the horizon by a factor that is the square root of this horizon. But, to the contrary, empirical evidence shows us that over the twentieth century, average U.S. equity volatility over 30-year periods typically represented about two-thirds of the average equity volatility over one-month periods. This observation relates to the phenomenon of *mean reversion* attributed to equity time series, which, over time, smoothes significant gains and losses incurred beyond the long-term risk premium level. Therefore, by looking repeatedly at short-term horizons for investment decisions, we are led to overestimate the "true" equity volatility that a long-term investor should really care about and tend to underweight the allocation to equity in the portfolio despite the fact that equities represent the strongest performance engine in the portfolio over the long term. In this sense, frequent myopic rebalancing should lead to suboptimality. The picture is not as clear as it seems, however, for at least two reasons. The first is related to the behavior of investors. The second corresponds to a change in the way we look at the financial time series themselves.

- Regarding the first aspect, the mean reversion property means that "it will be a bumpy ride," more bumpy than without any mean reversion, and one typically needs periods of time as long as 20 to 30 years to smooth this inconvenience.[25] From the perspective of the utility function of an individual who is an investor, a salary earner, and a consumer, such bumps in her wealth can prove difficult to accommodate from a consumption perspective because consumption is not a long-term, end-of-period decision but rather an on-the-run choice. Behavioral finance has much to say about this.
- The second point, even more important, is that following Ang and Bekaert's (2002, 2010) seminal papers, the way we tend to understand these time series has evolved. We no longer look purely at volatility but at volatility and correlation together. We know and show in this chapter that a conceptual framework related to regime shifts is more powerful than the traditional approach of mean-reverting time series. Let us consider a time series characterized by two regimes. What this means is that this time series can be decomposed into two "better behaved" subseries

corresponding more or less to bull and bear markets. In one regime, the volatility and correlation of this series will differ significantly from what is observed in the other regime. In addition, the shift from one regime to another does not happen very frequently, typically once or twice every 10 years. This reading is more sophisticated than the mean reversion assumption. It does not assume any iid property across regimes. On the contrary, because there is resilience in each regime, it is clear that the investor will be better off taking advantage of knowing which regime she is in, in a rigorous emotionless way, and by keeping a stable asset allocation and taking the blows during bear markets. Overall, by identifying a pattern in the time series, the long-term investor is no longer short-term myopic and is able to better take into account her newly acquired knowledge in comparison with a long-term investor who does nothing with it.

Our final observation is that frequent reestimation of the parameters (i.e., volatility, correlation, and distribution parameters) of the portfolio should help us to empirically identify which regime we are in and therefore to adapt the optimal vector of portfolio weights in a regime-conditional way. Under these conditions, frequent portfolio rebalancing displays better performance optimality than alternative static portfolio recipes.

Appendix B

A QUICK SURVEY OF SOME MACHINE-LEARNING TECHNIQUES

In this appendix we briefly discuss some statistical approaches to assessing the direction of asset return probabilities for a given period of time. Some of these approaches are based on techniques from classical statistics, whereas others resort to methods from machine learning (also called *statistical learning*).

In statistical learning, one often makes a distinction between supervised and unsupervised classification. These two approaches differ with respect to the data we learn from. In the first case, so-called labeled training data are available, and a supervised algorithm learns from historical observations of asset return series for which we know the class labels (loss/gain). Unsupervised learning algorithms, on the other hand, rely on so-called unlabeled data, that is, observations for which the class labels are unknown. While this type of learning can be used, we won't discuss unsupervised learning in this appendix.

Some approaches that can be used for modeling direction are[26]

1. Logistic regression and probit
2. Maximum-likelihood estimation
3. Bayesian estimation (e.g., naive Bayes' classifier),
4. Minimum-relative-entropy models
5. Fisher linear discriminant analysis
6. *K* nearest neighbor classifiers

7. Classification trees
8. Support-vector machines
9. Neural networks
10. Genetic algorithms

Some of the methods in this list are closely related to each other, and the methods in the list are not exclusive. For example, logistic regression can be viewed as a special case of methods 2, 3, and 4. However, all these methods are interesting in their own right and are applied by practitioners.

The first four of these methods provide conditional probabilities for the classes given the values of the factors. The remaining methods in the list are classifiers by design; that is, they assign a single class but no class probabilities to the direction of asset returns. This makes these methods less directly relevant for direction forecasting. However, some of these methods can be generalized to provide conditional probabilities. One way for doing this is to apply multiple, slightly different classifiers and assign class probabilities according to how often each class is assigned.

In what follows, we shall focus on asset return direction modeling and restrict ourselves to logistic regression, which is perhaps the most popular method for such modeling, and on a generalization that fits into the frameworks 2, 3, and 4.

Let us consider a vector X of factors, with $X \in R^d$. In a logistic regression, the probability of a positive direction (symbolized by a 1) in a given period of time (e.g., one month), conditional on the information X over the previous period, is written as the logit transformation of a linear combination of the feature functions $f_j(X), j = 1 \ldots J$, that is,

$$P(1|X) = \frac{1}{1 + e^{-\left[\beta_0 + \sum_{i=1}^{j} \beta_j f_j(X)\right]}}$$

where the β_j's are parameters. One can think of the feature functions as terms of a Taylor expansion of some appropriate function of X that reflects the dependency of the asset return on the factors. The logit transformation enables us to obtain a result located in the interval [0, 1].

There are various choices one can make for the feature functions. The simplest choice, which is frequently used, is a set of linear functions. In this case, we obtain the so-called linear logit model, that is,

$$P(1|X) = \frac{1}{1 + e^{-\left(\beta_0 + \sum_{i=1}^{d} \beta_i x_i\right)}}$$

Another, occasionally used choice for feature functions is the set of all first- and second-order combinations of factors; it results in

$$P(1|X) = \cfrac{1}{1 + e^{-\left(\beta_0 + \sum\limits_{i=1}^{d} \beta_i x_i + \sum\limits_{j=1}^{p} \sum\limits_{k=j}^{p} \delta_{jk} x_j x_k\right)}}$$

(We have renamed some of the β_j to δ_{jk} values here in order to simplify the notation.)

Another choice is to include additional cylindrical kernel features besides the first- and second-order terms of the form

$$f_j(X) = \frac{(x_i - a_j)^2}{\sigma^2}$$

where the a_j's are the selected centers and σ is a bandwidth corresponding to the decay rate of the kernels.

In order to specify a model of any of the preceding types, one has to estimate the model parameters, that is, the β_j's. The standard approach for doing so is to maximize, with respect to the β_j, the log-likelihood function:

$$L(\beta) = \sum_{i=1}^{N} \{Y_i \log P(1|X_i) + (1 - Y_i)\log[1 - P(1|X_i)]\}$$

where the (X_i, Y_i), $i = 1, \ldots, N$ are observed pairs of factors and direction indicators (1 for a positive direction and 0 for a negative direction). This approach is often called *logistic regression* (see, for example, Hosmer and

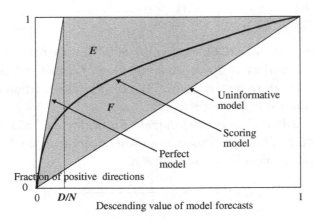

Figure 6B.1 The CAP curve.

Lemeshow, 2000). This maximum-likelihood approach is effective if there are relatively few feature functions and relatively many observations available for model training. Otherwise, it can lead to overfitting, that is, to a model that fits the training data well but performs poorly on out-of-sample data. In order to mitigate overfitting, one can use so-called regularization, that is, maximize a regularized likelihood, which typically takes the form

$$L(\beta) + R(\beta)$$

where $R(\beta)$ is a regularization term that takes a large value for large absolute β_j and a small value for small absolute β_j. Since smaller β_j correspond to smoother (as a function of the risk factors) probability P, the preceding regularization term penalizes nonsmooth P's. The result of the estimation is a probability that is smoother than the one we would obtain from the maximum-likelihood estimation. In practice, one uses regularization terms that are either quadratic or linear in the absolutes of the β_j. It is interesting to observe that regularization of linear in the absolutes of the β_j leads to automatic feature selection.[27]

Performance Analysis for Probability Forecasting Models

There are a number of measures that are used commonly to quantify the performance of probability models. Many of them, such as the Gini curve/cumulative accuracy profile (CAP) and the receiver operator characteristic (ROC) curve, which we discuss below, analyze how a direction model ranks individual asset return time-series direction observations. Other performance measures, such as the likelihood, which we also discuss below, don't explicitly focus on ranks but rather depend on the probability values that are assigned to the direction of asset returns.

The Gini/CAP and ROC Approaches[28]

A commonly used measure of classification performance is the *Gini curve* or *cumulative accuracy profile* (CAP). This curve assesses the consistency of the predictions of a scoring model to the ranking of observed gains. Directions are first sorted in descending order of direction probability, as produced by the scoring model (horizontal axis of Figure 6B.1). The vertical axis displays the fraction of series observations that actually have incurred a gain.

A perfect model would have assigned the D highest probabilities to the D series observations that actually have had a positive direction out of a sample of N. The perfect model therefore would be a straight line from the point $(0, 0)$ to the point $(D/N, 1)$ and then a horizontal line from $(D/N, 1)$ to $(1, 1)$. Conversely, an uninformative model would assign randomly the probabilities of defaults to high- and low-risk firms. The resulting CAP curve is the diagonal from $(0, 0)$ to $(1, 1)$.

Any real scoring model will have a CAP curve somewhere in between. The Gini ratio (or *accuracy ratio*), which measures the performance of the scoring model for rank ordering, is defined as $G = F/(E + F)$, where E and F are the areas depicted in Figure 6B.1. This ratio lies between 0 and 1; the higher this ratio, the better is the performance of the model.

The CAP approach provides a rank-ordering performance measure of a model and is highly dependent on the sample on which the model is calibrated. For example, any model calibrated on a sample with no observed positive direction that predicts zero gain will have a 100 percent Gini coefficient. However, this result will not be very informative about the "true performance" of the underlying model. For instance, the same model can exhibit an accuracy ratio under 50 percent or close to 80 percent depending on the characteristics of the underlying sample. Comparing different models on the basis of their accuracy ratio, calculated with different samples, is therefore totally nonsensical.

A closely related approach is the receiver operator characteristic (ROC) curve. Here, one varies a parameter α and computes, for each α, the hit rate [percentage of correct positive direction prediction assuming that $P(1|X) > \alpha$ predicts a gain] and the false-alarm rate [percentage of wrong positive direction prediction assuming that $P(1|X) > \alpha$ predicts a gain]. The ROC curve is the plot of the hit rate against the false-alarm rate. There exists a simple relationship between the area ROC under the ROC curve and the Gini coefficient Gini, which is

$$\text{Gini} = 2(\text{ROC} - 0.5)$$

In order to give an idea for what ranges to expect for Gini or ROC, we quote Hosmer and Lemeshow (2000):

- If ROC $= 0.5$: this suggests no discrimination (i.e., we might as well flip a coin).
- If $0.7 < $ ROC < 0.8: this is considered acceptable discrimination.
- If $0.8 < $ ROC < 0.9: this is considered excellent discrimination.
- If ROC > 0.9: this is considered outstanding discrimination.

- In practice, it is extremely unusual to observe areas under the ROC curve greater than 0.9.

All the preceding model performance measures focus exclusively on how a model ranks the probability of gains of an asset return time series at different periods in time. They provide very valuable information and often work well in practice. However, they neglect the absolute levels of the probabilities. That is, if, for example, all probabilities for a given set of asset return directions are multiplied by 10 (or any other monotone transformation is applied), the preceding performance measures do not change their values. Thus it seems advisable to supplement these measures, for example, with the likelihood.

Log-Likelihood Ratio

Among statisticians, perhaps the most popular performance measure for probabilistic models is the *likelihood*. We have discussed it in the preceding section as a tool to estimate model parameters. For the purpose of measuring the relative performance of two probability models, one often uses the following log-likelihood ratio (the logarithm of the ratio of the two model likelihoods):

$$L(P_1, P_2) = \sum_{i=1}^{N} \left[Y_i \log \frac{P_1(1|X_i)}{P_2(1|X_i)} + (1 - Y_i) \log \frac{1 - P_2(1|X_i)}{1 - P_2(1|X_i)} \right]$$

where the (X_i, Y_i), $i = 1, \ldots, N$ are observed pairs of factors and direction indicators (1 for a gain and 0 for a loss) on a test data set (as opposed to the model training data set) here.

The preceding log-likelihood ratio has a number of interpretations:

- It measures the relative probabilities the two models assign to the observed data (by construction).
- It is the natural performance measure from the standpoint of Bayesian statistics (see, for example, Jaynes, 2003).
- It is the performance measure that generates an optimal (in the sense of the Neyman-Pearson lemma) decision surface for model selection (see, for example, Cover and Thomas, 1991).

Number of Factors and Robustness

There exist several criteria, based on likelihood, devised to compare different models. They tend to consider both likelihood and the number of parameters required to fit the model. The ultimate objective is to include what is called the *minimum description length principle*,[29] which advantages the model having the shortest or more succinct computational description.

There are, among others,

The Akaike (1974) information criterion (AIC): $\text{AIC} = -2\ln L(\hat{\theta}_k) + 2k$
The Schwarz (1978) Bayesian information criterion (BIC): $\text{BIC} = -2\ln L(\hat{\theta}_k) + k\ln N$

where k is the number of parameters, N is the size of the sample, and $\hat{\theta}$ is the k-dimensional vector of parameter estimates. The best model is supposed to minimize the selected criterion. Both BIC and AIC penalize models with many parameters and thereby reduce overfitting.

Notes

1. Making the assumption of normality here also enables us to temporarily step aside from the discussion in the preceding chapter on investor preferences and use standard performance measures (e.g., the Sharpe ratio) to assess whether the methodologies we test in this chapter result in improved performance. As long as asset returns are Gaussian, then the efficient frontier depends only on expected returns and volatility, two fund-separation holds, and the Sharpe ratio of the market portfolio can be used as a measure of the effectiveness of different general approaches to estimating the dynamics of asset returns over time.
2. Depending on the sign of the return over the preceding 13 months, the investment strategy is either long or short over the next month. It always leads to outperformance over a purely long-only investment strategy.
3. Even this is not entirely knowledge-free because there is de facto an implicit selection of asset classes.
4. This latter framework is no more knowledge-free because it assumes an unknown implicit utility function based on a relative appetite for volatility in the absence of any knowledge on mean returns. The claim that there is no pattern here is therefore not entirely correct.
5. A *copula* is an elegant representation of the dependency structure of different series that is neutral to the distribution and characteristics of each of the series considered individually. For more on copulas, see McNeil, Frey, and Embrechts (2005).

6. It is worth noting that relying on recent asset return information rather than on long-term historical averages is already a way of taking advantage of momentum effects.

7. Time-varying transition matrices can be estimated. The more parameters introduced, however, the weaker is the robustness of the full estimation process.

8. The transition matrix gives the probability, from any regime, of moving in the next period to each of the other regimes.

9. It is likely that this local maximum will coincide with the global maximum, although it may not because we are not trying to solve a convex problem.

10. We have assumed in this chapter that asset returns are Gaussian to more easily isolate and examine the effects of methodologic differences that are of interest to us here. This means that we can abstract from the discussion about risk and performance measures in Chapter 5 and adequately rely on volatility as a risk measure. However, in Chapter 5 we showed that a portfolio can exhibit a higher Sharpe ratio and yet have lower risk-adjusted performance (i.e., it lowers expected utility), so for completeness, we note here in addition the desirability scores for each of our three example investors, with risk tolerances of $T = 0.5$, $T = 1$, and $T = 1.5$, respectively. As a quick reminder, the desirability of an investment is the excess return minus the compensation the investor requires to take on the risk of the investment, which for Gaussian investments is simply the variance divided by risk tolerance. For the methodologies we examine in this chapter, however, we draw the same conclusions regardless of whether we use the investor's performance measure (desirability) or the more traditional Sharpe ratio. In Chapter 7 we will go beyond volatility, using the findings of Chapter 5.

11. This feature will be analyzed in Chapter 7, where we will use a measure of risk more appropriate to handle tail risk.

12. We have tested different decay factors. Very intuitively, this level of decay factor, which enables us to take into consideration the previous two months, does a better job than higher decay factors that correspond to relying almost exclusively on the most recent observation.

13. This level corresponds relatively well to an efficient risk level for the average investor. In addition, it corresponds to a sweet spot from a diversification perspective.

14. These results are computed without transaction costs. Using exchange-traded funds (ETFs) or futures, the impact on the Sharpe ratio of monthly rebalancing has been found to be of the order of magnitude of approximately -0.1. Transaction costs are taken into account later on in this chapter.

15. The indicator is $D = 1/ctWc$, where c is the vector of weights, and W is the correlation matrix. On a relative basis, it can be seen as the square of equivalently independent assets.

16. This remains true if we use the Desirability measure for all three levels of Risk Tolerance, so we don't show these here. Although not necessarily the case, particularly if asset returns are significantly non-Gaussian, for the most part if portfolios have similar risk levels (which will be the case here since all target the same volatility level), then a significantly higher Sharpe ratio must come from higher average returns, which will also mean greater Desirability. It is only when comparing portfolios with both very different risk and return levels that the rank ordering given by Sharpe ratios may deviate significantly from the true preference ordering deriving from the risk and return preferences of investors (given by Desirability).

17. As with the four-asset-class example, this holds true when we use Desirability to measure risk-adjusted performance for each investor.

18. For a moderate risk portfolio—for a portfolio with an annualized volatility of 8 percent, a difference in Sharpe ratios of 0.1 corresponds to annualised rebalancing costs of 80bps.

19. It is worth noting that conditional/dynamic factor models represent state-of-the-art techniques, with a real challenge for econometricians to provide robust selection tests. In this respect, we can mention very recent papers such as on the percentile t (moving blocks bootstrap) technique by Goncalves and Vogelsang (2008) or tests of conditional factors by Ang and Kristensen (2010).

20. A forward stepwise regression including at each step the variable with the highest predictive power/highest fit.

21. A forward stepwise regression weighting each constituting variable as a result of its correlation with the other variables and with the residual.

22. A technique to shrink the number of selected factors by penalizing factors with low predictive power. The LASSO technique can be used in the context of the two previous approaches as part of a "regularization" process.

23. An allocation choice is said to be myopic if it ignores what happens beyond its defined horizon. See Samuelson (1963, 1969), Mossin (1968), Merton (1969), and Fama (1970). See Campbell and Viceira (2002) for a more detailed discussion of the topic.

24. The Samuelson and Merton conditions are that investors with a power utility over many periods ahead can rebalance their portfolios frequently if asset returns are iid or if their utility takes a log form—but Chapters 2 and 5 invite us not to make any such heroic assumption about the utility function of investors.

25. Note that at the 5- to 10-year horizon, the mean reversion is not yet fully effective, which means that holders of static portfolios at this horizon risk being disappointed by the performance of their portfolios as they were over the 2000–2010 period.
26. See, for example, Hastie, Tibshirani, and Friedman (2003), Jebara (2004), Mitchell (1997), or Witten and Frank (2005).
27. See, for example, Hastie, Tibshirani, and Friedman (2003) for the general idea of regularization.
28. For a more detailed discussion of ROC, see, for example, Hosmer and Lemeshow (2000).
29. See Rissanen (1989).

Chapter 7

COMBINING BEHAVIORAL PREFERENCES WITH DYNAMIC RISK/RETURN EXPECTATIONS

We now attempt to bring together the advances suggested in Chapters 5 and 6. In Chapter 6 we explained how to best describe the expected joint distribution for the assets we were considering. Before that, in Chapter 5, we looked at how to combine these assets to ensure that the resulting portfolio provided the best possible risk/return tradeoff for the rational long-term objectives of each investor. Combining these two strands allows us to create a new framework for optimal portfolio construction. Each of these two components adds something on its own, but the full benefit is achieved only when combining them.

In this chapter we present some specific examples of this new approach in practice, examining the resulting portfolios' characteristics using two illustrative past months as examples. We also examine portfolios over the full period of the last 10 years to complement this illustration. But, as we argue in the conclusion to this chapter, we now have a methodology and approach applicable to any set of assets for which we can establish a multivariate distribution of future expected returns and applicable regardless of the shape or dynamics of this returns distribution or the methodology used to estimate it.

In Chapter 5 we defined a utility function for an investor with stable long-term preferences that was "cleaned" of the sorts of short-term behavioral responses that a rational investor, focused exclusively on the best long-term risk/return tradeoff, would wish to avoid. From the utility function of any investor, we showed how we could define the expected risk and return for any portfolio or investment—analogous to the standard mean variance model but with the crucial difference that the risk measure encompasses not just volatility but also the investor's preferences for all higher moments of the returns distribution, as reflected in his *risk tolerance*. This is of paramount importance for nonnormally distributed investments.

Chapter 5 also showed how, having determined the subjective risk of an investment or portfolio, each investor would trade off risk and return to determine the *desirability* of this investment. The best portfolio for each investor would be that which, of all available portfolios, has the highest desirability, which is equivalent to determining the portfolio with the highest *expected utility* or the best risk-adjusted performance.

Thus, armed with the techniques in Chapter 5, and given an "accurate" description of the distribution of returns for a number of assets, it would be possible to compute the desirability of all possible combinations of these assets and thereby both to produce an efficient frontier showing the lowest behavioral risk portfolio for any level of returns and also to pick the specific point on this frontier that best satisfied the investors' preferences for long-run risk and return.

But what Chapter 5 did not show us in any way was how to establish a reasonable joint distribution of asset returns that could be used as an input into the expected utility optimization. Our examples in Chapter 5 simply used estimates of expected risk and return derived from historic time series to illustrate the mechanics of the behavioral approach to trading off risk and return. It was left to Chapter 6 to examine various ways of arriving at a sensible forward-looking assessment of the joint distribution of future returns.

The challenge of Chapter 6 was to balance simplicity with accuracy. To reach this tradeoff effectively, we made some simplifying assumptions. First, we assumed a world where the joint distribution of returns until the next rebalancing period was Gaussian (i.e., had a normal distribution). This assumption was made considerably more plausible by our use of short-term rebalancing horizons, where the asset universe could largely be characterized as being entirely *within* a single *regime* and so did not as frequently experience the asymmetries and fat tails that arise from us crossing from one economic regime to another. Second, to a large extent, we measured differences in portfolio performance using a simpler method than assessing full preference satisfaction through the use of measures of desirability—instead, we relied more heavily on the traditional Sharpe ratio to determine whether our competing methodologies improved risk-adjusted performance. This was partly to maintain a separation between our development of methods to more accurately forecast the world of *investments* (the multiasset dynamics) and methods to combine these more accurately to satisfy the preferences of specific *investors* (the utility framework).[1]

Given these assumptions, Chapter 6 established that we could reap significant risk-adjusted performance improvements by using a program of more frequent estimation of the joint distribution of asset returns over shorter time horizons coupled with more frequent rebalancing to take advantage of the changes in the optimal portfolio this causes. Such a program recognizes the key point that in a context of time-switching pricing regimes, a stable long-term specification of asset returns simply does not exist and that trying to resort to such a through-the-cycle estimation results in the portfolio's being "right" only occasionally (much in the sense that a stopped clock is right twice per day) and poorly optimized through most of the cycle.

In this chapter we shall combine the dynamic rebalancing approach we identified in Chapter 6 with the full utility framework of Chapter 5. This will allow us to dynamically vary the optimal risk level for each investor at each rebalancing period rather than targeting an assumed constant risk level. This allows each investor to make maximal use of his risk budget at each point in time. In the process, we will also drop the assumption of Gaussian returns used in Chapter 6, which will allow us to better characterize the multivariate distribution during those more changeable periods when the world is shifting from one regime to the next.[2]

This chapter contains five sections. The second section describes the theoretical and practical benefits we should expect to see from combining the insights from Chapters 5 and 6 and makes clear what we are *not* trying to achieve by this. The third section illustrates the effect of this combined approach on the efficient frontier available to investors by examining two particular time periods in detail, combining the dynamic estimation approach with the exponential utility function to generate efficient frontiers for August 2010 (a benign period) and November 2008 (a recessionary period). The fourth section then extends this illustration by determining the optimal portfolios for different investors at these times and comparing their characteristics. The final section uses the full framework to track two alternative investment strategies from January 2001 to September 2010 as an illustration of a specific benefit of using the utility approach together with frequent rebalancing: the chance to dynamically vary the risk of the portfolio in an optimal way rather than exogenously imposing a target risk level.

The Expected Benefits of Combining the Behavioral and Dynamic Frameworks

Moving Beyond the Assumption of a Fixed Level of Risk

We should not necessarily expect further large increases in performance over and above those already achieved by the dynamic approach of Chapter 6. In a world with Gaussian returns, behavioral risk will be identical to standard deviation, and the efficient frontier will be identical for all investors regardless of their risk tolerance.

The main improvement that the utility approach of Chapter 5 brings us in the initially assumed Gaussian environment is to enable us to precisely determine the optimal point on this efficient frontier. In principle, this was also possible in Markowitz's mean variance model because we could use the quadratic utility function to describe the investor's indifference curve in risk/return space. However, since the quadratic function does not provide a good description of long-term stable preferences, it was never clear how this should be parameterized to reflect these preferences accurately. In practice, this element of the mean variance framework has been largely ignored. Instead, the approach we took in Chapter 6 was often the one followed: to fix a volatility target exogenously that we assumed to be an appropriate level of risk for a given investor (e.g., around 8 percent volatility for a moderately risk-tolerant investor) and then to optimize the portfolio to attain the highest possible return for this level of risk.

While this may give a portfolio that is in the right ballpark for the investor's optimal risk/return combination, it cannot be correct that a fixed level of risk (i.e., 8 percent volatility) is always the optimal level for any given investor regardless of the investment opportunities on offer. For example, if we find ourselves in a regime where the marginal expected return for taking additional risk is higher at all risk levels (i.e., the efficient frontier is steeper), then it must be reasonable for this investor to increase risk above 8 percent volatility because the rewards for taking risk are higher. Similarly, in a bad regime, where the marginal returns to risk-taking are poor, the same investor should optimally reduce risk levels. This can be seen by examining Figure 7.1.

This ability to use the behavioral utility framework to pick off an optimal risk/return *combination* rather than just an optimal return level for a given fixed amount of risk should provide some further performance uplift over and above the techniques of Chapter 6. Despite the fact that at any point in time the utility framework merely allows us to pick a more accurately optimal point on the

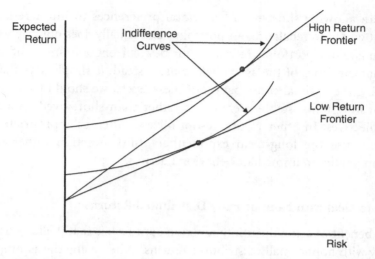

Figure 7.1 Optimal risk level (for the same investor) changes between regimes as the efficient frontier shifts.

same efficient frontier (with Gaussian returns), this can nonetheless add up to considerably greater benefits over time. It provides the investor with the flexibility to dynamically vary the risk of the portfolio optimally in response to the investment environment rather than require a constant volatility regardless of regime (as we assumed in Chapter 6). This is particularly valuable when combined with the dynamically changing estimates of expected risk and return used in Chapter 6: At each rebalancing period, the efficient frontier will change to reflect the current regime, and the utility approach allows us to pick off the optimal risk/return combination dynamically at each time rather than just fixating on a single static risk level.

Stable Long-Term Preferences Should Not Preclude Appropriate Rebalancing

At this point there may seem to some readers to be a contradiction in our attempt to bring together our conclusions from these two quite different branches of finance that we should address up front. In Chapter 5 we made much of the importance of ensuring that the utility function coded only the investor's stable long-term preferences over total wealth. And yet, with the move to dynamically changing assessments of the expected returns and dependency structure between assets, we may appear to be advocating a short-term view. In fact, there is no inconsistency here. The need to focus on long-term preferences and objectives rather than allowing short-term behavioral preferences to interfere need not imply that we fail to rebalance our portfolios and equally does not imply that we do not update our portfolios to reflect our best current assessment of the risk/ return characteristics of the assets before us. Instead, it simply says that when determining the optimal combination of these assets, we should focus on satisfaction of long-term, stable preferences rather than short-lived, emotionally driven objectives. In other words, re-optimize as often as appropriate, but at every point use the long-term exponential utility function rather than be tempted to pander to immediate behavioral desires.

Capacity to Deal with Nonnormally Distributed Returns

The final benefit of using the utility function approach is that it allows us to deal effectively with nonnormally distributed returns. When using the assumption of a stable, through-the-cycle distribution and high-level asset classes, the deviations from normality may be slight, and we gain little from moving to the exponential utility approach. However, with frequent dynamic updating of the expected returns distribution over shorter time periods, we would expect greater deviations from the normal distribution. Even then, in those times when the economic environment finds itself securely within a single regime, it may be the case that expected risks and returns can be fairly well expressed using a multivariate Gaussian distribution. However, when the world is shifting between regimes, this fit could be considerably poorer, with the "true" distribution exhibiting significant fat tails and skewness. In addition, although we have used high-level asset classes represented by diversified indices, which tend not to display large deviations from normality, as we showed in Chapter 5, the use of derivatives can cause behavioral variance to deviate substantially from variance. This framework thus allows us to incorporate asymmetric, synthetic, and other highly nonnormal distributions.

In Chapter 6 we showed that using dynamic rebalancing adds to performance, even when we constrain the joint distribution of expected returns to be Gaussian. To the extent that this assumption is a poor representation of "true" expectations we should be able to eke out some further improvement to the investor's risk/return tradeoff at each point, particularly in periods of transition between regimes. There is a vast range of sophisticated techniques that can be deployed to try to attain ever more accurate assessments of the multivariate distribution of expected returns. We discussed some of these that come from the field of machine learning in Chapter 6. Clearly, the better our assessment of the future risk and return at any point, the better the optimal expected utility

portfolio will reflect reality. However, in the mean variance framework, much of
the value of these methods is lost because "risk" reduces to just variance.

Using Student's *t* Distribution Is One Possible Approach

It is not our intention here to examine these techniques but rather to show how
use of the exponential utility framework permits nonnormal returns distributions to be fully utilized in the optimization. In this chapter we shall relax the
normality assumption somewhat by employing a fit using Student's *t* distribution in addition to relying on the regime-switching dynamics. While this does
not permit any exploration of the direct effects of skewness,[3] it does allow for a
measurement of fat tails at each time period (typically captured by kurtosis,
which is well represented by Student's *t* distributions) and thus drives a wedge
between the standard assumption of risk as variance and the behavioral variance
measure we introduced in Chapter 5. This will allow us to examine how all the
components of the framework work together, even though more sophisticated
multivariate assessment methodologies may extract even more "juice" than we
demonstrate here.

The detailed manner of how we estimate Student's *t* multivariate distribution of asset returns is reported in the Appendix. Our chosen approach has been
to use an estimation process as close as possible to the Gaussian approach presented in Chapter 6 in order to offer reasonable comparability. Our aim in using
it here is simply to provide a practical example of the combined framework
using a plausible distribution that permits illustration of how non-Gaussian
components can be dealt with consistently by the framework.

The Efficient Frontier Can Change Quickly during Periods of Regime Change

An implication of continual dynamic updating of the assessments of expected
risk, return, and the dependency between assets from Chapter 6 is that the efficient frontier will evolve over time to reflect the current regime. In times of relative stability, this evolution should be fairly minimal because risk and return
estimates remain stable from one period to the next. However, when comparing
different regimes, the efficient frontier may be quite different, and these shifts
could happen fairly rapidly in periods of transition between regimes.

Throughout this chapter we will use two models to fit the data at each period to a multivariate distribution. The first is simply the dynamic Gaussian

model of Chapter 6, whereby at each period we have both a vector of expected returns and a covariance matrix. This allows us to vary expected asset correlations, volatility, and returns over time but not to consider any expectations of fat tails. The second will be a dynamic multivariate *t* distribution that permits fat tails; we have, at each point, a vector of expected returns, a covariance matrix derived directly from the Gaussian estimation, and an estimate of the degrees of freedom. To simplify the exposition, we consider only two different degrees of freedom ($v = 3.5$ and $v = 5$) corresponding to two different regimes, both exhibiting fatter tails relative to the Gaussian, but in the former (corresponding to recessionary periods), the chance of extreme movements is particularly pronounced.[4] In the latter, the environment is more benign.[5] The methodology by which we estimate the multivariate *t* distribution is provided in Appendix 7A; here, we wish to focus on the effects these departures from the mean variance framework have on the efficient frontier and then the optimal portfolios and investor performance.

Efficient Frontiers during a Growth Period

First of all, let us examine the distributions and resulting efficient frontiers at a single recent point in time. To begin with, we have chosen a recent period, August 2010, when the estimates of risk and return for the next month were particularly benign.

Table 7.1 provides the estimated exponentially weighted moving average (EWMA) univariate monthly expected total log returns for each asset class and the covariance matrix under each of the two assessment methodologies.[6] At this time period, only commodities had a negative expected return. For the *t* distribution, the degrees of freedom for this period are 5. Note that the variance and covariance values are, in general, higher for the *t*-distribution fit, which would make them *appear* higher risk for the same returns in a mean variance world.

From each of these methods we can compute a number of similar efficient frontiers—one for the mean variance investor (assuming Markowitz's quadratic utility function) and three that represent the efficient frontier for each of the three exponential utility investors with varying degrees of risk tolerance ($T = 0.5, 1,$ and 1.5). To recap briefly from Chapter 5, the T parameter governs the degree of curvature of the exponential utility function and thus the degree of risk aversion of the investor. The higher the value of T, the more risk tolerant is the investor.[7]

Recall that the efficient frontier shows the constrained solutions to the portfolio-optimization problem at every possible risk or return level. That is, it

Table 7.1

EWMA Expected Returns and Covariance Matrices for Asset Classes in August 2010—Both Gaussian and Student's t Distribution

Aug 2010	CashTB	Gov Bond	IG Bond	HY Bond	Dev Equity	EM Equity	Commodities	Real Estate	Hedge Funds
EWMA mean	0.02%	0.67%	1.19%	1.64%	0.54%	1.57%	-0.31%	2.39%	0.43%
Variance/covariance (Gaussian)									
CashTB	0.000%	0.000%	0.000%	0.000%	0.000%	0.000%	0.000%	0.000%	0.000%
Gov bond	0.000%	0.016%	0.005%	-0.016%	-0.029%	-0.033%	-0.031%	-0.038%	-0.012%
IG bond	0.000%	0.005%	0.024%	0.033%	0.058%	0.057%	0.049%	0.044%	0.015%
HY bond	0.000%	-0.016%	0.033%	0.101%	0.175%	0.189%	0.151%	0.193%	0.051%
Dev equity	0.000%	-0.029%	0.058%	0.175%	0.451%	0.442%	0.374%	0.455%	0.114%
EM equity	0.000%	-0.033%	0.057%	0.189%	0.442%	0.476%	0.385%	0.460%	0.122%
Commodities	0.000%	-0.051%	0.049%	0.151%	0.374%	0.385%	0.512%	0.338%	0.107%
Real estate	0.000%	-0.038%	0.044%	0.193%	0.455%	0.460%	0.338%	0.754%	0.127%
Hedge funds	0.000%	-0.012%	0.015%	0.051%	0.114%	0.122%	0.107%	0.127%	0.036%
Variance/covariance (t distribution with $\nu = 5$)									
CashTB	0.000%	0.000%	0.000%	0.000%	0.000%	-0.001%	0.000%	-0.001%	0.000%
Gov bond	0.000%	0.027%	0.009%	-0.027%	-0.048%	-0.055%	-0.051%	-0.063%	-0.020%
IG bond	0.000%	0.009%	0.040%	0.055%	0.097%	0.095%	0.081%	0.073%	0.024%
HY bond	0.000%	-0.027%	0.055%	0.168%	0.291%	0.314%	0.252%	0.321%	0.086%
Dev equity	0.000%	-0.048%	0.097%	0.291%	0.752%	0.736%	0.623%	0.758%	0.190%
EM equity	-0.001%	-0.055%	0.095%	0.314%	0.736%	0.793%	0.642%	0.766%	0.203%
Commodities	0.000%	-0.051%	0.081%	0.252%	0.623%	0.642%	0.853%	0.564%	0.178%
Real estate	-0.001%	-0.063%	0.073%	0.321%	0.758%	0.766%	0.564%	1.257%	0.211%
Hedge funds	0.000%	-0.020%	0.024%	0.086%	0.190%	0.203%	0.178%	0.211%	0.060%

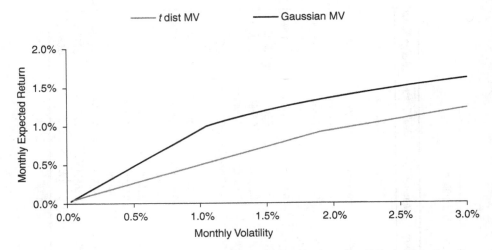

Figure 7.2 Mean variance efficient frontiers for August 2010 based on 10 years of historical data (Gaussian and t distribution).

shows the highest possible return for each level of risk, or alternatively, it shows the lowest possible risk that needs to be taken on to get any particular level of return. By definition, each point on the frontier has the greatest possible utility, or desirability, given the constraint. Figure 7.2 shows the mean variance efficient frontiers for both distribution assumptions.

Using the t-distribution fit, we appear to have a worse risk/return tradeoff, in that for each risk level the Gaussian curve would suggest that we can obtain higher expected returns. The t distribution may well be a more accurate expression of the future returns distribution, but an efficient frontier in mean and volatility space fails to make full use of this fit. To examine the risk/return efficient frontier using the complete distribution, we have to turn to the behavioral variance measure of Chapter 5, which incorporates all moments of the distribution.

Using the terminology of Chapter 5, the efficient frontier requires solving either

1. For all c,

    $\max \bar{r}$
    $s.t. \sigma_B = c$

    or

2. For all c,
    $\min \sigma_B$
    $s.t. \bar{r} = c$

where

$$\sigma_B^2 = \frac{T^2}{2} \ln E\left(e^{(2/T)(\bar{r}-r)}\right)$$

which depends on T. In the mean variance case, we simply have $\sigma_B = \sigma$.

For the Gaussian case, these four frontiers are identical because risk is completely captured by variance. For Student's t case, this will not quite be the case—recall that the behavioral risk measure incorporates the investor's preferences for all higher moments of the distribution and that the effect of these higher moments depends on the investor's degree of risk tolerance T:

$$\sigma_B^2 \approx \sigma^2\left(1 - \frac{2\sigma}{3T}\,\text{skew} + \frac{\sigma^2}{3T^2}\,\text{kurtosis}\right)$$

Using the t distribution means that our estimates do not display skewness, but they do display kurtosis, and this will have a greater affect on the risk of low-risk-tolerance investors (with $T = 0.5$). This means that each level of risk tolerance will have a slightly different efficient frontier, with the difference from the mean variance frontier being greater when the asset set contains fewer normally distributed assets.

Figure 7.3 shows that for high-level asset classes of this sort, in this relatively stable period, the effects of the fat tails of the t distribution are relatively slight.[8] Of course, if the investor had a quadratic utility function and therefore

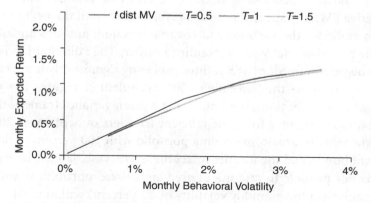

Figure 7.3 Student's t distribution efficient frontiers for August 2010 based on 10 years of historical data—mean variance and $T = 0.5$, 1, and 1.5.

cared only about the mean variance tradeoff and not fat tails, then the mean variance frontier in Figure 7.3 would be appropriate for all investors. However, since investors should, and do, care about fat tails when considering risks, we find that the true risk/return efficient frontiers are marginally different.

Note that although each investor has a slightly different efficient frontier, reflecting the degree to which he individually incorporates fat tails in his subjective risk measure, these differences are bound to be slight unless the assets are highly assymmetric and nonnormal. Although our asset classes exhibit kurtosis, the degree to which this changes the efficient frontier is useful but of secondary importance. The primary benefit of the utility approach is in determining *which point* on the frontier is optimal: Without a well-calibrated utility function that determines the optimal tradeoff between risk and return, the approach to selecting a single portfolio on the frontier is somewhat arbitrary and usually accomplished by exogenously selecting a target risk level. As we shall see below, our framework allows for a precise specification of the optimal risk level for each investor at each time.

The Efficient Frontiers during a Recessionary Period

To see the effect of the dynamic approach from Chapter 6, let us examine the same set of efficient frontiers at an alternative date, one at which the markets are in a quite different regime. We have chosen as an illustration November 2008, a few months into the financial crisis when our exponentially weighted approach provides expected distributions that are heavily influenced by negative events (Table 7.2).

In this environment, all asset classes except cash and government bonds have negative EWMA expected returns for the period until the next rebalancing period. In addition, the variance and covariance values are substantially larger than in the period of relative calm examined earlier. The *t* distribution is fit with the lower degrees of freedom of 3.5, thus displaying significantly fatter tails.

Figure 7.4 shows the November 2008 equivalent of Figure 7.2—with the Gaussian and *t* distributions, but both using a mean variance framework. These are dramatically different from the efficient frontiers of September 2010. The highest attainable returns come from a portfolio with 100 percent in developed government bonds, and the frontier mixes these with cash. Under these assumptions, it is not possible to attain a desired annualized portfolio volatility of 8 percent (equivalent to a monthly volatility of 2.3 percent) without using leverage to buy more government bonds. A conventional strategic asset allocation using through-the-cycle estimates of average returns and covariance would, by

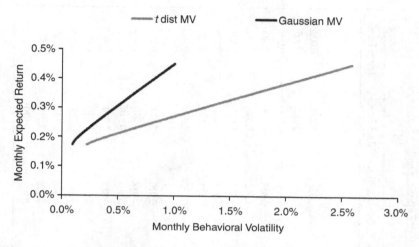

Figure 7.4 Mean variance efficient frontiers for November 2008 based on 10 years of historical data–Gaussian and *t* distribution.

contrast, still be allocating substantial amounts to equities to reach the volatility target. Also notable is the fact that the variance of government bonds estimated using the *t* distribution is substantially below that from the Gaussian.

Figure 7.5 shows the mean variance *t* distribution frontier and the three "personal" frontiers of each investor when using the *t* distribution, where there are slight differences owing to the fat tails.

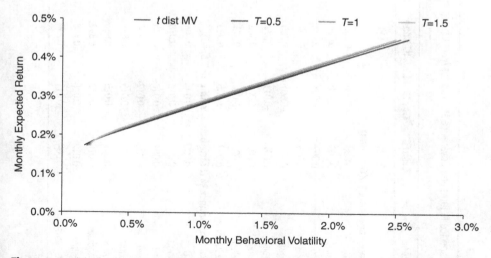

Figure 7.5 *t*-Distribution efficient frontiers for November 2008 based on 10 years of historical data–Mean Variance and *T* = 0.5, 1, and 1.5.

Table 7.2

EMMA Expected Returns and Covariance Matrices for Asset Classes in November 2008–Both Gaussian and Student's t Distribution

Nov 2008	CashTB	Gov Bond	IG Bond	HY Bond	Dev Equity	EM Equity	Commodities	Real Estate	Hedge Funds
EWMA mean	0.17%	0.45%	-2.12%	-3.93%	-6.62%	-8.66%	-6.13%	-6.21%	-2.14%
Variance/covariance % (Gaussian)									
CashTB	0.000	0.000	0.002	0.003	0.005	0.007	0.007	0.005	0.002
Gov bond	0.000	0.010	0.008	0.005	-0.007	-0.011	0.005	0.020	-0.005
IG bond	0.002	0.008	0.122	0.209	0.280	0.372	0.382	0.321	0.099
HY bond	0.003	0.005	0.209	0.440	0.578	0.781	0.807	0.848	0.189
Dev equity	0.005	-0.007	0.280	0.578	0.837	1.152	1.096	1.046	0.282
EM equity	0.007	-0.011	0.372	0.781	1.152	1.637	1.554	1.424	0.394
Commodities	0.007	0.005	0.382	0.807	1.096	1.554	1.972	1.431	0.398
Real estate	0.005	0.020	0.321	0.848	1.046	1.424	1.431	2.108	0.291
Hedge funds	0.002	-0.005	0.099	0.189	0.282	0.394	0.398	0.291	0.105
Variance/covariance % (t distribution with $\nu = 3.5$)									
CashTB	0.000	0.001	0.004	0.008	0.011	0.017	0.016	0.012	0.004
Gov bond	0.001	0.024	0.018	0.012	-0.015	-0.025	0.012	0.046	-0.011
IG bond	0.004	0.018	0.285	0.488	0.653	0.868	0.892	0.748	0.230
HY bond	0.008	0.012	0.488	1.026	1.350	1.822	1.883	1.978	0.441
Dev equity	0.011	-0.015	0.653	1.350	1.952	2.688	2.558	2.440	0.659
EM equity	0.017	-0.025	0.868	1.822	2.688	3.819	3.627	3.322	0.919
Commodities	0.016	0.012	0.892	1.883	2.558	3.627	4.602	3.338	0.929
Real estate	0.012	0.046	0.748	1.978	2.440	3.322	3.338	4.918	0.679
Hedge funds	0.004	-0.011	0.230	0.441	0.659	0.919	0.929	0.679	0.245

In this case of November 2008, the efficient frontier consists solely of combinations of two assets—developed government bonds and cash. Thus the highest attainable risk is given by the 100 percent allocation to bonds, shown by the top-right endpoint of each frontier. This endpoint thus shows the risk/return combination of a single asset class and enables us to see how this changes as we reflect risk using only volatility or as we use the three behavioral volatility measures for each level of T.

Determining the Optimal Portfolio

The Optimal Risk/Return Tradeoff in Mean Variance Theory and Practice

In theory, the optimal portfolio should be determined from the set of efficient portfolios by determining the single point on the frontier with the best risk/return tradeoff (or equivalently, the highest expected utility or highest desirability). Graphically, this is the point where the indifference curve in risk/return space is highest, which occurs where it is tangential with the efficient frontier. In the mean variance framework with quadratic utility, this indifference curve is defined by the equation

$$(\bar{r} - r_f) = \frac{\sigma^2}{\lambda} + I$$

where the left-hand side is expected excess returns (the value on the y axis of the risk/return diagram), λ is a risk-aversion parameter that governs the curvature of the utility function and thus the steepness of the indifference curve (higher values of λ mean greater risk tolerance and thus a flatter indifference curve), and I is the elevation of the indifference curve (the higher the better).

The optimal portfolio is found where this line is tangential to the efficient frontier (Figure 7.6). The trouble is that because quadratic utility was never a particularly plausible function for defining investors' risk/return preferences, it was never quite clear how to parameterize λ. As a result, practical uses of mean variance theory have frequently glossed over this element, preferring instead to impose a desired level of volatility exogenously for different levels of risk tolerance and then simply to choose the portfolio on the frontier with this level of risk. For a moderate- or balanced-risk portfolio, this level is typically defined at around 8 to 10 percent volatility. Over a long period of time, this may well be close to the average volatility level appropriate to a moderately risk-tolerant

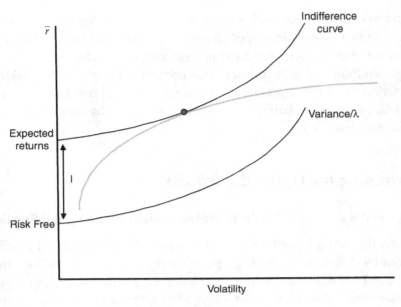

Figure 7.6 Quadratic utility indifference curve with efficient frontier.

investor, but in a world where we are attempting to optimize the portfolio dynamically to suit the current market environment, imposing a static target risk level is generally sub-optimally low because responding dynamically to regimes as they happen allows us to make more effective use of any given risk budget—which raises the expected benefits of risk-taking and thus the optimal level of risk.

Examining the mean variance efficient frontier for the two dates we looked at earlier, we see that fixing an annual EWMA volatility target of 8 percent[9] resulted in expected monthly returns in September 2010 of 2.31 percent (Figure 7.7).

In the crisis period of November 2008, it was not possible to attain this volatility level, and we would either have to leverage a single asset class substantially to attain this or settle for 100 percent government bonds (Figure 7.8).[10] This target volatility approach implies that instead of the optimal portfolio changing to reflect the changing environment, it is the investor's risk tolerance that changes to suit the "optimal" portfolio![11] Of course, it is possible that risk tolerance changes somewhat over time and that the optimal portfolio should adapt to accommodate this, but it is highly unlikely that this would ever occur in precisely such a way as to keep the optimal portfolio always at exactly 8 percent.[12]

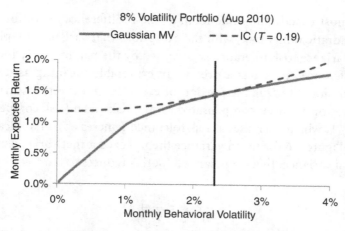

Figure 7.7 Mean variance efficient frontier (August 2010) and 8 percent target EWMA behavioral volatility portfolio and implied aggregate indifference curve (IC).

The Optimal Risk/Return Tradeoff in a Gaussian World

As noted earlier, even if we assume a Gaussian world, we can do better than simply impose an exogenous and somewhat arbitrary volatility target. In the exponential utility world of Chapter 5, the indifference curve that governs the tradeoff between risk and return is very similar to the mean variance one:

$$(\bar{r} - r_f) = \frac{\sigma_B^2}{T} + D$$

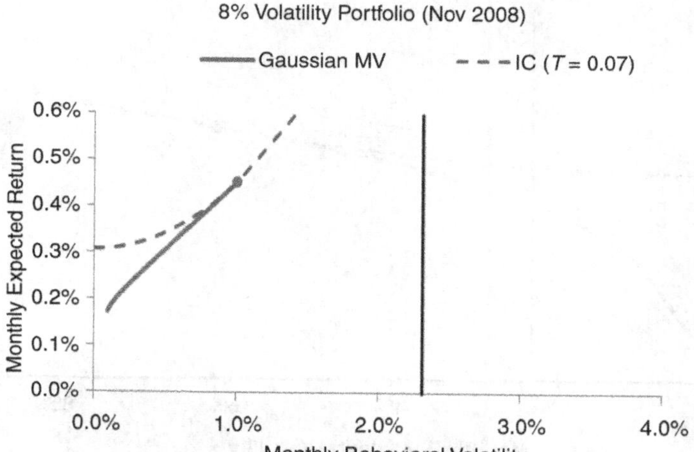

8% Volatility Portfolio (Nov 2008)

Gaussian MV   - - - IC (*T* = 0.07)

Figure 7.8 Mean variance efficient frontier (November 2010) and 8 percent target EWMA behavioral volatility portfolio and implied aggregate indifference curve (IC).

This has almost exactly the same form as the indifference curve for the mean variance quadratic utility case, with the exceptions that variance is replaced with behavioral variance, risk tolerance is governed by the parameter T, and the level of the indifference curve has a precise, interpretable meaning as desirability. Recall that desirability D is the portion of expected excess returns that remains once the investor has been compensated for the risk taken (risk compensation is the term σ_B^2/T, which decreases as risk tolerance T increases). Graphically, this is identical to Figure 7.6 for mean variance theory, except that variance is replaced by behavioral variance. In a Gaussian world, this reduces to

$$(\bar{r} - r_f) = \frac{\sigma^2}{T} + D$$

Since we are on firmer footing with regard to providing reasonable calibrations of T for long-term preferences over total wealth (see Chapter 5), we can employ this to pick off optimal portfolios for each of our three levels of investor risk tolerance. This is shown in Figures 7.9 and 7.10.

For September 2010, we see that each level of risk tolerance will pick the portfolio where the indifference curve is tangential to the efficient frontier, that is, the portfolio that optimizes expected utility or, equivalently, desirability. Notice in

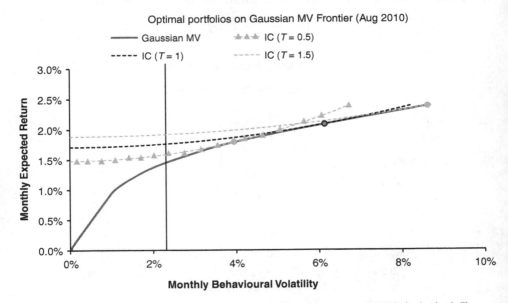

Figure 7.9 Mean variance efficient frontier (August 2010) with 8 percent target EWMA behavioral volatility portfolio and three optimal portfolios for investors with $T = 0.5$, 1, and 1.5.

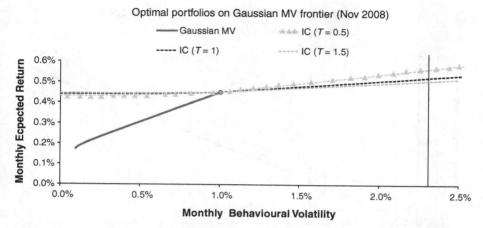

Figure 7.10 Mean variance efficient frontier (November 2008) with 8 percent target EWMA behavioral volatility portfolio and three optimal portfolios for investors with $T = 0.5$, 1, and 1.5.

particular that the portfolio chosen by the middle investor with $T = 1$ has monthly volatility of 6.1 percent (annual volatility of 21.2 percent), which is substantially higher than the constant 8 percent annual target. This may seem extremely risky for a moderate-risk investor, but recall that we deliberately selected this period because it represented a period of high expected returns. In this benign environment, when expected returns are high relative to risks, all investors should be taking more risk than usual rather than being stuck at an exogenously imposed constant level—in fact, even the low-risk-tolerant ($T = 0.5$) investor has an optimal portfolio with an annual volatility of 13.7 percent. This level will change optimally from period to period rather than being constrained by a constant target volatility that would be imposed without having the use of an appropriate indifference curve mapped to risk tolerance. Thus, even if we impose variance as a risk measure on the *assets* in our investment universe, the utility framework can still improve expected performance by choosing the right level of variance endogenously.

For November 2008, by contrast, it makes no difference which indifference curve we use. For long-only portfolios, they all choose the same one. Where we allow leverage, however, the indifference curves once again become valuable in determining how much leverage is optimal given the environment. Figure 7.11 is an illustration of this[13]—it captures the intuition that when investors can borrow freely in regimes in which low-risk assets will benefit from a flight to safety, then the rational response is to take on risk through leveraging these safe assets.

From these combinations of the efficient frontiers and indifference curves we can determine the expected risk and return, the proportion of returns that

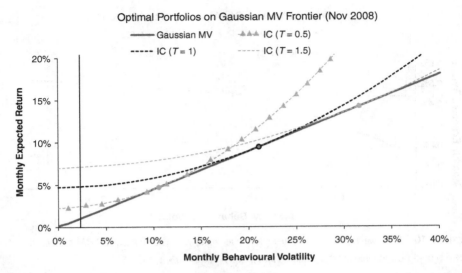

Figure 7.11 Mean variance efficient frontier (November 2008) with an 8 percent target EWMA behavioral volatility portfolio and three optimal portfolios for investors with $T = 0.5$, 1, and 1.5–leverage allowed.

each investor requires to compensate himself for taking the risk (risk compensation σ^2/T), and the proportion of returns that remains after this compensation (desirability $D = (\bar{r} - r_f) - \sigma^2/T$).

Tables 7.3 and 7.4 examine six cases demonstrating how the optimal portfolios may be characterized in terms of their expected risk and return, the

Table 7.3

Statistics Representing the Expected Performance of Optimal and Target Volatility–Efficient Portfolios in August 2010

August 2010 (Gaussian)	Risk-Free Rate	Expected Return	Behavioral Volatility (monthly)	Risk Compensation	Desirability	Sharpe Ratio
8% annualized volatility ($T = 0.5$)	0.01%	1.45%	2.31%	0.11%	1.34%	0.63
8% annualized volatility ($T = 1$)	0.01%	1.45%	2.31%	0.05%	1.39%	0.63
8% annualized volatility ($T = 1.5$)	0.01%	1.45%	2.31%	0.04%	1.41%	0.63
Optimal ($T = 0.5$)	0.01%	1.79%	3.95%	0.31%	1.47%	0.45
Optimal ($T = 1$)	0.01%	2.09%	6.13%	0.38%	1.70%	0.34
Optimal ($T = 1.5$)	0.01%	2.38%	8.62%	0.50%	1.87%	0.27

Table 7.4

Statistics Representing the Expected Performance of Optimal and Target Volatility–Efficient Portfolios in November 2008

November 2008 (Gaussian)	Risk-Free Rate	Expected Return	Behavioral Volatility (monthly)	Risk Compensation	Desirability	Sharpe Ratio
8% annualized volatility ($T = 0.5$)	0.02%	0.45%	1.00%	0.02%	0.41%	0.42
8% annualized volatility ($T = 1$)	0.02%	0.45%	1.00%	0.01%	0.42%	0.42
8% annualized volatility ($T = 1.5$)	0.02%	0.45%	1.00%	0.01%	0.42%	0.42
Optimal ($T = 0.5$)	0.02%	0.45%	1.00%	0.02%	0.41%	0.42
Optimal ($T = 1$)	0.02%	0.45%	1.00%	0.01%	0.42%	0.42
Optimal ($T = 1.5$)	0.02%	0.45%	1.00%	0.01%	0.42%	0.42

compensation required for this risk, and desirability. These figures will vary both according to the portfolio chosen and according to the risk tolerance of the investor evaluating the portfolio. The primary conclusion is that investors do better by choosing the optimal risk level in this period than by resorting to the static target risk level—the desirability is higher. We also show how the optimal portfolio may often be different from that with the highest Sharpe ratio.

The first three rows show the expected risk, expected return, risk compensation, and desirability of the 8 percent annual EWMA behavioral volatility target portfolio for each of the three investors ($T = 0.5$, 1, and 1.5). Since we are using completely normal distributions here, the expected risk and return will be the same for all three investors, but each will require different risk compensation and thus will perceive this portfolio to be differentially desirable.

The bottom three rows show the characteristics of the portfolio that each investor would optimally choose (although still under the constraint of Gaussian distributions). Here, each investor picks a different portfolio on the efficient frontier, and each is different from the portfolio with a target annual EWMA behavioral volatility of 8 percent.

From Table 7.3 we can observe some interesting features of the optimal portfolios in August 2010. First, although the 8 percent annual EWMA behavioral volatility portfolio has been designed to be appropriate on average for the $T = 1$ investor, we can see how it is viewed by each of the three investors. For each, the expected return and volatility, and thus the Sharpe ratio, are the same, but the more risk-tolerant investors require less compensation for this risk and so have higher desirability.

Even the $T = 0.5$ investor would prefer a slightly more risky portfolio than the target volatility portfolio (with monthly volatility of 3.95 percent rather than 2.31 percent) because the expected return is somewhat higher (1.79 percent rather than 1.45 percent). Interestingly, this portfolio has a lower Sharpe ratio than the target volatility portfolio, though higher desirability! The moderate ($T = 1$) investor would actually prefer a portfolio with a substantially worse Sharpe ratio. The $T = 1$ optimal portfolio has a Sharpe ratio of 0.34 rather than 0.63—which would cause many investors to assume that it has worse performance. For this investor, though, the higher risk is more than compensated for by the higher return, and this drop in Sharpe ratio actually raises desirability (and thus expected utility) from 1.39 to 1.70 percent.[14] This is so because the increase in expected return outweighs the increase in risk compensation (σ_B^2/T) for this investor.

For November 2008, the situation is as reflected in Figure 7.10: Because the expected returns on so many of the asset classes are negative, the highest risk point on the efficient frontier is that with 100 percent in government bonds. This means that all three optimal portfolios and the target risk portfolio are the same in every case.

The Optimal Risk/Return Tradeoff with *t* Distributions

Where we drop the restrictive assumption of normal distributions, we can use the full specification of the indifference curve

$$(\bar{r} - r_f) = \frac{\sigma_B^2}{T} + D$$

with the added proviso that the indifference curve for any particular value of T needs to be matched with the efficient frontier that is derived using the appropriate behavioral risk measure. This section will examine exactly the same optimal portfolios as earlier, but now with the t distribution. The results are not dissimilar from those earlier, although the ability to model nonnormality leads to different portfolios and a more accurate risk/return tradeoff. In particular, nonnormal distributions mean that the behavioral volatility of each asset is slightly different depending on the risk tolerance of each investor. Each investor faces his own efficient frontier, and thus even the 8 percent target volatility portfolios may be slightly different.

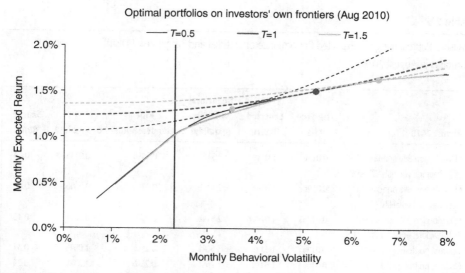

Figure 7.12   Risk/return *t*-distribution efficient frontier (August 2010) with 8 percent target risk portfolio and three optimal portfolios for investors with $T = 0.5$, 1, and 1.5.

In Figures 7.12 and 7.13, we see the equivalent charts on the *t* distributions to Figures 7.9 and 7.10 (for the Gaussian case). A key difference here is that in addition to having a different optimal risk/return tradeoff, as reflected in the indifference curve, the efficient frontiers themselves are slightly different owing to differential degrees of aversion to the fat tails of the *t* distribution (although

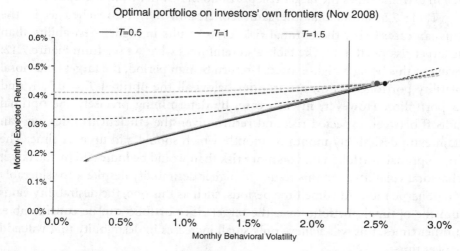

Figure 7.13   Risk/return *t*-distribution efficient frontier (November 2008) with 8 percent target risk portfolio and three optimal portfolios for investors with $T = 0.5$, 1, and 1.5.

Table 7.5

Statistics Representing the Expected Performance of Optimal and Target Risk *t*-Distribution–Efficient Portfolios in August 2010

August 2010	Risk-Free Rate	Expected Return	Behavioral Volatility (monthly)	Risk Compensation	Desirability	Sharpe Ratio
t-Distribution 8% annualized behavioral volatility (*T*=0.5)	0.01%	1.03%	2.31%	0.14%	0.91%	0.44
t-Distribution 8% annualized behavioral volatility (*T* = 1)	0.01%	1.03%	2.31%	0.07%	0.96%	0.45
t-Distribution 8% annualized behavioral volatility (*T* = 1.5)	0.01%	1.02%	2.31%	0.03%	0.98%	0.45
Optimal portfolio (*T* = 0.5)	0.01%	1.31%	3.50%	0.25%	1.05%	0.37
Optimal portfolio (*T* = 1)	0.01%	1.51%	5.25%	0.28%	1.23%	0.29
Optimal portfolio (*T* = 1.5)	0.01%	1.64%	6.56%	0.29%	1.35%	0.25

without introducing synthetic asymmetric assets, the differences are small). We now find that in the absence of leverage, although all three investors as in the Gaussian case select the same 100 percent government bond portfolio, with the *t*-distribution fit, this portfolio has somewhat higher risk than the target risk portfolio, which has 91 percent government bonds and 9 percent cash.[15] Thus even in extreme times the target risk portfolio may differ from the optimum.

Table 7.5 shows that the same conclusion may be reached as in the Gaussian case: Using the optimal risk levels results in higher desirability than the target risk portfolios. The table also reinforces what we see from Figure 7.12: Owing to this being a high-expected-return benign period, the target behavioral volatility portfolio lies on the frontier below all the optimal $T = 0.5$, 1, and 1.5 portfolios. However, in each case, by determining precisely the optimal tradeoff between expected risk and return given the efficient frontier, we can attain extra desirability month by month, which should add up over time. The $T = 1$ optimal portfolio takes on more risk than would be indicated by the target behavioral volatility, and this results in higher desirability despite a considerably lower Sharpe ratio. At some time periods, such as this one, the desirability gains from the optimal portfolio over the target risk portfolio can be considerable. At other times, this will achieve only small increases in desirability that will add up over time.

In November 2008, as with the Gaussian case, the optimal portfolio is identical in each case—100 percent government bonds. The only difference

Table 7.6

Statistics Representing the Expected Performance of Optimal and Target Risk *t*-Distribution–Efficient Portfolios in November 2008

November 2008	Risk-Free Rate	Expected Return	Behavioral Volatility (monthly)	Risk Compensation	Desirability	Sharpe Ratio
t-Distribution 8% annualized behavioral volatility ($T = 0.5$)	0.02%	0.42%	2.31%	0.107%	0.29%	0.17
t-Distribution 8% annualized behavioral volatility ($T = 1$)	0.02%	0.43%	2.31%	0.053%	0.35%	0.17
t-Distribution 8% annualized behavioral volatility ($T = 1.5$)	0.02%	0.43%	2.31%	0.036%	0.37%	0.17
Optimal portfolio ($T = 0.5$)	0.02%	0.45%	2.59%	0.134%	0.29%	0.16
Optimal portfolio ($T = 1$)	0.02%	0.45%	2.53%	0.064%	0.36%	0.16
Optimal portfolio ($T = 1.5$)	0.02%	0.45%	2.50%	0.042%	0.38%	0.16

from the Gaussian case is that because of the existence of fat tails, each investor will have a slightly different risk measure for the same asset. For the investor with the low risk tolerance ($T = 0.5$), the monthly behavioral volatility is 2.59 percent versus 2.50 percent for the high-risk-tolerant investor ($T = 1.5$). In addition, the higher the risk tolerance, the less compensation is required for the risk. This leads to small differences in desirability of the same asset. The target risk portfolios are not 100 percent government bonds but close to it (91 percent in the case of the $T = 1$ investor).

The *t* distribution allows us to consider fat tails and to use the behavioral volatility measure, so we do not need to restrict the efficient frontier to be mean variance–efficient. Instead of all portfolios being different selections from a single efficient frontier, each investor faces his own frontier (although these may be very similar in practice).

Comparing the Optimal Portfolios

Table 7.7 shows the composition of the optimal portfolio for eight of the portfolios examined earlier for September 2010: the optimal portfolio for each investor and the target (behavioral) volatility portfolios for both the Gaussian and the *t* distributions. The optimal Gaussian solutions for this period are simply a split between high-yield bonds and real estate, with the proportion of the latter rising

Table 7.1

Composition of Optimal and Target Risk Portfolios in August 2010

Optimal Asset Allocation (August 2010)	CashTB	Gov Bonds	IG Bonds	HY Bonds	Dev Equity	EM Equity	Commodities	Real Estate	Hedge Funds
Gaussian 8% annualized volatility	0.0%	0.0%	48.0%	48.4%	0.0%	0.0%	0.0%	3.6%	0.0%
Gaussian Optimal $T = 0.5$ investor	0.0%	0.0%	0.0%	80.1%	0.0%	0.0%	0.0%	19.9%	0.0%
Gaussian Optimal $T = 1$ investor	0.0%	0.0%	0.0%	40.5%	0.0%	0.0%	0.0%	59.5%	0.0%
Gaussian Optimal $T = 1.5$ investor	0.0%	0.0%	0.0%	1.0%	0.0%	0.0%	0.0%	99.0%	0.0%
t-Distribution 8% annualized behavioral volatility ($T = 1$)	0.0%	45.7%	37.9%	16.5%	0.0%	0.0%	0.0%	0.0%	0.0%
t-Distribution optimal portfolio ($T = 0.5$)	0.0%	0.0%	74.6%	25.4%	0.0%	0.0%	0.0%	0.0%	0.0%
t-Distribution optimal portfolio ($T = 1$)	0.0%	0.0%	29.6%	70.4%	0.0%	0.0%	0.0%	0.0%	0.0%
t-Distribution optimal portfolio ($T = 1.5$)	0.0%	0.0%	0.2%	99.8%	0.0%	0.0%	0.0%	0.0%	0.0%

from 19.9 to 99.0 percent as the level of risk increases. Being lower risk, the target risk portfolio favors an allocation to investment-grade credit.[16]

When using the t distribution, the solution changes considerably to reflect the implications of fat tails: Risks are acknowledged by the model to be higher than under Gaussian assumptions, and the relative risk/return tradeoff between asset classes changes because the covariance matrix is different. The target risk portfolio achieves greater safety by allocating 45.7 percent to government bonds—not an allocation that appears optimal for any of the three investors in this benign period. At this specific point in time, the portfolios appear quite undiversified, although the particular assets the methodology selects for will change over time.[17]

When we consider the traumatic period of November 2008, the portfolio composition is much less complex: In the absence of leverage, all portfolios allocated 100 percent to government bonds for optimal portfolios in this period and slightly under 100 percent for the target risk portfolios.

The analysis in this section shows how the optimal portfolios differ depending on whether we allow our expectations of future returns to follow a t distribution or a Gaussian distribution but more crucially on how we characterize the risk/return tradeoff of investors. We have seen that this can make a considerable difference to the chosen portfolio but have so far examined only two quite different time periods.

Portfolio Performance Over Time

Extending the Analysis Beyond Single-Month Comparisons

In what follows we will explore the dynamics of two portfolios over time to see the contribution of each to long-term performance. Using the t-distribution estimates, we will examine the dynamic portfolio distributions and performance over time. We should not necessarily expect a dramatic improvement in fit when moving from a Gaussian to a t distribution here because we are examining broad asset classes within short time periods that largely correspond to a single economic regime and do not deviate dramatically from normality.[18] However, since a key feature of the exponential framework is that it permits us to incorporate non-Gaussian assets with complete consistency, we feel that it is important to illustrate how the framework works using nonnormal distributions.

We have focused in this book on identifying a few features of the overall approach that should lead us to attain better realized performance, assuming that we have a good assessment of a dynamic regime-specific starting distribution with which to work. The idea is not, however, to make every effort to capture the most accurate representation of the joint dynamics of the joint behavior of the asset classes but to offer a sensible and tractable setup.[19]

The two portfolios are the *optimal portfolio* using the *t*-distribution fit for the middle investor with $T = 1$ and the *target risk portfolio*, which gives the optimal returns for a steady target level of risk (annualized EWMA behavioral volatility) of 8 percent[20] (again using the *t*-distribution fit). We will stick to long-only portfolios so that when an expected annualized behavioral volatility of 8 percent cannot be reached, we will simply use the highest-available-volatility portfolio.[21]

For each portfolio, we will examine a number of performance and outcome measures, adapting those used in Chapter 6 to evaluate the effectiveness of dynamic risk and return modeling.

Overall Portfolio Performance Characteristics Over a Given Time Period

What we see from the analysis that follows is that the benefits of using the optimal risk level from period to period are not restricted to the two specific months we examined earlier but to use of the approach over a long period of time. Relative to the constant target risk approach, the ability to pick the optimal risk levels dynamically over time results in greater long-term risk-adjusted performance (higher desirability). The optimal portfolios do result in higher risk levels over time, but this is more than compensated for by higher realized returns. That is, the optimal portfolios take more risk but use it substantially more efficiently to produce better risk-adjusted performance. We also find that the optimal portfolio performance displays lower kurtosis and less negative skew.

Let's first examine the overall characteristics of the realized performance of each portfolio over the whole period under examination, from January 2001 to September 2010. So far we have examined two specific months from this period in detail, but Table 7.8 shows how each portfolio approach fares over the whole period.

The first thing to note from this table is that the dynamically optimal portfolios do indeed attain a higher realized desirability over the entire period than the target risk portfolios—of 6.6 percent rather than 4.5 percent. By the definition of desirability, then, the distribution of realized returns from the optimal portfolios have a higher expected utility for investors with a long-term rational exponential utility function with risk tolerance of $T = 1$.[22]

Table 7.8

Realized Characteristics of *t*-Distribution $T = 1$ Optimal and Target Risk Portfolios—January 2001 to September 2010

t-Distribution Portfolios for Moderate-Risk-Tolerance $T = 1$ Investor	Target Risk Portfolio	Optimal Portfolio
Average annual total return	7.42%	10.90%
Average risk-free return	2.51%	2.51%
Average excess return	4.90%	8.39%
Annual realized volatility	6.06%	13.33%
Skewness	−1.36	−0.56
Kurtosis	7.04	1.82
Annual behavioral volatility	6.08%	13.37%
Average annual risk compensation	0.37%	1.79%
Average annual desirability	4.53%	6.60%
Sharpe ratio	0.86	0.65
Proportion of loss months	39%	38%
Maximum 1-month gain	4.76%, September 2007	10.20%, October 2007
Maximum 1-month loss	−8.97%, April 2004	−12.66%, April 2004
Maximum 12-month drawdown	−9.66%, April–July 2004	−14.96%, April–September 2004

Figure 7.14 shows the distribution of monthly returns for each approach. The increase in desirability comes from taking more risk (behavioral volatility of 13.4 percent versus 6.1 percent) but using this risk more effectively, concentrating risk-taking on the times when the economic environment means that it has the greatest likelihood of being rewarded. This results in the optimal portfolios having higher realized excess returns (8.4 percent versus 4.9 percent). The optimal portfolios have a much higher spread of realized monthly returns but also a significantly higher mean and a modal monthly return of around 2 percent. The target risk portfolios are not immune to substantial monthly losses (although this is less frequent, with only one extreme loss of 9.0 percent) but also have no monthly returns at all above 4.8 percent, and the vast majority (56 percent) of all monthly returns are around 0 to 1 percent.

For this level of risk tolerance ($T = 1$), the increase in risk is more than compensated for by the additional returns: The risk compensation increases

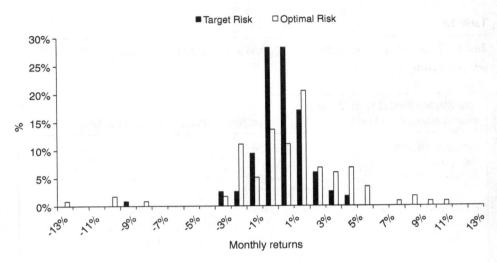

Figure 7.14 Distribution of monthly returns for each approach.

from 0.4 percent in the case of the target risk portfolios to 1.8 percent for the optimal portfolios. It is worth reiterating here the intuition of what risk compensation measures: It is the amount of returns that a given investor will require to precisely compensate for the risk of holding the asset—an asset with expected returns exactly equal to its risk compensation will have the same expected utility as the risk-free asset (and zero desirability). Desirability is the expected returns that are in excess of risk compensation and is maximized in optimization of expected utility.

We also note from Table 7.8 that the realized returns of both portfolios show negative skewness and positive kurtosis (fat tails) but that the returns of the optimal portfolios are significantly more normal in both regards. That said, even for the realized returns of the target risk portfolios, these deviations from the normal distribution are insufficient to increase the realized behavioral volatility for this $T = 1$ investor much from simple volatility (6.08 percent from 6.06 percent)—this is so because we're using only broadly diversified indices for which the deviations from the Gaussian distribution are relatively slight. This difference could be much larger if we were using asymmetric derivatives on these assets.

Here is an occasion where the Sharpe ratio would lead to an incorrect assessment of which of the two approaches has better risk-adjusted performance. The optimal portfolio approach leads to a lower Sharpe ratio (0.65) than the

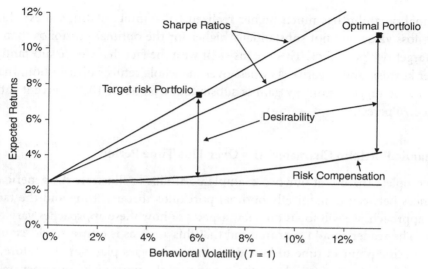

Figure 7.15 Sharpe ratio versus desirability for optimal and target risk *t*-distribution portfolios. Sharpe ratio is greater for target risk portfolios, but desirability is greater for optimal portfolios.

target risk portfolio approach (0.86). Figure 7.15 shows how this situation arises: The target risk portfolios realize a higher Sharpe ratio, but for the $T = 1$ investor, risk compensation rises with the increased risk by less than the realized returns increase.

Lastly, we examine some indicators of how comfortable the investment journey is with each of these two approaches. These, of course, should not feature in the decision making of a purely rational long-term investor—the risk/return preferences for this investor are completely captured by the risk/return tradeoff inherent in the desirability calculation—but as we will explore in more detail in Chapter 8, the investor's psychological ability to stick with the rational solution may depend heavily on how turbulent the journey is. Here we see that the probability of observing a loss in any given month is just below 40 percent in both cases—this is commensurate with what we observe in major equity indices. As we might have expected from its higher risk, the optimal portfolio program does require deeper psychological reserves: The maximum monthly loss is higher at −12.66 percent compared with −8.97 percent for the constant-behavioral-volatility portfolio (both in the same month), the greatest 12-month peak-to-trough drawdown is higher at −14.96 percent rather than −9.66 percent, and this drawdown lasted 6 months rather than 4 months. However, given that the optimal portfolio has much higher realized behavioral volatility, these short-term-loss values are not substantially higher for the optimal portfolios than for the target risk portfolios. This is consistent with the fact that we see substantially lower kurtosis and negative skewness over the whole returns distribution. In addition, the biggest monthly gain is substantially larger at 10.20 percent rather than 4.76 percent.[23]

Dynamic Portfolio Characteristics Over This Time Period

To complete the use of our two example portfolios to illustrate the generic differences between dynamically optimal portfolios through time and the target risk approach, we will focus on a few aspects of how these approaches vary over time. The reader should bear in mind that this analysis is only a single example at a specific point in time of how these methodologies play out. Therefore, we will not focus too intensively on the specifics of the portfolios but rather on the more revealing generic differences between them.

This shows that the risk levels of the optimal portfolios are consistently higher than the target risk level of 8 percent commonly imposed—the optimization, coupled with the dynamic estimations of risk and return, allows us to use each investor's risk budget more effectively and thus to benefit from taking more risk over time. We also show that the optimal combinations lead to greater desirability in the majority of years we examine in this example, although in two of the 10 years (2002 and, in particular, 2004), the increased risk levels were not compensated for adequately by realized returns. Finally, we show that the increase in both risk levels and realized returns comes both from the optimal portfolios holding more risky assets on average and from shifting them more responsively in and out of risky assets altogether from period to period.

Portfolio Risk Over This Time Period

We saw earlier that the optimal portfolios show substantially higher risk, on average, over the whole period. As a general point, the optimal risk levels for the optimal portfolios are always higher than the somewhat arbitrary level of 8 percent EWMA behavioral volatility that we imposed as an exogenous risk target in terms of both the targeted risk and the ex post realized risk. This is consistent with what we observed during our in-depth explorations of August 2010 and November 2008—in both cases, even the low-risk-tolerance ($T = 0.5$) optimal portfolio had anticipated risk levels of above 8 percent per year. The annual realized behavioral volatility levels for each year over the period of our example are

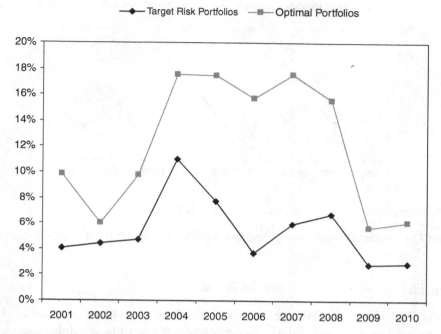

Figure 7.16 Realized (ex post/out-of-sample) behavioral volatility for both optimal and target risk portfolios over time.

shown in Figure 7.16. We see that the 8 percent target level is seldom reached in practice but also that the realized optimal levels are always higher than the realized target risk level.

The primary reason for this is that the level of 8 percent was set because it is around what is often used as a target risk level for moderate-risk portfolios in the world where we used long-term through-the-cycle estimates of expected risk and return. When we estimate these dynamically and adjust portfolios frequently to take account of the more regime-specific and thus precise estimates, we can use the expected risk/return tradeoff much more efficiently. Thus a level (say 8 percent) that is an appropriate risk/return tradeoff for an investor using long-term estimates may be highly inefficient for a more nimble investor able to respond effectively to the environment. More precision about the expected risk and return of the immediate future allows us to optimally take more risk along the journey. By contrast, if the optimization is performed using risk expectations that reflect the average over very long periods of time, with no secure basis on which to ground tactical rebalancing, then the expected risk/return balance at any date will be less beneficial, and the optimal risk level thus should be kept lower.

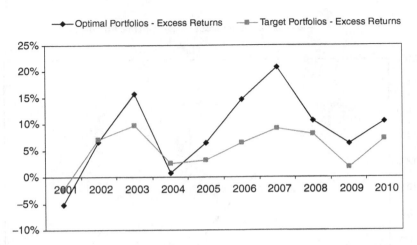

Figure 7.17   Realized (ex post/out-of-sample) average excess returns for optimal and target risk portfolios over time.

Portfolio Performance Over This Time Period

Figure 7.17 shows the average annual realized excess returns over time. Unsurprisingly, given its generally higher risk levels, the optimal portfolio approach outperforms the target risk approach in seven of 10 years but also shows greater variability in excess returns.

Although the optimal approach requires greater risk compensation (Figure 7.18), the average annual risk compensation required for these positions is

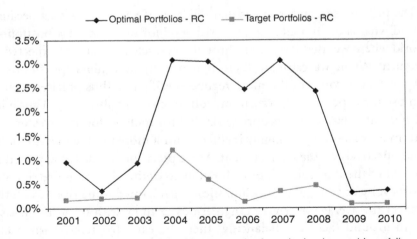

Figure 7.18   Realized (ex post/out-of-sample) risk compensation for optimal and target risk portfolios over time ($T = 1$ investor).

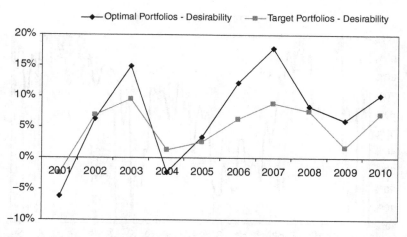

Figure 7.19 Realized (ex post/out-of-sample) desirability for optimal and target risk portfolios over time ($T = 1$ investor).

actually relatively small compared with the realized excess returns. Again, this is unsurprising because the point of the optimization is precisely to attain the greatest gap between excess returns and risk compensation. This gap, desirability, is shown in Figure 7.19.

As we can see from the combination of these charts, in most years, the risk taken is more than compensated for by the realized excess returns. In 2001, average returns of the optimal approach were an outright loss and so had negative desirability despite not having particularly high required risk compensation. In 2004, however, the realized excess returns, though positive, were outweighed by relatively high required risk compensation and so also posted negative desirability.

Portfolio Composition Over This Time Period

Both these portfolio-optimization approaches achieve their goal of high desirability by being highly responsive to the current economic environment and rebalancing to the new optimal portfolio composition every month. This enables the optimization to make maximal use of the most effective risk/return tradeoff every month.

As a simple comparison between the two approaches, in Figure 7.20 we examine the proportion of the total portfolio in cash, government bonds, and investment-grade credit over time. The target risk portfolios have, on average, two-thirds of the portfolio in these asset classes (66 percent), whereas the

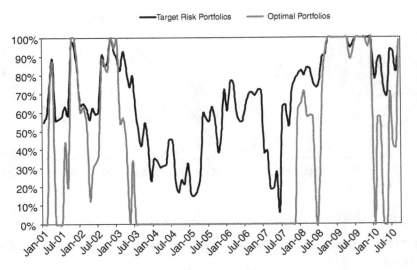

Figure 7.20 Proportion of target risk and optimal portfolios in safe assets ($T = 1$ investor).

optimal portfolios have only 34 percent. More important, the two approaches do not differ that much in recessionary periods, with both approaches approaching 100 percent in safe assets when required. But the optimal portfolios have less than 2 percent in safe assets in fully 54 percent of months over the whole period (as opposed to none for the target risk portfolios) and, in particular, benefit from a long patch between July 2003 and November 2007 when they are 100 percent in risky assets. This failed to pay off in 2004 but allowed the optimal approach to benefit substantially from this prolonged and stable benign period from 2005 to 2007.

Figures 7.21 and 7.22 show the average portfolio composition over the nine asset classes. The target risk portfolios are constrained by the need to keep risk levels constant and so show somewhat less dramatic asset shifts and greater diversification than the optimal portfolios. They also have particularly high allocations to cash and/or government bonds for long periods of time in order to keep expected risk sufficiently low.

The dynamically optimal portfolios, by contrast, have frequent allocations to only a single asset class and quite dramatic shifts between them. This lack of diversification at any time may be cause for concern, although, as we have seen, over the time period of the analysis it has served extremely well in terms of out-of-sample risk-adjusted performance. As we see from Figure 7.22, the allocations are using all asset classes (with the exception of hedge funds) in quite diversified proportions, but the diversification is largely happening over time rather than at each point in time.

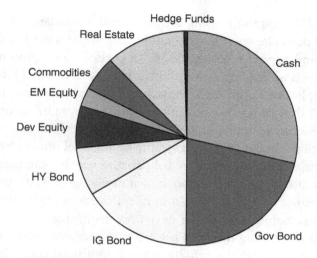

Figure 7.21 Average portfolio composition of target risk portfolio ($T = 1$ investor).

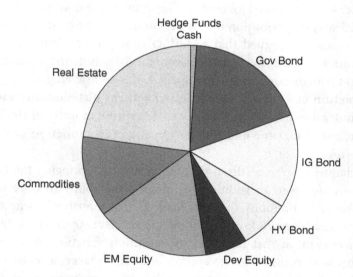

Figure 7.22 Average portfolio composition of optimal portfolio ($T = 1$ investor).

Conclusion

The methodology and approach are applicable to any set of assets regardless of the shape of the expected returns distributions.

This chapter has brought together the dynamic rebalancing framework of Chapter 6 with the utility-optimization approach of Chapter 5. Although we have illustrated the approach using the same nine-asset-class data set over the last decade as used elsewhere in this book, it is important to realize that the methodology and approach are applicable to portfolio allocation using *any* set of assets for which we can establish a multivariate distribution of future expected returns and applicable regardless of the shape of this returns distribution.

Chapter 5 showed how we can employ thinking from behavioral finance to improve the somewhat implausible risk/return tradeoff inherent in mean variance optimization. One of the features of the exponential utility framework with the most potential is the construction of a risk measure that can measure the risk of any returns distribution, no matter how non-Gaussian. With the nine high-level and diversified asset classes used in our illustration, this feature does not add considerable value because the deviations from normality are not sufficiently large to cause a big disparity between variance and behavioral variance. However, this does raise the possibility of using additional assets that are highly non-Gaussian by construction—in particular, options—and incorporating them into a rational portfolio-optimization model with complete consistency.

Chapter 6, by contrast, focused not on how to form an optimal portfolio given a multivariate distribution but rather on how to arrive at this distribution in the first place. We argued that a shifting economic environment required more dynamic and therefore precise assessments of this distribution than could be arrived at through using long-term through-the-cycle averages.
The combination of dynamic estimation or returns distributions and utility-driven optimization provide the ability to determine to optimal risk level relevant to each specific time and for the specific utility function of each individual investor.

This chapter combined the two components, thus bringing the benefits of each together. However, in addition to bringing the ability to cope with non-Gaussian returns distributions, the combination offers a further benefit: the ability within a dynamic framework to determine the risk level optimal for the specific distribution relevant at that time and for the utility function of the individual investor. This is in contrast to the approach generally taken to determining the optimal risk level, which is to fix a target risk level exogenously, regardless of the combinations of expected risk and return assumed to be available at that time.

We showed in this chapter how using dynamic risk and return estimates causes the efficient frontier to shift from period to period and (slightly) for the different levels of risk tolerance of different individuals as they place different degrees of importance on the higher moments of non-Gaussian distributions. We then demonstrated how the indifference curves in risk/return space implied by the individual utility functions may be used to pick off the optimal portfolios on these frontiers rather than simply accepting the efficient point at a constant risk level.

Additional risk taken on through this optimal approach should be more than compensated for by higher realized returns over time.

In the later sections of this chapter we used real data from the last decade on nine high-level asset classes to provide an illustrative example of the effects that this combined methodology may have in practice. We further employed a multivariate t distribution fitted dynamically at each period to make some use of the non-Gaussian aspects of the framework and computed the optimal portfolios assuming both a target annual risk level of 8 percent and dynamically optimal risk levels. All optimizations in the illustrative example were performed for an investor with moderate risk tolerance. This showed that there was indeed a considerable benefit to dynamically optimal risk targets: Over 10 years, the optimal portfolios achieve considerably greater realized returns than the target risk portfolios. To do so, they also consistently took on considerably more risk. This was perhaps unsurprising because the target risk level of 8 percent is one that is typically employed for average through-the-cycle methodologies—a dynamic approach should permit much more nimble and efficient use of the risk budget and thus generally higher optimal levels of risk. Most important, though, the additional risk taken on in the optimal approach was more than compensated for by the additional returns: The risk-compensated performance, or desirability, of the optimal portfolios was significantly higher for the moderate-risk-tolerance individual. **The dynamic approach and higher risk levels mean that funding liquidity is crucially important, as is psychological resilience to the investment journey.**

To conclude, it is worth reflecting briefly on two particular aspects of the resulting optimal portfolios. First, we only permitted long-only portfolios, with no leverage. Depending on the cost of credit, the models suggest that significantly greater long-term desirability could be achieved by employing leverage in benign periods (the average cash proportion in the optimal portfolios is only 0.9 percent). This would increase both expected risk and return but lead to better expected desirability—although it further raises the dangers of inaccurate expected multivariate returns distributions, as well as of ensuring that liquidity requirements are closely attended to.

Although it is a crucial consideration for *all* investing, the increased risk levels that follow from frequent dynamic expectations assessment and rebalancing mean that the importance of funding liquidity is even higher than normal. Although long-term performance is greatly improved, short-term losses and drawdowns can be significant, particularly when transitioning between regimes, and it will be essential not to have to withdraw funds at such times. We have kept to long-only portfolios in this analysis, but even then, investors will need to ensure that external cash-flow requirements are adequately met.

Finally, as important as financial liquidity is having the psychological resilience to withstand the same potential drawdowns along the journey—the dynamic approach requires considerable tenacity to follow effectively over time. This is something we'll discuss in much more detail in Chapter 8.

Appendix

ESTIMATION METHODOLOGY FOR PARAMETERS OF THE MULTIVARIATE STUDENT'S *t* DISTRIBUTION

In Chapter 6 we made the assumption that the difference between the ex post realized monthly return and the corresponding ex ante monthly EWMA estimated return would be normally distributed. If this were the case, then by capturing regimes through regular monthly reestimation of these EWMA returns, we should account for the fat-tail effects. Essentially, the fat tails we observe in the data series would then be due to the existence of multiple regimes in these series and caused by switches *between* these regimes. We should not expect to see fat tails in the EWMA estimates that occur *within* single regimes.

Table 7A.1 shows the first four moments of these differences between the estimated mean and realized returns. It is apparent that this assumption—that regimes are fully captured through a dynamic EWMA process—does not hold fully. The differences still exhibit skewness and kurtosis. In general, we should not be too worried about the skewness in the sense that it is always positive, rather low, and much lower than when looking at the skewness of these asset returns directly (Table 7A.2). However, the kurtosis clearly lies outside the

Table 7A.1

Moments of the difference between EWMA estimated and realized returns

	CashTB	Gov Bonds	IG Bonds	HY Bonds	Dev Equity	EM Equity	Commodities	Real Estate	Hedge Funds
Mean	0.0%	0.0%	0.0%	−0.1%	−0.1%	−0.3%	0.1%	0.0%	0.0%
Variance	0.0%	0.0%	0.0%	0.1%	0.3%	0.6%	0.6%	0.6%	0.0%
Skew	0.12	0.59	0.46	0.35	0.10	0.36	0.71	0.30	0.40
Kurtosis	−0.75	1.26	4.51	6.76	1.74	1.56	2.29	7.37	1.21

assumption of normality and looks particularly high for investment-grade bonds, high-yield bonds, and real estate.

To address this, as a second step, we fitted univariate Student's t distributions on these series resulting from the differences between ex ante EWMA estimated and realized returns. We then estimated the corresponding degrees of freedom (v). This allows us to account somewhat for the fat tails but here maintains the assumption of zero skewness of these series. In Table 7A.3 we display the results we obtained for v. As expected, the asset classes with the highest kurtosis of the realized differences are those with the lowest degrees of freedom.

At this stage, to preserve the principle of dynamic expected risk and return estimates identified in Chapter 6 as a key source of performance, we would like to estimate the degrees of freedom of the multivariate Student's t distribution corresponding to each time period while relying on the monthly EWMA covariance matrices estimated in Chapter 6. Unfortunately, it is not mathematically possible to draw simultaneously on the degrees of freedom extracted from the univariate series presented in Table 7A.2 and on these monthly EWMA covariance matrices. We therefore decided on a simple approximation that captures the spirit of different regimes but which is suitable for use in the

Table 7A.2

Moments of realized returns

	CashTB	Gov Bonds	IG Bonds	HY Bonds	Dev Equity	EM Equity	Commodities	Real Estate	Hedge Funds
Skew	0.40	−0.30	−1.41	−1.64	−1.02	−1.10	−0.89	−1.67	−1.05
Kurtosis	−1.19	1.26	6.21	8.60	2.57	2.85	2.44	7.84	2.50

Table 7A.3

Degrees of Freedom on the Difference Between the Estimated and Realized Returns for Each Asset Class

Cash	Gov Bonds	IG Bonds	HY Bonds	Dev Equity	EM Equity	Commodities	Real Estate	Hedge Funds
ν 6.24.E+06	5.23	2.83	1.74	3.77	5.50	5.96	2.33	7.56

A low degree of freedom means a departure from the Gaussian. (A degree of freedom above 5 begins to approximate "Gaussianity.")

illustrative example in this chapter—to differentiate the full period in two sub-periods based on the analysis undertaken in Chapter 6.

Considering the Gaussian optimizations over the nine asset classes of Chapter 6, we divided all periods between those when risky asset classes[24] constituted greater than 50 percent of the optimal portfolio and those whose share was under 50 percent. Each of these two periods could be said to correspond roughly to either a benign/growth or a recessionary regime. We then estimated different ν parameters separately for these growth periods (risky assets above 50 percent) and the recessionary periods (risky assets below 50 percent). In the first instance, the data were fit best by a parameter ν of around 5, which is not too far from normality. In the recessionary regime, we found a ν parameter of 3.5, which exhibits considerably more kurtosis.

In the final stage, these ν values were used in this chapter to fit a multivariate t distribution instead of a Gaussian distribution at every point. For this distribution, we employed (1) the EWMA Gaussian estimates of the mean, (2) the EWMA (Gaussian) covariance matrix adjusted to account for the shift between a Gaussian and a t distribution, and (3) the appropriate degrees of freedom depending on which of the two regimes the period has been assigned to. These fitted multivariate distributions thus use the same estimates of expected return as in the Gaussian model but allow for fat tails at each rebalancing period.

Notes

1. In addition, when assuming Gaussian returns, risk can be completely described by volatility (as used in the Sharpe ratio to represent risk), so a significantly higher Sharpe ratio will also result in higher desirability for most investors. We tested the performance uplift with both the Sharpe ratio and desirability and got the same results.

2. In Chapter 6 we noted that when targeting an exponentially weighted moving average (EWMA) volatility level of 8 percent, we implicitly target a historical volatility of around 10 percent, given the decay factor selected. This slight change does not change the substance of this paragraph, which is that, whatever the level, a fixed volatility target is bound to be suboptimal. However, in this chapter, on dropping the Gaussian assumption, we apply this target to behavioral volatility instead of volatility using the *t* distribution— our analysis shows that when using this combination, the realized behavioral volatility is actually lower than targeted. Thus, although use of the EWMA volatility may indicate that a higher target behavioral volatility of 10 percent should be used, in fact, the combination of this with the behavioral risk measure on the *t* distributions means that targeting 8 percent is approximately correct in practice on our data set.

3. What is, over long periods, measured as skewness is, however, taken care of to a large degree through the existence of multiple regimes. Skewness in this framework is largely an artifact of averaging expected distributions at multiple time periods rather than a feature of the expected returns distribution at any single point of time as is clear from looking at the Appendix.

4. An ideal fit would estimate the degrees of freedom dynamically over time, without having to restrict them to only two levels, and also to allow different degrees of freedom on each asset class at each point. The idea here is not to maximize complexity but to ensure tractability.

5. The choice of these two parameters has been obtained by a conditional estimation process. Periods in Chapter 6 during which risky assets represented more than 50 percent of all assets have been designated as a benign environment, and periods during which risky assets represented less than 50 percent of all assets have been designated recessionary periods.

6. Our methodology for arriving at the fitted *t* distributions ensures that the EWMA expected returns (in Appendix 7A) are the same as for the Gaussian—this enables us to have a more direct comparison of the two approaches than if the two distributions were fitted entirely independently. In addition, it ensures that when a fixed volatility target is defined, there is full comparability between the two approaches.

7. One could argue that by using an EWMA approach, we modify the dynamics of the assets somehow, which, in turn, could lead the investor to slightly underestimate the riskiness of the investment program. There is, however, no certainty here because we should keep in mind that the optimization process and the resulting moments of the realized performance are always

predicated on the ambitious assumption that the multivariate distribution of expected returns is a good description of the future.

8. It also shows us that the discrepancies that we could have expected through use of the EWMA technology are not material at this level of analysis.

9. Corresponding to a monthly volatility target of 2.3 percent.

10. For these analyses, we will assume a long-only portfolio. This will benefit the performance of the traditional approach relative to the utility-function approach because in periods such as November 2008 when returns are low and risks high, all approaches will pick the same corner solution portfolio. However, the same arguments hold a fortiori when the efficient frontiers are extended upward by allowing short cash positions. Here, the traditional approach will be forced to take high leverage to meet the 8 percent target, whereas the indifference curves of the utility approach will still pick a risk/return tradeoff appropriate to the time and the investor's utility function.

11. We can use the equation for the indifference curve to solve for the degree of curvature of the utility function, λ, which would make this combination optimal. For our two time periods this gives two different values of $\lambda = 0.19$ and $\lambda = 0.07$. However, note that due to the no-leverage constraint in November 2008 the "optimal" portfolio would be chosen by all investors with $\lambda \geq 0.07$, so the fact that this indifference curve is tangential only for highly risk-averse individuals is not, by itself, a requirement that risk tolerance changes from one period to the next. In a Gaussian world these levels of risk tolerance in the mean-variance framework exactly correspond to the degree of risk tolerance, T, which governs the curvature of the utility function.

12. And considerable evidence suggests that risk tolerance is, in fact, largely stable over time (e.g., Weber, Weber, and Nosic, 2010). Insofar as risk appetite changes from time to time, this is more due to changes in risk perception than risk tolerance—in other words, it is investors' perception of how risky assets are that forms their subjective efficient frontier that changes, not the indifference curve. These issues are discussed in more detail in Chapters 2 and 8.

13. Notwithstanding that it is somewhat unrealistic in that it assumes that significant leverage can be obtained at zero cost.

14. This improvement is lower than it could be owing to our restriction on leverage. If we permitted leverage, then the investor would be able to increase risk without so dramatically decreasing the Sharpe ratio, and this would lead to substantially higher desirability.

15. We will not examine the case with leverage again at this point. Very similar conclusions may be drawn as from the Gaussian case.

16. These allocations are at present driven exclusively by the model, and we have used the same asset classes throughout. Clearly, in this dynamic environment where our allocations are optimized only for the next period ahead, we may need to place restrictions on the magnitude of allocations to inherently more illiquid asset classes in particular. This is not something we tackle in this book, but it is worth bearing in mind that the quantitative results from the models must always be seen in the context of liquidity requirements and rebalancing costs.

17. In addition, we are here using a quite blunt, brute-force methodology for fitting the distributions using only historic data, without the inclusion of any subjective forward-looking views that could add further sophistication and diversification to the optimal solutions.

18. This is especially true using our simplified t-distribution fits, which allow for only two different values of the degrees of freedom that are applied to all asset classes simultaneously.

19. There are many thorough explorations of the various technical approaches to obtaining the most accurate multivariate estimations of expected returns distributions. See, for example, McNeil, Frey, and Embrechts (2005).

20. Monthly behavioral volatility of 2.31 percent.

21. Although this reduces the effect of moving from the Gaussian to the t distribution. The difference is most marked in recessionary periods, where the lower degrees of freedom lead to fatter tails, and yet without leverage at such periods, all methods are likely to lead to an identical portfolio.

22. We may also note that the realized volatility in the target portfolio is below the 8 percent target, giving us confidence that the combination of volatility overshooting (through the EWMA technique) and volatility undershooting (through adoption of the t distribution and the behavioral risk measure) compensate each other and result in a slight volatility undershooting in the portfolio.

23. By *skittish*, we refer to short-term behavioral responses to the investment journey, not to general risk tolerance. Differences in long-term risk tolerance should be reflected in changes in the optimal portfolios themselves using different values of T.

24. High-yield bonds, developed equity, emerging-market equity, commodities, real estate, and hedge funds.

Chapter 8

PORTFOLIO OPTIMIZATION FOR THE ANXIOUS INVESTOR

The last few chapters have all been about how we should structure the best portfolio for an investor who wishes to trade off risk and return optimally so as to meet his long-term preferences. In Chapters 5 and 7 we developed both a risk measure and a risk/return tradeoff function under the assumption that we could use a utility function to represent the cleaned long-term "rational" preferences of an investor with a specific degree of stable risk tolerance. In Chapter 6 we described how a dynamic rebalancing of portfolios should deliver a sequence of risk/return optimal portfolios given the information we have at any point in time and result in improved long-term performance.

In so doing, we deliberately excluded two categories of observed *behavioral* tendencies: decision-making errors or biases and decision making based on unstable short-term preferences.

The first of these categories—decision-making errors or biases—we would always wish to exclude from consideration when building a portfolio because they necessarily lead to poor decision making over time. But we excluded the second category—decision making based on unstable short-term preferences—because, on the face of it, it makes little sense for investors to seek to pursue long-term investment goals by optimizing utility that reflects behavioral responses to their current frame and reference point.

282 • Behavioral Investment Management

However, although investors can ignore these short-term behavioral effects in their formal model of what an investor should do, in reality, these perceptions and short-term behavioral responses *will* affect them, no matter how determined they are to focus exclusively on long-term framing-free objectives. In fact, an investor's short-term behavioral preferences will start to interfere at the first hurdle of implementing a portfolio. Figuring out what an optimal portfolio for her long-term preferences looks like is only a small (yet difficult) part of actually achieving the best possible risk-adjusted returns over the long term. Thereafter, the investor has to be able to stick with the investment program and maintain this portfolio over long periods of time while being constantly beset with interim investment successes and failures that can lead to innate behavioral responses.

We therefore need to refine the portfolio-optimization approach we have developed so far, which ignores all these behavioral responses and short-term preferences and assumes that the investor is able to robotically implement the normative portfolio. This is so because we know that no matter how perfect his portfolio is, an investor can easily throw away a substantial amount of this performance through his emotionally driven and short-term behavioral responses.

This chapter will therefore extend the utility model of Chapter 5 to account for some of the more universally observed behavioral deviations from purely rational long-term frame-invariant preferences. In particular, we will explore how we can examine the effect of these on the desirability of investments (a concept first discussed in Chapter 5) and look at some of the more common ways that such behavioral features might cause us to want to deviate from the optimal portfolios outlined in previous chapters. We will also explore some of the strategies we might use to try to overcome those behavioral effects that cause difficulties in either implementing or sticking with a portfolio optimized for our long-term rational preferences.

Modeling Short-Term and Behavioral Preferences

All the optimization analyses of Chapter 7 used the exponential utility function on log asset returns to pick out the most desirable portfolio for investors who focus purely on their long-term preferences for risk and return. However, for the reasons outlined earlier, we need to examine the effect that short-term preferences have on the desirability of their optimal portfolios. In many cases, investors deviate from optimal investment choices because at the time of decision making, their short-term preferences make these investments seem considerably less desirable than they actually are. In this section we will use some aspects of the formal descriptive models of decision making to illustrate how these short-term behavioral preferences may be brought into our risk, return, and desirability framework while not ignoring investors' primary long-term preferences for achieving maximal utility from investing.

We have already incorporated one ubiquitous finding of behavioral science, which is that humans tend to view outcomes as gains and losses from a reference point: By modeling utility on *returns* instead of total wealth, we have provided a zero point dividing the possible outcomes into gains and losses. This gives us the ability to treat gains and losses differently—a key feature of descriptive decision models.

The exponential function that we have used until now implies that a very smooth and well-behaved utility function is applied directly to potential log returns:

$$u(r) = 1 - e^{-2r/T}$$

It is not reference-dependent; that is, the utility applied to outcomes decreases smoothly over the entire range, and there is nothing special about the zero point in how outcomes above and below are treated. So the position of the zero point has made little difference in our model until now. Indeed, in the last two chapters, for practical purposes, we have typically been working with our zero point at zero *excess returns* rather than total returns. Unless preferences are genuinely reference-dependent, this makes no difference to the desirability of the portfolios.

However, when we start to introduce reference-dependent preferences, the ability to treat gains and losses differently becomes very important. We saw in Chapter 2 that the most commonly used descriptive model of choice, *cumulative prospect theory* (CPT), treats gain and losses quite differently.

Adjusting the Utility Function

So how do we adjust our exponential utility function so that it incorporates behavioral features as well as the long-term risk/return preferences? The key here is to build such distortions directly into the utility model. We can do this simply by assuming that the long-term self is forced to make rational decisions not on the actual asset returns r but rather on *perceived* returns that are distorted by first passing the returns through a behavioral value function $v(r)$ that transforms actual outcomes according to features observed in descriptive contexts. Thus the long-term self, instead of being able to use $u(r) = 1 - e^{-2r/T}$ is unable to completely isolate the outcomes of their shorter-term psychological import and instead maximizes utility using asset returns distorted by behavioral biases: $u(r) = 1 - e^{-2v(r)/T}$. This reflects the separation we discussed in Chapter 2 of human decision making into two separate systems: the intuitive and the deliberative. The behavioral distortions encoded in $v(r)$ represent the functioning and preferences of the emotional/intuitive brain; and the utility function into which $v(r)$ is inserted reflects the functioning of the deliberative long-term preferences. The normative model is still fully functioning . . . but operates on descriptive inputs that are distorted by our short-term selves.

The strength of the distortion will depend on the individual and on the environment. In small-scale, immediate, isolated choices given to participants in psychology experiments where there is little attempt by the decision maker to suppress these effects in favor of long-term goals, the effects of framing and reference dependence may be quite strong, leading to the sort of descriptive features that formed part of prospect theory outlined in Chapter 2.

In environments where we are making large-scale, long-term decisions over total wealth, and where we attempt to control our reference-dependent behavioral responses, we would hope that our utility function would look more like the exponential function in Chapter 5, where $v(r) = r$. The reality, of course, probably usually is somewhere in the middle: The more the decision is immediate, small scale, and emotionally driven, the more the behavioral distortions come to dominate. Certainly, some individuals will be more affected by the short-term decision frame than others.

In principle, we could make $v(r)$ as complicated as our knowledge of individual behavioral distortions would allow, but we shall limit the discussion here to some simple illustrations of the effect of commonly observed features.[1]

Recall the prospect theory value function from Chapter 2 shown in Figure 8.1. The combination of our long- and short-term preferences tends to display these features for small experimental gambles. Typical features of

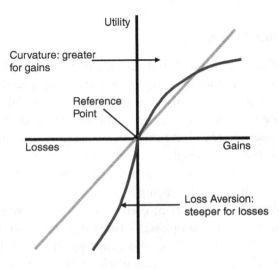

Figure 8.1 The CPT descriptive value function.

observed experimental choices are (1) risk aversion in the domain of gains, (2) risk-seeking in losses, but (3) less curvature in losses than gains (the function is more linear), and (4) loss aversion.

We have isolated idealized long-term preferences through the exponential utility function. But how do we now isolate the distortions in order to see the effects of long- versus short-term preferences separately? Let us start by imagining that short-term preferences distort the long-term rational exponential utility function in just one simple way—*that investors display diminishing sensitivity to outcomes away from their reference point.* Diminishing sensitivity is intuitive to explain—it is much easier to discern differences between outcomes close to your existing situation than it is between outcomes that are a long way from where you are currently. For example, it is relatively easy to perceive a difference between a gain of £0 versus £1, but the difference between £1,000 and £1,001 does not seem particularly significant. The same is true for losses: The difference between losing nothing and losing £1 is far more psychologically salient than the difference between losing £1,000 and losing £1,001.

We can model this very simply by $v(r) = sgn(r)|r|^c$. This is the same function used by Kahneman and Tversky (1979) in their prospect theory, except that we ignore loss-aversion, concentrating only on diminishing sensitivity away from the reference point. The parameter c governs the degree of diminishing sensitivity,[2] which we will assume is the same for both gains and losses. Note that when $c = 1$, $v(r)$ simplifies back to $v(r) = r$ (i.e., there are no short-term behavioral distortions). Figure 8.2 shows how $v(r)$ distorts the underlying returns before these are used to determine the optimal risk/return tradeoff through the exponential preference function. The straight line represents no behavioral distortion [$v(r) = r$], and the curved lines are $v(r)$ with $c = 0.85, 0.9$, and 0.95. In essence, the effect is to increase the influence of small gains and small losses relative to larger outcomes. Notice that this form displays the first two features of observed decisions described earlier: (1) risk aversion for gains and (2) risk-seeking for losses.

Let's now see what effect this distortion has on the rational exponential utility function. The distorted perceptions of returns $v(r) = sgn(r)|r|^c$ form *inputs* into the exponential function $u(r) = 1 - e^{-[2v(r)]/T}$. After combining the two equations, we can determine the utility function used by investors who wish to make sensible, rational long-term decisions but face short-term behavioral features that distort exponential utility to form somewhat different short-term behavioral preferences:

$$u(r) = 1 - e^{-(2/T)sgn(r)|r|^c}$$

Again, when $c = 1$, this simply collapses to the usual long-term exponential utility function, but with $c < 1$, the investor shows the behavioral feature of

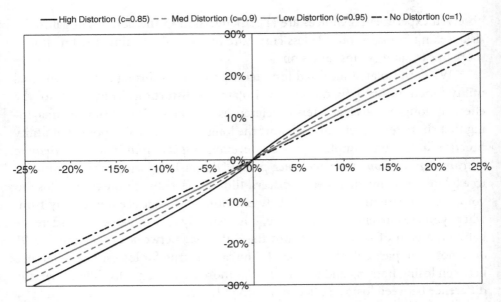

Figure 8.2 Short-term behavioral value functions $v(r)$ (with different values of c) transform actual potential returns (the straight line, which represents undistorted returns) into perceived returns as they are apprehended by investors who display diminishing sensitivity away from the reference point (the curved lines).

short-term diminishing sensitivity away from the reference point, which distorts long-term preferences.

Figure 8.3 shows this function for an investor with risk tolerance of $T = 0.5$—both the original exponential function (with $c = 1$) and the resulting de facto function that the investor might actually be using after accounting for behavioral distortions with $c = 0.85$. The exponential function is the universally smooth and concave function, whereas the distorted combined function results in outcomes having distorted utility values everywhere except at the reference point.

Above the reference point, the concavity of the exponential function is reinforced by diminishing sensitivity. The utility of small gains is accentuated relative to larger gains, and risk aversion is stronger. In losses, the effects of the behavioral distortion are particularly interesting. First, for small losses, we obtain precisely what is observed in laboratory studies with small gambles: risk-seeking behavior for losses (owing to the initial convexity of the distortion curve for negative returns). Second, for large losses, the global exponential function starts to dominate, and the function is once again risk-averse—we would not commonly expect to see investors exhibiting risk-seeking behavior in gambles that constituted a very large portion of their total wealth.

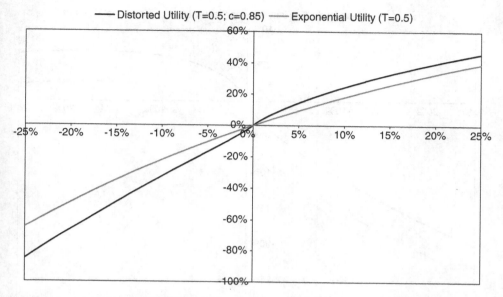

Figure 8.3 A rational exponential utility function is globally concave, smooth, and unaffected by the reference point at 0 percent. The distorted utility line shows the combined effect of rational exponential utility and short-term diminishing sensitivity away from the reference point. To arrive at the combined effect, the distorted perceived returns v(r) shown in Figure 8.2 form inputs into the exponential utility function instead of just using returns r, as a perfectly rational investor would.

Most interestingly, though, the fact that the behavioral distortions make small gains more positive and small losses more negative, combined with the exponentially increasing attention on the downside, actually leads to *loss aversion*. Note that we have not imposed loss aversion in the value function specifically.[3] Instead, loss aversion arises naturally as a combination of rational long-term risk-averse preferences and short-term psychophysical distortions owing to diminishing sensitivity. This raises the interesting speculation that what researchers have typically observed as loss aversion is in fact an artifact of our natural short-term behavioral responses combining with more rational and stable long-term risk aversion.

Thus the investor faced with short-term perceptions of possible outcomes will make investment decisions *as if* using the distorted utility function, even where long-term preferences are perfectly well behaved.

Introducing the Anxiety Measure

While these combined effects are interesting, what we really wish to achieve is to be able to separate the effects of rational responses to risk owing to long-term

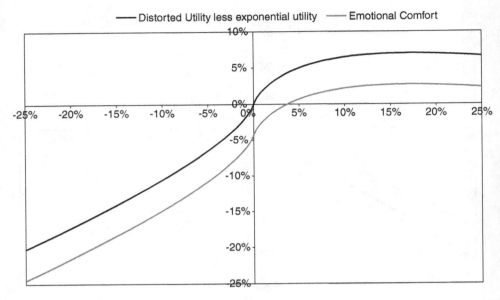

Figure 8.4 The effect of short-term distortions to exponential utility. The top line shows the difference between the distorted short-term utility function and the undistorted exponential function. The lower line shows a parallel downward shift of the upper line to reflect the contribution of each returns outcome to short-term anxiety—the downward shift is to ensure that the risk-free rate has a zero contribution to anxiety.

preferences from the behavioral effects. To this end, it is worth looking at one more graphic (Figure 8.4) showing the difference between the two functions. The top line isolates the effect due only to the interference of short-term preferences—we may think of this as being the contribution each level of returns makes to the *emotional comfort*, for, conversely, the *anxiety* of the investor. Returns where this line is positive will add to the behavioral investor's emotional comfort (or detract from anxiety), and returns where the line is negative will decrease emotional comfort (increase anxiety). The bottom of the two lines is lowered to ensure that the risk-free rate (3.7 percent) passes through zero—this normalizes the difference such that the risk-free rate shows zero anxiety. From this we see that anything below 3.7 percent increases anxiety relative to the risk-free asset but that it is those outcomes just below 0 percent where the contribution to anxiety increases fastest.

The behavioral distortion exaggerates the utility of both gains and losses, but the effect on gains is smaller (particularly so for large outcomes). The aversion to losses induced by these short-term perceptions is demonstrated by the fact that for losses, the difference between the distorted utility and exponential utility (and thus the contribution to anxiety) keeps increasing in size even for very large losses.

The effect of this distortion on the desirability of the investment naturally depends on the distribution of outcomes. In the same way as the risk measure is a result of the combination of the risk aversion of the utility function and the distribution of outcomes, we may think of these behavioral distortions as determining the short-term *anxiety* induced by the investment. In the Appendix to this chapter we show how this difference between the exponential utility function and the combined function can be used to calculate the anxiety of any investment such that we can now decompose total excess returns into three components: the compensation for risk (as before), the compensation required to cope with anxiety, and desirability. The formula for desirability when short-term behavioral distortions are accounted for by the anxiety measure is

$$D = (\bar{r} - r_f) - \frac{\sigma_B^2}{T} - A$$

Where there are no behavioral distortions, $A = 0$, so desirability is determined solely by expected risk and return as before. The anxiety measure then gives us a direct way of investigating the effect of short-term preferences and biases on the desirability of portfolios. The risk-free investment, by definition, has zero anxiety.[4] The general effect of anxiety is to decrease the desirability of investments relative to what they would have been if evaluated from a purely rational long-term perspective. This means that investors will turn down several investments that actually are beneficial for meeting their long-term preferences. In Figure 8.5 we see how the existence of short-term anxiety creates a zone of risk/return combinations that are falsely rejected by the investor—making that investor worse off in the long run.[5]

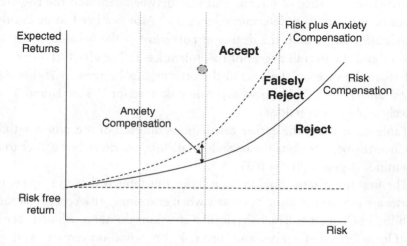

Figure 8.5 The impact of anxiety on biasing investment decisions.

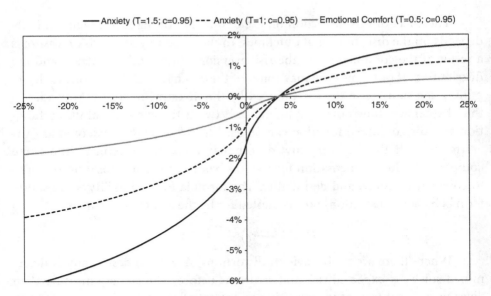

Figure 8.6 The combined effect of short-term distortion and long-term risk aversion on the measure of anxiety (increasing risk aversion leads to higher sensitivity to losses in the figure). All lines have $c = 0.95$ and varying values of $T = 0.5$, 1, and 1.5.

Measuring Anxiety across the Nine Asset Classes

We now return to the monthly asset class data we used in earlier chapters to give some precise values for anxiety. Because the shape of $v(r)$ is reference-dependent, it is important for us to work on total returns rather than excess returns: The slice of returns that falls between zero and the risk-free return can be important in determining anxiety.[6] Also, we need to be aware that anxiety is affected by both the degree of curvature of the behavioral distortion function c and the overall degree of risk tolerance T. The effect of different values of risk tolerance on the overall distortions can be seen in Figure 8.6 for $c = 0.95$ and $T = 0.5$ (the most extreme risk aversion), $T = 1$, and $T = 1.5$ (relatively slight risk aversions).

Table 8.1 extends the earlier calculations on each of the nine asset classes for an investor who exhibits the behavioral distortions described earlier to a relatively minor degree with $c = 0.95$.

The first important thing to note about this table is that the figures in the first rows are exactly the same as we saw when examining risk compensation and desirability in Chapter 5. The behavioral distortions do not at all affect the measures of long-term preferences, and thus risk compensation remains as it was. If we set $c = 1$, then the behavioral function would not distort returns at all, and

Table 8.1

Measuring Anxiety on Asset Classes

	Cash	Gov Bonds	IG Bonds	HY Bonds	Dev Equity	EM Equity	Commodities	Real Estate	Hedge Funds
Return	3.7%	6.7%	7.4%	8.7%	4.5%	10.2%	4.0%	11.9%	11.3%
Risk-free rate	3.7%	3.7%	3.7%	3.7%	3.7%	3.7%	3.7%	3.7%	3.7%
Standard deviation	0.6%	4.6%	5.4%	9.1%	17.8%	24.9%	22.0%	21.2%	7.1%
Risk compensation ($T = 0.5$)	0.0%	0.4%	0.6%	1.8%	6.7%	14.0%	10.2%	10.7%	1.0%
Risk compensation ($T = 1$)	0.0%	0.2%	0.3%	0.9%	3.2%	6.5%	4.9%	4.8%	0.5%
Risk compensation ($T = 1.5$)	0.0%	0.1%	0.2%	0.6%	2.1%	4.3%	3.3%	3.1%	0.3%
Desirability ($T = 0.5$)	0.0%	2.7%	3.2%	3.3%	-5.8%	-7.4%	-9.9%	-2.5%	6.6%
Desirability ($T = 1$)	0.0%	2.9%	3.5%	4.2%	-2.4%	0.0%	-4.6%	3.4%	7.1%
Desirability ($T = 1.5$)	0.0%	2.9%	3.6%	4.5%	-1.3%	2.3%	-2.9%	5.1%	7.3%
Anxiety ($T = 0.5$)	0.1%	-0.1%	-0.2%	-0.2%	2.1%	2.6%	3.0%	1.4%	-0.7%
Anxiety ($T = 1$)	0.1%	-0.2%	-0.3%	-0.5%	1.1%	0.8%	1.7%	0.1%	-0.9%
Anxiety ($T = 1.5$)	0.0%	-0.2%	-0.4%	-0.6%	0.8%	0.3%	1.3%	-0.3%	-1.0%
Anxiety-adjusted desirability ($T = 0.5$)	-0.1%	2.8%	3.4%	3.4%	-7.9%	-10.0%	-12.9%	-3.9%	7.3%
Anxiety-adjusted desirability ($T = 1$)	0.0%	3.1%	3.8%	4.7%	-3.5%	-0.8%	-6.3%	3.3%	8.0%
Anxiety-adjusted desirability ($T = 1.5$)	0.0%	3.2%	4.0%	5.0%	-2.1%	2.0%	-4.2%	5.4%	8.3%

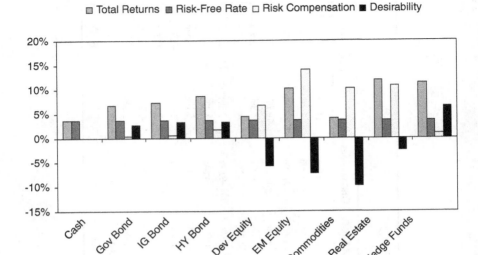

Figure 8.7 Decomposition of total returns of each asset class into risk-free rate, risk compensation, and desirability for investor with $T = 0.5$ and $c = 1$.

only the long-term rational preferences would be operational. In this case, anxiety would simply reduce to zero for all asset classes.

Figure 8.7 illustrates this situation, showing the decomposition of overall expected return into risk-free returns, risk compensation, and desirability for an investor with $T = 0.5$. This simply shows the situation for the rational investor discussed in Chapter 5.

Now examine the rows with the anxiety figures and Figure 8.8, which illustrates the effect of risk tolerance on anxiety for each asset class. The compensation required for anxiety is always greater for those who are also less risk tolerant (i.e., have lower T scores). Low risk tolerance accentuates the effect of anxiety, so behavioral distortions will have a more negative (or less positive) effect on those for whom the desirability of investments is already low because of compensation required for risk itself.

Compensation for anxiety does not always make the investment less favorable—in a number of cases, investing in some asset classes can *reduce* anxiety. Recall, however, that compensation for anxiety is *in addition* to the compensation required for risk. A negative value for anxiety means that the variability in asset returns is dispersed in a way that reference-dependent preferences distort in a positive way. In particular, referring back to Figure 8.6, we see that the distortion is positive for outcomes above the risk-free rate.

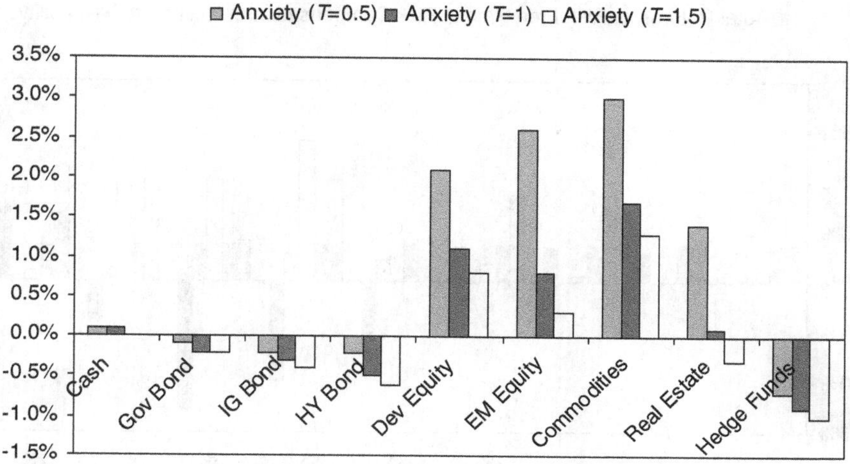

Figure 8.8 Compensation required for anxiety of investors with $c = 0.95$ and three levels of risk tolerance ($T = 0.5$, 1, and 1.5).

Investment-grade credit illustrates this. The asset class has an expected return of 7.4 percent with a relatively low standard deviation of 5.4 percent. This means that quite a substantial portion of the probability mass lies above the risk-free rate, falling into the zone where the behavioral distortion *adds* to desirability. The relatively small portion of probability mass below the risk-free rate does not extend very far below and thus does not incur the extreme anxiety of large negative returns. Thus, for this asset class, the net effect of the behavioral distortions is to make it appear better than it actually is for all three levels of risk tolerance. For a risk-averse investor ($T = 0.5$), this makes desirability look 0.2 percent better that it actually is; for a risk-tolerant investor, the behavioral distortion of 0.4 percent actually dominates the risk compensation of 0.2 percent.

All the bond asset classes, as well as the alternative trading strategies in the hedge fund index, share this characteristic of short-term distortions making the investments look better from the short-term perspective than they actually are for a long-term investor.

The opposite is true for equities and commodities: Here, some compensation is required to overcome anxiety, and the assets appear worse to a short-term behavioral investor than they do to the same investor who focuses exclusively on long-term objectives. Indeed, for commodities, anxiety reduces desirability by as much as 3 percent, and in the case of emerging-market equities for the middle ($T = 1$) investor (which had a desirability of exactly 0 percent), the anxiety

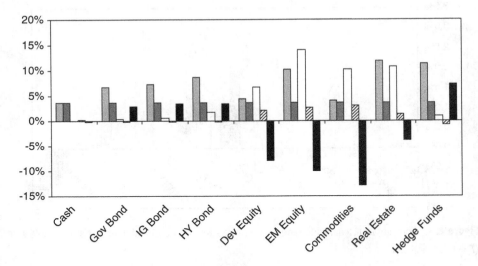

Figure 8.9 Decomposition of total returns of each asset class into risk-free rate, risk compensation, anxiety, and desirability for an investor with $T = 0.5$ and $c = 0.95$.

compensation of 0.8 percent pushes the asset into the reject zone of the risk/return chart. Finally, real estate is particularly interesting because behavioral distortions make the asset appear worse than it really is for low-risk-tolerance investors but actually make it look excessively good to risk-takers. These effects of anxiety on desirability are show in Figure 8.9.

Thus, even with a very simple version of the short-term behavioral distortions that reflects solely diminishing sensitivity to outcomes away from the reference point, we observe significant potential effects of anxiety on the perceived desirability of different investments. For investors whose short-term behavioral preferences were a larger component of their immediate decision making, these effects would be even stronger. In Table 8.2 is an equivalent table with $c = 0.9$, and Figure 8.10 shows the difference between the compensation for anxiety required by low-risk-tolerance ($T = 0.5$) investors with either $c = 0.9$ or $c = 0.95$. Notably, the effects of anxiety for many asset classes are much larger than for the more composed investor shown in Figure 8.8. For example, the compensation for the anxiety induced by commodities for a low-risk-tolerance investor ($T = 0.5$) is now 7 percent rather than 3 percent.

We can see the reason for this in Figure 8.11, which shows a comparison between the utility function distortion with $c = 0.95$ and $c = 0.9$ for the

Table 8.2

The Effect of a Higher Degree of Anxiety on the Adjusted Desirability of Asset Classes

	CashTB	Gov Bonds	IG Bonds	HY Bonds	Dev Equity	EM Equity	Commodities	Real Estate	Hedge Funds
Desirability 1	0.0%	2.7%	3.2%	3.3%	-5.8%	-7.4%	-9.9%	-2.5%	6.62%
Desirability 2	0.0%	2.9%	3.5%	4.2%	-2.4%	0.0%	-4.6%	3.4%	7.14%
Desirability 3	0.0%	2.9%	3.6%	4.5%	-1.3%	2.3%	-2.9%	5.1%	7.31%
Anxiety 1	0.1%	-0.1%	-0.3%	-0.2%	5.0%	6.0%	7.0%	3.5%	-1.3%
Anxiety 2	0.1%	-0.3%	-0.6%	-0.9%	2.7%	2.1%	4.0%	0.5%	-1.8%
Anxiety 3	0.1%	-0.4%	-0.7%	-1.1%	2.0%	0.8%	3.1%	-0.4%	-2.0%
Anxiety-adjusted desirability 1	-0.1%	2.7%	3.5%	3.4%	-10.8%	-13.4%	-16.9%	-6.0%	7.9%
Anxiety-adjusted desirability 2	-0.1%	3.2%	4.1%	5.1%	-5.1%	-2.0%	-8.6%	2.9%	8.9%
Anxiety-adjusted desirability 3	-0.1%	3.3%	4.3%	5.6%	-3.3%	1.4%	-6.0%	5.5%	9.3%

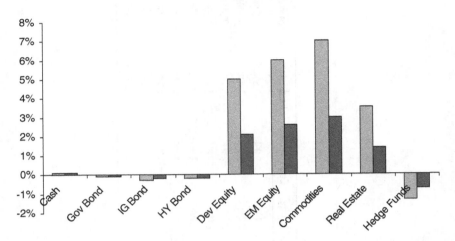

Figure 8.10 Compensation required for anxiety of investors with $T = 0.5$ and either $c = 0.90$ or $c = 0.95$.

low-risk-tolerance investor with $T = 0.5$. The latter shows much greater effects of short-term behavioral distortions.

Lastly, in Figure 8.12 we see the effect of these higher levels of anxiety (with $c = 0.9$) on desirability. This provides a direct comparison with Figure 8.9, where $c = 0.95$.

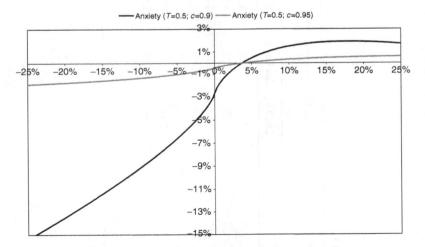

Figure 8.11 Higher anxiety leads to higher distortions of the utility function. In each line, $T = 1$, but the less sensitive line has $c = 0.95$, whereas the more sensitive line has stronger behavioral distortions with $c = 0.9$.

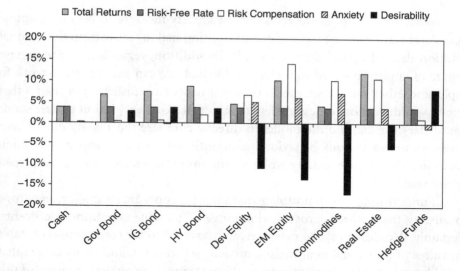

Figure 8.12 Decomposition of total returns of each asset class into risk-free rate, risk compensation, anxiety, and desirability for an investor with $T = 0.5$ and $c = 0.9$.

Instability of Behavioral Distortions Argues against Precise Calibration

It is not our intention in this chapter to provide or even argue for the validity of any particular calibration of c. The strength of short-term preferences certainly may vary from individual to individual depending on his degree of composure, of self-control, of experience, or the intensity of his emotional involvement with the short term. However, it could also vary strongly *within* an individual from moment to moment depending on all sorts of environmental and emotional factors. For example, we might expect greater degrees of behavioral distortion at times of stress or excitement. Or these effects may increase for particularly important decisions or perhaps for particularly unimportant decisions when the deliberative mind is not given the opportunity to override intuitive decision making because it's simply not worth the cognitive effort.

In short, unlike long-term global risk tolerance T, we do not believe that the behavioral distortions are stable from time to time or from situation to situation. In addition, we have used a fairly simple model of the behavioral distortions encoded in $v(r)$ that reflects only symmetric diminishing marginal sensitivity to returns away from the reference point—in reality, it may be possible to specify far more complex functional forms for $v(r)$ that are more accurate reflections of true behavioral distortions. Therefore, we do not wish to place too much weight on the precise values of c to be employed or on the anxiety values that emerge.

What we can do, however, is use the anxiety measure to help us examine how short-term preferences may distort decision making away from the rational solution desired by the short-term self. In addition, regardless of the precise degree of anxiety induced in a given individual, we can use this framework to explore whether some asset classes or investments have distribution shapes that reliably produce more or less anxiety than others. So, even without precise stable parameters, we can use the model to directly compare the anxiety of different investors under various behavioral assumptions—this can help us to design portfolios that reduce anxiety while having minimal effects on long-term risk/return tradeoffs.

Furthermore, we can postulate that some investors are naturally more prone to anxiety than others across a wide range of possible situations and events. Certainly, decades of psychometric research have led to the construction of stable measures of individual neuroticism, anxiety, self-control, and many others that could be reflected to a greater or lesser degree through an anxiety measure of this sort. In this case, we can use comparisons of the effect of anxiety on desirability of different degrees of curvature c to understand the way in which different investors may find their decision making distorted by short-term preferences.

Anxiety and Framing

How Avoiding Narrow Framing Lowers the Anxiety Measure

There are a few particularly important aspects of framing that the anxiety measure can help us to get a grip on. The first is the question of narrow framing in the portfolio—that is, the strong tendency to view investments one by one rather than together as a portfolio. We already know that this has negative effects on financial decision making, even before the introduction of behavioral distortions through $v(r)$: Failure to consider the big picture when combining assets causes us to ignore the quite significant value of diversification because combining assets causes the combined risks to be lower than a linear combination of the two. However, the existence of behavioral distortions gives us further reason to be concerned about this. Quite aside from the effect that combining assets has on reducing risk, if investors can rise above the tendency to monitor each asset individually, they can also considerably reduce the perceived anxiety from the portfolio.

This can be seen in Table 8.3, where we examine the anxiety of an equally weighted portfolio of the nine asset classes versus the simple average anxiety of the nine asset classes themselves. Although the return, risk-free rate, and risk compensation are the same regardless of whether viewed independently or not

Table 8.3

The Effect of Narrow Framing on Anxiety

Monthly, $c = 0.9$	Equally Weighted Portfolio	Average of Independent Asset Classes
Return	7.6%	7.6%
Risk-free rate	3.7%	3.7%
Risk compensation ($T = 0.5$)	1.6%	1.6%
Risk compensation ($T = 1$)	0.8%	0.8%
Risk compensation ($T = 1.5$)	0.5%	0.5%
Anxiety ($T = 0.5, c = 0.9$)	0.3%	2.2%
Anxiety ($T = 1, c = 0.9$)	−0.4%	0.6%
Anxiety ($T = 1.5, c = 0.9$)	−0.6%	0.2%
Desirability ($T = 0.5, c = 0.9$)	2.0%	0.1%
Desirability ($T = 1, c = 0.9$)	3.5%	2.5%
Desirability ($T = 1.5, c = 0.9$)	4.0%	3.3%

(combining them into a portfolio produces diversification benefits regardless of the framing), the difference in the required compensation for anxiety can be significant. Viewed at the detailed level of individual assets, on average, they all require compensation for anxiety—an average of 2.2 percent compensation is required for the lowest risk profile. If investors can take a broader frame, however, and focus only on the big picture of the portfolio as a whole, then the same collection of assets requires anxiety compensation of only 0.3 percent.

For investors with higher risk tolerance levels, observing the combined assets actually increases desirability relative to the optimum. In theory, this would itself be suboptimal because it would lead investors to take on slightly too much risk, but we've already seen that frequently the problem is the opposite: Too much anxiety leads to taking on too little risk, so a slight inducement in the opposite direction is unlikely to be too harmful at most periods.

Despite this, it is crucial to note that although combining assets into a portfolio will reduce the risk of that portfolio through diversification regardless of whether the investor perceives this to be the case or not, this is not true of the reduction of anxiety. Because anxiety is inherently about perception, behavioral responses, and framing, merely combining assets will not necessarily reduce anxiety—it is also necessary that investors overcome narrow framing and actually focus on the bigger picture rather than the returns of the individual assets or investments. In other words, having a diversified portfolio will do nothing to reduce anxiety if the investor still focuses on the details and tracks the investments line by line instead of concentrating only on the overall portfolio performance. This gives a sense of the effect the narrow framing can have on the perceived desirability of investments.

A Longer-Term Focus also Reduces the Anxiety Measure

In the preceding tables we have assumed that investors use monthly data as their frequency frame. For long-term (exponential) preferences, this will not make much difference, but as we saw in Chapter 2, myopia combined with loss aversion can cause investors to perceive the same investment quite differently. Since anxiety reflects the effects of such short-term preferences on the evaluation of the investment, we should see a significant difference in anxiety depending on the time horizon over which the investments are framed. In particular, we saw that the time horizon used to examine the distribution of outcomes considerably affects the proportion of outcomes that appear as a loss relative to the reference point rather than a gain. Since losses have a much greater effect on anxiety than gains, we should expect to see anxiety dropping off considerably as myopia decreases and investors focus more on the long term. Figure 8.13 shows how the annualized anxiety measure for developed-market equities changes as we consider longer and longer holding periods.[7]

Dealing with Investor Anxiety Over the Investment Journey

In addition to determining the appropriate portfolio, we also need to consider how best to manage it over an extended period. To do this, we need to

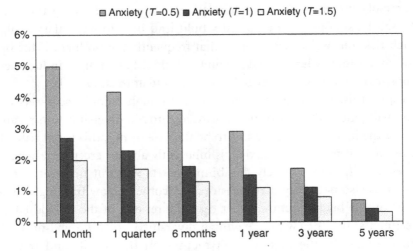

Figure 8.13 Anxiety measure for developed-market equities at different time frames ($c = 0.9$).

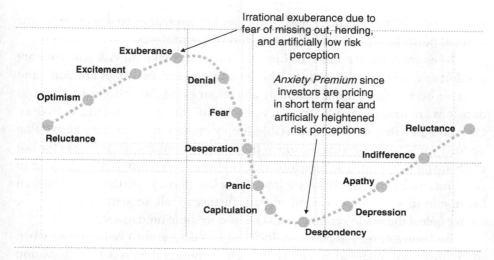

Figure 8.14 The cycle of market emotions.

understand something about how behavioral short-term preferences and perceptions may vary over time and how this can lead us to deviate from the most well-intentioned portfolio path. Having the emotional fortitude to *implement* an optimal portfolio solution is in many respects the easy part. Typically we take the time to think about and construct an optimal long-term portfolio in times of relative calm, when emotional and behavioral influences on our decisions are likely to be at their least intrusive. The difficult part is in maintaining the optimal portfolio over time.

Some version of Figure 8.14 is often brought into play whenever popular discussion turns to the role of emotions in driving investment decisions and therefore the investment cycle. As with so many well-intentioned and sensible discussions about the realities of investing, it seems to find the light of day most intensively shortly after crashes, substantial market drops, and financial crises, and then investors (and particularly the financial media) pay little attention to it thereafter. This is a pity because it would be much more useful as a warning on the way up.

In fact, this sort of description holds insights and warnings for us at every part of the cycle and is closely intertwined with how we behaviorally perceive the menu of investment options before us. The optimal portfolio we have already described should, with appropriate knowledge and insight about current market conditions, lead to the best portfolio at any point in the cycle. We've already seen how anxiety can make this difficult to implement—but the cycle of market emotions has very direct effects on the degree to which we are affected by anxiety in investment decision making, as well as on our very perceptions of expected return and risk. Both of these lead to very strong tendencies to deviate from the optimal portfolio over the market cycle in very harmful ways.

In essence, we are more inclined to invest and take on risk when we are comfortable, when anxiety is low. This could be so because times are calm, and we have been able to think rationally about our portfolio and ensure that our decisions are framed broadly enough to be in line with our long-term objectives. Or it could be that we feel comfortable simply because markets have been going up for a while, we're nearing the top of the cycle of emotions, memories of the last crash are far behind us and therefore anxiety is low, high recent returns look set to continue, and perceived risks are low. (This last point is particularly mistaken because in these conditions, markets have further to fall, so actual risks must be higher unless the world genuinely has changed in some fundamental way.[8])

By contrast, we are naturally inclined to safety and to reduce risks when we're uncomfortable—when anxiety is high. Although the preceding discussion shows that as a general rule narrow framing means that we usually have a certain degree of distorting anxiety to overcome, this typically becomes extreme when we're very focused on the short term, when we're concerned about the implications of every detailed piece of news, and when we're stressed and emotionally primed—in other words, after a market crash.

Unfortunately, our natural psychology therefore inclines us to procyclical investing: putting a greater share of our wealth at risk at the top of the market than at the bottom. This need not be as blatant as actually buying assets at higher prices than you sell them for it to accrue large hits to long-term performance—although in extreme conditions this certainly happens too. Simply, if we put a larger portion of our dollars into risky assets when we feel comfortable, toward the top of the market, than we do when we feel uncomfortable at the bottom, by definition our long-term performance will be worse than the average buy-and-hold performance of the same assets over the same period.

There have been a number of studies illustrating this effect,[9] but let us consider here only one recent study. Researchers at Cass Business School examined data on investors' performance in U.K. equity funds over the period from 1992 to 2009 and showed that investors, on average, have fared worse than the buy-and-hold performance of these funds by just under 1.2 percent per year. This is a substantial amount, particularly when you would hope that the capacity to judiciously time your investments would lead to *better*, not worse, performance than a static buy-and-hold strategy. It is also important to note that this is the *average*—some investors do fare much better, but then those who are more affected by short-term behavioral biases and anxiety will throw away considerably more. When we consider the effects of compounding this *investor behavior penalty* over the course of an investor's lifetime, the final effect on total wealth can be enormous.[10] Over just five years, this already amounts to a difference of over 7 percent in total wealth, and over the 18 years under analysis, it means an average loss of 20 percent of wealth.

Understanding the Psychological Sources of Shifting Emotions

To know how to combat these costly behavioral tendencies, we need to understand how they arise. We will now explore some of the ways that these shifts in emotions over time can be viewed within the utility framework we've already developed. Within our model, there are essentially five different moving parts that could shift over the course of the cycle to influence the decision making of investors.

Risk Tolerance Stability (T)

The most commonly used explanation for the dramatic shifts in risk-taking we observe over the economic cycle is also, unfortunately, the one least likely to be the correct explanation. We often read in the press after a particularly good or bad day in the markets that "risk tolerance has increased" or "risk tolerance has decreased."

Insofar as risk tolerance is taken to mean our long-term, stable psychological willingness to trade off risk and return, which in our model is reflected by the parameter T, this is highly unlikely to be true. It is true that substantial shifts in T over time would induce investors to take very different amounts of risk, but can this explain the procyclical behavior we observe? By its very definition, T is long term in nature and completely independent of short-term framing effects. We might expect our long-term preferences to shift gradually over time: we may become less risk tolerant as we become older, or we may become more risk tolerant as we gain knowledge and experience with investing and, perhaps, as our wealth increases (although the opposite can happen, too). We also may find some permanent shifts in long-term willingness to take on risk after being badly burned by investing—there is evidence that people's financial decision making continues to be affected over their whole lives by the economic conditions that prevailed when they were young.[11] But this will not provide an adequate explanation for the large short-term, cyclical fluctuations in risk-taking that we observe.

This was examined in detail in a recent study by academics in Mannheim, Germany, using data from a survey designed and run by the Barclays Wealth behavioral finance team. From September 2008 to September 2010, every three months a group of Barclays Stockbrokers' clients was monitored, tracking their attitudes toward risk, return, and investment as the financial crisis unfolded. This allowed the researchers to explore the extent to which financial behavior is driven by personality or by rational responses to the market.[12] The respondents were largely experienced investors who make their own investment decisions using the online Barclays Stockbrokers' trading platform. The time period over which the survey was run was particularly interesting because the first round by chance almost exactly coincided with the collapse of Lehman Brothers and the start of the financial crisis.

Among many other things, the investors were asked psychometric questions used to determine their level of long-run risk tolerance, and the same questions were used throughout the two years of the survey. These two years were some of the most turbulent in financial history, and *risk-taking intentions* shifted dramatically over the period. For example, responses to the question of how much of a hypothetical £100,000 the respondents said they were prepared to place at risk in the market (FTSE All-Share) for the next three months, with the remainder to be held in cash, shifted substantially from quarter to quarter. However, investors' responses to the psychometric measures of their long-term risk tolerance were almost entirely steady. We simply cannot explain investors' short-term shifts in risk-taking by shifts in their fundamental levels of risk tolerance. The latter are far too stable and deep seated to explain the former.

Figure 8.15 shows the percentage change in investors' (notional) allocation to the FTSE from one round to the next for the first five rounds of the survey. In all rounds, more than 50 percent of respondents shifted their allocations by

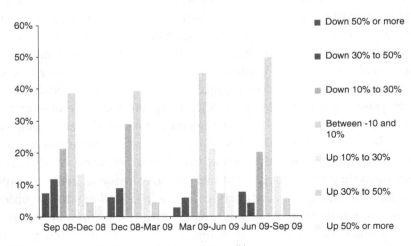

Figure 8.15   Investment intentions in turbulent market conditions.

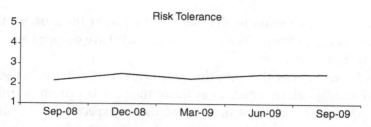

Figure 8.16 Evolution of the average risk tolerance of investors during the same period.

more than 10 percent from round to round. For example, between September and December 2008, 27 percent of respondents shifted their allocation by more than 30 percent up or down, a marked change in risk-taking that matched the dramatic shifts in the market that were occurring. Figure 8.16, on the other hand, shows the average response to a measure of psychological risk tolerance over the same period—it is remarkably stable in very extreme market conditions.

Changing Expectations of Returns and Risk

Thus, if these shifts cannot be ascribed to changes in risk tolerance, where do they come from? One factor could be changing expectations of risk and returns. No matter how objective we think we are, our expectations of future returns and risks are affected by the current environment and by the opinions and expectations of the media and friends and colleagues around us—and these tend to be highly cyclical. The study referred to earlier also asked for investors' expectations of returns and risks every quarter. Unlike the measures of risk tolerance, these did vary substantially over time, and these expectations were predictive of changes in risk-taking.[13] Investors increased risk, as expected, when subjective anticipated returns increased and reduced risk when anticipated market risks increased.

These are not changes to any aspect of the utility function used by investors, nor to long-term changes in risk tolerance, nor to the effect of short-term reference-dependent behavioral preferences. They are changes to investors' *beliefs*—to the anticipated shape of the returns distributions that are used as subjective inputs to the optimization. These changes thus will affect the investment decisions of investors even if their preferences and utility functions remain entirely unchanged. Of course, to some degree, these shifts in returns and risk expectations may be entirely rational and reflect the changing environment— this would lead to good tactical adjustments to the portfolio to take advantage of short- to medium-term shifts in market conditions. However, these perceptual changes are unlikely to be entirely rational and will rely to some extent on *momentum*—when we examine the risk expectations at the least, we find that they largely increase *after* periods where the markets have dropped and decrease when things have gotten better.

This is not to deny that intuitive judgments have validity, but without a systematic framework in which to evaluate them, it is extremely difficult to know to what degree changes in risk and return expectations are driven by changes in one's fundamental assumptions, by changes in the market environment given constant assumptions, or simply by emotional and perceptual responses to the recent past and the influences of media and peer opinions.

This is not a purely semantic issue. If our long-term risk tolerance changes, then it is absolutely the right answer for our portfolio to change as a result. If the investing environment changes, then it is also appropriate that our portfolios change in response, even if risk tolerance is unchanged. If, on the other hand, our changes in risk-taking are driven solely by temporary shifts in risk and returns expectations that are grounded in perceptual or emotional responses that are not supported by genuine shifts in information (as often appears to be the case), then the correct response is to correct our perceptions rather than change our portfolios.

Shifts in Anxiety

Another variable that could cause risk tolerance to vary over time is the force of behavioral distortions to long-term preferences themselves. We have already seen that anxiety can vary considerably as we vary the curvature of $v(x)$, the function that codes short-term behavioral distortions from long-term objectives, depending on the value of c.

While the degree of behavioral distortion may vary from investor to investor, it is also highly likely that the effects of short-term concerns, framing, and emotions vary considerably over time for any given individual. We are all familiar with times when particular decisions start to become emotionally charged for us. There are times when we're able to put aside any short-term worries and concerns and devote time and thought to achieving our long-term goals—at such times, we respond to decisions as though there were little or no behavioral distortion (with $c = 1$). At other times, framing, loss aversion, hope, and fear come to dominate, and we respond to decisions as though we're using a behavioral distortion function that is highly curved. Anxiety may vary from time to time . . . or even from decision to decision: Some decisions, particularly those relating to investments we've owned for some time or on which we've made previous gains or losses, are more emotionally charged than others.

In fact, anxiety is most likely to adversely affect our decision making at precisely the times when we'd most like to eliminate short-term distortions and respond rationally to our environment—in times of great excitement or stress or after recent large gains or losses. So variations over time in the extent to which our short-term selves come to impinge on our long-term objectives can be a key reason for the difficulties in keeping to a rational program of investing over time. The last section of this chapter will examine some of the techniques and strategies we may deploy to protect ourselves against our own desires in those future moments when anxiety comes to dominate our investing behavior.

Shifts in the Reference Point

We now need to face up to the final variable that could lead to shifts in risk-taking over the cycle. Until now, we have assumed that the reference point that divides psychological gains from losses when calculating compensation for anxiety is at a return of zero. For the most part, this assumption seems quite reasonable—if returns are negative, wealth has been reduced; if they are positive, wealth has increased.[14]

However, there are a number of aspects of the way we respond to past returns or the perceived performance of the markets or of friends and peers that could lead us to make decisions based on alternative reference points. Indeed, the way investment products are presented to investors by the industry is often designed to induce other natural reference points. The whole use of benchmarks against which performance is to be evaluated can cause investors to feel the pain of a loss if they've not beaten the benchmark regardless of whether the benchmark itself has returned a positive or negative absolute result.

Ultimately, we should be rationally concerned about increasing wealth in absolute terms over the long term and optimize our portfolios to achieve this. The fact that other investors are doing better than we are may be a signal that they are taking more risk or that our own portfolio is inefficient—but we should not care about relative returns as a goal in itself. If we do so, our portfolios, by definition, will be suboptimally invested for the long-term objective of achieving the best possible returns relative to the risk taken on, or of maximizing desirability. Instead, we will be irrationally devoting substantial parts of our risk budget to beating other investors' performance regardless of whether that performance is good or bad. Because the reference point has a strong role to play in behavioral distortions, this focus on relative returns will also mean that the returns of the benchmark have enormous sway over how we feel, and this will lead us to conform our portfolios to the benchmark (whichever benchmark it is) rather than to the genuinely optimal portfolio.

The problem of a shifting reference point can become particularly pernicious at the top of the cycle. In what we've considered up to now, the effect of behavioral preferences has largely been to cause investors to shy away from taking enough risk owing to narrow framing and short-term time horizons. For most of the market cycle, this is probably the case for most investors. After the bottom of the cycle and for some time thereafter, investors are more likely to be nervous than exuberant and may well also be perceiving the risks in available investments to be much higher than reality. But the nervousness and fear engendered by the recent poor market conditions are also likely to cause investors to fear getting back into the market and getting it wrong. This effect of *anticipated regret* may well be one of the contributing factors to anxiety because despite aphorisms to the contrary, most of the time we fear the regret of doing something and failing more than we fear the regret of not doing something.

However, this state of affairs cannot be permanent. After markets have been rising consistently for some time, a number of factors lead us gradually back into the market. But something else can happen too: More and more exposure to media stories of investors realizing great returns and to the stories of braver friends and colleagues around the dinner party table of how well they've been doing, and we start to shift our reference point. Rather than regret getting it wrong by taking risks, we start to fear missing out. The environment has started to shift our viewpoint such that sitting comfortably on risk-free assets no longer appears as a gain relative to our absolute reference point of 0 percent. This starts instead to feel like a loss relative to the returns we think we *could* be getting. With our reference point reset at 10 percent rather than 0 percent, what should be a placid positive return of 5 percent starts to feel like a *loss* of 5 percent. Gradually, more and more risky assets come to require negative compensation for anxiety relative to the risk-free rate simply because the risk-free rate itself starts to cause us anxiety. The shift in reference point can induce large increases in risk-taking in a rising market.

Figure 8.17 shows how returns contribute to anxiety for the investor with $T = 1$. The lower line is the normal behavioral distortion line for those who have a reference point at 0 percent. The upper line shows the effect of a reference point at 10 percent rather than 0 percent. The kink in the curves between gain and loss now occurs at 10 percent. Anything below this is perceived as a loss. Since our anxiety measure fixes the risk-free rate to have zero anxiety, we see that with the risk-free rate still at 3.7 percent, all outcomes above this add to utility through the behavioral distortions. In other words, they *reduce* anxiety:

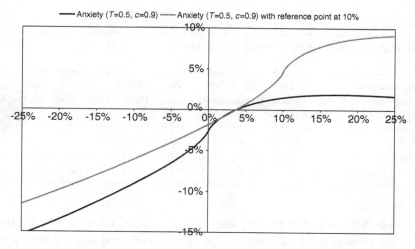

Figure 8.17 The change in reference point from 0 to 10 percent has massive implications for the profile of the anxiety curve.

If we perceive the risk-free rate to be equivalent to a *loss* of 6.3 percent, then risky assets with outcomes above this start to feel very desirable. Assuming that the expected distribution of returns has not itself shifted as the investor's reference point shifts, this means that compared with the risk-free asset, most risky assets offer negative anxiety. To put it simply, when our expectations of high returns cause our reference point to shift up, behavioral distortions lead us to take on far more risk.

This means that as markets do better and better over the cycle, our expectations of what we should get are at risk of increasing too. This makes low returns feel like losses. And as a result everything else (i.e., the risky assets) starts to contribute negative anxiety, making them appear far more desirable than they are to our long-term objectives. Thus, far too late, we start investing heavily near the top of the market—with the obvious accompanying risks. Table 8.4 compares the anxiety measure for each asset class for investors with $c = 0.90$ and the reference point at 10 percent rather than 0. And in Figure 8.18 we observe the dramatic effect this has on anxiety. If investors perceive any returns less than 10 percent as a loss, then they will actually be substantially more anxious holding cash than holding bonds of all types and hedge funds (which at least offer the option of getting closer to a gain). The short-term anxiety normally caused by holding equities and commodities is reduced substantially, and real estate now decreases anxiety rather than adding to it.

Table 8.4

The Effect of an Upward Shift of the Reference Point on Anxiety

Monthly Returns w. Reference Point at 10%	Cash	Gov Bonds	IG Bonds	HY Bonds	Dev Equity	EM Equity	Commodities	Real Estate	Hedge Funds
Anxiety ($T = 0.5, c = 0.9$)	0.0%	−2.4%	−2.7%	−3.0%	0.9%	1.5%	2.7%	−0.8%	−4.3%
Anxiety ($T = 1, c = 0.9$)	0.0%	−2.6%	−3.1%	−3.8%	−1.4%	−2.4%	−0.2%	−3.7%	−4.8%
Anxiety ($T = 1.5, c = 0.9$)	0.0%	−2.7%	−3.2%	−4.0%	−2.1%	−3.6%	−1.2%	−4.5%	−5.0%

It is possible too that the opposite effect happens. Closer to the bottom of the market we actually find ourselves perceiving potential returns with a negative reference point. This would have the opposite effect, the risk-free asset would appear highly appealing and anxiety would increase for all risky assets. This effect is also likely to be muted for another reason: It is more difficult to convince oneself to perceive a negative return as a gain than it is to adjust expectations such that we're disappointed by small gains. Even if markets are doing very badly, a negative return may still feel like the loss that it is. Although people are swayed by relative returns to different degrees, we are all more likely to chase the benchmark when things are going well, but we simply to want positive absolute returns when they're going badly.

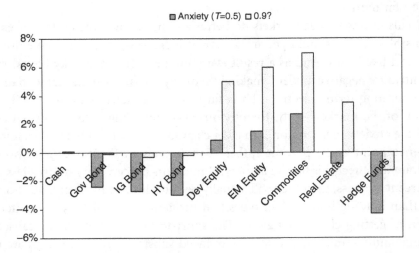

Figure 8.18 The effect of changing the reference point from 0 to 10 percent on the anxiety contribution of each asset class. Anxiety is reduced considerably across the board.

Strategies for Dealing with Anxiety

. . . [B]ut you must bind me hard and fast, so that I cannot stir from the spot where you will stand me . . . and if I beg you to release me, you must tighten and add to my bonds.

—Homer, *The Odyssey*

We humans are inherently emotional, subject to hopes, fears, social pressures, and cognitive biases—in short, as rational beings, we are fallible. Even after accounting for future liquidity needs, sticking with an investment policy is difficult psychologically. But behavioral finance gives us one key advantage—increasing awareness of our own fallibility and knowledge to overcome it.

This idea is not new. In Homer's *Odyssey*, Ulysses knows that when he sails past the island of the Sirens, no matter how strong his resolve ahead of time, in the heat of the moment, he will be unable to resist their enchanting song. To prevent disaster for himself and his crew, he has them bind him firmly to the ship's mast with ropes and then stop up their own ears with beeswax so that they will not be tempted by the Sirens. Being aware of his own fallibility, he *constrains* the possible actions of his future self. Likewise in investing, there are times when good intentions will not be enough to overcome the intensity of our short-term desires. At these times, we are most in danger of making decisions based on anxiety or hope, which can be calamitous for our long-run performance—pulling out of the market in fear after a crash, thereby locking in the losses, or plunging in near the top for fear of missing out. To stop ourselves from buying high and selling low, we need some ropes to bind ourselves to the mast.

As we have seen in this chapter, there are four broad contributing factors to overall anxiety:

1. Relative strength of short-term behavioral distortions to long-term preferences
2. Narrow framing on individual investments
3. Narrow framing on short time periods
4. Instability of reference point

Although, as we've seen, an upward shift of the reference point can encourage investors to take too much risk, the dominant effect of short-term behavioral distortions is to induce anxiety, and this causes almost all risky assets to appear less desirable than they should from the perspective of long-term objectives.[15] Thus, at any point in time, we should expect real investors with reference-dependent behavioral preferences and a reference point at 0 percent to undervalue risky investments—and therefore to be in less risky portfolios than would be optimal for their long-term investments. In addition, they will shy away from some assets more than others and will find taking the appropriate degree of risk more difficult at some times than others, depending on their current framing.

This will mean that investors will be in suboptimal portfolios and will not achieve optimal risk-adjusted returns in the long run. Are there things we can do to help us overcome these biases? The answer is yes. For most investors, though, these things will not come naturally—they require conscious thought and active steps to overcome the very natural tendency to avoid investments that cause us short-term anxiety. The following subsections will outline a number of strategies that may be employed to constrain our short-term emotional selves: aligning our decision frame to our objectives; purchasing emotional comfort in various ways; avoiding short-term information; using investment processes and rules; and lastly eliminating our future options.

Align Decision Frames with Long-Term Objectives

The most obvious way of overcoming these biases is by taking conscious steps to align the framing of investment decisions with one's long-term objectives. We have already seen how taking a short-term perspective or focusing too narrowly on individual investments can accentuate anxiety. To combat this, we need to ensure that when setting up and implementing our long-term optimal portfolio, we intentionally focus only on long-term outcomes and on the big picture.

If you establish your level of risk tolerance as an input into a quantitative portfolio model and then build your portfolio to match the output recommendations, you have forced a long-term and big-picture view. When it comes to implementation, you are simply following a program. However, even here doubts can exist. We consider below how to overcome them.

Purchase Emotional Comfort

Successfully implementing one's optimal portfolio requires emotional comfort, and shying away from risky assets and sitting on cash is one way of acquiring this comfort. However, if you are naturally inclined toward narrow framing (see above) or have particularly strong behavioral distortions (e.g., a low value of distortion parameter c), it can be a very expensive way of doing so because it means that your portfolio will have dramatically lower risk and return than is optimal. Some of the strategies that can help to overcome anxiety do cost something—but these more sophisticated ways of insuring yourself may be much cheaper than the alternative of sitting on the sidelines altogether. In other words, there may be cheaper ways of achieving the same emotional comfort with your portfolio than simply pandering to your short-term behavioral preferences.

Using Hedging and Protection to Lower Anxiety Directly

The most direct ways to purchase the emotional comfort required are to respect behavioral distortions to a degree and directly seek products and strategies that reduce anxiety—just sufficiently to give one the confidence to get fully invested, but with minimal deviations from the optimal portfolio. Dampen the Sirens' song by reducing the anxiety measure of your portfolio—increase the weight of low-anxiety assets and use downside protection to eliminate the effect of the worst-case scenarios. These can reduce the anxiety measure of the portfolio as a whole without reducing the long-term risk/return tradeoff too much. A number of asset features may contribute to this and in many cases can be implemented either through dynamic active management or through the passive use of derivatives, structuring, or dynamic trading strategies:

- *Downside protection may increase your level of comfort with your portfolio.* In particular, if this protection only eliminates the far-left tail of the distribution, then it would affect the overall risk/return characteristics less and thus provide cheaper emotional comfort.
- *Dynamic hedging to smooth the variation in short-term returns relative to long-run risk.* Also, funds that have infrequent mark-to-market valuations or for which the short-term variation in value cannot be observed easily, give the perception of a smoother journey and thus lead to less anxiety about the portfolio as a whole.[16]
- *Asset distributions with a relatively low monthly probability of loss.* The most dramatic increases in the marginal contribution of returns to the anxiety score occur just below the gain/loss reference point, so products that have uncharacteristically low probability of loss would provide cheaper reductions of portfolio anxiety.[17]
- *Funds that bundle a wide diversity of assets together into a single reported return.* These products provide a natural big-picture frame and thus reduce the perceived anxiety of the portfolio.

Using Delegation and Advice

A different strategy to get around anxiety is to use a trusted advisor, something that often can strengthen an investor's resolve and get him to implement choices that suit his long-term preferences but overcome his short-term anxiety.

An even more effective—if initially unnerving—device is for investors to abrogate responsibility entirely and hand the whole issue of portfolio implementation and management over to a professional who is tasked with taking a long-term, big-picture, rational perspective on their behalf. This can put you at a greater emotional distance from your portfolio and also limits the detail in which you observe your portfolio holdings and transactions—both of which lead to a broader framing and therefore reduced anxiety. However, as we note below, advisers will also be vulnerable to their own behavioral biases. In addition, this comes at a cost because one has to pay for such advice and professional management—but if this cost of purchasing emotional comfort is lower than the inefficiency costs that stem from the effects of anxiety when trying to implement a portfolio oneself, then this could be a cost worth paying.

Phasing Investments Gradually Over Time

One of the most difficult concerns to overcome when implementing a portfolio is that the timing may be wrong. As a result, we often sit on the sidelines with chunks of our wealth in cash, missing out on the positive returns we should expect from being in the market.

If the optimal portfolio has positive expected returns (which it should), then keeping any part of an investor's wealth uninvested simply reduces long-term performance, has lower expected utility, and produces, by definition, a suboptimal portfolio. This reasoning is why what is called *dollar cost averaging* (investing equal amounts regularly over a specified time period) is never a theoretically optimal strategy from a rational perspective—the loss in expected utility from leaving a portion of wealth uninvested outweighs the gain in expected utility arising from the small probability that we inadvertently get the timing very wrong in initiating the portfolio. However, jumping into the markets all at once can be very difficult, and rather than leaving a substantial amount of one's portfolio uninvested indefinitely, it may well be better to accept the reduction of expected returns that comes from a program of dollar cost averaging over time in exchange for the emotional security that comes from a fixed program of gradual investment over time.

Like all strategies we discuss in this section, this is an example of where it might be beneficial for an anxious investor to pursue a strategy that would be suboptimal for a completely rational long-term investor. In so doing, the investor purchases the emotional comfort to overcome the inefficiency costs of anxiety. For less anxious or more rational individuals or for those who can keep their focus on the long term, dollar cost averaging introduces a suboptimality that has no compensating beneficial effects. For an anxious, behaviorally driven investor, though, the reduction in anxiety that it delivers may make the small inefficiencies of dollar cost averaging a price worth paying.

Avoid Information that Is Too Focused on the Short Term

Trying to determine what is going on in the world by reading newspapers is like trying to tell the time by watching the second hand of a clock.

—Ben Hecht

We are constantly bombarded by information that induces a narrow frame—in the media, through detailed reports of investment performance, and through friends and family discussing specific decisions or issues in isolation. More information may mean we are better informed, but the benefits for decision making, like everything, diminish incrementally—and at the same time it also has the negative effect of causing us to focus more and more on the short term and on specific details in isolation from the larger perspective. Often we are simply better off without so much detailed information: It becomes noisy, confusing, and triggers emotional and behavioral responses rather than allowing us to focus on achieving longer-term perspectives.

The financial media are particularly dangerous in this regard because they frequently attempt to provide exciting, emotionally engaging explanations for extremely short-term and detailed market movements that are either (1) simply random noise or (2) quite irrelevant for what we are genuinely trying to achieve through our investment portfolio. In the choice between additional and potentially contradictory information on the one hand and trying to overcome short-term behavioral hurdles to taking the right overall level of risk in one's portfolio on the other, the latter easily dominates in importance for long-term performance. A policy of deliberately avoiding information or media that are too focused on short-term or detailed asset price movements (or the explanations for them) can be one of the most beneficial ways of overcoming undesired behavioral tendencies.

Establish and Follow a Robust Investing Process

If we rely purely on our intuitions and perceptions at any point in time to evaluate risk/return tradeoffs, we are very likely to respond to noise rather than genuine information. We are also likely to find that short-term whims and preferences come to dominate our decision making. The result will be too frequent trading and decisions based more on subjective perceptions and emotional responses than on accurate analysis of information. This is not to say that we should become robotic in our approach to investing—intuition and emotion can be valuable signals that we should not ignore when making decisions. However, it is essential that we establish a good investment framework and decision-making process to boost the chance that our decisions are aligned with our long-term objectives and not just based on immediate whim.

One reason that professional investors conventionally outperform individual investors is not that they are smarter or have better data, models, and analytic capabilities[18] but rather that they have to work within a systematic set of rules, guidelines, procedures, sign-offs, and risk limits for what they're allowed to do and not do. Rigorous performance measurement and evaluation (where used) also mean that traders get accurate feedback on performance over time and need to be rigorous to succeed in the long run. By contrast, the vast majority of individual investors has absolutely no idea of their true performance at a big-picture portfolio level. All manner of psychological biases (e.g., hindsight bias, confirmation bias, attribution bias, overconfidence, and availability bias, to name a few) lead us to systematically overestimate our own performance and thereby to the dangerous conclusion that our intuitive, reactive, narrow framing approach to investing is actually serving us well!

A solid decision-making process is not as extreme as binding oneself completely, but it can still be effective (after all, Ulysses could have chosen to block his own ears rather than be tied down). One example is to use a sign-off process for big investment decisions to avoid making major investing decisions on a whim. Requiring yourself to reflect for a few days as a cooling-off period and to seek a second opinion for big decisions are examples of this.

Eliminate Your Range of Options

Finally if, like Ulysses, you want to be fully exposed to the Sirens' song but nonetheless control your behavior, you could seek more extreme measures such as deliberately seeking investments that lock you in completely or have low liquidity and so are difficult, expensive, or time-consuming to exit.

Conclusion

Investing is too often seen as a purely quantitative problem with right and wrong answers and a single "rational" way of doing things that everyone should strive equally to follow. We started this chapter by showing how to incorporate short-term behavioral preferences into our modeling framework and introduced the concept of an anxiety measure for the investor to accompany the investment desirability and risk compensation measures introduced in previous chapters. As we demonstrated, while this anxiety measure helps us to better understand investor behavior, the instability of behavioral distortions makes us reluctant to try to calibrate it precisely.

Looking at the problem of anxiety over the longer term, it is clear that our natural psychology inclines us to procyclical investing, something that carries a number of risks. When we try to identify the factors that encourage the dramatic shifts in risk-taking that we observe over the economic cycle, it is clear that these cannot be ascribed to changing risk tolerance. Instead, we should consider changing expectations of risk and return, as well as the changing force of behavioral distortions on long-term preferences themselves. Shifts in the reference point against which we intuitively measure investment performance are also likely to be very important and often pernicious.

If there is one message to be taken from this chapter, it is that individual investors should be aware of all the multiple factors that can affect their decision making and that they should attempt to create processes to contain those factors that may prove most disruptive. In Chapter 9 we consider the same problem of improving investment returns, but from a quite different perspective—that of the wealth-management industry itself.

Appendix

DERIVATION OF ANXIETY MEASURE

The utility function may be rewritten as follows:

$$
\begin{aligned}
E[u(r)] &= 1 - E\!\left(e^{-(2/T)v(r)}\right) \\
&= 1 - E\!\left(e^{-(2/T)[(v(r)-\bar{r}+\bar{r})]}\right) \\
&= 1 - E\!\left(e^{-(2/T)\bar{r}}e^{(2/T)[\bar{r}-v(r)]}\right) \\
&= 1 - E\!\left(e^{-(2/T)\bar{r}}\right)E\!\left(e^{(2/T)[\bar{r}-v(r)]}\right) \\
&= 1 - e^{-(2/T)\bar{r}}E\!\left(e^{(2/T)[\bar{r}-v(r)]}\right)
\end{aligned}
$$

This follows exactly the methodology of Chapter 5 except that r has been replaced everywhere with $v(r)$. Now, in order to further separate out the behavioral effects from the rational risk aversion, we wish the total variability to be expressed by two component parts. The first is the risk R, as before. The second is the effect of behavioral distortions reflected in the transformation $v(r)$—let us term it B. Thus, where before we defined R such that

$$
e^{(2/T)R} = E\!\left(e^{(2/T)(\bar{r}-r)}\right)
$$

and thus

$$
R = \frac{T}{2}\ln E\!\left(e^{(2/T)(\bar{r}-r)}\right)
$$

we now replace the more complex expression

$$E\left(e^{(2/T)[\bar{r}-v(r)]}\right)$$

with

$$e^{(2/T)(R+B)} = E\left(e^{(2/T)[\bar{r}-v(r)]}\right)$$

which allows us to express the *total deviation* from the mean as the sum of risk and of the behavioral distortion induced by the investment. As before, we can solve for $R + B$ as

$$R + B = \frac{T}{2}\ln E\left(e^{(2/T)[\bar{r}-v(r)]}\right)$$

Since the risk of the investment should not change because of these behavioral distortions, we still have

$$R = \frac{T}{2}\ln E\left(e^{(2/T)(\bar{r}-r)}\right) = \frac{\sigma_B^2}{T}$$

as before. This means that in order to cleanly separate the effects of risk, expected return, and anxiety, the latter must be

$$B = \frac{T}{2}\ln E\left(e^{(2/T)[\bar{r}-v(r)]}\right) - \frac{\sigma_B^2}{T}$$

Total expected utility, with behavioral distortions, can now be given as a function of expected return, risk, and B, which reflects the extent to which the investment triggers behavioral effects such as disparities between gains and losses:

$$E[u(r)] = f\left(\bar{r}, \sigma_B^2, B\right) = 1 - e^{-(2/T)\left[\bar{r}-(\sigma_B^2/T)-B\right]}$$

A positive value for B implies that these behavioral distortions decrease the overall expected utility.

This can be seen more intuitively if we put these distortions into the framework of desirability. Recall that desirability is the value that makes the investor indifferent between holding the asset or the risk-free investment, so we find it by equating the utility of the investment with that of the risk-free rate plus desirability. We need to also account for the fact that the risk-free rate itself will be subject to a small amount of behavioral distortion, which we denote by B_{rf}.

Thus, desirability is the solution to

$$1 - e^{-(2/T)\left(r_f + D - B_{r_f}\right)} = 1 - e^{-(2/T)\left[\bar{r} - (\sigma_B^2/T) - B\right]}$$

$$r_f + D - B_{r_f} = \bar{r} - \frac{\sigma_B^2}{T} - B$$

$$D = (\bar{r} - r_f) - \frac{\sigma_B^2}{T} - \left(B - B_{r_f}\right)$$

Unfortunately, B_{r_f} makes the resulting equation for desirability more awkward than we'd like. However, a precise formulation for B_{r_f} can be determined by plugging the risk-free rate into B, which, since there is no variability in the risk-free rate, simplifies considerably:

$$B_{r_f} = \frac{T}{2} \ln E\left(e^{(2/T)[r_f - v(r_f)]}\right) - \frac{\sigma_{B_{r_f}}^2}{T}$$

$$= r_f - v(r_f)$$

This is simply the difference between the risk-free rate and the behaviorally distorted risk-free rate.

Let us define the term $A = B - B_{r_f}$ as *anxiety*:

$$A = B - B_{r_f}$$

$$= \frac{T}{2} \ln E\left(e^{(2/T)[\bar{r} - v(r)]}\right) - \frac{\sigma_B^2}{T} - [r_f - v(r_f)]$$

Examining the equation for anxiety shows how it represents completely and exclusively the behavioral distortions. The first term is the *overall* effect on utility of the combined rational and behavioral distortions, and the second subtracts from this the effect of variations from the mean that are accounted for by the rational risk/return preferences, leaving only the effect of the behaviorally induced distortions. The last term is simply a correction to ensure that the risk-free rate itself has zero anxiety by definition.

With this we can see that desirability is simply made up of three components:

$$D = (\bar{r} - r_f) - \frac{\sigma_B^2}{T} - A$$

It is comprised of the excess return less the compensation for risk required by the rational long-term investor and less compensation required to cope with anxiety.

Notes

1. Notably, this formulation will not permit us to account for the probability-distortion feature of CPT.
2. Equivalently, the curvature of $v(r)$.
3. As is the case, for example, in CPT, where a specific loss-aversion parameter is imposed precisely in order to induce a kink in the value function at zero.
4. There may well be investments out there that have negative anxiety. However, such investments would have to have a strong positive skew because, as shown in the figure, behavioral distortions tend to have a much stronger effect on negative outcomes.
5. Note that the risk compensation plus anxiety curve is purely stylistic in this diagram to give a sense of the effects of anxiety. Unlike risk compensation, it is not purely a function of risk and thus is not necessarily smoothly increasing in risk. The precise amount of anxiety induced by each investment will be specific to that investment and to the time horizon over which the returns outcomes are measured. Thus two investments with the same behavioral risk could have different anxiety scores.
6. Recall that anxiety also has been calibrated to ensure that the risk-free rate itself exhibits $A = 0$.
7. We have calculated these using overlapping rolling windows of each different holding period. This does add some degree of artificial autocorrelation to the data, so, as with all calculations of anxiety numbers, we should not take the precise values too seriously. However, this clearly illustrates the main trend, which is that anxiety decreases substantially as the time frame of evaluation increases.
8. At which point it is always worth bearing in mind the aphorism from Sir John Templeton that the four most dangerous words in investing are: *This time it's different.*
9. Clare and Motson (2010). See also Dichev (2007).
10. Note that this behavioral effect exists alongside a more rational reason for increasing net flows into risky assets after good times, which is simply that investors typically have more funds at their disposal in good times. However, this should not necessitate an increase in the relative allocation to risk.
11. Malmendier and Nagel (2011).
12. Weber, Weber, and Nosic (2011).
13. To be precise, respondents' subjective assessments of risk and return (i.e., assessments of risk and return on a scale from 1 to 7) were predictive of changes in risk-taking. The survey also asked for numerical assessments of

risk and return (i.e., what percentage return do you expect the FTSE 100 to deliver over the next three months?). The correlations between the subjective and numerical assessments were not high, and the numerical assessments were not predictive of stated risk-taking intentions. This reinforces the difficulty, often found in the literature, faced by investors when providing firm numerical assessments of risk and returns expectations.

14. It is true that opportunity costs of investing are better considered by using the risk-free rate as the point of comparison, but the anxiety score already makes an adjustment to ensure that the risk-free rate has zero anxiety by definition, and it is less natural for us to think of a return that is below the risk-free rate but is nonetheless positive as a loss.

15. Indeed, only outcomes above the risk-free rate detract from anxiety, and then not as substantially as returns below the risk-free rate add to it—so any investment with negative anxiety would also be likely to have extraordinarily high expected returns relative to its level of risk. In other words, the sort of investment that arbitrage arguments would cause us to doubt the existence of.

16. It is interesting that many companies manage the reporting of annual earnings in a way that seems analogous to anxiety reduction. They will frequently use leeway in accounting assumptions to ensure that a gain is posted rather than a loss wherever possible—if they have to post a loss, they typically will make it as large as possible (taking the big bath) in order to get all the bad news out of the way at once.

17. For example, product structuring using derivative instruments could be used to shift some probability mass from negative 1 percent to positive 1 percent where there is a big difference in anxiety contribution in exchange for a compensating shift in probability mass from, say, 11 percent to 9 percent where the difference in anxiety contribution is minimal. This could be constructed to maintain the expected value of the portfolio while maximally reducing anxiety—the cost of structuring comprises the payment for anxiety reduction.

18. Although these may be true too and should always give individual investors pause before trying to "beat the market" in active trading.

Chapter 9

THE IMPACT OF BEHAVIORAL INVESTMENT MANAGEMENT ON WEALTH AND PENSION MANAGEMENT

In this chapter we review carefully the implications of the new paradigm defined by this book for the wealth-management and pension fund industries. These two sectors have been seriously challenged by the recent crisis in ways that are not fundamentally dissimilar. Both sectors were focused on the long-term horizon and were unprepared for the necessity of adapting to a market crash. We believe that these two sectors should not treat recent history as an accident but should use it instead to assess and reengineer their core operating principles. Their aim should be to adapt these principles to include a more advanced understanding of individuals and of the dynamics of financial markets.

Wealth-Management Reengineering

The wealth-management industry needs to improve its performance in two key areas. First, it needs to have a thorough understanding of clients in order to be able to act in accordance with their expectations. Second, it needs to incorporate advanced money-management skills within organizations.

Looking at the current practices in the wealth-management sector, we observe four common pillars:

1. A simple risk classification of clients primarily meant to accommodate regulatory requirements
2. Stock-picking capabilities often presented as a central offering in order to differentiate firms from competitors
3. A search for profitability that encourages the distribution of high-margin products (i.e., mutual funds, hedge funds, and structured products)
4. In the most sophisticated companies, the definition of a quasi-static asset-allocation framework that broadly guides diversification recommendations

An emphasis on one or another of these four pillars is usually meant to express the differentiated/competitive edge of the individual wealth-management firm.

This book does not set out a variation on these four pillars. Instead, we propose something fundamentally new and different that should contribute to a profound reshaping of this industry.

More Systematic Use of Client Information for Better Risk Management

Wealth management is probably the only industry, outside of health care, where clients are ready to be fully cooperative and to disclose considerable information about who they are, what they aspire to, and what they would like to avoid. They are ready to do so because they are generally convinced that it is in their best interest.

In addition, the large number of clients serviced by the bigger wealth managers should lend itself particularly well to the use of statistical techniques in order to better understand the patterns of clients' core characteristics and needs. An obvious comment is that what Amazon is doing impressively well with very little insight on clients could be done much more thoroughly in the wealth-management space. Being able to tell a client, "We understand who you are and what you might be looking for" is a good way of differentiating your firm from the competition.

Wealth managers are also prone to forget that there is more than one style of investment in the investment world. The current static asset-allocation approach favored by wealth managers often leads to a single, restrictive approach to investing. A recent book compiled by Lomdard Odier Darier Hentsch & Cie[1] focuses on describing how different money managers have been successful relying on diverse investment philosophies and how these investment philosophies should be available to clients. The identification of clients' varying financial attitudes and the acknowledgment of different investment styles should enable wealth-management firms to offer a more bespoke match. There are many roads to go down here: One could think of using client segmentation, peer groups, special information, or risk alerts.

The next point concerning the need for a more systematic use of client information relates to risk management. As a private bank, you may not deliver out-of-the-ordinary investment performance, but you are generally expected to be the "risk manager" for the client. But is it possible to do this when you rely on a single grid, typically segmented as low/medium/high risk, and with a large majority of clients in any case ending up in the medium-risk category? We have already discussed two quite distinct sources of risk attitude for individuals extensively in Chapters 2, 5 and 8: the structural, long-term, rational perspective on risk and the shorter-term, more emotional aspect of risk.

In addition to these two dimensions, which are purely centered on the investor, we believe that there is a third important dimension of risk to take into consideration that deals both with investor preferences and investment specifics. This is *liquidity risk*.

As Keynes put it, "[T]here is nothing so dangerous as the pursuit of a rational investment policy in an irrational world," and he was also correct that markets can certainly stay irrational for longer than clients can remain solvent. So the inclusion of liquidity risk is not an invitation to irrational investing; it is rather a suggestion that one should fully consider liquidity when making investment decisions. This liquidity focus should, in fact, incorporate two distinct features related to solvency. There is a technical solvency aspect—in plain words, Will it be possible for an investor to cover future expenditures and liabilities with his assets given current market conditions without being forced into an inefficient portfolio allocation owing to liquidity concerns? But there is also an emotional solvency perspective, that is, the investor's perception that even if the portfolio can effectively meet required expenditures (possibly via some reduction and rebalancing), there remains a solvency risk in the future, something that could lead to an investor selling anticipatively at the worst moment for misguided precautionary reasons. To put it another way, we frequently do not have sufficient emotional liquidity to see us through the bad times.

The overall point here is that the financial solvency required to remain invested in bad times is client-specific and requires rigorous analysis. This was one lesson learned from the 2007–2010 crisis. We also suggest that a range of products, such as private equity funds, hedge funds, and closed-end real estate funds, should not be considered liquid. During bull markets, liquidity is seldom perceived to be an issue, but during the last crisis, liquidity conditions deteriorated rapidly—and forced selling results in a massive discount. As a consequence, these assets should be incorporated with care within clients' portfolios because they constrain the capability to rebalance the portfolio over time in a flexible manner.

There are certainly other secondary dimensions to be considered beyond these three primary risk categories, but we believe that these three risk features—structural risk, emotional risk, and liquidity risk—offer a sound basis on which to evaluate clients' risk profiles and therefore to be able to act as an effective risk manager. And yet, all too often, only the first is considered in any systematic way throughout the cycle. Emotional risks and liquidity risks tend to recede from view precisely when they become most important—at the top of the market cycle.

Using Behavioral Analysis to Better Understand Risk

But what does it mean to be the *risk manager* of a client? Let us start with a little bit of methodologic background. In earlier chapters of this book we discussed the use of behavioral analyses to provide either a normative or a descriptive perspective on investing by individuals. As we have explained, since the mid-1950s, modern portfolio theory (MPT) has offered a purely normative framework for doing this, but one that fails to describe realistically fundamental investor preferences. We strongly believe that relying on such a normative approach, even it were to include a more realistic depiction of client preferences, will fail to deliver a fully suitable and sustainable investment experience to all clients. This is so because it could lead most market-reactive clients to experience a difficult emotional journey, meaning there is an associated risk that they will leave the investment trip at the worst moment.

More recently, cumulative prospect theory (CPT) has provided a more descriptive perspective of how investors typically react because of their behavioral biases. But relying on a purely descriptive (rather than normative) approach to investing, even though it might better accommodate to some extent the client investment journey, could seriously damage investment performance. Observing that investors have a lower than normal tolerance to losses because of short-term emotional biases will lead either to a severe underweighting of risky assets or to selling low when prices slide as a result of emotional stress.

In this book we have very consciously taken a different, intermediate view. Our view is that state-of-the-art investing should rely on the combination of a realistic normative approach (based on elicitation of each client's degree of risk tolerance and subjective risk measures) with the option of actively mitigating the behavioral biases of more emotionally sensitive individuals through the payment of an "insurance premium" related to protection against temporary downside risk events. This approach is only possible if the risk characterization of each client is sufficiently detailed along all the various risk dimensions. Understanding who the client is from the perspective of all three aspects of risk and setting the corresponding portfolio construction framework as described earlier corresponds to acting as the risk manager of the client.

Because we have a more detailed understanding of the risk dimensions of an individual, we can articulate a more refined and tailored asset-allocation framework. We also offer a technical breakthrough in that we have clarified the "missing link" between advanced but simple measures of risk and the behavioral understanding of individuals.

Of course, there have already been many articles in the financial literature arguing that volatility is not a suitable measure of risk. As a result, new paradigms such as value-at-risk (VaR) and conditional-value-at-risk (CVaR) have been presented as alternative measures, only to be criticized shortly thereafter because they are either weak from an axiomatic perspective or because it is extremely difficult objectively to set an optimal confidence level at which an investor can reliably assess them.

These latter measures, however, have had the merit of establishing a focus on downside risk. In this book we have made good progress on defining risk measures by considering specific ones individually that are robust from a methodologic perspective, as well as simple to use and to parameterize. With this toolkit, we are much better able to deal with new financial instruments within portfolios. Of relevance here are the more exotic, nonnormally distributed asset classes, such as credit, or instruments meant to express an investment view through an asymmetric payoff, such as options.

Redefining Risk-Management Targets

We believe that this approach of combining behavioral finance with investment management may well come to influence current best practices. At present, two main risk-management targets are typically defined by fund managers: either the definition of a target level of volatility or the definition of a target VaR level. We suggest that neither of these two objectives, especially the second, is optimal from a performance perspective.

As regards volatility, it provides no means within the mandate to understand how to focus on the preservation of wealth and, ultimately, on the sustainability of the consumption capabilities of the investor. This is so because, as we have shown in previous chapters (in particular, in Chapter 5), no accurate link exists between the utility function of the investor, on the one hand, and the volatility and expected return of the assets in a fund or in a portfolio, on the other, as would be required to express complete preferences for risk and return adequately.

There are also problems surrounding the definition of a target VaR level. Because the VaR and CVaR measures of risk are discontinuous around the selected confidence level, they trigger discrete reactions from portfolio managers. In practice, portfolio managers are bound to implement a stop-loss approach: Below a certain level of risk, the situation remains under control, but as soon as the predefined limit is reached, positions need to be cut immediately. Because of the mean reversion inherent in financial markets, sell-offs are usually synonymous with "selling low." It is both intuitive and well documented in the financial literature that stop losses lead to underperformance.

Behavioral measures of risk constitute a significant advance for several reasons: They are directly investor-related, and they are technically suitable because they are continuous measures that have no arbitrary points of discontinuity.[2]

From a fund-management perspective, this measure of risk is superior to the other measures of risk in the sense that it naturally leads one to see risk management as a gradual leveraging/deleveraging of risk over time in order to deliver a stabilized degree of satisfaction to the investor instead of having to brutally react when a risk trigger is breached. It is worth noting that some market participants have already implemented a similar type of strategy purely based on intuition and without relating it to behavioral measures of risk. They have defined an asset allocation that is dynamically leveraged/deleveraged depending on the level of gain/loss in the portfolio.[3]

Establishing New Investment Best Practice

Innovation in wealth management not only involves a better understanding of clients but must also lead to a very noticeable modification of investment best practice.

The Current Investment Paradigm

The current investment paradigm within wealth-management organizations is usually twofold.

1. Less sophisticated organizations emphasize stock picking, although empirical evidence suggests that outperforming benchmark indices through active stock picking is difficult to achieve over the long run. As has already been noted in Chapter 1, the percentage of mutual funds in developed economies outperforming their benchmark over a cumulative period of three years is only just over 5 percent. As a consequence of this poor performance, there is a strong trend in the direction of direct investment in passive indices through low-cost vehicles called *exchange-traded funds* (ETFs). This trend has started to affect the investment industry significantly, as can be seen in Figure 9.1. The future does not look bright for stock-picking organizations both in terms of loss of market share and in terms of market pressure on active management fees.

2. More sophisticated organizations tend to rely on a fundamentally static asset-allocation process, more or less derived from MPT. By doing so, they are able to define a stable investment framework that can be populated with in-house or third-party products. The beauty of this approach is that it enables large firms to distribute products and advice on a large scale in a disciplined manner within a preestablished, industrially scalable, and centrally defined asset-allocation guiding framework. This framework guarantees a certain level of diversification within clients' portfolios while not necessarily meaning that the wealth-management firm must rely on professionals with particularly strong

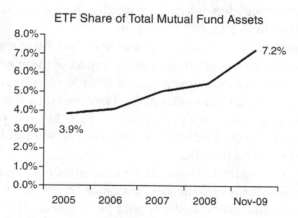

Figure 9.1 The market share for ETFs is growing.
(Indexuniverse.com.)

investment qualifications providing advice. This is so because by setting a limited range of reference static asset-allocation portfolios, many wealth-management firms have been able to reap the benefits of some economies of scale, focusing on distribution while not investing heavily in dedicated asset-management skills.

Why a Static Approach to Asset Allocation Is Becoming Irrelevant

On the face of it, such a static approach to asset allocation should also be advantageous because it forces the wealth manager to clearly define, together with the client, the static investment benchmark that it aims to outperform. In reality, though, this framework can prove quite time-consuming for relationship managers because there is a constant need to reconcile the qualitative aspirations of the clients with the often unexpected performance of their assigned asset allocation (not to mention the performance of the agreed-upon benchmark). There is a structural issue here, as has been outlined in Chapters 7 and 8: Because many clients will typically fail to judge events against a static benchmark, they will judge performance more closely to a market benchmark during growth periods but feel much closer to a cash benchmark during recessionary periods.

In addition, the idea of a static asset-allocation investment is rapidly becoming challenging simply because the evaluation horizon of clients has been constantly shortening over the past years (which may not be considered to be an improvement, though!). In practice, the number of clients still ready to wait between 5 and 10 years before reassessing their investments and hence the value added by their wealth managers is becoming smaller and smaller. The evaluation horizon of wealthy people is getting closer to 2 to 3 years rather than 5 to 10.[4]

At the same time, it is becoming clearer and clearer that ever-longer time periods are necessary to smooth the annoying impact of mean reversion within equities. As Figure 9.2 shows, a time period of 20 to 30 years is now required for equity's volatility to come close to that of fixed income rather than 5 to 10 years. If you are thinking in terms of a period shorter than 20 to 30 years, then you need to expect a high level of volatility. In other words, you will have to experience significant peaks and troughs.

As a result, the dislocation between the conceptual offering of many of the wealth-management firms (a static asset allocation at a 5- to 10-year horizon) and the realities of investment results in poor performance. This has created an increasingly unsustainable situation where wealth managers' confidence and credibility risk serious damage.

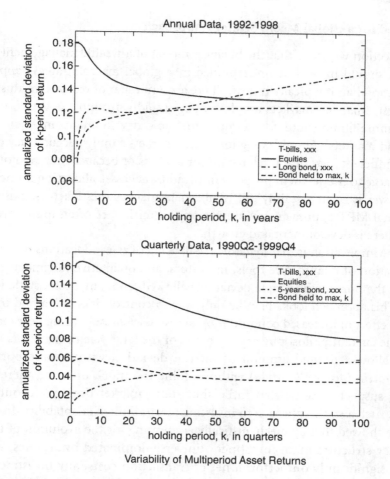

Figure 9.2 The benefit of decreasing equity volatility takes many years to be substantial. (*Campbell and Viceira, 2001.*)

Earlier in this book, especially in Chapter 4, we showed that the poor performance of such static asset allocations (which rely to varying extents on MPT) is not the result of unexpected bad luck. In fact, the foundations for such approaches look weak at best both from an understanding of the dynamics of assets and from a risk-management perspective. So they will generally fail to deliver palatable investment performance. Chapters 4 and 6 have established that the poor performance of static portfolios following a benchmark over the past 15 years has been due to a limited understanding of the dynamics of asset classes over the period.

The Need for a Global Macro Strategy Approach

In this section we argue that the business model of a wealth-management organization should instead be underpinned by a global macro strategy[5] approach much more than it typically is now. There are a number of reasons for this.

First, financial markets are developing rapidly around the world and are getting more liquid (note, for example, the rapid developments in Asian equity and bond markets). Should we ignore these markets simply because they do not have a sufficient historical track record for analysis or because they are not sufficiently large to model them properly in a traditional asset-allocation framework? The answer is most certainly no, whatever headaches these factors cause for a traditional MPT approach. Investment opportunities are often found precisely where there is development and growth.

The implication is that dynamic rebalancing of asset allocations relying on a combination of quantitative tools, indicators, and qualitative judgments should become the norm, with ample deviations allowed from any preset static benchmark. This approach looks like the only way to control risks better and to mitigate the effect of increased concentration across asset classes during bear markets.

The current philosophy among many of the large wealth managers is usually to allow a limited amount of tactical deviation within static portfolios (called *tactical asset allocation*) without doing too much of it and thereby becoming suspect of somewhat futile short-term market timing.[6] In our view, though, such a static approach to investing means limited adaptability. In Chapter 6 we showed that by mechanistically accounting for the evolution of the dependency structure in an investment universe dominated by regimes, we can already significantly outperform, net of transaction costs, any investment approach based on a static through-the-cycle dependency structure estimated over long periods of time.

The implication of this is that dynamically rebalancing portfolios does not need to be supported by strong subjective investment views and/or track records to already improve performance substantially. It is important to note in passing here that a more dynamic rebalancing of the portfolios, even on a monthly frequency, should not require an extremely high level of turnover in the portfolio. Looking at the world from a regime-switching perspective, the big shifts typically take place two to five times every 10 years. This means that a large discontinuity in the asset-allocation process should be expected only every other year at most. Such discontinuities in the portfolio will result from identified shifts in the world equilibrium and will not stem from short-term market bets or any second-guessing of the risk aversion of other market participants.

Second, complementing this dynamic rebalancing by quantitatively selected factors carrying predictive power and by qualitative views informed by a lasting macroeconomic perspective should help to enhance performance further. These factors and views should be expressed in a variety of ways, typically directional long/short plays or asymmetric plays through options. Expressing these views while maximizing the outcome from a risk-management perspective requires increasing flexibility of implementation. If the claim that we have now entered a period of low growth holds water, especially among the developed economies facing the negative impact of aging and other increasing structural imbalances, we will inevitably have to select and implement investment ideas with a lot of care. This is another argument for high implementation flexibility and more accurate risk management: This is much easier to achieve within a global macro type of organization than with the rigid framework of static asset allocation.

Fixing the Problems Surrounding a Total-Wealth Approach

When put in the context of the wealth-management industry, some of the abstract assumptions that we have made need to find a practical interpretation to ensure that the active investment portfolio of a client is also appropriate to her financial circumstances or risk capacity. This requires looking a little more closely at two elements—the assumption (as in previous chapters) that the optimization is applied to total wealth and the need to accommodate liquidity (as mentioned earlier).

It is important for a wealth manager to respect the fact that risk/return efficiency is not by a long shot the only objective that clients have for their wealth. Two categories of assets reasonably can fall outside such calculations: assets from which consumption or enjoyment benefits are derived and assets that investors have invested in their own entrepreneurial and business interests. No wealth manager should be in the business of telling his clients that the house they live in and love is an inefficient investment and that they should sell it and redeploy those assets more effectively in an optimal investment portfolio. In addition, as regards the second category, it is also not the place of the wealth-management industry to advise clients in their own area of expertise—entrepreneurial activities may have highly concentrated risks, but these are generally how the entrepreneur became wealthy in the first place and activities in which she is expert.

There are many possible approaches to dealing with this problem. The simplest solution may be to take extremely conservative haircuts on all external assets to reflect the risks of each but thereafter to treat the remainder as a fixed allocation to risk-free assets in the overall asset allocation. Alternatively, a wealth manager could keep these assets outside the asset allocation but would then need to make adjustments to the risk-tolerance parameter to account for the outside assets.

In addition to adjusting for assets held outside the optimal portfolio, a wealth manager must also adjust for an investor's *liabilities*—either by incorporating them into the portfolio optimization itself as leverage or by reducing the risk-tolerance parameter to account for the increased risk levels of total wealth.

A further, often ignored aspect of total wealth when making portfolio recommendations to a client is the effect of future income and expenditures. Although, because of the inherent uncertainty of future cash flows, it is difficult to model precisely, there is a large difference between the risk capacity of high-earning investors who are many years away from retirement and those who have already retired and need to fund all future expenditure from their current asset base. The former may be seen as having a human capital asset in addition to current wealth, substantially reducing these investors' current investment portfolios as a portion of their total wealth (i.e., including their human capital). Since our utility function approach is supposed to apply to total wealth, this means that these investors can take on significantly more risk with their investment portfolio. The opposite, of course, is true of investors as they approach retirement. We shall return to this notion briefly in our discussion of pension funds later in this chapter.

Finally, a total-wealth approach needs to include a reasonable cash buffer to cover possible expenditure requirements until the next rebalancing period. This is essential not only to prevent the need to meddle in the portfolio between rebalancing periods but also to avoid the costs of having to sell portions of the portfolio at short notice without being able to rebalance the portfolio effectively.

Implications for the Wealth-Management Industry

The consequences of this analysis are multiple. The first is that instead of looking like a very mature, even perhaps boring and cynical product brokerage industry, largely reliant on the old discredited conceptual bases of conventional investment advice related to "modern finance," wealth management looks like a very young business that is just about to gain maturity on the basis of new sciences such as behavioral finance as well as on a fascinating combination of advanced quantitative analytics and state-of-the-art macroeconomics.

As a result, we anticipate that in the near future the acquisition of a significant competitive advantage by a wealth-management firm will be directly linked with its capability to enhance or develop and integrate high-quality behavioral and investment platforms. Such an endeavor requires a critical mass to bear the associated costs, and only large, innovative organizations will be able to take advantage of this new trend. In a context where, as noted earlier, fees related to traditional management of money (i.e., stock picking, profiled asset-allocated funds) are getting eroded by low-cost products, this new direction truly offers a way ahead where what gets remunerated is a fair combination of (1) demonstrable services to clients and (2) performance.

Some Possible Points of Contention

We are conscious of the fact that the views held here will not be welcome to all and will face multiple ingrained habits and industry hurdles. The principal points of contention may be summarized as follows.

Fees and Costs

- *Fees.* The current fee structure in the wealth-management industry is much more product- than service-centric. In contrast, client behavioral analysis and dynamic portfolio management are primarily a service, typically respectively based on statistical intelligence and the trading of low-cost liquid underlying assets. Moving away from a product tariff to a service fee will be necessary to be able to fund the costs of upgrading and maintaining the behavioral and investment environment.
- *Implications of multiple risk dimensions for costs.* By introducing more risk dimensions to service clients adequately, a firm automatically has to maintain more reference portfolios/funds, which presupposes a critical mass of assets under management to be able to mitigate the associated costs.

Rebalancing Concerns

- *Tax penalties for higher rotation of assets.* In certain jurisdictions, such as the United States, the tax structure typically penalizes any very frequent rotations of assets. This increases the need for the wealth-management industry to pursue sound investment and portfolio management services within efficient tax advisory and wealth structuring frameworks.
- *Booking capabilities.* A related point is that more frequent adjustment/rebalancing of portfolios typically means that one needs more expensive advanced booking capabilities in order to execute orders in a timely fashion, to contain transactions costs, and to limit slippage.

- *Incorporation of the more illiquid asset classes.* Dynamically rebalanced portfolios do not usually live well with more illiquid asset classes. These illiquid asset classes, however, are interesting because they tend to remunerate a different type of risk than market risk, that is, illiquidity risk. Client holdings of such instruments typically remain dormant for a long number of years. This segment could either be isolated from the more liquid assets or incorporated into the main portfolio with appropriate flags.

Client Service

- *Quality control.* Many wealth-management firms have not yet put in place a mechanism of objective quality control, whereby the firm can demonstrate to its clients that it follows carefully defined value-adding processes leading to performance in a way that shows the value of the investment service it provides. As a consequence, moving from a product-fee to a service-fee approach may not prove easy so long as the quality of the service is not fully apparent to clients.
- *Communication.* Dynamic rebalancing of clients' portfolios also requires a heavier focus on communication to explain the rationale and intuitions behind these rebalancing decisions. This does not necessarily imply more communication (indeed, this would often be counter-productive) but much more consideration of what constitutes appropriate communication.
- *Enabling individual clients to benefit from the framework while conducting their own trades.* A particular challenge is to enable engaged clients who want to operate on their own to be able to benefit from such a dynamic asset-allocation environment without being affected by execution delays.

Suitability and Regulatory Concerns

- *Portfolio suitability.* Until now, the suitability of portfolios for clients has been determined largely by vague notions of risk tolerance and risk capacity, with little clarity around what exactly these are or how they should be measured. Many of the tools used to measure risk tolerance are woefully inadequate from a behavioral perspective, and the role of short-term behavioral responses and anxiety in establishing a portfolio suitable to each client is so far completely ignored by the framework.
- *Moving away from static benchmarks.* The adoption of dynamic portfolio rebalancing should lead to a distancing from static benchmarks,

which are well embedded in industry standards and constitute the basis for client protection, as typically understood by regulators.

Lastly, effective use of behavioral analysis implies organizational changes. The establishment of an advanced behavioral analysis platform needs to overcome several organizational challenges with respect to confidentiality related to access to client information, as well as education about the relationship of managers to their role as risk advisors to their clients.

These multiple hurdles demonstrate that innovation in wealth management not only constitutes a methodologic challenge but also requires significant operational changes if the organization is to be able to execute the new approach properly, as well as to communicate clearly and educate clients about the benefits of these improvements.

Advantages from the Perspective of a Client

Let us now look at the preceding proposition from the perspective of the client. Table 9.1 presents a list of the main areas of focus/concerns typically expressed

Table 9.1

Client Criteria	Traditional Approach	New Recommended Approach
Alignment of incentives between the client and the wealth manager	Limited in the case of brokerage	Yes, as service rather than product focus
Existence of an investment quality-control process	Generally limited	Relies on clear explanation of the process followed and reporting on performance and suitability
Bespoke service corresponding to client's expectations	In practice, limited by lack of sophisticated client risk analysis	Multiple behavioral dimensions to articulate client needs in a more tailored fashion
Limited surprises from a risk perspective	Difficult to control risk with a static asset allocation, when there is one	A time-varying asset allocation combined with tail-risk measures does a good job at stabilizing risk
Focus on diversification	Yes, but often too limited during bear markets and inadequately applied in bull markets	Time-varying recipes improve diversification
Adequate surveillance/maintenance of portfolio over time	Needs strong rules to account for portfolio drifts	Closely monitored through regular rebalancing

by clients and how the traditional and new recommended approaches attempt to respond to them.

Overall, turning wealth-management firms from large-scale product-distribution platforms into recognized investment houses that are focused on performance and have demonstrable expertise in understanding the expectations/constraints/mandates expressed by their private clients must be the industry's main objective in coming years.

The Implications for the Pension Industry

The defined-contribution pension industry faces the problem of devising an optimal asset allocation for long-term investors. The objective is to maximize, with a high degree of predictability, the value of the terminal portfolio of the investor at the age of his retirement in such a way that he can benefit from the highest possible annuities once having retired.

This industry has followed an approach based on the life cycle of individuals. The degree of sophistication of the recommended asset-allocation rules may vary, but the underlying principle seems to be to reduce one's allocation to the high risk-premium-yielding risky assets when getting closer to retirement to compensate for the fact that the hedge constituted by discounted future labor income from the individual tends to shrink during this period. In addition, as has already been discussed and presented in Figure 9.2, when we consider very long holding periods, thanks to assumed mean reversion of equity returns, the annualized volatility of equities reduces massively. Hence, over such long periods, the risk/return tradeoff for equities appears significantly better than that for bonds. This automatically triggers a very large initial asset allocation to equities when one derives the allocation from the MPT framework. This allocation gradually reduces over time as the volatility of equity increases along with the reduction of the investment period to retirement.

To implement this approach, some very simple deterministic rules have been promoted such as the *age rule*, which is as straightforward as setting the total equity holdings in one's portfolio to 100 minus the age of the individual, all divided by 100. Other similar linear rules posit holding 100 percent equity when starting to work and progressively scaling down the allocation to hold 35 percent of stocks at the age of retirement. Individuals who have challenged these approaches, such as DeMiguel, Garlappi, and Uppal (2009) have done so with respect to MPT and show that these rules of thumb also typically underperform the so-called $1/N$ naive rule in the defined-benefit universe.[7]

Why Pension Asset Allocation Is Complex

Optimizing pension asset allocation is complex for at least two reasons. It is a multiperiod problem, and—a point overlooked by many people—the size of the portfolio should grow over time as a result of regular contributions, which means that these multiperiod allocation decisions are made over size-varying portfolios. As Shiller[8] puts it, "A lifecycle plan that makes the percent allocated to stocks something akin to the privately offered lifecycle plans may do much worse than a 100 percent stocks portfolio since young people have relatively little income when compared to older workers. . . . The lifecycle portfolio would be heavily in the stock market (in the early years) only for a relatively small amount of money, and would pull most of the portfolio out of the stock market in the very years when earnings are highest." It is therefore not obvious that this massive formulaic shift into fixed-income instruments, once taking into account the size effect and the equity risk premium (Figure 9.3), will deliver a maximized terminal wealth at retirement. Little work seems to have been done on the topic, as far as we know. However, Basu (2010) shows in his Ph.D. thesis that this strategy is bound to underperform more balanced portfolios.

In addition to being complex, this defined-contribution optimization problem cannot be considered to be a purely rational one. The recent 2007–2010 crisis has showed us that when risky asset classes collapse, individuals tend to change their savings behavior as a result of what is called the *wealth effect*. They reduce their consumption, and they increase and shift their savings into "safe" assets as a precautionary measure to compensate for the drop in value of their stock and housing value-repository assets. Their pension plan forms part of their savings. This means that it is not realistic to consider individuals as neutral vis-à-vis nonterminal values of their pension plans and focusing only on this medium-/long-term terminal value. The problem is compounded by the fact that money managers are themselves prone to emotional reactions. Several pension plan managers reacted to the recent financial crisis by deviating from the recommended formulaic/life-cycle asset-allocation scheme. Instead of reloading equities in the portfolio to keep up with the predefined proportion, they deleveraged defined-contribution pension plans by fleeing to safer assets, sometimes at the worst time to do so. They were subject to their own emotional responses, in addition to clients' criticisms. In other words, even the managers found it difficult to ignore the short-term horizon and to focus on terminal values.

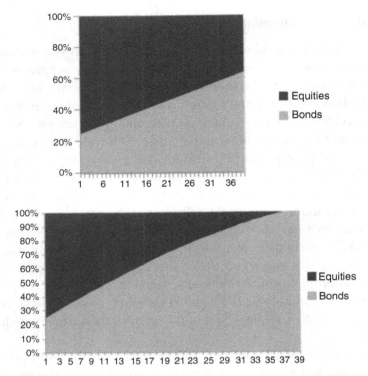

Figure 9.3 The impact of regular contributions on distorting one of the naive equity bond allocation rules mentioned earlier. The bottom figure shows what actually takes place once the variation in the size of the portfolio and an equity premium of 4 percent are taken into account, whereas the top figure represents the rule: In actual fact, individuals focus more heavily on bond investments than they think.

Performance Issues Surrounding Fixed Income

There are also some combined emotional/performance issues to take into consideration. Fixed income is often seen a safe asset in the short run. This is less true in the longer run, especially when considering instruments with a long duration. Figure 9.2 shows us in this respect that as the investment horizon increases, the volatility of fixed-income instruments tends to increase too, thereby worsening their risk/return tradeoff. In addition, from a forward-looking perspective, the expected return of these fixed-income instruments is likely to be poor in the coming years, again reducing desirability. From the current macroeconomic perspective, interest rates can only move up over time as a result of the degradation of sovereign credit risks in developed economies owing to growing debt and deficit imbalances, combined at some stage with some increasing inflation fears and, ultimately, the general context of aggressive monetary policies undertaken by many central banks at the risk of compromising their perceived independence from governments. It is worth noting that over long periods of time, 100 years and above, fixed income has not often proved a very solid repository of value.

Does this focus on fixed income correspond to a methodology mistake? To provide an answer, the first question we need to ask is: What is the duration of a typical defined-contribution pension account after considering ongoing contributions? This obviously depends on the amount by which these contributions will grow over time, as well as on the return expected from each investment. A simple set of simulations shows us that 40 years of contributions, growing at a steady pace, gives us an equivalent duration of the portfolio of between 10 and 20 years.

As a consequence, it appears that in reality, defined pension plans have an effective time span that is much lower than it appears at first sight. It is important to notice that this true investment period is well below the 30 to 40 years required to be able to securely benefit from the effect of volatility reduction on risky assets resulting from the mean reversion effect. This explains why these life-cycle plans are in reality so much geared toward fixed income and so cautious about equity holdings.

If the objective is to minimize the uncertainty regarding the final value of the pension portfolio of the investor, the only traditional alternative we know of that does not require any specific investment skill is to invest in fixed income. In this simple formulaic approach, the individual funding her pension plan has in fact to pay a costly insurance premium to obtain certainty about the future, overinvesting in fixed income. From a forward-looking perspective, the problem, by the way, could be exacerbated in the future by the fact that with aging of the population in the developed economies, the cost of this insurance premium may well increase over the coming decades as a result of growing supply and demand imbalances on some portions of the yield curve.

Until now, these deterministic/formulaic approaches to investing have enabled the pension fund industry to provide a limited set of low-cost solutions that require little understanding of the aspirations and reactions of individuals, as well as only limited asset-management skills. In addition, from a commercial perspective, these simple approaches look misleadingly easy to explain to clients. Saying that these are both suboptimal and too expensive for individual investors is equivalent to stating that the defined-contribution pension fund industry requires some important and extensive reengineering. In the next section we suggest some possible alternatives.

Applying Behavioral Analysis to the Defined-Contribution Pension Fund Industry

The eight previous chapters in this book have taught us that there are two main aspects to establishing a coherent investment approach:

1. Establish a detailed behavioral analysis of the client in order to capture the different dimensions of risks, both rational and behavioral.
2. In order to gain confidence about performance, move from a static asset-allocation process to a dynamic one, especially when the maturity of the planned investment program is below 30 to 40 years.

What would these two points mean in practice? There are two main areas where they could improve on the current standard—risk and performance.

Risk

There is a wide range of uncertainties surrounding pension provision. Many relate to the macroeconomic environment and others to the risk of professional/personal accidents in life. These sorts of uncertainties are difficult to predict and deal with. But there are, however, some parameters that we are in a better position to control.

First, with regard to emotional risk: Will the degree of investor concern about the smoothness of the defined-contribution fund performance journey cause adverse responses that will detrimentally affect the long-term value of the pension? In other words, will investors be unsettled by changes in the value of their pension portfolio?

Calvet, Campbell, and Sodini (2009) show, on the basis of a review of the total wealth behavior of all Swedish households, that the less wealthy a household is, the more prone it is to make the wrong investment decisions (typically to buy high and sell low). As regards pensions, such incorrect decisions would include changing one's asset-allocation preferences to plump for a 100 percent fixed-income allocation right after a financial crisis. Being able to identify clearly the emotional risk of the individual—as well as of the pension fund manager—would seem to be very important and would allow us to mitigate possible irrational decisions by either, offering some fully "arm's length" management solutions or by agreeing up front with individuals to purchase an adequate insurance premium program that makes the investment journey acceptably free of sharp downward movements.

Second, there may be some investor concern related to whether or not the size of the final portfolio is perceived to be sufficient to buy an acceptable value of annuities in a satisfactory way.[9] There will be a temptation to increase the risk or the leverage, especially during benign market periods, in order to compensate for the individual's inability to predict exactly what portfolio value will be necessary to fund a reasonable level of income from annuities. This desire to adjust risk levels to chase desired goals puts the cart before the horse. It is irresponsible to sell investors pension portfolios that are more risky than they are able or willing to cope with by convincing them that this is the only way to achieve certain future levels of annuity income—in doing so we also magnify the risk of them falling far short of these goals. Instead, this emphasizes the need for an objective and prior assessment of investors' long-term risk tolerance. If the optimal asset allocation looks unlikely to achieve desired long-term objectives, then advisors need to help investors do one of three things: save more, retire later, or reevaluate future goals. All these will help to achieve alignment between objectives and the realm of the possible. Increasing risk levels is an appeal to hope over reason and gets in the way of hard but necessary choices.

Strategic risk should not be totally ignored either, in the sense that individuals may look at their total wealth rather than just at their pension portfolio. In the case where other assets located outside of their defined-contribution funds can provide regular income during retirement, the appetite for risk on defined-contribution fund investments may well be different from what it would be were the defined-contribution fund the investor's only resource.

A further consideration in regard to the right level of risk to take on with pension assets is related to the discussion of time horizons. In the paradigm of life-cycle investing, it is generally argued that it is optimal that risk is reduced as the investor approaches retirement owing to shortening of the time horizon. However, with frequent rebalancing, the optimal portfolio is exactly that: It is the optimal investment portfolio until the next rebalancing period for the level of risk that the investor is prepared to take given the degree of risk tolerance. The expected returns from investing fully for one more period are an optimal compensation for risks taken, and this is true for every period approaching retirement. Any reduction in risk in this regard will be, by definition, suboptimal. Thus, reducing risk in the portfolio in the years approaching retirement cannot be justified on the basis of time horizon alone.

So where does this intuition come from? There are good reasons for gradually reducing risk toward retirement, but with constant rebalancing, this is not because of a shortening time horizon. Rather it is because of something we discussed earlier in this chapter—the role of human capital in defining total wealth. When a long way from retirement, investors typically have a surplus of future income over future expenditure. This human capital asset means that they should in fact be taking on more risk than indicated by a straight optimization of expected utility based only on current wealth. With conservative estimates of the net present value of future savings, this human capital is equivalent to holding an additional quasi-risk-free asset.

When retirement approaches, this reasoning reverses. The net present value for future income dwindles to zero, whereas expenditure must be maintained over the rest of the investor's lifetime—which with the extended life expectancy at retirement in the modern world can be substantial. At some point before retirement, the human capital asset flips into a liability, the size of which peaks more or less at retirement. It is the effect of this liability on the investment portfolio as a proportion of total wealth that is the reason that portfolio risk should be reduced as retirement approaches. But note that this, combined with continual rebalancing of an optimal portfolio, provides the possibility of a much more targeted approach to appropriate investing over the life cycle.

Performance

Turning now to the second aspect of behavioral investment management, it is clear that dynamic portfolio management with its associated focus on more accurate and responsive characterization of the dependency between asset classes improves diversification, reduces volatility in the portfolio, and also allows us to establish better control over the tail of the distribution of returns. Dynamic rebalancing therefore reduces the need to minimize risks in a portfolio by blunt means such as, inter alia, overweighting fixed income relative to the optimum. If needed, for clients seeking to minimize either the risk along the investment journey or the risk related to the final outcome (and thus the ability to purchase annuities), several options exist, such as, respectively, buying downside risk protection or deleveraging the portfolio with cash-like instruments.

Overall, our view is that there is no good reason why defined-contribution pension fund management should not truly correspond to an optimal asset-management/portfolio-construction approach and that there can be risks of underperformance associated with current "one size fits all" and formulaic offerings, however appealing they may look.

Conclusion

In this book we have reviewed current common standards in the wealth-management industry. We have assessed as honestly as we could the methodologic and economic shortfalls of this approach in the light of recent financial crises and of the growing body knowledge that has been accumulated both by academic studies and as a result of empirical experiments within the industry.

We believe that we are at an interesting period, potentially a turning point, for the wealth-management industry. We think that the industry could—and should—aspire to much higher standards of best practice. The evolution of the industry to these new levels of best practice, will, however, as frequently happens, be conditioned and challenged by the weight of conservatism within the companies, the limits set by regulation, and industry professionals' reluctance to rethink their operating model and their marketing strategy. We have discussed such possible improvements in relation to the case of wealth management and defined-contribution pension fund management. However, we believe that the suggestions in this book also could be applied when dealing with more institutional investors such as family offices, endowments, and so on.

Investing, of course, is inherently uncertain—and there is no silver bullet that will guarantee returns without risk. But it is our contention that we can do better in coping with uncertainty than the standard portfolio-optimization models would have us believe. In particular, they make three large-scale errors that result in poorer risk-adjusted performance than investors could and should be able to expect.

The first error relates to our knowledge of the world or lack of it: The traditional approach is to assume that the best we can do to assess risk and particularly dependency is to assume long-run average stability in correlations. It is not. By paying attention to shifting patterns of interaction between asset classes from one regime to the next and rebalancing to account for this, we can do better.

The second error relates purely to our assumptions about investors rather than our assumptions about the world. We assume that investors are rational and that the portfolio solution for a rational investor is the same as a rational solution for a human investor. Again, it is not. We are all subject to conflicting preferences, particularly between our short-term behavioral responses and the preferences that reflect our rational long-term objectives. If we attempt to invest for the latter while ignoring the former, we will find ourselves with actual performance that lags our expectations. Our short-term responses easily can interfere with our attempts at rational investing and cause us to deviate, in small or large ways, from the optimal portfolio.

The last large-scale error is one that straddles both our knowledge of the world and our knowledge of investors. The measures of risk in traditional modern portfolio theory are neither able to completely characterize the true risk of assets that do not have normally distributed returns, nor do they accurately reflect the notion of risk as it matters to investors, either individual or institutional. Risk is inherently downside and therefore asymmetrical, and it is inherently subjective because different investors will trade off different return distributions in different ways. If portfolio theory is to bridge the essential gap between our best forecast of the distribution of asset returns in the investment world and our best model of human preferences over these distributions, then it has to do a lot better in measuring risks in a way that copes consistently with complex distribution and complex preferences.

In this book we have sought to provide some ways of rectifying these errors. This last issue is resolved by moving to a risk measure that is derived from a more reasonable expression of rational long-term preferences, expressed through a realistic utility function. In so doing, the risk measure becomes both inherently subjective and relevant to the preferences of each individual investor. At the same time, though, we acquire a measure that can be used to rank all investments regardless of the shape of the distribution, leading to a more accurate representation of the actual investment world.

To increase the accuracy of our modeling of future investment returns, we also move away from the traditional paradigm of assuming a stable long-term dependency structure between asset classes to one of constant updating of our assessment of how assets relate to each other in the current investment environment and then rebalancing frequently to ensure that the portfolio remains optimal in a shifting market environment.

The last extension to the traditional framework that we have sought to introduce in this book is purely behavioral—to recognize that establishing what constitutes the optimal portfolio is only the first stage of the problem and that a complete solution to investment management also requires us to consider the difficulties of implementing this solution consistently over many years. We are humans, not robots, and investing involves taking risks with amounts that can meaningfully cause us distress. To assume that an "optimal" investment strategy for our long-term preferences is necessarily optimal when we consider our own human fallibility is flirting with investment disaster. To achieve good investment returns often requires us to deliberately deviate from the narrowly optimal solution in favor of some strategies that help us, at some small cost to long-term returns, to control our own future behavior and remain emotionally comfortable with our portfolio.

In short, what we have tried to do in this book is establish a rigorous systematic approach to understanding, measuring, and controlling the risks that really matter to us—and to controlling our own behavior. This can help us to achieve much better performance than failing to follow effectively a current framework that is itself based on unrealistic assumptions. Better wealth management depends on this.

Notes

1. Aeschlimann, Apffel, and Lombard (2009).
2. This is so because they are meant to reflect the rational utility of the investor, which is continuous with respect to both its risk and return parameters: The higher the loss, the increasingly higher the dissatisfaction of the investor will be, with the first derivative of this dissatisfaction constantly increasing.
3. Consider, for example, the Tap 4 fund from Barclays Capital.
4. This should not be taken to imply that their genuine time horizon for growing their wealth has diminished. For the most part, this is indefinite because we generally want to keep our overall wealth growing over our whole life and beyond. However, the ability of wealth managers to shelter behind a "long-term investment horizon" as an excuse for poor medium-term performance is limited, which calls for more active responses to changing market conditions than can be provided through a static long-term strategic allocation.
5. Wikipedia definition: "*Global macro* is defined as the process of investing, on a large scale, around the world using economic theory to justify the decision-making process. The term *global macro* is used to classify the strategy of certain hedge funds—those which take positions in financial derivatives and other securities on the basis of movements in global financial markets. The strategies typically are based on forecasts and analysis about interest-rate trends, movements in the general flow of funds, political changes, government policies, intergovernment relations, and other broad systemic factors."
6. "Most of the time, stocks are subject to irrational and excessive price fluctuations in both directions as a consequence of the ingrained tendency of most people to speculate or gamble . . . to give way to hope, fear and greed"

(Benjamin Graham, *The Intelligent Investor*. New York: Harper Business, 1973).
7. See Bagliano, Fugazza and Nicodano (2009).
8. Shiller and Robert (2005).
9. Concerns here also will be related to perceptions of the annuities' capability to match personal deferred liabilities.

BIBLIOGRAPHY

Abdellaoui, Mohammed. 2000. Parameter-free elicitation of utility of probability weighting functions. *Management Science* 46, 1497–1512.

Aeschlimann, Anne, Arnaud Apffel, and Thierry Lombard. 2009. *De l'expérience à l'expertise*. Geneva: Lombard Odier.

Akaike, H. 1974. A new look at the statistical model identification. *IEEE Trans. Automat. Contr. AC* 19, 16°23.

Allais, M. 1953. *Le comportement de l'homme rationnel devant le risque, critique des postulats et axiomes de l'école Américaine. Econometrica* 21, 503–546.

Andreou, Elena, and Eric Ghysels. 2002. Detecting multiple breaks in financial market volatility dynamics. *Journal of Applied Econometrics* 17, 579–600.

Ang, A., and D. Kristensen. 2010. Testing conditional factor models. Working paper, Columbia University, New York.

Ang, Andrew, and Geert Bekaert. 2002. International asset allocation with regime shifts. *Review of Financial Studies* 15, 1137–1187.

Arrow, Kenneth. 1965. *Aspects of the Theory of Risk Bearing*. Helsinki: Yrjo Jahnssonin Saatio.

Arrow, Kenneth, and Gerard Debreu. 1954. Existence of an equilibrium for a competitive economy. *Econometrica* 22, 265–290.

Bagliano, Fabio C., Carolina Fugazza, and Giovanna Nicodano. 2009. Pension funds performance evaluation: a utility based approach. University of Tonrino, Italy. Working paper.

Bai, Jushan, and Serena Ng. 2005. Tests for skewness, kurtosis, and normality for time series data. *Journal of Business and Economic Statistics* 23, 49–60.

Barberis, Nicholas, and Ming Huang. 2001. Mental accounting, loss aversion, and individual stock returns. *Journal of Finance* 56, 1247–1295.

Barro, Robert J., and David B. Gordon. 1983. A positive theory of monetary policy in a natural-rate model. *Journal of Political Economy* 91, 589–610.

Basu, A. K. 2010. *Essays on Asset Allocation Strategies for Defined Contribution Plans*. Brisbane, Australia: School of Economics and Finance, Queensland University of Technology.

Bell, David E. 1995. Risk, return, and utility. *Management Science* 41, 23–30.

Benartzi, Shlomo, and Richard H. Thaler. 1995. Myopic loss aversion and the equity premium puzzle. *Quarterly Journal of Economics* 110, 73–92.

Best, M. J., and R. R. Grauer. 1991. On the sensitivity of mean-variance-efficient portfolios to changes in asset means: some analytical and computational results. *Review of Financial Studies* 4, 315–342.

Biggs, Barton. 2008. *Wealth, War, and Wisdom*. Hoboken, NJ: Wiley.

Birnbaum, Michael H. 2004. Tests of rank-dependent utility and cumulative prospect theory in gambles represented by natural frequencies: effects of format, event framing, and branch splitting. *Organizational Behavior and Human Decision Processes* 95, 40–65.

Black, Fischer, and Robert Litterman. 1992. Global portfolio optimization. *Financial Analysts Journal* 48, 28–43.

Boeckh, Anthony. 2010. *The Great Reflation: How Investors Can Profit from the New World of Money*. Hoboken, NJ: Wiley.

Bontemps, Christian, and Nour Meddahi. 2005. Testing normality: a GMM approach. *Journal of Econometrics* 124, 149–186.

Brennan, M. J., and Alan Kraus. 1978. Necessary conditions for aggregation in securities markets. *Journal of Financial and Quantitative Analysis* 13, 407–418.

Calvet, Laurent E., John Y. Campbell, and Paolo Sodini. 2009. Measuring the financial sophistication of households. *American Economic Review* 99, 393–398.

Campbell, John Y., and Luis M. Viceira. 2002. *Strategic Asset Allocation: Portfolio Choice for Long-Term Investors.* Oxford, United Kingdom: Oxford University Press.

Carhart, Mark M. 1997. On persistence in mutual fund performance. *Journal of Finance* 52, 57–82.

Clare, Andrew, and Nick Motson. 2010. Comparing the performance of retail unit trusts and capital guaranteed notes. Working paper, Cass Business School, London.

Coval, Joshua D., and Tobias J. Moskowitz. 1999. Home bias at home: local equity preference in domestic portfolios. *Journal of Finance* 54, 2045–2073.

Cover, Thomas M., and Joy A. Thomas. 2001. *Elements of Information Theory.* Hoboken, NJ: Wiley.

Davies, Greg B. 2006. Rethinking risk attitude: aspiration as pure risk. *Theory and Decision* 61, 159–190.

Davies, Greg B., and Stephen E. Satchell. 2006. The behavioural components of risk aversion. *Journal of Mathematical Psychology* 51, 1–13.

DeMiguel, Victor, Lorenzo Garlappi, and Raman Uppal. 2009. Optimal versus naive diversification: how inefficient is the $1/N$ portfolio strategy? *Review of Financial Studies* 22, 1915–1953.

Dichev, Ilia D. 2007. What are stock investors' actual historical returns? Evidence from dollar-weighted returns. *American Economic Review* 97, 386–401.

Doornik, Jurgen A., and Henrik Hansen. 2008. An omnibus test for univariate and multivariate normality. *Oxford Bulletin of Economics and Statistics* 70, 927–939.

Estrada, Javier. 2007. Black swans and market timing: how not to generate alpha. Working paper. http://ssrn.com/abstract=1032962

Fama, Eugene F. 1970. Efficient capital markets: a review of theory and empirical work. *Journal of Finance* 25, 383–417.

Fama, Eugene F., and Kenneth R. French. 1992. The cross-section of expected stock returns. *Journal of Finance* 47, 427–465.

Fama, Eugene F., and Kenneth R. French. 1993. Common risk factors in the returns on stocks and bonds. *Journal of Financial Economics* 33, 3–56.

Fama, Eugene F., and Kenneth R. French. 1995. Size and book-to-market factors in earnings and returns. *Journal of Finance* 50, 131–155.

Fama, Eugene F., and Kenneth R. French. 1996. Multifactor explanations of asset pricing anomalies. *Journal of Finance* 51, 55–84.

Fama, Eugene F., and Merton H. Miller. 1972. *The Theory of Finance.* New York: Holt, Rinehart and Winston.

French, Kenneth R., and James M. Poterba. 1991. Investor diversification and international equity markets. *American Economic Review* 81, 222–226.

Friedman, C., and S. Sandow. 2003. Model performance measures for expected utility maximizing investors. *International Journal of Theoretical and Applied Finance* 6, 355.

Friesen, Geoffrey C., and Travis R. A. Sapp. 2007. Mutual fund flows and investor returns: an empirical examination of fund investor timing ability. *Journal of Banking & Finance* 31, 2796–2816.

Goncalves, S., and T. Vogelsang. 2008. *Block Bootstrap HAC Robust Tests: The Sophistication of the Naive Bootstrap.* Montreal, Canada: University of Montreal.

Guidolin, Massimo, and Allan Timmermann. 2007. Asset allocation under multivariate regime switching. *Journal of Economic Dynamics and Control* 31, 3503–3544.

Harris, Judith Rich. 2006. *No Two Alike: Human Nature and Human Individuality.* New York: Norton.

Hastie, T., R. Tibshirani, and J. Friedman. 2003. *The Elements of Statistical Learning: Data Mining, Inference, and Prediction.* New York: Springer.

He, Xue Dong and Zhou, Xun Yu, Portfolio choice under cumulative prospect theory: An analytical treatment (September 13, 2010). Management Science. Available at SSRN: http://ssrn.com/abstract=1479580

Head, Alex, Gary Smith, and Julia Wilson. 2009. Would a stock by any other ticker smell as sweet? *Quarterly Review of Economics and Finance* 49, 551–561.

Hodges, S. D., and R. A. Brealey. 1972. Portfolio selection in a dynamic and uncertain world. *Financial Analysts Journal* 28, 58–69.

Hosmer, David W., and Stanley Lemeshow. 2000. *Applied Logistic Regression.* Hoboken, NJ: Wiley.

Huberman, Gur. 2001. Familiarity breeds investment. *Review of Financial Studies* 14, 659–680.

Jaynes, E. T. 2003. *Probability Theory: The Logic of Science.* Cambridge, England: Cambridge University Press.

Jebara, T. 2004. Multi-task feature and kernel selection for SVMs. International Conference on Machine Learning. http://dl.acm.org/citation.cfm?id=1015330.1015426

Jegadeesh, N., and S. Titman. 1993. Returns to buying winners and selling losers: implications for stock market efficiency. *Journal of Finance* 48, 65–91.

Jegadeesh, N., and S. Titman. 2001. Profitability of momentum strategies: an evaluation of alternative explanations. *Journal of Finance* 56, 699–720.

Kahneman, Daniel, and Amos Tversky. 1979. Prospect theory: an analysis of decision under risk. *Econometrica* 47, 263–291.

Leijonhufvud, Axel. 2011. Nature of an economy. Centre for Economic Policy Research Policy Insight No. 53.

Lintner, John. 1965. The valuation of risk assets and the selection of risky investments in stock portfolios and capital budgets. *Review of Economics and Statistics* 47, 13–37.

Lo, Andrew. 2004. The adaptive markets hypothesis: market efficiency from an evolutionary perspective. *Journal of Portfolio Management* 30, 15–29.

Malmendier, Ulrike, and Stefan Nagel. 2011. Depression babies: do macroeconomic experiences affect risk taking? *Quarterly Journal of Economics* 126, 373–416.

Mankiw, N. Gregory, and Stephen P. Zeldes. 1991. The consumption of stockholders and nonstockholders. *Journal of Financial Economics* 29, 97–112.

Markowitz, Harry. 1952. Portfolio selection. *Journal of Finance* 7, 77–91.

McNeil, Alexander J., Rudiger Frey, and Paul Embrechts. 2005. *Quantitative Risk Management: Concepts, Techniques, and Tools*. Princeton, NJ: Princeton University Press.

Merton, R. C. 1969. Lifetime portfolio selection under uncertainty: the continuous time case. *Review of Economics and Statistics* 51, 247–257.

Merton, Robert C. 1972. An analytic derivation of the efficient portfolio frontier. *Journal of Financial and Quantitative Analysis* 7, 1851–1872.

Michaud, R. 1989. The Markowitz optimization enigma: is optimized optimal. *Financial Analysts Journal* 45, 31–42.

Minsky, Hyman. 2008. *Stablizing an Unstable Economy*. New York: McGraw-Hill.

Mishkin, Frederic S. 1999. International experiences with different monetary policy regimes. NBER Working Paper No. 6965.

Mitchell, T. 1997. *Machine Learning*. New York: McGraw-Hill.

Mossin, Jan. 1968. Aspects of rational insurance purchasing. *Journal of Political Economy* 76, 553–568.

Rabin, Matthew. 2000. Diminishing marginal utility of wealth cannot explain risk aversion, in Daniel Kahneman, and Amos Tversky, eds., *Choices, Values, and Frames*. Cambridge, England: Cambridge University Press.

Rashes, Michael S. 2001. Massively confused investors making conspicuously ignorant choices. *Journal of Finance* 56, 1911–1927.

Reinhart, Carmen M., and Kenneth S. Rogoff. 2009. *This Time Is Different: Eight Centuries of Financial Folly*. Princeton, NJ: Princeton University Press.

Rissanen, Jorma. 1989. *Stochastic Complexity in Statistical Inquiry Theory*. New York: World Scientific Publishing Co.

Rubinstein, Mark. 1974. An aggregation theorem for securities markets. *Journal of Financial Economics* 1, 225–244.

Sahm, Claudia. 2007. How much does risk tolerance change? Finance and Economics Discussion Series, Divisions of Research and Statistics and Monetary Affairs, Federal Reserve Board, New York.

Samuelson, Paul A. 1963. Risk and uncertainty: a fallacy of large numbers. *Scientia* 98, 108–113.

Samuelson, Paul A. 1969. Lifetime portfolio selection by dynamic stochastic programming. *Review of Economics and Statistics* 51, 239–246.

Schacter, Daniel L. 1987. Implicit memory: history and current status. *Journal of Experimental Psychology: Learning, Memory, and Cognition* 13, 501–518.

Schwarz, Gideon. 1978. Estimating the dimension of a model. *Annals of Statistics* 6, 461–464.

Shefrin, Hersh. 2008. *A Behavioral Approach to Asset Pricing*. New York: Elsevier.

Shiller, R. 2005. The life-cycle personal accounts proposal for social security: a review. NBER Working Paper No. 11300.

Shleifer, Andrei. 2000. *Inefficient Markets: An Introduction to Behavioral Finance*. Oxford, England: Oxford University Press.

Shleifer, Andrei, and Robert W. Vishny. 1997. The limits of arbitrage. *Journal of Finance* 52, 35–55.

Sloman, Steven A. 2002. Two systems of reasoning, in Thomas Gilovich, Dale Griffin, and Daniel Kahneman, eds., *Heuristics and Biases: The Psychology of Intuitive Judgment*. Cambridge, England: Cambridge University Press.

Slovic, Paul. 1991. The construction of preference. *American Psychologist* 50, 364–371.

Takats, Elod. 2010. Ageing and asset prices. BIS Working Paper No. 318.

Thaler, Richard H., and Shlomo Benartzi. 2004. Save more tomorrow: using behavioral economics to increase employee saving. *Journal of Political Economy* 112, 164–186.

Tobin, J. 1958. Liquidity preference as behavior towards risk. *Review of Economic Studies* 25, 65–86.

Tversky, A, and D Kahneman. 1981. The framing of decisions and the psychology of choice. *Science* 211, 453–458.

Tversky, Amos, and Daniel Kahneman. 1992. Advances in prospect theory: cumulative representation of uncertainty. *Journal of Risk and Uncertainty* 5, 297–323.

Weber, Martin, Elke U. Weber, and Alen Nosic. 2011. Who takes risks when and why: determinants of changes in investor risk taking. Working paper.

Witten, Ian H., and Eibe Frank. 2005. *Data Mining: Practical Machine Learning Tools and Techniques*. New York: Elsevier.

INDEX

defining inputs to, 146–151
and errors/biases, 144–145
and long-term stable preferences,
 145–151
quadratic, 46, 46*f*, 49–50
and short-term preferences, 145,
 283–287
total wealth levels and, 146–147

V

Value at risk (VaR), 36, 183n6,
 327–328
Value function, 55
Variance, 49
Volatility:
 notation for, 72–73
 and risk-management targets,
  327–328

W

Weakly dependent data, 122
Wealth, War and Wisdom (Biggs), 31
Wealth effect, 339

Wealth levels, total, 146–147
Wealth management, 323–337
 and client service, 336
 current practices in, 324, 328–331
 and entrepreneurial/business
  interests, 333–334
 fees/costs for, 335
 and increasing irrelevance of static
  approach, 330, 331
 and investor's liabilities, 334
 need for global macro strategy
  approach to, 332–333
 and portfolio suitability, 336–337
 and rebalancing, 335–336
 and regulatory concerns, 337
 and risk tolerance, 326–327
 and risk-management targets,
  327–328
 and systematic use of client
  information, 324–326

Y

Yen, 24